FOCUS ON People and Migration

2005 edition

Editor Roma Chappell

First published 2005 by
PALGRAVE MACMILLAN
Houndmills, Basingstoke, Hampshire RG21 6XS and 175 Fifth
Avenue, New York, NY 10010, USA
Companies and representatives throughout the world.

PALGRAVE MACMILLAN is the global academic imprint of the
Palgrave Macmillan division of St. Martin's Press, LLC and of
Palgrave Macmillan Ltd. Macmillan® is a registered trademark
in the United States, United Kingdom and other countries.
Palgrave is a registered trademark in the European Union and
other countries.

ISBN 1-4039-9327-0

This book is printed on paper suitable for recycling and made
from fully managed and sustained forest sources.

A catalogue record for this book is available from the British
Library.

10   9   8   7   6   5   4   3   2   1
14   13   12   11   10   09   08   07   06   05

Printed and bound in Great Britain by William Clowes Ltd,
Beccles, Suffolk.

A National Statistics publication
National Statistics are produced to high professional standards
set out in the National Statistics Code of Practice. They are
produced free from political influence.

About the Office for National Statistics
The Office for National Statistics (ONS) is the government
agency responsible for compiling, analysing and disseminating
economic, social and demographic statistics about the United
Kingdom. It also administers the statutory registration of births,
marriages and deaths in England and Wales.

The Director of ONS is also the National Statistician and the
Registrar General for England and Wales.

Contact points
For enquiries about this publication, contact the Editor, Roma
Chappell
Tel: 01329 813490
E-mail: roma.chappell@ons.gsi.gov.uk

For general enquiries, contact the National Statistics Customer
Contact Centre.
Tel: 0845 601 3034
(minicom: 01633 812399)
E-mail: info@statistics.gsi.gov.uk
Fax: 01633 652747
Post: Room 1015, Government Buildings,
Cardiff Road, Newport NP10 8XG

You can also find National Statistics on the Internet at:
www.statistics.gov.uk

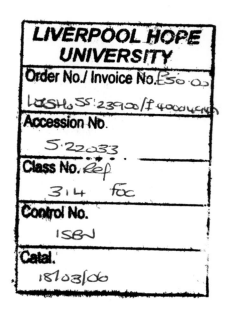

Contents

List of figures, tables and maps

3: The UK's major urban areas

List of contributors

Authors:

Francesca Ambrose
François Carlos-Bovagnet (Eurostat)
Jessica Chamberlain
Tony Champion (University of Newcastle upon Tyne)
Roma Chappell
Baljit Gill
Mike Hawkins
Giles Horsfield
Julie Jefferies
David Pearce
Graham Pointer
Michael Rendall
John Salt (University College London)
Kate Shaw
Steve Smallwood
Chris Smith
Denis Till
Cecilia Tomassini
Gary Wainman

Editorial team:

Francesca Ambrose
Roma Chappell
Julie Jefferies
Gary Wainman

Typesetting:

ONS Desktop Publishing Unit

Acknowledgements

The editors wish to thank all authors who have helped in the production of *Focus On People and Migration*. Special thanks go to our colleagues in the Office for National Statistics (ONS) for their invaluable support in the preparation of this report.

We have received expert advice from our independent referees: David Coleman (University of Oxford); Danny Dorling (The University of Sheffield); Christian Dustmann (University College London); Andrew Hinde (University of Southampton); John Salt (University College London); John Stillwell (University of Leeds).

We are grateful to our colleagues from the following departments, devolved administrations and the armed forces: Defence Analytical Services Agency; Department for Education and Skills; Department of Enterprise, Trade and Investment; Central Statistics Office Ireland; Eurostat; Government Actuary's Department; General Register Office for Scotland; Greater London Authority; Home Office; Northern Ireland Statistics and Research Agency; Northern Ireland Office; Office of the Deputy Prime Minister; Scottish Executive; United States Air Force; Welsh Assembly Government.

Introduction

Focus on People and Migration is part of the 'Focus on' series of publications from the Office for National Statistics (ONS). The series combines data from the 2001 Census and other sources to illustrate various topics, and provides links to further information. Other reports in the series cover social inequalities, families, gender, ethnicity and identity, religion, health and older people. Each report consists of a short overview of the topic, followed by a full report containing more comprehensive analysis. The overviews and full reports can be viewed or downloaded from the National Statistics website: www.statistics.gov.uk/focuson

Focus on People and Migration provides an up-to-date and comprehensive description of the UK population at the start of the 21st century. It presents a wealth of information on how the population is changing over time and the demographic forces driving these trends. An understanding of population size and population change is crucial for those involved in planning and decision-making at the national and local level. At the individual level, this volume also contains a fascinating insight into the wider significance of milestones that affect us all, such as birth, death and moving house.

The following chapters bring together data from a variety of sources to describe the characteristics of the UK population. The report covers the population of the UK as a whole, and geographical variations in population characteristics and trends are highlighted throughout.

The report is aimed at people who want to deepen their understanding of the UK population and its dynamics, be they students, teachers, researchers, policy makers or members of the general public. It is designed to be accessible to a general audience, with text, charts, maps and tables that are easy to understand, and an appendix for those who want more information on data and methods.

The structure of *Focus on People and Migration*

Chapter 1, The UK population: past, present and future, describes how the UK's population has evolved and how it is expected to continue to change in the near future. It also provides an introduction to some of the features of the UK's population and its characteristics at the beginning of the 21st century. Subsequent chapters explore in more detail many of the issues touched on in Chapter 1.

Chapters 2 and 3 focus on the regional distribution of the UK population. Chapter 2, Where people live, describes how the population's characteristics differ across the country and discusses why people may choose to live in certain areas. It highlights regional and district-level differences in age structure, employment and other characteristics. Chapter 3, The UK's major urban areas, focuses on the largest urban areas identified by the 2001 Census and looks at how these have changed since the 1991 Census. This chapter also explores the characteristics of people who were living in large urban areas in 2001.

Chapter 4, The changing age structure of the UK population, focuses on people who are aged under 16, of working age and of retirement age. It explores how the UK's age structure is projected to change during the next four decades. And, finally, it shifts its attention to Japan, for a comparison with a population whose age structure has changed more rapidly.

Chapters 5 to 7 focus on the components of population change in the UK. Chapter 5, Fertility and mortality, examines how births and deaths have shaped the population size and structure. It discusses various aspects of childbearing from both the male and female perspective, and presents analyses of trends and patterns in mortality over time, by age and by sex. The chapter closes by summarising the consequences of changing fertility and mortality patterns on the UK population.

Chapter 6, Population movement within the UK, looks at how many people change address each year, the types of people most likely to move and how far they go. It examines the impact of this internal migration on the populations of different areas of the UK. The chapter also investigates the migration patterns of particular groups of people such as students.

Chapter 7, International migration, deals with people moving into and out of the UK. It shows how migration flows have changed over the last three decades and discusses the possible impact of international migration on future population size. The chapter also presents information on the characteristics of those entering or leaving the UK for one year or more.

In Chapters 8 and 9 the focus shifts to specific groups within the UK population. Chapter 8, The foreign-born population, looks in detail at people resident in the UK who were born in a different country. Both the size and characteristics of the foreign-born population are explored using census data. Comparisons are made between those who had migrated to the UK during the year before the 2001 Census and those born abroad who had already been living in the UK for a year or longer.

Chapter 9, Special and communal populations, looks at four other groups within the UK population: people in the armed forces, prisoners, students and residents of communal establishments. As well as examining the size of these special populations, the chapter discusses characteristics such as their age and sex profiles, and how these compare with the UK population as a whole.

Finally, Chapter 10, The UK population in the European context, takes a wider perspective. At the beginning of 2004, the UK had the third largest population in the European Union. The chapter highlights similarities and differences between the UK and other European countries in terms of population growth, fertility, mortality and other demographic characteristics.

Data and classifications

More information on the data and classifications used in this report can be found in the appendix. The glossary provides useful explanations of the terminology used.

The UK population: past, present and future

Julie Jefferies

Chapter 1

Introduction

The United Kingdom consists of England, Wales, Scotland and Northern Ireland. In 2004, it was home to over 59.8 million people.[1]

This chapter provides an overview of the UK population, from its early origins to the present. It explores some of the characteristics of the people living in the UK at the start of the 21st century and describes briefly how the population of the UK is projected to change in the near future.

The UK population in the past

This section provides a very brief review of a complex topic: the way in which the population of the UK has changed over the centuries. The history of the UK population is not easy to explain for two main reasons.

First, the UK has only existed in its present form (England, Wales, Scotland and Northern Ireland) since 1922. Prior to the Act of Union 1800, Great Britain and Ireland were separate kingdoms but in 1801 the United Kingdom of Britain and Ireland came into existence. The United Kingdom (of Great Britain and Northern Ireland) as we know it today came about when the Irish Free State (now the Republic of Ireland) gained independence in 1922 following the Anglo-Irish war. To understand the population history of the UK prior to 1922, it is necessary to look at the populations of England, Wales, Scotland and Ireland.

Second is the scarcity of data sources, particularly before 1800. More is known about the population history of England before the 19th century than about Scotland, Wales or Ireland, due to the amount of research carried out and the availability of data sources.[2] Data from parish registers and historic tax records exist in many areas of the UK. As historic sources, these data are useful but imperfect: they may refer to localised areas or selected population groups only and thus conflicting conclusions may be drawn from the available data.[3]

A population can change in size via two main mechanisms: natural change (the difference between the numbers of births and deaths) and net migration (the difference between in-migration and out-migration). A larger number of births than deaths or a higher number of in-migrants than out-migrants in a particular year will add people to a population. Similarly, a greater number of deaths than births or more people migrating out of than into the population will reduce the number of people in a population.

In practice the combination of natural change and net migration will determine whether a population increases or decreases in size. The following sections track the changes in the size of the UK population over time and the reasons for these changes, a task that has become much easier in recent decades as data sources have improved.

Early history of the UK population

One of the earliest population data sources for the UK is the Gaelic document 'Senchus fer n'Alba' (an account of the men of Scotland). Attributed to the 7th century, it listed the numbers of men available for naval service and paying taxes.[4] Better known is the Domesday Book of 1086, which surveyed land and resources in England. From this source, England's population in 1086 is estimated to have been between 1.4 and 1.9 million. The exact number is uncertain as the estimated population depends on the assumptions made about the average number of people living in each household and the number of people not recorded in the Domesday Book.[5]

Between 1086 and 1750, the population of England experienced some periods of faster growth and some periods of stagnation and even decline. It is believed that the population grew quickly in the 12th and 13th centuries and reached between four and six million by the end of the 13th century.[6] However, the 14th century was a period where disease and the struggle to produce an adequate food supply prevented further population growth. A sustained agricultural crisis from 1315 to 1322 leading to famine was later dwarfed by the plague epidemic of 1348 to 1350. Commonly known as the Black Death, the latter probably caused the death of over one-third of the English population and was followed by other major epidemics, which kept population growth low.[7]

In 1377 King Edward III levied a poll tax on all people aged 14 or over in order to fund the Hundred Years War with France. The records from this tax collection were sufficiently robust to provide an estimate of the population of England in 1377. Depending on the proportion of the population assumed to be aged under 14, the total population is estimated to have been between 2.2 and 3.1 million, considerably lower than it had been at the start of the 14th century.[8]

Between 1377 and 1750 the English population grew slowly and unsteadily, with faster growth in the 16th century than in the 15th or 17th centuries. Long periods of civil war during the 15th century (the Wars of the Roses) and the mid-17th century (the Civil War) disrupted food supplies. These periods of political instability were characterised by relatively high mortality, late marriage and low marriage rates keeping fertility relatively low[9] and net out-migration of English people.[10] In contrast, the 16th century was a period of political stability under the Tudors, hence there were fewer socio-economic barriers to population growth.[11] By 1750 the English population is estimated to have been 5.74 million,[12] probably similar to the level prior to the mortality crises of the 14th century.

Other parts of what is now the UK are likely to have had slightly differing population histories, although further research is needed. For example, Scotland and Ireland experienced civil wars and mortality crises at different times from England[13] and were vulnerable to famine for longer, probably due to lower agricultural productivity and inadequate poor relief. In Scotland, population growth was relatively low in the late 17th and early 18th centuries. This is thought to be due to lower standards of living and thus higher mortality, particularly for infants, plus later marriage and childbearing than in England. In contrast, Ireland may have had higher fertility rates and hence higher growth rates than England or Scotland in the 17th century due to earlier marriage and higher fertility within marriage.[14]

Migration between areas also affected their total populations. The movement of an estimated 100,000 Scots to Ireland in the 17th century was a particularly notable outflow given that Scotland's population was estimated to be 1.23 million in 1691.[15] Significant emigration from the Scottish Highlands also occurred following the Second Jacobite rebellion in 1745.

The era of the census

Towards the end of the 18th century concerns were raised that the British population might be growing faster than the food supply. Thomas Malthus's 'Essay on the Principle of Population', published in 1798, articulated these concerns. By the end of the 18th century, the British Government began to see the need for reliable data to confirm the number of people living in the country.[16] The impetus for data collection was reinforced by the ongoing wars between Britain and France: both countries made plans to carry out their first census at the start of the 19th century[17] to ascertain their manpower and tax base.

The Census Act of 1800 paved the way for the first British census, which took place in March 1801 in England, Wales and Scotland.[18] The 1801 Census showed that England's population had grown to 8.3 million, while there were nearly 0.6 million people living in Wales and 1.6 million in Scotland, giving a total of 10.5 million people in Great Britain.[19]

Since 1801, a census has been taken in Great Britain every 10 years, except in 1941 during the Second World War.[20] In Ireland, the first census was taken in 1821, but the 1841

Census was the first where a complete enumeration of the population of Ireland was achieved.[21] In 1841 the population of Ireland stood at nearly 8.2 million.[22] As in Great Britain, the Irish census was taken every 10 years between 1841 and 1911. From the 1920s onwards censuses were taken in slightly different years in Great Britain, Northern Ireland and the Republic of Ireland, with five-yearly censuses taken in the Republic of Ireland since the 1950s.[23] The collection of census data has made it far easier to identify the changes taking place in the UK's population.

Figures 1.1 to 1.4 show how the populations of England, Wales, Scotland, Northern Ireland and the Republic of Ireland have changed between 1801 and 2001 according to the ten-yearly census. The population of England had more than doubled from 8.3 million in 1801 to 16.8 million in 1851 and, by 1901, had nearly doubled again to 30.5 million (Figure 1.1). The pace of growth slowed a little in the 20th century, with the English population reaching 41.2 million in 1951 and 49.1 million in 2001. However, England's population in 2001 was still nearly six times higher than the population 200 years earlier.

Figure **1.1**

Population on Census day, England, 1801 to 2001

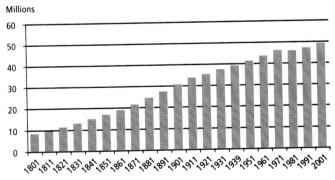

Source: Census – Office for National Statistics

Census data show that the populations of Wales and Scotland also grew substantially during the 19th century (Figures 1.2 and 1.3) though not quite so fast as England's population. The Welsh population grew from 0.6 million in 1801 to 2.0 million in 1901, while the number of people living in Scotland increased from 1.6 million to 4.5 million over the same period. The 20th century has seen more fluctuation in these populations, with some periods of slight decline. Overall the Welsh population increased by 0.9 million between 1901 and 2001, an increase of 44 per cent. The Scottish population grew by 13 per cent (0.6 million) over the same period.

Figure **1.2**

Population on Census day, Wales, 1801 to 2001

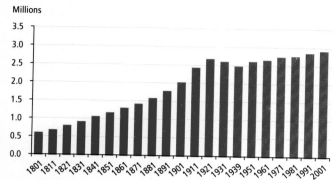

Source: Census – Office for National Statistics

Figure **1.3**

Population on Census day, Scotland, 1801 to 2001

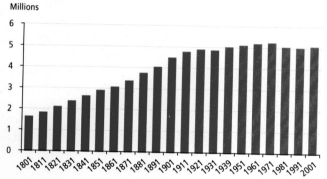

Source: Census – General Register Office for Scotland

In contrast, census data for the area that is now Northern Ireland (Figure 1.4) show a population falling from 1.6 million in 1841 to 1.2 million by 1901. During the 20th century the population of Northern Ireland started to increase slowly and by 2001 had reached nearly 1.7 million, only slightly higher than in 1841.

The population of what is now the Republic of Ireland also fell considerably, from 6.5 million in 1841 to 3.2 million at the start of the 20th century (Figure 1.4). However, unlike Northern Ireland's population, which began to increase slowly, the population of the Republic continued to fall during the 20th century to a low of 2.8 million in 1961. After 1961 it increased gradually, apart from a slight decline in the late 1980s, but, at 3.9 million in 2002, the population of the Irish Republic had still not recovered to anywhere near its size in 1841 (6.5 million).

The next two sections outline briefly some of the underlying reasons for the population trends shown by the censuses and the differences between the constituent countries of the UK.

Figure **1.4**

Population on Census day, Northern Ireland[1] and Republic of Ireland[2], 1841 to 2001

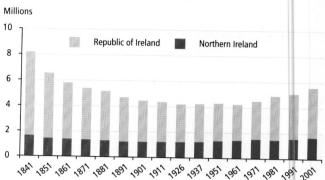

1   Data for 1841 to 1911 refer to the populations of areas currently defined as Northern Ireland and the Republic of Ireland.
2   For the Republic of Ireland, census data refer to 1936 rather than 1937 and 2002 rather than 2001; all other census years are identical to those for Northern Ireland.

Source: Census – Central Statistics Office Ireland; Northern Ireland Statistics and Research Agency

1750 to 1950: population growth and the demographic transition

The demographic transition model describes the stages a population goes through as it moves from a pre-industrial population with high fertility and mortality to a modern industrial country with low fertility and mortality.[24] The model is based on the experiences of Western European countries and a simplified version is shown in Figure 1.5.

In stage one (pre-transition) both birth and death rates are high so the population grows only slowly. In stage two, social and economic changes, most notably improvements in the quality and quantity of the food supply, lead to a fall in death rates. This in turn causes rapid population growth. By stage three, birth rates also start to fall and as a result population growth slows. Stage four represents the stable situation following the demographic transition, where both birth and death rates are low and the population size fairly constant. The model assumes that net migration is zero.

Census data are consistent with England's population moving from stage one to stage four of the demographic transition model during the period from 1750 to 1950. In the mid-18th century, England's population entered a period of sustained population growth, increasing rapidly from less than six million in 1750, to almost 17 million by 1851 and more than 41 million by the time of the 1951 Census (Figure 1.1).

The transition from low and intermittent population growth before 1750 to the period of high population growth after 1750 represents England entering stage two of the

Figure **1.5**

The demographic transition model

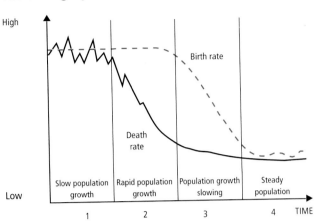

demographic transition. In the late 18th and early 19th centuries, improvements in agricultural productivity, and therefore a more reliable food supply, enabled this growth in population. However, the lack of reliable data sources for the early part of the period makes it difficult to be certain about why this population growth occurred.

It is generally agreed that mortality was an important factor. As well as a general fall in death rates, of particular note was the fact that mortality crises such as those caused by plague or famine had mostly been eliminated, especially in Scotland and Ireland.[25] An increasing birth rate may also have been an important factor contributing to population growth during this period, with increased agricultural productivity meaning that people could afford to marry earlier and begin having children at younger ages.[26]

After 1850 adult mortality rates began to fall more dramatically (as would be expected in stage two of the demographic transition model). The possible reasons for the fall in death rates in the 19th century are disputed but may include improved nutrition, rising standards of living, such as improved sanitation, and the introduction of the smallpox vaccination. Infant mortality in England remained high until 1900 but fell during the first half of the 20th century, probably due to improved public health and changing child-care practices.[27]

The decline in birth rates, identified as stage three of the demographic transition, took place in England from around 1870 to 1920. In 1871 the average woman was having 5.5 children but by 1921 this had fallen to 2.4 children.[28] Whereas previously, delayed marriage and non-marriage were the only factors reducing the number of children borne by each woman, by the late 19th and early 20th centuries the use of traditional methods of birth control (abstinence and withdrawal) within

marriage had become more widespread. The third stage of the demographic transition was therefore achieved almost totally without modern contraceptive methods and with no support for family planning from the major social institutions. By the 1930s an increased acceptance of birth control by medical and some religious institutions, plus the availability of modern methods such as condoms from around time of the First World War, enabled this decline in birth rates to continue.[29]

England's population would have grown even more rapidly during the demographic transition had it not been for increasingly large numbers of out-migrants leaving for countries including the United States, Canada, Australia and New Zealand. Although this was partly balanced by in-migration from other countries, there was net out-migration from England in every decade from 1840 to 1930.[30]

During the first half of the 20th century, England was moving into stage four of the demographic transition, with low birth rates, decreasing death rates and slower population growth. There were, however, some exceptions to these trends. For example, during the First World War, 723,000 British servicemen (mainly aged between 20 and 40) are estimated to have lost their lives.[31] Following the First World War, an influenza pandemic caused 152,000 deaths in England and Wales between June 1918 and May 1919.[32] Although Figure 1.1 shows the English population steadily increasing after 1901, the rate of growth as a percentage of the total population had slowed considerably.

The English experience shows that the conventional demographic transition model is a useful starting point for explaining the change in a population. However, a major limitation is that it does not take account of migration. According to the model, towards the end of stage four, birth rates will be equal to or lower than death rates, hence population growth will be very low. In practice, England's population has continued to grow due to net international in-migration, as described later in this chapter, and the population momentum built into the age structure (see Chapter 5 for an explanation of population momentum).

Individual countries and regions also vary in how closely they adhere to the process described in the model. Figures 1.2 and 1.3 show that the populations of Wales and Scotland also grew considerably during the period 1801 to 1901, although the pace of growth was slower in Scotland than in England. Scotland's growth may have been slower due to higher emigration[33] and episodes of high mortality, for example the typhus epidemics of 1837 and 1847.[34]

In line with the demographic transition model, decreasing mortality rates were the most likely cause of Ireland's rapid population growth after 1750, given that Ireland was producing enough food for its own population plus a surplus for export.[35] Ireland's population grew from an estimated 2.4 million in 1750 to over five million by 1800[36] and over eight million by the 1841 Census.

However, after 1841, the demographic transition model does not describe Ireland's experience well. As Figure 1.4 shows, the population of Ireland charted a very different course from that of England during the 19th century, falling sharply between 1841 and 1851 and continuing to decrease for the rest of the century. The failure of the potato crop through blight in 1845, 1846 and 1848 had serious consequences. The population was dependent on the crop, with most people unable to afford the limited alternative food that was available. Over the course of the resulting famine over one million people died and a further million emigrated from Ireland, mainly to Canada and the United States but also to Britain, swelling the population there.[37] These figures relate to Ireland as a whole but the area that is now Northern Ireland was affected to a lesser extent than other parts of the country, with the industrial areas centred around Belfast less susceptible to agricultural crises. Northern Ireland's population began to recover in the first half of the 20th century, increasing by 13 per cent between 1901 and 1951.

The UK population, 1950 to 2001

By the end of the Second World War, the UK had moved into the fourth stage of the demographic transition and was one of the first European countries to do so. In post-war England, birth rates were low (but fluctuating), death rates fairly low and population growth beginning to slow, particularly by the 1970s. During the second half of the 20th century death rates continued to fall (see Chapter 5), with the majority of deaths due to degenerative diseases such as heart disease, cancers and stroke. The population also began to age noticeably due to the improved chances of survival and low birth rates (see Chapter 4).

Other significant social changes took place during this period. The use of modern contraceptive methods became more widespread, particularly with the availability of the pill in Britain from the early 1960s and the legalisation of abortion in 1967 (in Great Britain but not Northern Ireland). The implementation of the 1969 Divorce Reform Act led to a large rise in the number of divorces in England and Wales from the 1970s onwards and similar increases in the number of divorces were seen in Scotland and Northern Ireland. The 1980s witnessed

large increases in the prevalence of cohabitation and the proportion of births taking place outside marriage in all parts of the UK.[38] These and other changes in society, that have resulted from a new emphasis on personal freedom of choice, are sometimes considered to represent a 'second demographic transition'.[39]

Figure 1.6 shows how the UK population grew over the five decades from 1951 to 2001. It rose from 50.3 million in mid-1951 to 59.1 million in mid-2001,[40] an increase of nearly nine million people. Although this might appear to be a large increase in absolute terms, the rate of growth is much slower than in the 19th century when the population was smaller and was doubling or nearly doubling every 50 years.

The UK's population growth from 1951 to 2001 did not occur at a steady pace. Between 1951 and 1961, the population increased by 5.0 per cent over the decade, with an even higher growth of 5.9 per cent in the following ten years from 1961 to 1971. However, the 1970s showed a different trend. Between 1974 and 1978 the population declined slightly, leading to overall growth of only 0.8 per cent in the period 1971 to 1981. In subsequent decades, the UK population continued to grow at an increasing pace, by 1.9 per cent between 1981 and 1991 and by 2.9 per cent between 1991 and 2001.

Between 1951 and 2001 the main cause of UK population growth was natural increase. The number of births in the UK exceeded the number of deaths every year during this period, except in 1976.[41] The number of births during the mid-1970s was particularly low (see Chapter 5) and this led to the slight population decline noted in the 1970s (Figure 1.6).

Figure **1.6**

Population estimates[1], 1951 to 2001

United Kingdom

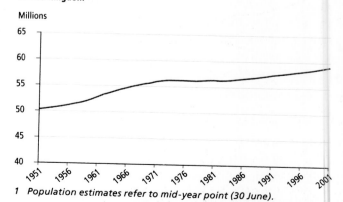

1 *Population estimates refer to mid-year point (30 June).*

Source: Population estimates – Office for National Statistics; General Register Office for Scotland; Northern Ireland Statistics and Research Agency

During the early and mid-1990s the number of births generally exceeded the number of deaths by over 100,000 per year (Figure 1.7). A lower level of natural increase was seen towards the end of the decade (in 1995–96 and from 1998 to 2001), when the number of births each year exceeded the number of deaths by between 62,000 and 77,000 per year. Although the annual numbers of both births and deaths decreased between 1991 and 2001, the decline in the number of births was faster, hence the lower level of natural increase in the more recent period.

In the early 1990s net international migration into the UK from abroad was making an increasingly important contribution to population growth. By 1998, net migration[42] had overtaken natural increase as the main driver of growth (Figure 1.7). During the late 1990s the UK experienced higher levels of both in-migration and out-migration than in previous years. The level of in-migration increased to a greater extent than the level of out-migration, resulting in an increase in net international migration to the UK during this period (see Chapter 7). In the year ending mid-2001, net international migration contributed approximately two-thirds of the UK's annual population increase.

The populations of Wales, Scotland and Northern Ireland grew at different rates from the populations of England and the UK as a whole in recent decades (Table 1.8). Between 1971 and

1981, the population of Wales grew the fastest of the constituent countries of the UK, with a 2.7 per cent increase over the decade, compared with 0.8 per cent for the UK as a whole. However, during the 1980s and 1990s, the population of Northern Ireland grew much faster than the rest of the UK (at over 5 per cent during the decade from 1991 to 2001, compared with less than 3 per cent for the UK as a whole). In contrast, Scotland's population decreased slightly, from over 5.2 million in 1971 to less than 5.1 million in 2001.

Table 1.9 shows population change and its components over the past decade for the four constituent countries of the UK, revealing the underlying causes of these different rates of growth. England's population growth between 1991 and 2001 was due to both natural increase and net migration.[43] In Northern Ireland, net migration made little difference to the population over the decade, but the population continued to grow due to natural increase (see Chapter 5).

In contrast, Scotland experienced a generally decreasing population, with more deaths than births each year from mid-1997 onwards, and net out-migration during the late 1990s. However, this trend changed in 2000, when the population began to increase slightly due to net in-migration. The Welsh population also saw natural decrease from mid-1998 onwards but this was outweighed by net in-migration, in particular from the rest of the UK,[44] leading to an increasing population between 1998 and 2001. Chapter 6 discusses in more detail the migration flows between different parts of the UK.

Figure **1.7**

Natural increase[1] and net migration[2] as components of population change, 1991 to 2001

United Kingdom

Thousands

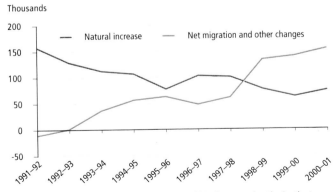

1 Natural increase refers to the excess of births over deaths in that year.
2 'Net migration and other changes' refers mainly to international migration. Other small changes include changes in the numbers of armed forces.

Source: Population estimates – Office for National Statistics; General Register Office for Scotland; Northern Ireland Statistics and Research Agency

Table **1.8**

Population of the UK and constituent countries, 1971 to 2001

Thousands

	1971	1981	1991	2001
UK	55,928.0	56,357.5	57,438.7	59,113.5
England	46,411.7	46,820.8	47,875.0	49,449.7
Wales	2,740.3	2,813.5	2,873.0	2,910.2
Scotland	5,235.6	5,180.2	5,083.3	5,064.2
Northern Ireland	1,540.4	1,543.0	1,607.3	1,689.3

Source: Population estimates – Office for National Statistics; General Register Office for Scotland; Northern Ireland Statistics and Research Agency

Table **1.9**

Population change and its components, 1991 to 2001

United Kingdom and constituent countries

Thousands

| Mid–year to mid–year | Population at start of period | Components of change (mid-year to mid-year) | | | | |
		Total change	Births	Deaths	Natural change[1]	Net migration and other changes[2]	Population at end of period
United Kingdom							
1991–92	57,438.7	+145.9	792.7	635.4	+157.3	−11.4	57,584.5
1992–93	57,584.5	+129.4	762.4	633.6	+128.8	+0.5	57,713.9
1993–94	57,713.9	+148.3	763.1	650.8	+112.3	+36.0	57,862.1
1994–95	57,862.1	+162.7	737.2	630.4	+106.9	+55.8	58,024.8
1995–96	58,024.8	+139.6	722.3	645.0	+77.3	+62.2	58,164.4
1996–97	58,164.4	+149.9	739.9	637.1	+102.8	+47.0	58,314.2
1997–98	58,314.2	+160.7	717.5	617.1	+100.4	+60.3	58,474.9
1998–99	58,474.9	+209.5	710.5	633.9	+76.6	+132.8	58,684.4
1999–2000	58,684.4	+201.6	688.0	625.7	+62.3	+139.3	58,886.1
2000–01	58,886.1	+227.4	673.5	599.2	+74.3	+153.2	59,113.5
England							
1991–92	47,875.0	+122.9	661.7	526.0	+135.7	−12.8	47,998.0
1992–93	47,998.0	+104.3	636.7	522.5	+114.2	−9.9	48,102.3
1993–94	48,102.3	+126.5	639.3	536.9	+102.4	+24.1	48,228.8
1994–95	48,228.8	+154.7	617.8	521.1	+96.8	+57.9	48,383.5
1995–96	48,383.5	+135.7	605.9	533.2	+72.6	+63.0	48,519.1
1996–97	48,519.1	+145.6	619.7	526.8	+92.9	+52.8	48,664.8
1997–98	48,664.8	+155.8	601.8	509.9	+92.0	+63.8	48,820.6
1998–99	48,820.6	+212.3	597.5	523.1	+74.5	+137.8	49,032.9
1999–2000	49,032.9	+200.4	580.1	516.1	+64.0	+136.4	49,233.3
2000–01	49,233.3	+216.4	568.2	495.3	+72.9	+143.6	49,449.7
Wales							
1991–92	2,873.0	+4.7	38.1	33.6	+4.5	+0.1	2,877.7
1992–93	2,877.7	+5.9	36.7	34.1	+2.6	+3.3	2,883.6
1993–94	2,883.6	+3.9	36.2	35.6	+0.6	+3.3	2,887.4
1994–95	2,887.4	+1.1	34.8	34.4	+0.5	+0.6	2,888.5
1995–96	2,888.5	+2.8	34.0	35.3	−1.3	+4.1	2,891.3
1996–97	2,891.3	+3.6	35.5	35.1	+0.3	+3.2	2,894.9
1997–98	2,894.9	+4.7	33.9	33.7	+0.2	+4.4	2,899.5
1998–99	2,899.5	+1.1	32.9	35.0	−2.0	+3.1	2,900.6
1999–2000	2,900.6	+6.3	31.5	34.3	−2.8	+9.1	2,906.9
2000–01	2,906.9	+3.4	31.0	33.0	−1.9	+5.3	2,910.2

Table **1.9** - continued

Population change and its components, 1991 to 2001

United Kingdom and constituent countries

Thousands

Mid–year to mid–year	Population at start of period	Components of change (mid-year to mid-year)					Population at end of period
		Total change	Births	Deaths	Natural change[1]	Net migration and other changes[2]	
Scotland							
1991–92	5,083.3	+2.3	67.0	61.1	+5.9	−3.6	5,085.6
1992–93	5,085.6	+6.8	64.3	61.9	+2.4	+4.4	5,092.5
1993–94	5,092.5	+9.8	63.1	62.6	+0.5	+9.2	5,102.2
1994–95	5,102.2	+1.5	60.6	59.6	+0.9	+0.5	5,103.7
1995–96	5,103.7	−11.5	58.9	61.2	−2.3	−9.2	5,092.2
1996–97	5,092.2	−8.9	60.2	60.1	+0.1	−8.9	5,083.3
1997–98	5,083.3	−6.3	58.0	58.5	−0.5	−5.8	5,077.1
1998–99	5,077.1	−5.1	56.6	60.3	−3.7	−1.4	5,072.0
1999–2000	5,072.0	−9.0	54.1	59.7	−5.7	−3.4	5,062.9
2000–01	5,062.9	+1.3	52.7	56.6	−3.9	+5.2	5,064.2
Northern Ireland							
1991–92	1,607.3	+16.0	25.9	14.7	+11.2	+4.8	1,623.3
1992–93	1,623.3	+12.3	24.7	15.1	+9.7	+2.6	1,635.6
1993–94	1,635.6	+8.2	24.5	15.7	+8.8	−0.7	1,643.7
1994–95	1,643.7	+5.4	24.0	15.3	+8.7	−3.3	1,649.1
1995–96	1,649.1	+12.6	23.6	15.2	+8.4	+4.2	1,661.8
1996–97	1,661.8	+9.5	24.6	15.0	+9.6	−0.1	1,671.3
1997–98	1,671.3	+6.5	23.8	15.1	+8.7	−2.2	1,677.8
1998–99	1,677.8	+1.2	23.4	15.5	+7.9	−6.7	1,679.0
1999–2000	1,679.0	+3.9	22.3	15.5	+6.8	−2.8	1,682.9
2000–01	1,682.9	+6.4	21.6	14.3	+7.2	−0.9	1,689.3

1. *Natural increase refers to the excess of births over deaths in that year. Natural decrease refers to the excess of deaths over births.*
2.' *Net migration and other changes' refers mainly to international migration. Other small changes include changes in the numbers of armed forces.*

Source: Population estimates – Office for National Statistics; General Register Office for Scotland; Northern Ireland Statistics and Research Agency

The UK population at the start of the 21st century

In 2004 the UK was home to over 59.8 million people. This makes it one of the largest countries in the European Union in terms of population size (see Chapter 10). The present size and characteristics of the UK population reflect many of the changes that have occurred in the population over the past 50 years. The following section explores some of the characteristics of the UK population at the start of the 21st century.

Geographical distribution and growth

In 2004 83.7 per cent of the UK's population was resident in England (Table 1.10). Between 2001 and 2004 England's population increased by 644,000 to 50.1 million. Two-thirds of this increase was due to net in-migration,[45] with the remainder a result of natural increase.

Scotland was home to 8.5 per cent of the UK's population in 2004. Despite a decreasing population during the 1990s, there is some evidence that the Scottish population is beginning to increase: between 2002 and 2004, the population grew by 23,600.[46] This growth is due to an increase in net in-migration, which has begun to outweigh Scotland's natural decrease.

Table **1.10**

Population size and density, 2004

United Kingdom and constituent countries

	Resident population (thousands)	Percentage of UK population	Land area (km²)	Population per km²
United Kingdom	59,834.9	100.0	242,495	247
England	50,093.8	83.7	130,279	385
Wales	2,952.5	4.9	20,733	142
Scotland	5,078.4	8.5	77,907	65
Northern Ireland	1,710.3	2.9	13,576	126

Source: Population estimates – Office for National Statistics; General Register Office for Scotland; Northern Ireland Statistics and Research Agency

Figure **1.11**

Population by age and sex, 2004

United Kingdom

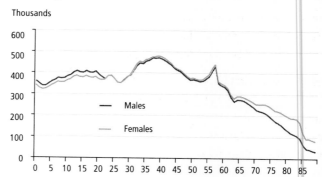

Source: Population estimates – Office for National Statistics; General Register Office for Scotland; Northern Ireland Statistics and Research Agency

Five per cent of the UK population lived in Wales in 2004. As is the case in Scotland, the Welsh population is increasing, despite the number of deaths exceeding the number of births each year. This is due to net in-migration, mainly from the rest of the UK, outweighing the population's natural decrease. Between 2001 and 2004, Wales has been in percentage terms the fastest growing constituent country of the UK.

Northern Ireland's 1.7 million residents made up 2.9 per cent of the UK population in 2004. This population has continued to grow into the 21st century due to natural increase; in contrast to the other UK countries, net migration did not make a large contribution to population change in Northern Ireland between 2001 and 2004.

The UK had an average population density of 247 people per km² of land in 2004 (Table 1.10). However the population is not evenly spread over the UK's land area of 242,495km². Scotland was by far the least densely populated, with 65 people per km². Northern Ireland and Wales had 126 and 142 people per km² respectively. England had the highest population density of 385 people per km², nearly six times higher than in Scotland. And, despite having over 80 per cent of the UK population, England makes up only 54 per cent of the land area.

Chapters 2 and 3 examine in more depth where people are living in the UK and focus on the characteristics of the UK's major towns and cities.

Age-sex structure

There are slightly more females than males living in the UK. In 2004 there were 30.6 million females and 29.3 million males, or 96 males for every 100 females.

Figure 1.11 shows that this pattern varies significantly by age. Normally more boys are born than girls, for example in 2004 there were 105 boys born for each 100 girls in England and Wales.[47] As a result, boys outnumber girls throughout childhood and the teenage years. The number of males relative to females decreases rapidly from around age 21 onwards due to differences in migration patterns and mortality rates.[48] At all ages above 30, women outnumbered men in 2004. At older ages, sex differentials in mortality lead to an increasingly female population. At age 65 there were 94 men for each 100 women, while at age 75 there were only 79 men per 100 women. At age 85 the contrast is even greater, with only 53 men per 100 women.

The average (median) age of the UK population in 2004 was 38.6 years. Figure 1.12 shows that there were slightly more

Figure **1.12**

Proportion of population in selected age groups, 2004

United Kingdom and constituent countries

Source: Population estimates – Office for National Statistics; General Register Office for Scotland; Northern Ireland Statistics and Research Agency

children aged under 16 in the UK in 2004 than people of retirement age (men aged 65 and above and women aged 60 and above). Almost one-fifth of the UK population (19.5 per cent) was aged below 16 while 18.6 per cent were in the retirement ages. Chapter 4 discusses in more detail how the proportion of children and older people in the UK has changed over time and is likely to change in the near future.

Wales and Scotland both have slightly more people of retirement age than children in their populations (Figure 1.12). Therefore, the average (median) age of their populations is higher than the UK average; 39.8 years in Scotland and 40.2 years in Wales compared with 38.6 years for the UK as a whole.

Northern Ireland stands out clearly from the rest of the UK as having the youngest population, with an average (median) age of only 35.8 years in 2004. This reflects the higher proportion of children aged under 16 in Northern Ireland (22.4 per cent compared with 19.5 per cent in the UK as whole). Northern Ireland's relatively youthful population is a result of its higher total fertility rate than the rest of the UK in recent years (see Chapter 5). Correspondingly Northern Ireland also has a lower proportion of people in the retirement ages (16.1 per cent compared with 18.6 per cent in the UK as a whole).

The population pyramid (Figure 1.13) shows the age-sex structure of the UK population in 2004 in more detail. The number of males and females of each age, and hence the shape of the UK pyramid, is determined by the numbers of births, deaths and migrants over the past century. The number of births each year over the past 90 years determines the initial size of each age group at birth, and the numbers surviving to each age are reduced by death, particularly at older ages. International migration also acts to increase or decrease the number of people of each age living in the UK.

The indent in the UK pyramid at around age 63 represents those born during the first half of the Second World War when fewer births took place than usual. In contrast, the spike in the pyramid at ages 54 to 57 reflects the large number of births occurring in the late 1940s, often referred to as the post-war baby boom. The large bulge in population for those in their late 30s and early 40s is a result of the high number of births that occurred during the 1960s. Similarly, the smaller bulge around ages 10 to 20 represents the children of the large number of women born in the 1960s.

Although some of these features are specific to the UK, the pyramid does follow the general pattern for a developed country: a stable or declining base to the pyramid and a large number of persons aged over 65 (see Chapter 10 for a comparison with the EU population pyramid). The interactive population pyramid available on the National Statistics website shows how the age structure of the UK population has changed since 1971.[49]

Figure **1.13**

Population pyramid showing age[1] and sex structure of the UK, 2004

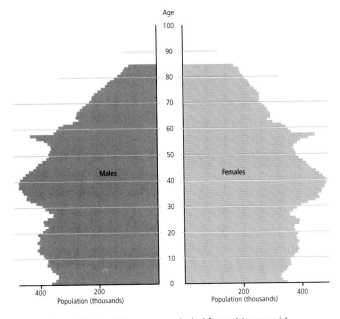

1   People aged 85 and above are excluded from this pyramid.

Source: Population estimates – Office for National Statistics; General Register Office for Scotland; Northern Ireland Statistics and Research Agency

Marital status and living arrangements

According to the 2001 Census, over half (53.3 per cent) the adults in the UK were married at the time. This figure includes the 7.1 per cent of adults who were remarried and 2.5 per cent who were separated. A further 30.2 per cent of adults were single (never married), 8.0 per cent were divorced and 8.4 per

Figure **1.14**

Population aged 16 and over by legal marital status, 2001

United Kingdom

Percentages

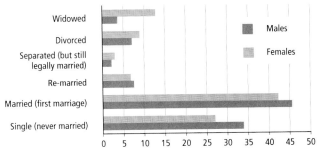

Source: 2001 Census – Office for National Statistics; General Register Office for Scotland; Northern Ireland Statistics and Research Agency

cent widowed. These figures refer to the legal marital status of people aged 16 and above on Census day.

The marital status composition of the population varies considerably by sex, as illustrated in Figure 1.14. In the UK in 2001, 34 per cent of men aged 16 and above were single compared with only 27 per cent of women. Men were also slightly more likely to be married or remarried at the time of the Census (53 per cent) than women (49 per cent): this percentage difference is due to the higher number of adult women than men in the population. However, 13 per cent of the female population was widowed at the time, compared with 4 per cent of the male population; this reflects the larger number of women than men in the population at older ages.

Women were also slightly more likely to be divorced or separated (12 per cent) at Census day than men (9 per cent), which may reflect differentials in remarriage patterns between the sexes. Chapter 4 describes in more detail how the legal marital status of the UK population varies by age and how it has changed over time.

Legal marital status does not always give a complete picture of people's living arrangements as many non-married people are actually cohabiting (living in a couple with a person they are not legally married to). Estimates of the extent of this cohabitation are available from the 2001 Census by combining information from the relationship matrix with a person's legal marital status. In April 2001 in the UK almost 4.4 million adults

aged 16 and over were cohabiting. This represents 10.0 per cent of men in households and 9.1 per cent of women in households.[50]

Although a small proportion of people in the UK live in communal establishments (1.8 per cent in 2001, see Chapter 9), the majority lives in private households. In 2004 there were 24.7 million households in the UK.[51]

The number of households in the UK has increased fairly steadily over recent decades, from 16.7 million households in 1961 to 20.6 million in 1981 and 24.7 million in 2004.[52] This reflects partly the increasing population over this period but also a decline in average household size over the past 40 years. In 1961 there were on average 3.0 people living in each household in Great Britain but, by 2004, this had fallen to 2.4.[53]

Nearly three in ten UK households (29 per cent) were one-person households in 2004. The number of one-person households has increased dramatically in recent decades. For example, in Great Britain, 12 per cent of households contained only one person in 1961 but this had risen to 23 per cent by 1981 and 29 per cent by 2004.[54] This increase is predominantly seen in one-person households containing an adult of working age. This household type has become more common due to both the growth in divorce rates during the 1970s and 1980s and, more recently, the postponement of marriage and childbearing by young adults.

Table 1.15

Family type and presence of children, 2004

United Kingdom and constituent countries

Percentages[1]

	England	Wales	Scotland	Northern Ireland	United Kingdom
Family type					
Married couple family	71	72	70	74	71
Cohabiting couple family	13	12	12	6	13
Lone-mother	13	14	16	18	14
Lone-father	2	2	2	2	2
All families	100	100	100	100	100
Presence of children					
With no children	43	43	42	31	42
With dependent children	43	43	41	50	43
With non-dependent children only	14	14	16	20	14
All families	100	100	100	100	100

1 Percentages may not add exactly to 100 due to rounding.

Source: Labour Force Survey, Spring 2004 – Office for National Statistics

A further 3 per cent of UK households in 2004 contained two or more people who were unrelated. However the most common UK household type was a household containing one or more families (68 per cent).

Families headed by a married couple are the most common family type in the UK, making up 71 per cent of families in 2004 (Table 1.15). A further 14 per cent of families were headed by a lone mother, 13 per cent by a cohabiting couple and 2 per cent by a lone father. Northern Ireland stands out in Table 1.15 as having a lower proportion of cohabiting-couple families (6 per cent) and higher proportions of married-couple families and lone mothers then other parts of the UK. In recent decades the proportion of families headed by a married couple has been declining while the proportions of families headed by a cohabiting couple or a lone mother have been increasing.

Not all families have dependant children living with them. In 2004, 43 per cent of UK families had dependent children, while in 14 per cent of families the only offspring living with the family were non-dependant children. The remaining 42 per

cent of families consisted of a married or cohabiting couple with no children living with them. Again, Northern Ireland stands out in Table 1.15 as having a lower proportion of families without children and higher proportions of families with dependent or non-dependent children. Further information on families in the UK can be found in *Focus on Families*.[55]

Ethnicity

The majority (92.1 per cent) of the UK population described themselves as White in the 2001 Census. The remaining 4.6 million people (7.9 per cent) belonged to non-White ethnic groups.[56]

Table 1.16 shows that the largest non-White ethnic group in 2001 was Indian, comprising 1.8 per cent of the UK population. Those of Pakistani origin were the second largest group (1.3 per cent), followed by 1.2 per cent of the population who described themselves as of mixed ethnic origin; for example, White and Black Caribbean or White and Asian.

Those from Black Caribbean and Black African backgrounds made up 1.0 per cent and 0.8 per cent of the UK population respectively. In addition, there were a large number of other ethnic minority groups represented in the census, accounting for the remaining 1.9 per cent of the UK population.

Of the four countries of the UK, England had the largest ethnic minority population in both absolute and percentage terms (Table 1.17), with nearly 4.5 million people or 9.1 per cent of its population being in an ethnic group other than White. This compares with 2.1 per cent of the population in Wales, 2.0 per cent in Scotland and 0.7 per cent in Northern Ireland.

In England, Wales and Scotland the largest generic ethnic minority population was Asian and Asian British (or Asian Scottish in Scotland). Within this category, those of Indian origin were the largest group in England with a population of over one million, while in Scotland the Pakistani population of 31,800 was the largest (although still much smaller than England's population of Pakistani origin). In Northern Ireland, the Chinese population of 4,100 made up nearly one-third of the small ethnic minority population (12,600). Further information on the geographical distribution of people in different ethnic groups is available in Chapter 2 or in *Focus on Ethnicity and Identity*.[57]

Those identifying with a White ethnic group come from a variety of backgrounds. In Great Britain, 50.4 million people, the majority of the White population, described themselves as White British or White Scottish in 2001. A further 0.7 million identified themselves as White Irish and 1.4 million as Other White.

Table **1.16**

Population by ethnic group, 2001

United Kingdom		Numbers and percentages
	Total population	
	(Numbers)	(Per cent)
White	**54,153,898**	**92.1**
Mixed	**677,117**	**1.2**
Indian	1,053,411	1.8
Pakistani	747,285	1.3
Bangladeshi	283,063	0.5
Other Asian	247,664	0.4
All Asian or Asian British	**2,331,423**	**4.0**
Black Caribbean	565,876	1.0
Black African	485,277	0.8
Other Black	97,585	0.2
All Black or Black British	**1,148,738**	**2.0**
Chinese	**247,403**	**0.4**
Any other ethnic groups	**230,615**	**0.4**
All minority ethnic population	**4,635,296**	**7.9**
All ethnic groups	**58,789,194**	**100.0**

Source: 2001 Census – Office for National Statistics; General Register Office for Scotland; Northern Ireland Statistics and Research Agency

Table **1.17**

Population by ethnic group, 2001[1]

United Kingdom and constituent countries

Numbers and percentages

	England		Wales		Scotland		Northern Ireland		United Kingdom	
	Numbers	Per cent	Numbers	Per cent	Numbers	Per cent	Numbers	Per cent	Numbers	Per cent
White[2]	44,679,361	90.9	2,841,505	97.9	4,960,334	98.0	1,672,698	99.3	54,153,898	92.1
British	42,747,136	87.0	2,786,605	96.0	*	*	*	*	.	.
Scottish	*	*	*	*	4,459,071	88.1	*	*	.	.
Irish	624,115	1.3	17,689	0.6	49,428	1.0	*	*	.	.
Other British	*	*	*	*	373,685	7.4	*	*	.	.
Other White	1,308,110	2.7	37,211	1.3	78,150	1.5	*	*	.	.
Mixed	643,373	1.3	17,661	0.6	12,764	0.3	3,319	0.2	677,117	1.2
White and Black Caribbean	231,424	0.5	5,996	0.2	*	*	*	*	.	.
White and Black African	76,498	0.2	2,413	0.1	*	*	*	*	.	.
White and Asian	184,014	0.4	5,001	0.2	*	*	*	*	.	.
Other Mixed	151,437	0.3	4,251	0.2	*	*	*	*	.	.
Asian or Asian British/ Scottish	2,248,289	4.6	25,448	0.9	55,007	1.1	2,679	0.2	2,331,423	4.0
Indian	1,028,546	2.1	8,261	0.3	15,037	0.3	1,567	0.1	1,053,411	1.8
Pakistani	706,539	1.4	8,287	0.3	31,793	0.6	666	0.0	747,285	1.3
Bangladeshi	275,394	0.6	5,436	0.2	1,981	0.0	252	0.0	283,063	0.5
Other Asian	237,810	0.5	3,464	0.1	6,196	0.1	194	0.0	247,664	0.4
Black or Black British/ Scottish	1,132,508	2.3	7,069	0.2	8,025	0.2	1,136	0.1	1,148,738	2.0
Black Caribbean	561,246	1.1	2,597	0.1	1,778	0.0	255	0.0	565,876	1.0
Black African	475,938	1.0	3,727	0.1	5,118	0.1	494	0.0	485,277	0.8
Black Other	95,324	0.2	745	0.0	1,129	0.0	387	0.0	97,585	0.2
Chinese or other ethnic groups	435,300	0.9	11,402	0.4	25,881	0.5	5,435	0.3	478,018	0.8
Chinese	220,681	0.5	6,267	0.2	16,310	0.3	4,145	0.3	247,403	0.4
Any other ethnic group	214,619	0.4	5,135	0.2	9,571	0.2	1,290	0.1	230,615	0.4
All ethnic groups	49,138,831	100.0	2,903,085	100.0	5,062,011	100.0	1,685,267	100.0	58,789,194	100.0

1. Cells in this table have been randomly adjusted to avoid the release of confidential data.
2. In Northern Ireland, this category includes 1,170 people who ticked 'Irish Traveller' box.
* Answer category not provided as a tick-box option in this country.
'.' not applicable.

Source: 2001 Census – Office for National Statistics; General Register Office for Scotland; Northern Ireland Statistics and Research Agency

The UK population in the future

In the near future, the UK population is projected to continue the gradual increase seen since the mid-1980s. The Government Actuary's Department (GAD) produces future projections of the population for the UK and its constituent countries.[58] These projections are based on assumptions relating to fertility, mortality and migration that are agreed in consultation with the statistical offices of England, Wales, Scotland and Northern Ireland.[59]

The UK population is projected to increase from 59.8 million in 2004 to an estimated 66.6 million by 2029[60] (Figure 1.18). Of this projected 6.8 million increase, 44 per cent (3.0 million) is projected to be natural increase (the excess of births over deaths), while 56 per cent (3.8 million) is the assumed total

Figure **1.18**

Population estimates and projections, 1981 to 2028

United Kingdom

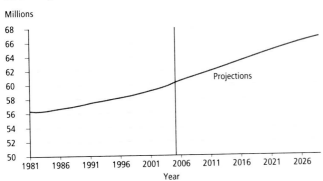

Source: Population estimates (1981–2004) – Office for National Statistics; General Register Office for Scotland; Northern Ireland Statistics and Research Agency. Population projections (2005–2028) – Government Actuary's Department

By 2031 there are projected to be 56.8 million people living in England, 3.3 million in Wales, 5.1 million in Scotland and 1.9 million in Northern Ireland. The proportion of UK residents living in England is, therefore, expected to be slightly higher than in 2004, while the proportions living in Wales, Scotland and Northern Ireland will have fallen slightly by 2031.

Notes and references

1. Population estimates for England and Wales are produced by the Office for National Statistics: www.statistics.gov.uk/statbase/Product.asp?vlnk=601&More=N

   Population estimates for Scotland are produced by the General Register Office for Scotland (GROS): www.gro-scotland.gov.uk

   Population estimates for Northern Ireland are produced by the Northern Ireland Statistics and Research Agency (NISRA): www.nisra.gov.uk/index.asp

number of net migrants. However, the projected numbers of future births and deaths are themselves partly dependent on the assumed level of net migration.[61] In the longer-term the UK's population is expected to continue rising until 2074, the end of the projection period.

Projected population trends differ between the constituent countries of the UK (Table 1.19) owing to differences in the assumptions made about future fertility and mortality (see Chapter 5) and expected net migration. The populations of England, Wales and Northern Ireland are expected to continue increasing up to 2031. Projections suggest that, during the early 2030s, the population of Northern Ireland will start to decline gradually in size, whereas the populations of England and Wales will continue rising slowly. In contrast, Scotland's population is expected to peak around 2019 and then resume the decrease seen during much of the 1990s, falling by nearly 0.3 per cent overall between 2004 and 2031.

2. Houston R A (1996) The Population History of Britain and Ireland 1500–1750, in Anderson M (1996) British Population History from the Black Death to the present day, Cambridge University Press: Cambridge.

3. For example, Hatcher J (1996) Plague, population and the English economy, 1348–1530, in Anderson M (1996) British Population History from the Black Death to the present day, Cambridge University Press: Cambridge. Hinde A (2003) England's Population: A History since the Domesday Survey, Hodder Arnold: London.

4. British Broadcasting Corporation: www.bbc.co.uk/history/state/nations/four_nations_01.shtml

5. Hinde A (2003) England's Population: A History since the Domesday Survey, Hodder Arnold: London.

Table **1.19**

Population estimates and projections, 2004 to 2031

United Kingdom and constituent countries

Thousands

	2004	2006	2011	2016	2021	2026	2031
United Kingdom	59,835	60,533	61,892	63,304	64,727	66,002	67,013
England	50,094	50,714	51,967	53,276	54,605	55,823	56,832
Wales	2,952	2,977	3,037	3,102	3,165	3,219	3,256
Scotland	5,078	5,108	5,120	5,126	5,127	5,109	5,065
Northern Ireland	1,710	1,733	1,767	1,800	1,830	1,851	1,860

Source: Population estimates (2004) – Office for National Statistics; General Register Office for Scotland; Northern Ireland Statistics and Research Agency. Population projections (2006–2031) – Government Actuary's Department

LIVERPOOL HOPE UNIVERSITY

6. See reference 5.

7. See reference 5.

8. See reference 5.

9. Coleman D and Salt J (1992) *The British Population: Patterns, Trends and Processes,* Oxford University Press: Oxford. Hinde A (2003) *England's Population: A History since the Domesday Survey,* Hodder Arnold: London.

10. See reference 9 and Houston R A (1996) The Population History of Britain and Ireland 1500–1750, in Anderson M (1996) *British Population History from the Black Death to the present day,* Cambridge University Press: Cambridge.

11. Coleman D and Salt J (1992) *The British Population: Patterns, Trends and Processes,* Oxford University Press: Oxford.

12. Wrigley E A and Schofield R S (1981) *The Population History of England 1541–1871: a Reconstruction,* Edward Arnold: London.

13. See reference 11 and Houston R A (1996) The Population History of Britain and Ireland 1500–1750, in Anderson M (1996) *British Population History from the Black Death to the present day,* Cambridge University Press: Cambridge.

14. Houston R A (1996) The Population History of Britain and Ireland 1500–1750, in Anderson M (1996) *British Population History from the Black Death to the present day,* Cambridge University Press: Cambridge.

15. See reference 14.

16. Office for National Statistics (2001) *200 Years of the Census.* On Census Bicentenary web pages: www.statistics.gov.uk/census2001/bicentenary/bicentenary.html

17. Clarke J I (1972) *Population Geography,* 2nd edn, Pergamon Press: Oxford.

18. See reference 16.

19. Office of Population Census and Surveys (1993*) 1991 Census Historic Tables – Great Britain,* OPCS: London.

20. Office for National Statistics 2001 Census pages: www.statistics.gov.uk/census2001/cb_8.asp

21. Northern Ireland Statistics and Research Agency: www.nisra.gov.uk/census/censushistory/censusireland.html

22. Central Statistics Office Ireland (2004) *Irish Statistical Yearbook 2004,* Chapter 1 and Northern Ireland Appendix: www.cso.ie/releasespublications/statistical_yearbook_ireland_2004.htm

23. See reference 22. In Northern Ireland, censuses were taken in 1926, 1937, 1951, 1961, 1966, 1971, 1981, 1991 and 2001. In the Republic of Ireland, censuses were taken in 1926, 1936, 1946, 1951 and then every five years (with the exception of 1979 instead of 1976 and 2002 instead of 2001, due to foot and mouth disease).

24. The demographic transition model was initially proposed by Warren Thompson in 1929 and has since been documented and modified by Frank Notestein and others.

25. McKeown T (1976) *The Modern Rise of Population,* Edward Arnold: London. Hinde A (2003) *England's Population: A History since the Domesday Survey,* Hodder Arnold: London.

26. See reference 5.

27. See references 11 and 25.

28. Woods R I and Smith C W (1983) The decline of marital fertility in the late 19th century: the case of England and Wales. *Population Studies* **37**, 207–226.

29. See reference 11.

30. Baines D (1985) *Migration in a Mature Economy: Emigration and Internal Migration in England and Wales, 1861–1900,* Cambridge University Press: Cambridge, cited in Hinde A (2003) *England's Population: A History since the Domesday Survey,* Hodder Arnold: London.

31. See reference 11.

32. Griffiths C and Brock A (2003) Twentieth Century Mortality Trends in England and Wales. *Health Statistics Quarterly* **18**, 5–17.

33. Baines D (1985) *Migration in a Mature Economy: Emigration and Internal Migration in England and Wales, 1861–1900,* Cambridge University Press: Cambridge, cited in Woods R I (1996) The Population of Britain in the nineteenth century, in Anderson M (1996) *British Population History from the Black Death to the present day,* Cambridge University Press: Cambridge.

34. Anderson M (1996) Population Change in North-western Europe, 1750–1850, in Anderson M (1996) *British Population History from the Black Death to the present day,* Cambridge University Press: Cambridge.

35. See reference 34.

36. See reference 34.

37. See reference 34.

38. See reference 11. Plus Northern Ireland Statistics and Research Agency and General Register Office for Scotland (for data on births and divorces).

39. Van de Kaa D (1987) Europe's second demographic transition, in *Population Bulletin* **42(1)**.

40. All population estimates from 1951 onwards refer to mid-year estimates (population as at 30 June).

41. Figure refers to the calendar year 1976.

42. 'Net migration' in this context refers to 'net civilian migration and other changes'. 'Other changes' refers to changes in the numbers of armed forces resident in the UK plus any adjustments made to reconcile differences between estimated population change and the figures for natural change and net civilian migration.

43. See note 42.

44. See Office for National Statistics National Health Service Central Register (NHSCR) inter-regional migration movements data:

www.statistics.gov.uk/STATBASE/Product.asp?vlnk=10191

45. See note 42.

46. General Register Office for Scotland: www.gro-scotland.gov.uk

47. Office for National Statistics (2005) *Birth Statistics 2004*. Series FM1 No.33. www.statistics.gov.uk/StatBase/Product.asp?vlnk=5768&Pos =1&ColRank=1&Rank=272

48. Office for National Statistics (2004) *Focus on Gender*: www.statistics.gov.uk/focuson/gender/

49. Office for National Statistics UK interactive population pyramid: www.statistics.gov.uk/populationestimates/svg_pyramid/ default.htm

50. 2001 Census data from Office for National Statistics, General Register Office for Scotland and Northern Ireland Statistics and Research Agency.

51. Labour Force Survey data – Office for National Statistics.

52. 1961 and 1981 estimates are Census data from the Office for National Statistics, General Register Office for Scotland, Northern Ireland Statistics and Research Agency. 2004 estimate is from the Labour Force Survey.

53. 1961 average household size is from Census data. 2004 average household size is from the Labour Force Survey.

54. 1961 and 1981 percentages are from Census data. 2004 estimates for household and family types are from the Labour Force Survey.

55. Office for National Statistics (2004) *Focus on Families*: www.statistics.gov.uk/focuson/families/

56. In this context, ethnic minority groups include those of Mixed, Asian (or Asian British/Scottish), Black (or Black British/Scottish), Chinese and other non-White ethnic origins.

57. Office for National Statistics (2004) Focus on Ethnicity: www.statistics.gov.uk/focuson/ethnicity/

58. For information on UK population projections, see Government Actuary's Department website: www.gad.gov.uk/

59. Responsibility for the production of national population projections is due to be transferred from the Government Actuary's Department to the Office for National Statistics in 2006.

60. Figures refer to the 2004-based projections: principal projection.

61. See note on *Migration and population growth* at www.gad.gov.uk/population/2003/methodology/mignote.htm

Chapter 1: The UK population: past, present and future

Focus on People and Migration: 2005

Where people live

Kate Shaw and Julie Jefferies

Chapter 2

Introduction

Chapter 1 provides an overview of the population of the UK and its four constituent countries. Such an overview is a useful starting point but a huge amount of diversity exists between different regions and local areas within the UK.

This chapter describes where people live within the UK and which areas have the highest and lowest concentrations of population. It highlights variations in the age and sex structure of the populations of different areas, as well as geographical differences in population characteristics such as ethnicity, religion and deprivation.

As well as providing a portrait of the geographical variations in population characteristics throughout the UK, the chapter also touches on the reasons for these variations. For people who are able to choose where they live, the characteristics of the population already residing in different areas will help them to make that choice. For example, retired people may decide to move to coastal areas with high concentrations of people of a similar age and thus a high level of service provision for their age group.

However, it is important to recognise that not everybody is able to choose where they live. For example, many people are unable to move out of their current area of residence due to financial or personal constraints. Factors such as the availability of employment or housing play a part in where people choose to live or are forced to live. The chapter finishes by looking at some of the variations in employment and housing patterns within the UK.

Population distribution and density

Of the 59.8 million people living in the UK in mid-2004,[1] 50.1 million were resident in England, 5.1 million in Scotland, 3.0 million in Wales and 1.7 million in Northern Ireland (Table 2.1). Among Government Office Regions (GORs) in England, the South East had the largest population at that time, with over 8.1 million residents, followed by London with 7.4 million residents. In fact over one-quarter (26 per cent) of the UK population was resident in London and the South East combined. The smallest English region in terms of population was the North East, with only 2.5 million residents.

The local government districts with the largest populations in mid-2004 were Birmingham (992,400), Leeds (719,600) and Glasgow City (577,700). London as a city does not feature here, because it consists of a number of separate boroughs for the purposes of local government administration. In a similar way, the population sizes of all areas depend on the boundaries of the local government areas in existence at the time.

Table **2.1**

Resident population and population density,[1] 2004

United Kingdom

	Total population (thousands)	Area Km^2	People per Km^2
United Kingdom	59,835	242,495	247
England	50,094	130,279	385
North East	2,545	8,573	297
North West	6,827	14,106	484
Yorkshire and the Humber	5,039	15,408	327
East Midlands	4,280	15,607	274
West Midlands	5,334	12,998	410
East	5,491	19,109	287
London	7,429	1,572	4,726
Inner London	*2,931*	*319*	*9,180*
Outer London	*4,498*	*1,253*	*3,591*
South East	8,110	19,069	425
South West	5,038	23,837	211
Wales	2,952	20,733	142
Scotland	5,078	77,907	65
Northern Ireland	1,710	13,576	126

1 Population estimates refer to mid-year point (30 June).

Source: Population estimates – Office for National Statistics; General Register Office for Scotland; Northern Ireland Statistics and Research Agency

The local districts with the smallest populations in mid-2004 were the Isles of Scilly, with 2,200 residents, the City of London with 8,600 residents and Moyle (Northern Ireland) with a population of 16,400. The City of London authority contains London's financial institutions and has a small resident population despite having a large daytime population.

On average, there were 247 people living in each square kilometre of the UK in 2004 (Table 2.1). Population density varies considerably between the countries and regions: the highest in 2004 being the London GOR, with 4,726 people per km^2, and the lowest in Scotland, with 65 people per km^2. Within England, the second most densely populated region was the North West (484 people per km^2) and the least densely populated was the South West (211 people per km^2). Within London, Inner London was far more densely populated, with 9,180 people per square kilometre, than Outer London (3,591 people per km^2 in 2004).

Map **2.2**

Population density: by local or unitary authority, 2004[1]

United Kingdom

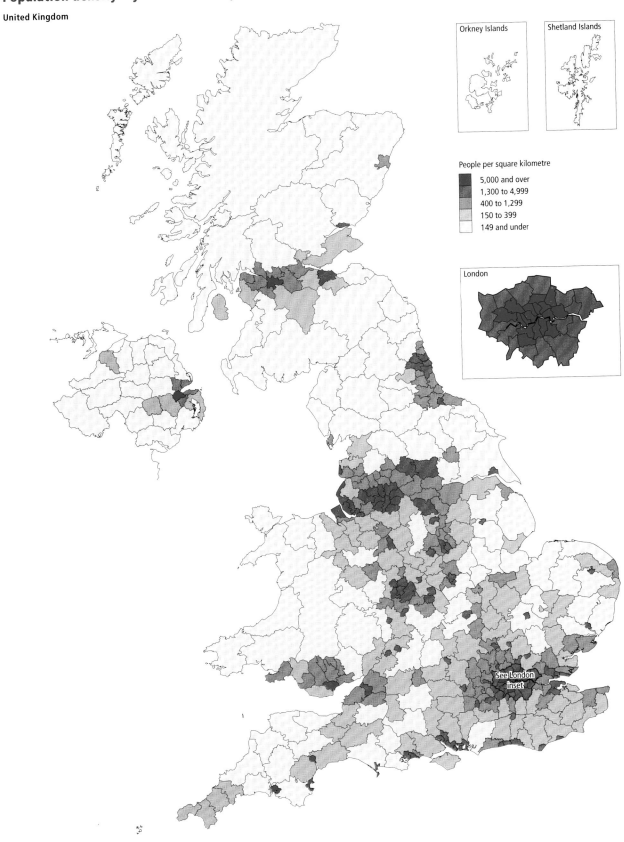

Orkney Islands

Shetland Islands

People per square kilometre

- 5,000 and over
- 1,300 to 4,999
- 400 to 1,299
- 150 to 399
- 149 and under

London

See London inset

1 Mid-2004 population estimates for the UK.

Source: Office for National Statistics; General Register Office for Scotland; Northern Ireland Statistics and Research Agency

Map 2.2 shows local variations in population density within the UK in 2004. The map illustrates clearly the areas with the highest population densities and also the large parts of the UK that have fewer than 150 residents per km^2.

Within England, the highest population densities are found in London. Table 2.3 shows that the ten local authorities with the highest population densities in the UK were all London boroughs, with the Royal Borough of Kensington and Chelsea home to over 15,000 persons per km^2. Every borough in Inner London, with the exception of the City of London, had a population density of over 6,000 people per km^2, higher than any other areas in the country.

Map 2.2 shows that the other areas of high population density (over 1,300 people per square kilometre) are spread throughout England but tend to be either clustered around large cities such as Birmingham, Manchester and Newcastle upon Tyne or consist of large towns, often with student populations. Outside London, Portsmouth Unitary Authority (UA) was the most densely populated area in England, with 4,683 people per km^2 in 2004, followed by Southampton UA (4,438 people per km^2). Eden (in the North West GOR) was the most sparsely populated area in England, with just 24 people per km^2 (Table 2.3). The North East and Yorkshire and the Humber GORs both had high numbers of sparsely populated districts compared with other English regions.

Wales, Scotland and Northern Ireland are all sparsely populated in comparison with the English regions, but each has areas of higher population density clustered around their cities. Wales had 142 people per km^2 on average in 2004, ranging from 2,263 in Cardiff to 25 in Powys. Northern Ireland contained 126 residents per km^2 on average, ranging from 2,454 in Belfast to 33 in Moyle.

Eight of the ten most sparsely populated districts in the UK were in Scotland (Table 2.3), with only eight people per km^2 in Highland and nine in Eilean Siar. Although Scotland's average population density of 65 people per km^2 was the lowest of the four UK countries, Scotland does contain some areas of higher population concentration. The most densely populated districts in Scotland in 2004 were Glasgow City (3,308), Dundee City (2,371) and Edinburgh (1,723 persons per km^2).

As with the other factors discussed in this chapter, the population density of an area is both a result of where people choose to live and, in some cases, a determinant of where they choose to live. Given the choice, some people would rather live in a high-density city area near to employment and leisure facilities, while others would choose a more remote area. The type of areas people choose to live in are likely to change over time as they age and their circumstances alter. For example, people often move when they are seeking employment, bringing up a young family or retiring, or when their children leave home. The links between age and where people live are discussed further in the next section.

Table **2.3**

Population density: highest and lowest ten districts in the UK, 2004

People per km^2

Rank	Most densely populated		Least densely populated	
1	Kensington and Chelsea	15,174	Highland	8
2	Islington	12,105	Eilean Siar	9
3	Hammersmith and Fulham	10,861	Argyll and Bute	13
4	Hackney	10,776	Shetland Islands	15
5	Westminster	10,709	Orkney Islands	20
6	Tower Hamlets	10,589	Dumfries and Galloway	23
7	Lambeth	9,996	Scottish Borders	23
8	Camden	9,959	Eden	24
9	Southwark	8,826	Powys	25
10	Wandsworth	8,070	Perth and Kinross	26

Source: Population estimates – Office for National Statistics; General Register Office for Scotland; Northern Ireland Statistics and Research Agency

Age and sex structure

In describing the age and sex structure of the UK population, Chapter 1 notes that the key determinant of population structure at the national level is fertility, with mortality and international migration also playing a part. At the local level, internal migration tends to be the most important determinant of a population's age and sex composition (Chapter 6), although international migration also plays an important role in some areas (Chapter 7).

This section examines regional and local variations in the age and sex structure of the population, starting at the regional level. The focus then moves to three age groups of specific interest and the local authorities in which they are concentrated. Finally, variations in the proportions of males and females in different areas are considered.

Regional patterns

Table 2.4 shows regional variations in age structure within the UK. In 2004, one-fifth (19.5 per cent) of the UK's population was aged under 16 years. Scotland had the lowest proportion of children (18.4 per cent), closely followed by the South West (18.5 per cent). Northern Ireland had by far the highest proportion of children (22.4 per cent), with the West Midlands having the highest proportion of children among the English GORs (20.1 per cent).

At the opposite end of the age spectrum, 18.6 per cent of the UK's population was of pensionable age in mid-2004. The proportion of older people was highest in the South West (21.7 per cent), followed by Wales (20.4 per cent). In contrast, London had the lowest proportion of its population in the retirement ages (13.9 per cent) and Northern Ireland the second lowest at 16.1 per cent.

Table 2.4

Resident population:[1] by age and sex, by UK country and Government Office Region, 2004

Percentages, thousands

	Percentages[2]				Resident population, all ages (thousands)
	0 to 15	16 to 24 years	16 to pensionable age[3]	Pensionable age and above[3]	
All Persons					
United Kingdom	19.5	11.6	61.9	18.6	59,835
England	19.5	11.5	62.0	18.5	50,094
North East	18.9	12.2	61.7	19.4	2,545
North West	19.8	11.9	61.5	18.7	6,827
Yorkshire and the Humber	19.7	12.3	61.6	18.8	5,039
East Midlands	19.3	11.6	61.7	18.9	4,280
West Midlands	20.1	11.7	61.0	18.9	5,334
East	19.6	10.6	60.9	19.4	5,491
London	19.4	12.2	66.7	13.9	7,429
South East	19.5	11.0	61.4	19.1	8,110
South West	18.5	10.8	59.9	21.7	5,038
Wales	19.4	11.7	60.2	20.4	2,952
Scotland	18.4	11.6	62.5	19.1	5,078
Northern Ireland	22.4	13.0	61.5	16.1	1,710

1 Population estimates refer to mid-year point (30 June).
2 Percentages may not add exactly to 100 due to rounding.
3 Pensionable age is defined as ages 65 and above for men and 60 and above for women.

Source: Population estimates – Office for National Statistics; General Register Office for Scotland; Northern Ireland Statistics and Research Agency

Map **2.5**

Population of pensionable age:[1] by local or unitary authority, 2004[2]

United Kingdom

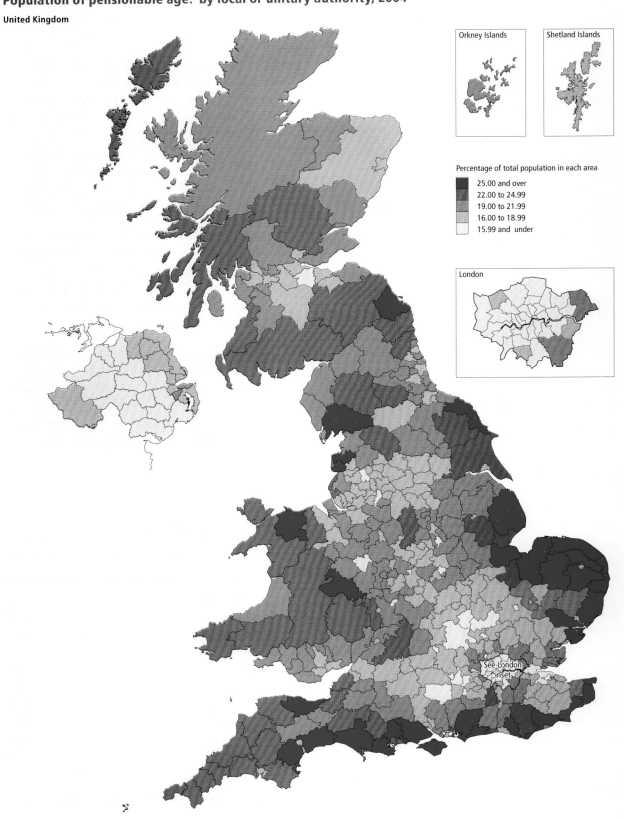

Orkney Islands

Shetland Islands

Percentage of total population in each area

	25.00 and over
	22.00 to 24.99
	19.00 to 21.99
	16.00 to 18.99
	15.99 and under

London

See London inset

1 State pension age is age 65 and older for men and age 60 and older for women.
2 Mid-2004 population estimates for the UK.

Source: Office for National Statistics; General Register Office for Scotland; Northern Ireland Statistics and Research Agency

The South West's population has a high proportion of older people and a low proportion of children, due to the in-migration of large numbers of retired people. This illustrates how particular age groups migrating to certain areas of the country can change the structure of the communities they live in. However, Northern Ireland has a low proportion of those above pensionable age in its population because its above-average fertility keeps the proportion of children high (see Chapter 5 for further information on fertility rates).

London's population contains a low proportion of people above retirement age, but the highest proportion of working age people of all the constituent countries and regions: 66.7 per cent compared with the UK average of 61.9 per cent. This is due to a combination of factors but, in particular, London attracts large numbers of young adults migrating from other parts of the UK and abroad to take up study and employment opportunities. This illustrates the influence of employment on where people live. Further discussion of this can be found under 'Employment patterns' later in the chapter.

Older people

Map 2.5 shows geographical variations in the concentrations of residents over retirement age in 2004. With a few exceptions (West Somerset, South Shropshire, Fylde, Wyre and South Lakeland in England and Conwy in Wales), the authorities with over a quarter of their population above pensionable age are predominantly on the southern and eastern coastlines of

England. Christchurch (33.2 per cent) and Rother (32.1 per cent), both on the south coast, have the highest proportions of older people in the UK (Table 2.6). Map 2.5 also highlights other areas with relatively older populations, including Cornwall, North and mid-Wales and southern Scotland.

The ten areas with the lowest proportions of older people in 2004 were all Inner London boroughs (Table 2.6), with Tower Hamlets the lowest at 9.8 per cent. Inner London in general had a low proportion of pensioners, with no boroughs having more than 14 per cent of their population over pensionable age, considerably lower than the UK average of 18.6 per cent. Correspondingly, Inner London boroughs are home to an above average proportion of working age people: 70.2 per cent on average compared with a UK average of 61.9 per cent.

Outside London, Milton Keynes UA and Bracknell Forest UA (both South East) had the lowest proportions of older people among English local authorities, at 12.3 and 13.3 per cent respectively. These authorities are in the broad band of areas in 'middle' England with a low proportion of population of pensionable age, as seen in Map 2.5.

Northern Ireland also stands out clearly on the map as having a low proportion of pensioners in virtually all its districts. The lowest proportions of older people in Northern Ireland in 2004 were seen in Limavady (12.4 per cent) and Derry (12.5) per cent. Only North Down (19.5 per cent) and Castlereagh (19.6 per cent) had a higher proportion of older people than the UK average.

Table 2.6

Percentage of population of pensionable age:[1] ten highest and lowest districts in the UK, 2004

Percentages

Rank	Highest		Lowest	
1	Christchurch	33.2	Tower Hamlets	9.8
2	Rother	32.1	Newham	10.0
3	West Somerset	30.8	Lambeth	10.4
4	East Devon	30.3	Hackney	10.5
5	Tendring	30.1	Haringey	11.0
6	North Norfolk	30.0	Islington	11.4
7	East Dorset	29.7	Camden	11.4
8	Arun	29.3	Wandsworth	11.6
9	West Dorset	28.3	Hammersmith and Fulham	11.6
10	Eastbourne	26.9	Southwark	11.7

1 Pensionable age is defined as ages 65 and above for men and 60 and above for women.

Source: Population estimates – Office for National Statistics; General Register Office for Scotland; Northern Ireland Statistics and Research Agency

Map **2.7**

Population under 16 years: by local or unitary authority, 2004[1]

United Kingdom

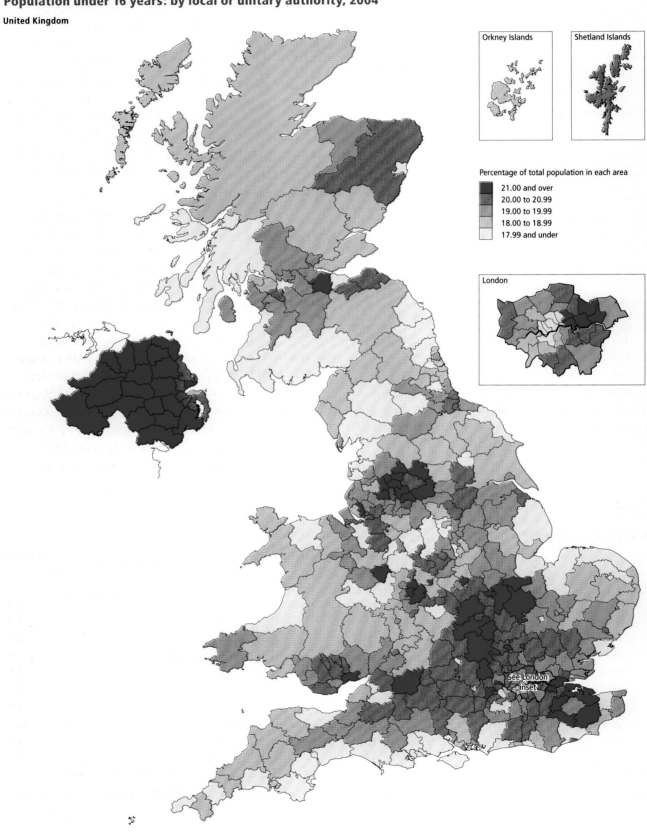

Orkney Islands

Shetland Islands

Percentage of total population in each area

- 21.00 and over
- 20.00 to 20.99
- 19.00 to 19.99
- 18.00 to 18.99
- 17.99 and under

London

See London inset

1 Mid-2004 population estimates for the UK.

Source: Office for National Statistics; General Register Office for Scotland; Northern Ireland Statistics and Research Agency

Children

Map 2.7 shows local variations in the proportion of the population aged under 16. Northern Ireland in particular stands out as having an above average proportion of children. As noted earlier, 22.4 per cent of Northern Ireland's population was aged under 16 in 2004, a figure around three percentage points higher than for England or Wales (Table 2.4).

The highest proportions of children in the UK were found in the two Northern Irish districts, Newry and Mourne, and Derry, where over one-quarter of the population was aged under 16. Table 2.8 shows that eight out of 10 districts with the highest proportions of children in the UK in 2004 were in Northern Ireland. Only one district in Northern Ireland (North Down) had a lower proportion of children (18.9 per cent) than the UK average of 19.5 per cent. Northern Ireland's younger population is a result of fertility rates in Northern Ireland being higher than those in other parts of the UK (Chapter 5).

Within the rest of the UK the pattern is less clear. Blackburn with Darwen UA in the North West had the greatest percentage of children under 16 in Britain (24.6 per cent), followed by Newham in London (24.4 per cent). Map 2.7 also shows above average proportions of children in various areas such as parts of Kent, Northamptonshire and Buckinghamshire, as well as pockets around Manchester, Birmingham and Newport in South Wales.

The capital exhibits an interesting pattern with London boroughs featuring among areas with both the highest and lowest proportions of children. Newham had the fifth highest proportion of children under 16 in the UK in 2004 (24.4 per cent), while the City of London (9.2 per cent) and Westminster (13.2 per cent) had the lowest (Table 2.8). Other areas with low proportions of children in their populations fall into two categories, the first being university towns such as Oxford and Cambridge where the proportion of young adults (those aged 16 to 24) is high. The second is those districts with particularly 'old' populations such as North Norfolk and West Somerset, which have a correspondingly low proportion of children.

These complex patterns illustrate the variety of factors that underlie the proportion of children in a particular area. Fertility rates and the age structure of the population will impact on the number of children born. However, the migration of children and other age groups in and out of districts will also have a considerable impact on the age structure of each area. As the majority of children live with a parent or parents, exploring where children live closely equates to exploring where adults with dependent children live. Residential choices among parents are likely to reflect the provision of suitable housing and services such as education, as well as employment opportunities and personal preferences about suitable locations for bringing up children. The high proportions of children seen in the Home Counties (Map 2.7) may in part result from the migration of families out of London to surrounding areas (Chapter 6).

Table **2.8**

Population under 16: highest and lowest ten districts in the UK, 2004

Percentages

Rank	Highest		Lowest	
1	Newry and Mourne	25.4	City of London	9.2
2	Derry	25.1	Westminster	13.2
3	Magherafelt	24.7	Cambridge	13.7
4	Blackburn with Darwen UA	24.6	Kensington and Chelsea	15.0
5	Newham	24.4	Oxford	15.3
6	Dungannon	24.2	Durham	15.4
7	Cookstown	24.1	Wandsworth	15.5
8	Armagh	24.1	West Somerset	15.5
9	Strabane	24.1	City of Edinburgh	15.6
10	Limavady	24.1	North Norfolk	15.7

Source: Population estimates – Office for National Statistics; General Register Office for Scotland; Northern Ireland Statistics and Research Agency

Map **2.9**

Population aged 16 to 24 years: by local or unitary authority, 2004[1]

United Kingdom

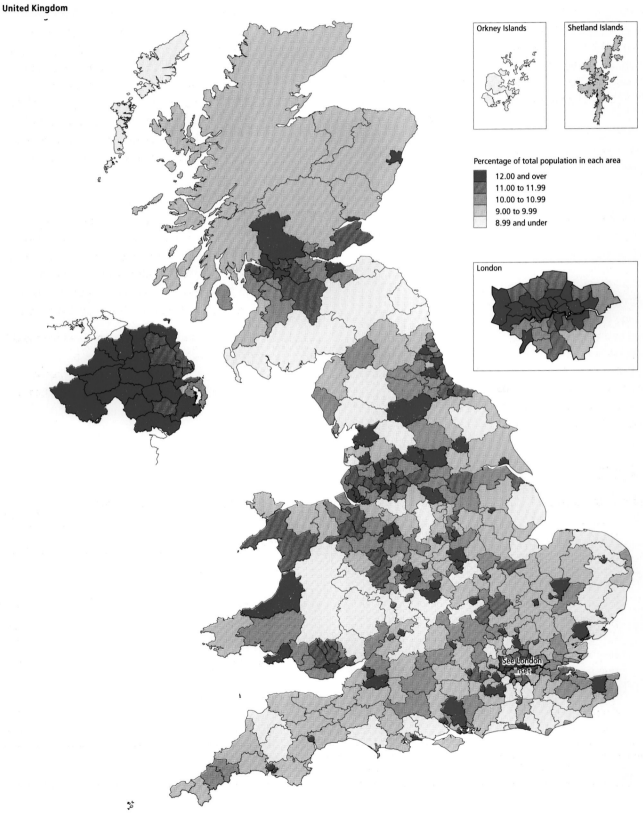

Orkney Islands

Shetland Islands

Percentage of total population in each area

- 12.00 and over
- 11.00 to 11.99
- 10.00 to 10.99
- 9.00 to 9.99
- 8.99 and under

London

See London Inset

1 Mid-2004 population estimates for the UK.

Source: Office for National Statistics; General Register Office for Scotland; Northern Ireland Statistics and Research Agency

Young adults

Young adults are considered separately here because of the high proportion (over 40 per cent) of the UK's 16 to 24-year-olds who were full-time students at the time of the 2001 Census.[2] The movement of students to and from higher education institutions greatly influences the geographic distribution of this age group. Higher education is an increasingly important determinant of where this age group lives, given the rising participation in higher education in recent years. The number of full-time students in higher education in the UK has increased from 748,600 in 1990/91 to 1,386,700 in 2002/03.[3] The student population is considered in detail in Chapter 9.

Table 2.4 shows that 11.6 per cent of the UK population was aged 16 to 24 in 2004. Regional variations were fairly small, with the proportion in this age group ranging from 10.6 per cent in the East region of England to 13.0 per cent in Northern Ireland. Map 2.9 again shows Northern Ireland standing out clearly with a high proportion of 16 to 24-year-olds as well as children, emphasising its 'younger' population compared with the rest of the UK.

Within regions, the variation in the proportion of 16 to 24-year-olds is far greater, hence Map 2.9 shows a far more fragmented picture than the maps for children and older people. Apart from in Northern Ireland and London, there is no clear pattern for areas with high proportions of young adults.

The lowest proportions of young adults were spread throughout different regions but were particularly prominent in rural areas in the South East and South West of England.

This fragmented pattern occurs because young adults are found in particularly high numbers in towns and cities with higher education institutions. Table 2.10 clearly shows that the areas with high percentages of young adults are those with large, established universities, with Oxford and Cambridge both having almost one quarter of their populations aged 16 to 24. In fact the 20 authorities with the highest proportions of young adults all contain higher education institutions and are, therefore, home to substantial numbers of students during term-time.

In contrast, the areas with very low proportions of young adults are likely to be either those sending large numbers of young adults to study in other areas or those with generally older populations. Table 2.10 shows that South Shropshire had the lowest proportion of young adult residents in the UK in 2004 (7.6 per cent), followed by the retirement areas of East Dorset, West Dorset, Christchurch and Rother (all 7.8 per cent).

The migration of higher education students both within the UK and from abroad clearly has a large impact on the age structure of different areas and is discussed further in Chapters 6 and 7 in the context of overall migration patterns.

Table **2.10**

Population of young adults aged 16 to 24 years: highest and lowest ten districts in the UK, 2004

Percentages

Rank	Highest		Lowest	
1	Oxford	23.9	South Shropshire	7.6
2	Cambridge	23.1	East Dorset	7.8
3	Nottingham UA	20.7	West Dorset	7.8
4	Durham	20.0	Christchurch	7.8
5	Southampton UA	18.9	Rother	7.8
6	Manchester	18.8	Wealden	8.0
7	Exeter	17.7	Mole Valley	8.1
8	Newcastle upon Tyne	17.7	Derbyshire Dales	8.2
9	Ceredigion UA	17.2	Craven[2]	8.3
10	Cardiff UA[1]	16.9	Isles of Scilly[2]	8.3

1 *Lincoln and Norwich also have 16.9 per cent of their populations in this age group.*
2 *South Holland and Tendring also have 8.3 per cent of their populations in this age group.*

Source: *Population estimates – Office for National Statistics; General Register Office for Scotland; Northern Ireland Statistics and Research Agency*

Data from higher education institutions can provide more information on the movement of UK students between regions when starting a higher education course. Table 2.11 shows that a student's home country or region has an influence on the region in which they choose to study. Scotland had the highest proportion of its students studying in their 'home' area in 2002/03 (94.2 per cent) while the East of England had the lowest, with only 41.1 per cent of its students staying in the region and 59.9 per cent studying elsewhere.

This may partly relate to the availability of places to study within the region. For example, London had the greatest number of higher education institutions in 2005, with 55 possible places to study.[4] It follows that many students from London (70.2 per cent) would study in London as their home region and others would be attracted there. In contrast, the East of England had only 13 higher education establishments in 2005, giving students from this region less choice, which may account for only 41.1 per cent remaining there to attend university in 2002/03. However, the North East had only five establishments but among the English regions had the highest proportion of students staying in their area of previous residence (73.0 per cent), confirming that local availability is not the only factor to consider when choosing where to study.

Students who did leave their home region were most likely to attend higher education in a nearby region. For example, students from the East Midlands were more likely to go to Yorkshire and the Humber (17.6 per cent) than London (4.2 per cent). These patterns suggest that only a minority of students

Table 2.11

Higher education students living in the UK prior to starting higher education:[1] by country and Government Office Region of current study and country and Government Office Region of previous residence, 2002/03

Percentages[2] and thousands

						Region of study							All students (=100 per cent) (thousands)
	North East	North West	Yorkshire and the Humber	East Mid-lands	West Mid-lands	East	London	South East	South West	Wales	Scotland	Northern Ireland	
Region of previous residence													
United Kingdom	4.7	11.3	10.0	6.6	8.3	5.3	15.3	10.3	7.0	5.8	12.3	3.0	1,779.2
England[3]	5.7	13.5	12.3	8.1	10.1	6.6	18.8	12.6	8.4	2.4	1.4	-	1,414.6
North East	73.0	5.2	9.7	2.5	1.3	1.2	1.6	1.5	0.6	0.5	2.8	0.1	71.3
North West	3.1	68.9	10.6	3.1	4.1	1.5	2.2	2.0	1.1	1.8	1.7	0.1	189.8
Yorkshire and the Humber	6.1	8.0	68.6	5.2	2.7	1.5	2.3	2.0	1.0	1.0	1.6	0.1	130.3
East Midlands	2.6	6.1	17.6	48.5	8.5	3.5	4.2	3.9	2.3	1.6	1.1	-	106.8
West Midlands	1.2	6.6	5.6	7.8	61.4	1.8	3.4	3.7	3.8	3.9	0.9	-	145.5
East	1.9	3.5	6.5	9.2	4.9	41.1	15.9	9.9	4.0	1.8	1.3	0.1	131.3
London	0.9	2.3	2.5	2.7	2.7	5.1	70.2	9.0	2.4	1.0	1.1	-	253.8
South East	1.5	2.9	3.9	5.2	4.2	4.2	16.9	48.5	8.1	3.0	1.4	-	217.5
South West	1.0	2.9	3.0	3.3	4.6	2.3	6.2	12.3	56.3	6.8	1.1	-	130.1
Wales	0.6	5.7	2.4	2.0	3.3	1.0	2.5	3.0	5.0	73.8	0.6	-	93.5
Scotland	0.8	1.0	0.7	0.4	0.4	0.4	0.7	0.6	0.3	0.4	94.2	0.1	205.2
Northern Ireland	1.3	4.1	1.1	0.8	0.7	0.8	1.5	1.1	0.5	0.8	8.4	78.9	65.8

1 Table refers to 'home domiciled' higher education students and excludes those living abroad prior to starting higher education. Open University students are also excluded.
2 Percentages may not add exactly to 100 due to rounding.
3 Includes students from the Channel Islands and Isle of Man and students whose region of domicile was unknown or unclassified.

Source: Department for Education and Skills; Higher Education Statistics Agency; National Assembly for Wales; Scottish Executive; Northern Ireland Department for Employment and Learning

will migrate a very long distance to go to university. However, Table 2.11 does not give the full picture of distances moved by students starting higher education, since regions differ in size. For example, a student from Scotland attending a university in Scotland may have migrated over a longer distance to participate in higher education than an English student crossing a regional border.

The courses offered and their length, university ratings, facilities available, finance and personal preferences all feature in a student's decision about where to study, as well as the location of the establishment. Students from Scotland and Northern Ireland may be particularly likely to study in their home country because of the different educational systems in those countries; for example, Scottish qualifications will be recognised more easily by Scottish institutions. In addition, potential students are constrained by various factors, including their expected or actual grades and the decisions of universities about which students to admit. All these factors influence both the internal and international migration patterns of young adults entering higher education.

A different range of factors (such as employment opportunities) will influence where young adults leaving higher education choose to live and this is discussed later in the chapter.

Sex differences

In 2004 almost half (48.9 per cent) of the UK population was male and 51.1 per cent female. As noted in Chapter 1, this higher proportion of females is due mainly to their higher life expectancy. There is very little regional variation in the sex structure of the population, with the proportion of females ranging from 50.6 per cent in London to 51.8 per cent in Scotland.

More pronounced differences are visible at a local level. Table 2.12 shows that the highest proportions of females in the UK were found in Eastbourne (53.3 per cent) and Rother (53.1 per cent), both in East Sussex, as well as in Belfast (53.1 per cent). In fact, five of the areas with the highest proportions of females were located on the south coast of England. In many cases, local authorities with a high percentage of females are also those with a high percentage of older people, since those of pensionable age are disproportionately female. For example, Eastbourne, Rother, Christchurch and Arun all appear in both the top ten for local authorities with the highest percentages of females (Table 2.12) and the highest percentages of people of pensionable age (Table 2.6).

In a handful of areas, men clearly outnumbered women in 2004. Low proportions of females were seen in the City of London (46.1 per cent) and the Isles of Scilly (48.3 per cent) but these results should be treated with caution given the small populations of these two authorities. In Richmondshire, Forest Heath and Rutland UA, men outnumbered women due to the presence of armed forces boosting their male populations. Finally, in other areas, a low proportion of females was related to a low proportion of people in the retirement ages. For example, Tower Hamlets had the lowest proportion of older people among UK authorities (9.8 per cent) and Lambeth the third lowest (10.4 per cent), and both are home to more males than females. In Tower Hamlets, the above average proportion of children (21.3 per cent) exacerbates the male bias of the

Table 2.12

Percentage of females: highest and lowest districts in the UK, 2004

Percentages

Rank	Highest		Lowest	
1	Eastbourne	53.3	City of London	46.1
2	Belfast	53.1	Richmondshire	48.1
3	Rother	53.1	Isles of Scilly	48.3
4	Christchurch	52.8	Rutland UA	48.3
5	Arun	52.7	Limavady	48.6
6	North Ayrshire	52.7	Tower Hamlets	48.7
7	Worthing	52.7	Forest Heath	48.7
8	Dundee City	52.7	Lambeth	48.8
9	Sefton	52.6	Reading UA	48.9
10	West Dunbartonshire[1]	52.6	Cambridge	49.0

1 Knowsley and Wirral also have 52.6 per cent females in their populations.

Source: Population estimates – Office for National Statistics; General Register Office for Scotland; Northern Ireland Statistics and Research Agency

population since boys outnumber girls throughout childhood (see Figure 1.11 in Chapter 1).

Diversity and deprivation

The populations of different local areas of the UK differ in many characteristics as well as age and sex. This section examines briefly some of the geographical variations in three selected characteristics: ethnicity, religion and deprivation.

Ethnic group

People living in the UK identify themselves as coming from a wide range of ethnic backgrounds, as confirmed by the 2001 Census. Chapter 1 shows that people from non-White ethnic groups are considerably more likely to be living in England than in the other constituent countries of the UK (Table 1.17). In 2001 people from ethnic groups other than White made up 9.1 per cent of England's population, compared with only 2.1 per cent in Wales, 2.0 per cent in Scotland and 0.8 per cent in Northern Ireland.

At a regional level, large variations are evident in the proportion of the population giving an ethnic group other than White in the census (Table 2.13). Almost 29 per cent of London's population was of a non-White ethnic origin, the largest groups being those describing themselves as Indian (6.1 per cent) and Black African (5.3 per cent). The West Midlands had the second highest proportion of its population in ethnic groups other than White (11.3 per cent), with those from Indian or Pakistani backgrounds making up over half of these. In contrast, the North East and South West had very low proportions of their populations from ethnic groups other than White (2.4 and 2.3 per cent respectively).

The non-White population of the UK is concentrated in the large urban centres, with 45 per cent living in the London GOR in 2001. Within London, high concentrations of non-White ethnic groups can be found in certain boroughs. Newham had the highest proportion of its population in ethnic groups other than White (61 per cent). Brent was the only other authority with a higher proportion of its population being non-White (55

Table 2.13

Ethnic group:[1] by country and Government Office Region, 2001

United Kingdom

Percentages[2] and thousands

	White	Mixed	Asian or Asian British				Black or Black British			Chinese	Other Ethnic Group	All people (thousands)
			Indian	Pakistani	Bangla-deshi	Other Asian	Caribbean	African	Other Black			
United Kingdom	92.1	1.2	1.8	1.3	0.5	0.4	1.0	0.8	0.2	0.4	0.4	58,789.2
England	90.9	1.3	2.1	1.4	0.6	0.5	1.1	1.0	0.2	0.5	0.4	49,138.8
North East	97.6	0.5	0.4	0.6	0.3	0.1	0.0	0.1	0.0	0.2	0.2	2,515.4
North West	94.4	0.9	1.1	1.7	0.4	0.2	0.3	0.2	0.1	0.4	0.2	6,729.8
Yorkshire and the Humber	93.5	0.9	1.0	3.0	0.3	0.3	0.4	0.2	0.1	0.3	0.2	4,964.8
East Midlands	93.5	1.0	2.9	0.7	0.2	0.3	0.6	0.2	0.1	0.3	0.2	4,172.2
West Midlands	88.7	1.4	3.4	2.9	0.6	0.4	1.6	0.2	0.2	0.3	0.3	5,267.3
East	95.1	1.1	1.0	0.7	0.3	0.3	0.5	0.3	0.1	0.4	0.3	5,388.1
London	71.2	3.2	6.1	2.0	2.2	1.9	4.8	5.3	0.8	1.1	1.6	7,172.1
South East	95.1	1.1	1.1	0.7	0.2	0.3	0.3	0.3	0.1	0.4	0.4	8,000.6
South West	97.7	0.8	0.3	0.1	0.1	0.1	0.3	0.1	0.1	0.3	0.2	4,928.4
Wales	97.9	0.6	0.3	0.3	0.2	0.1	0.1	0.1	0.0	0.2	0.2	2,903.1
Scotland	98.0	0.3	0.3	0.6	0.0	0.1	0.0	0.1	0.0	0.3	0.2	5,062.0
Northern Ireland[3]	99.3	0.2	0.1	0.0	0.0	0.0	0.0	0.0	0.0	0.3	0.1	1,685.3

1 Ethnic categories used are based on those used in the 2001 Census.
2 Percentages may not add exactly to 100 due to rounding.
3 Northern Ireland figures for White category include White Irish travellers.

Source: 2001 Census – Office for National Statistics; General Register Office for Scotland; Northern Ireland Statistics and Research Agency

per cent) than White. One-third of Newham's population described themselves as Indian, Pakistani, Bangladeshi or other Asian, while one-fifth classed themselves as Black African or Black Caribbean. One-third of the population of Tower Hamlets was Bangladeshi, with this borough being home to almost one-quarter of England's Bangladeshi population.

Geographical clustering of people with the same ethnic backgrounds also tends to occur within other regions. For example, two-thirds of the West Midlands Pakistani population were living in Birmingham in 2001. These clusters often occur in places where in-migrants from particular countries originally settled during the 20th century[5] and may then be reinforced by in-migration of family members and other factors such as social support networks and the provision of specialist services in particular areas. However, there is also some evidence of dispersal of minority ethnic populations from urban areas[6] (Chapter 6).

Outside London, Slough UA and Leicester UA had the highest proportions of their populations in non-White ethnic groups in 2001 (36 per cent), followed by Birmingham (29 per cent). In Leicester UA, the largest group was those of Indian origin

(26 per cent of the total population), while Slough UA was home to sizeable proportions of both Indians (14 per cent) and Pakistanis (12 per cent). Birmingham's population was more diverse with large numbers from Pakistani, Indian and Black Caribbean backgrounds.

This section has shown briefly that areas of the UK differ greatly in the composition of their populations by ethnic group. It has also suggested that in some cases ethnicity may be a factor in where people choose to live or are constrained to live. An in-depth discussion of the ethnic background of the population in different parts of the UK is outside the scope of this chapter but further information can be accessed in *Focus on Ethnicity and Identity*,[7] which also presents information on the interface between ethnicity and religion.

Religion

In Great Britain as a whole, 71.8 per cent of the population identified their religion as Christian according to the 2001 Census, while 5.5 per cent stated a religion other than Christian (Table 2.14). A further 15.1 per cent stated that they had no religion and 7.8 per cent chose not to answer the religion question (which was voluntary).

Table **2.14**

Religion:[1] by country and Government Office Region, 2001

Great Britain

Millions and percentages

	Total (millions = 100 per cent)	Percentage[2] of people stating religion as:								
		Christian	Buddhist	Hindu	Jewish	Muslim	Sikh	Other religions	No religion	Religion not stated
Great Britain	57.1	71.8	0.3	1.0	0.5	2.8	0.6	0.3	15.1	7.8
England	49.1	71.7	0.3	1.1	0.5	3.1	0.7	0.3	14.6	7.7
North East	2.5	80.1	0.1	0.2	0.1	1.1	0.2	0.2	11.0	7.1
North West	6.7	78.0	0.2	0.4	0.4	3.0	0.1	0.2	10.5	7.2
Yorkshire and the Humber	5.0	73.1	0.1	0.3	0.2	3.8	0.4	0.2	14.1	7.8
East Midlands	4.2	72.0	0.2	1.6	0.1	1.7	0.8	0.2	15.9	7.5
West Midlands	5.3	72.6	0.2	1.1	0.1	4.1	2.0	0.2	12.3	7.5
East	5.4	72.1	0.2	0.6	0.6	1.5	0.2	0.3	16.7	7.8
London	7.2	58.2	0.8	4.1	2.1	8.5	1.5	0.5	15.8	8.7
South East	8.0	72.8	0.3	0.6	0.2	1.4	0.5	0.4	16.5	7.5
South West	4.9	74.0	0.2	0.2	0.1	0.5	0.1	0.4	16.8	7.8
Wales	2.9	71.9	0.2	0.2	0.1	0.7	0.1	0.2	18.5	8.1
Scotland	5.1	72.6	0.1	0.1	0.2	0.8	0.1	0.2	17.5	8.4

1 For England and Wales, responses represent answers to the question 'what is your religion?' In Scotland two questions were asked on religion in the 2001 Census. Responses shown here are to the question 'what religion, religious denomination or body were you brought up in?'
2 Percentages may not add exactly to 100 due to rounding.

Source: 2001 Census – Office for National Statistics; General Register Office for Scotland

In 2001 people from non-Christian religions made up 6.0 per cent of the population in England compared with less than 2 per cent in Wales and Scotland. Within England there is great diversity between regions, with 17.3 per cent of London's population stating a religion other than Christian in the 2001 Census compared with only 1.4 per cent in the South West (Table 2.14).

London was clearly the most diverse region of Great Britain in terms of religion, with 8.5 per cent of its population describing themselves as Muslim, 4.1 per cent Hindu, 2.1 per cent Jewish, 1.5 per cent Sikh and 0.8 per cent Buddhist (Table 2.14). In fact, London was home to 56.0 per cent of the Jewish population of Great Britain, 52.3 per cent of the Hindu population and 38.2 per cent of the Muslim population. Muslims and Sikhs were the only minority religious groups with large regional populations outside London. For example, almost 104,000 Sikhs and more than 216,000 Muslims were living in the West Midlands in 2001.

These figures illustrate the way in which people identifying with particular non-Christian religions tend to be clustered in terms of where they live. Examining differences at the regional level masks the even greater concentration of particular groups in some local areas. For example, in 2001, Muslims made up 36.4 per cent of the population in the London Borough of Tower Hamlets, while Hindus made up 14.7 per cent of Leicester's population. In Scotland and Northern Ireland, 2001 Census data also showed geographical clustering among Christian sub-groups.[8] For example, in Northern Ireland, 85 per cent of the population of Carrickfergus had a Protestant community background, while 81 per cent of people living in Newry and Mourne were from the Catholic community.[9]

Although a detailed look at the religious make-up of the population in different local areas is outside the scope of this chapter, further information on this topic can be found in Focus on Religion.[10] Unlike Table 2.14, Focus on Religion also covers Northern Ireland, where the Census questions on religion were different from those used in Great Britain.[11]

Quality of life

Hart in Hampshire was the least deprived district in England, according to the English Indices of Deprivation 2004.[12] The second least deprived was Surrey Heath and the third, Wokingham UA. Of the ten least deprived local authorities in England, eight were located in the South East GOR and two in the East GOR (Table 2.15).

The most deprived local authorities in England were more spread out, with three in the North West GOR, three in the London GOR and two in the North East GOR. According to the index (Table 2.15), Liverpool was the most deprived authority in England, with neighbouring Knowsley in third place, and Manchester, the second most deprived. In London, Tower Hamlets was ranked as the most deprived borough, followed by Hackney and Islington, with these three authorities ranking as the fourth, fifth and sixth most deprived in England.

The 50 most deprived local authorities in England, according to the English Indices of Deprivation 2004, were not evenly spread across the country. Fifteen were located in the North West GOR, 12 in the London GOR and 10 in the North East GOR. None of the 50 most deprived authorities was in the South West or East of England and only one was in the South East (Hastings, ranked 38th).

Table 2.15

English Indices of Multiple Deprivation 2004: ten highest and lowest districts in England

Rank of average of ward scores

Highest		Lowest	
Hart	354	Liverpool	1
Surrey Heath	353	Manchester	2
Wokingham UA	352	Knowsley	3
Mole Valley	351	Tower Hamlets	4
Waverley	350	Hackney	5
Chiltern	349	Islington	6
East Hertfordshire	348	Nottingham UA	7
West Oxfordshire	347	Easington	8
Mid Sussex	346	Kingston upon Hull, City of UA	9
South Cambridgeshire	345	Middlesbrough UA	10

Source: Office of the Deputy Prime Minister

These figures show clearly that quality of life varies throughout England. Although deprivation is a difficult concept to measure, various indices have been produced to assess the differences in quality of life between areas. The rankings shown here are from the English Indices of Deprivation 2004,[13] which combines 37 different indicators into an index of multiple deprivation so that areas can be ranked. These indicators assess areas with respect to seven factors affecting quality of life: income, employment, health, education, housing and services, living environment and crime. The local authority deprivation scores shown here are ranked according to the average score for all wards within each authority. Depending on the exact measure of deprivation used, differences will emerge in the ranking of districts. In addition, there are large differences in deprivation between wards within each local authority, which these figures do not show.

Similar indices of deprivation have also been produced in the other constituent countries of the UK: the Welsh Index of Multiple Deprivation 2005,[14] Scottish Index of Multiple Deprivation 2004[15] and Northern Ireland Multiple Deprivation Measure 2005.[16] It is not possible to compare the relative deprivation of authorities in the different countries, because the components used to make up the indices for each country are slightly different. For example, although Strabane was identified as the most deprived local government district in Northern Ireland and North Down was found to be the least deprived (according to the rank of average ward scores from the Northern Ireland Multiple Deprivation Measure 2005), it is not possible to ascertain from the scores how these districts compare with the most and least deprived areas of England.

More in-depth information on quality of life in different parts of the UK can be found on the Internet, by accessing the links for the four country indices given in the 'Notes and references' at the end of this chapter, and in *Focus on Social Inequalities*,[17] part of the ONS's 'Focus on' series.

Employment patterns

Employment is a key determinant of where people live. At the individual level, many people choose to live near their place of work and may also migrate for employment purposes. At the aggregate level, areas with low unemployment or high earnings are likely to attract in-migrants, while areas with high unemployment or low earnings are much less likely to gain population in this way. In addition, people already living in areas with high unemployment or low earnings may not be able to afford to move, so have limited choice about where

they live. The following section examines briefly some of the differences in employment across the UK, by looking at rates of employment and unemployment, male and female earnings and the types of jobs available in different areas of the UK.

Employment and unemployment rates

The employment rate[18] in the UK was 74.2 per cent in the 12 months ending in December 2004. This indicates that almost three-quarters of the working-age population[19] were in employment, with the remainder either unemployed or economically inactive (for example, studying, looking after the home or permanently unable to work). The UK unemployment rate[20] for the same period was 4.7 per cent, showing that one in 20 economically active people were seeking employment.

Employment and unemployment rates differ across the UK, as Maps 2.16 and 2.17 illustrate. Employment rates in 2004 tended to be higher in Scotland (74.7 per cent) and England (74.6 per cent average) than in Wales (71.2 per cent) and Northern Ireland (67.6 per cent). Within England, the South East had the highest employment rate of the GORs (78.9 per cent) and London the lowest (69.1 per cent).

Map 2.16 shows larger differences at the local level. The lowest employment rates in the UK in 2004 were seen in the London boroughs of Tower Hamlets, Newham, Hackney and Haringey, as well as Manchester, all of which had employment rates of less than 60 per cent. Of the 20 authorities with the lowest employment rates in Great Britain, ten were London boroughs and four were in Wales. The UK's highest rates of employment in 2004[21] were found in the City of London (100.0 per cent) and in South Northamptonshire, the Shetland Islands, Dacorum, the Orkney Islands all with 85 to 86 per cent employed, although the result for the City of London may not be reliable due to its small population.

The unemployment rate of an area is not directly related to the employment rate and may be more closely associated with rates of economic inactivity. In 2004 England had the lowest unemployment rate of the UK countries (4.7 per cent) and Northern Ireland the highest (5.4 per cent). At a regional level, the South West had the lowest unemployment rate within England (3.4 per cent) and London, the highest (7.1 per cent). Unemployment rates and economic inactivity rates tend to vary more within regions than between regions. Map 2.17 shows no particularly clear pattern in unemployment rates by county,[22] although large swathes of southern England appear to have low rates of unemployment.

Map **2.16**

Employment rates:[1] by local or unitary authority,[2] 2004[3]

United Kingdom

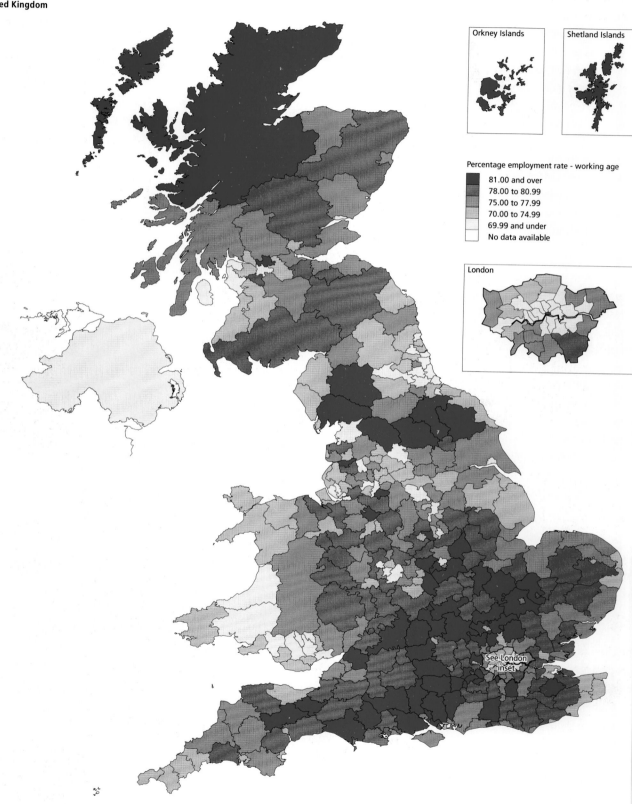

Orkney Islands

Shetland Islands

Percentage employment rate - working age

- 81.00 and over
- 78.00 to 80.99
- 75.00 to 77.99
- 70.00 to 74.99
- 69.99 and under
- No data available

London

See London inset

1 The employment rate refers to the total number of people of working age in employment divided by the total number of people of working age.
2 Northern Ireland data are shown at country level only.
3 Data cover the period January to December 2004.

Source: Annual Population Survey - Office for National Statistics

Map **2.17**

Unemployment rates:[1] by county or unitary authority,[2] 2004[3]

United Kingdom

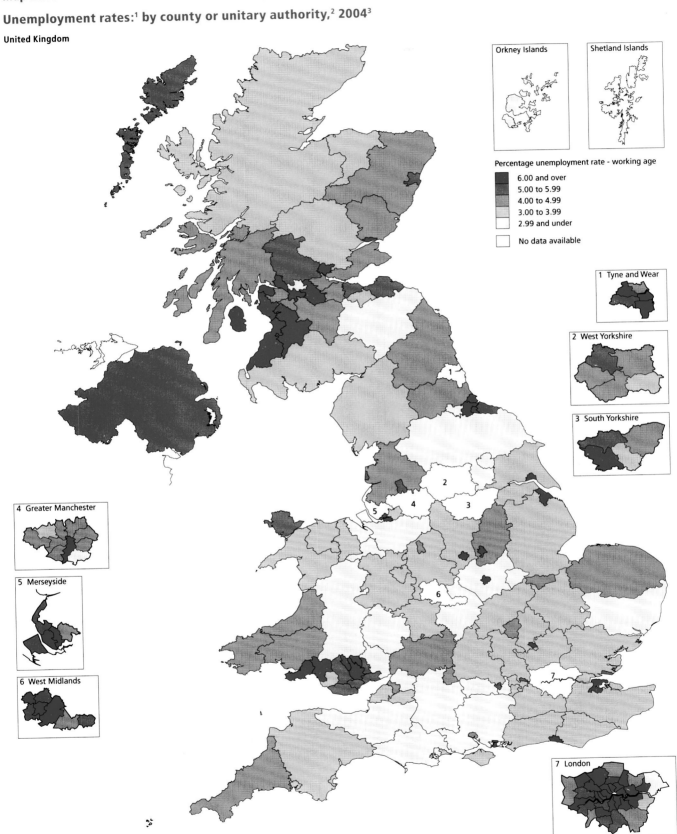

Orkney Islands

Shetland Islands

Percentage unemployment rate - working age

- 6.00 and over
- 5.00 to 5.99
- 4.00 to 4.99
- 3.00 to 3.99
- 2.99 and under

No data available

1 Tyne and Wear

2 West Yorkshire

3 South Yorkshire

4 Greater Manchester

5 Merseyside

6 West Midlands

7 London

1 The unemployment rate refers to the total number of unemployed people (ILO definition) aged 16 and above divided by the economically active population aged 16 and above.
2 Northern Ireland data are shown at country level only. Data for Metropolitan Counties and Greater London are shown at Metropolitan borough or London borough level (see insets).
3 Data cover the period January to December 2004.
Source: Annual Population Survey - Office for National Statistics

The London Borough of Tower Hamlets had Great Britain's highest unemployment rate in 2004 (12.6 per cent) and four other London boroughs (Hackney, Southwark, Lambeth and Haringey) made up the remaining five authorities with the highest unemployment rates (all above 11 per cent). Map 2.17 confirms that Inner London boroughs generally had high unemployment rates. North Ayrshire, Hammersmith and Fulham, Sandwell and Lewisham also experienced unemployment rates of double the UK average or higher.

Earnings

In 2004, the average[23] male full-time employee in the UK earned £462 per week (gross) while the average full-time female employee earned £358. The reasons for this discrepancy are outside the scope of this chapter but are related mainly to the types of jobs carried out by men and women and historical patterns of inequality in pay associated with jobs normally undertaken by men or women.[24]

Figure 2.18 shows variations in male and female earnings between the constituent countries of the UK in 2004. For men, average full-time earnings were highest for those working in England (£470 per week) and lowest in Northern Ireland (£402 per week), a difference of £68 per week. The differentials are smaller for women, with full-time workers in England earning £363 per week on average compared with only £322 per week in Wales. Within England, the London GOR had the highest average gross weekly earning for both men (£597) and women (£478), while Yorkshire and the Humber had the lowest earnings for full-time male employees (£393) and the East Midlands the lowest earnings for women (£317).

Figure **2.18**

Average gross weekly pay for full-time employee jobs:[1] by sex, country and Government Office Region, April 2004

United Kingdom

£pounds

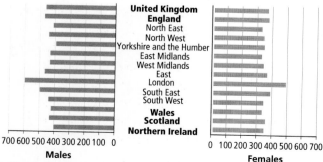

| Males | | Females |

1 *'Employee jobs' is a measure, obtained from surveys of employers, of jobs held by civilians, excluding the self-employed. These data cover employees on adult rates whose pay for the survey pay-period was not affected by absence. Figures are median measures of the average weekly pay.*

Source: Annual Survey of Hours and Earnings – Office for National Statistics

At district level,[25] women's average gross weekly earnings ranged from £230 for full-time workers in Berwick-upon-Tweed in the North East to £604 for those working in the London Borough of Tower Hamlets. London boroughs accounted for nine of the ten highest earning areas for women in Great Britain. Although men's full-time weekly earnings were significantly higher than women's in 2004, the range shows a similar pattern, from £309 in Penwith to £937 for those employed within the City of London. Outside London, Bracknell Forest UA, Mole Valley, Wokingham UA and Three Rivers had the most highly paid jobs for men in 2004 and also featured in the top ten areas outside London for female earnings. In general, both men and women's full-time earnings were higher in the London, South East and East regions than in other parts of the UK.

Industry of employment

In the UK as a whole, one half of all jobs in 2005 were in 'service industries' including 'distribution, hotels and restaurants' (24.3 per cent) and 'banking finance and insurance' (19.8 per cent). One quarter of jobs were in 'public administration, education and health' (26.0 per cent). However, there were notable regional variations in the types of employment available (Table 2.19). This is one of the factors that may influence where people of working age choose to live when they have specialist skills required by particular industries. Research has shown that nearly one-third of moves made between regions during the 1990s were for job-related reasons and that such migrations were more common among the more educated and highly skilled workers.[26]

The East Midlands and West Midlands had larger proportions of their jobs in the manufacturing industries in 2005 than other parts of the UK (17.9 per cent and 17.3 per cent respectively, compared with the UK average of 12.1 per cent). Of the English regions London had the lowest proportion of its jobs in 'manufacturing' (5.5 per cent) but a very high proportion in 'service industries' (61.7 per cent compared with the UK average of 50.2 per cent). In particular London had a high proportion of jobs in 'banking, finance and insurance' and is therefore likely to attract in-migrants with skills in these areas. In contrast, Northern Ireland had the lowest proportion of its employees in 'service industries' (39.1 per cent) but the highest proportion in 'agriculture, forestry and fishing' (2.1 per cent).

To a lesser extent, industry will have an impact at the local level on where people live; nearly one-fifth of moves between local authorities but within regions of Great Britain during the 1990s were job-related.[27] Particular types of job are often very concentrated in specific areas. For example, 80 per cent of employee jobs in the City of London in 2003 were in 'banking,

Table **2.19**

Employee job estimates by industry:[1] by country and Government Office Region, June 2005[2]

United Kingdom
Percentages and thousands

	Agriculture, Forestry & Fishing	Mining, Energy & Water supplies Industries	Manufacturing Industries	Construction	Service Industries[3]	Other Industries[4]	All Jobs
United Kingdom	0.9	0.7	12.1	4.9	50.2	31.3	26,413
England	0.8	0.6	12.0	4.8	51.3	30.5	22,343
North East	0.4	1.2	13.9	5.6	41.3	37.6	1,003
North West	0.5	0.3	14.0	5.0	48.5	31.7	3,012
Yorkshire and the Humber	0.8	0.6	15.3	5.6	46.5	31.3	2,175
East Midlands	1.2	0.8	17.9	4.5	44.8	30.8	1,744
West Midlands	0.8	0.6	17.3	5.2	45.5	30.5	2,310
East	1.4	0.6	12.3	5.8	51.8	28.1	2,336
London	0.1	0.2	5.5	4.2	61.7	28.3	3,952
South East	1.1	0.7	9.6	4.3	54.6	29.6	3,621
South West	1.3	0.7	12.1	4.4	49.3	32.2	2,190
Wales	1.1	0.7	16.2	4.1	40.4	37.4	1,102
Scotland	1.3	1.6	10.3	6.8	46.5	33.4	2,277
Northern Ireland	2.1	0.7	12.5	5.4	39.1	40.1	692

1 'Employee jobs' is a measure, obtained from surveys of employers, of jobs held by civilians. It excludes the self-employed. Figures here have not been seasonally adjusted. Industry categories used are based on Standard Industrial Classification 1992.
2 Figures refer to the period April 2005 to June 2005.
3 Includes 'distribution, hotels and restaurants,' 'transport and communications' and 'banking, finance and insurance.'
4 Includes 'public administration, education & health' and 'other services'.

Source: **Employer surveys – Office for National Statistics**

finance and insurance', by far the highest proportion in Great Britain.[28] The Isles of Scilly had the highest proportion of jobs in 'distribution, hotels and restaurants' (47 per cent) followed by two authorities in neighbouring Cornwall, Penwith and Caradon, both with 39 per cent of their jobs in this industry.

Two districts with small populations, Eilean Siar in Scotland and the Isles of Scilly, had the highest proportions of jobs in 'agriculture, forestry and fishing' in 2003 (16 per cent and 9 per cent respectively). Close behind were Boston and South Holland, both in Lincolnshire, one of the country's largest agricultural areas, with almost 9 per cent of jobs in this sector. Castle Morpeth in Northumberland had over 50 per cent of its jobs in 'public administration, education and health'. Corby in Northamptonshire had the second lowest proportion in this sector (10 per cent) but the highest proportion of jobs in manufacturing in Great Britain (37 per cent).

This chapter has described some of the variations in employment patterns within the UK. It has also suggested possible ways in which these variations may influence where

people choose to live. This is a very complex topic, as illustrated by the contrasts described for the London GOR – very high earnings and a large financial services sector side by side with high rates of unemployment.

Housing and households

An investigation of where people live would not be complete without reference to the types of household and housing they live in. This final part of the chapter notes some regional variations in how people live, in terms of household size, tenure and house building. At the local level, housing provision influences where people choose to live, as most will not move to areas with a shortage of appropriate housing or lack of affordable homes. A study of migration within Britain during the 1990s found housing to be the most frequently cited reason for moving, given by 45 per cent of those surveyed.[29]

In 2001 there were over 24 million households in the UK. London and the South East had the largest numbers, with over three million households in each region in 2001, while

Northern Ireland had the fewest (0.6 million). These figures reflect the number of people living in each country or region, but also the average number of people living in each household.

Average household size in England in 2001 was 2.36 people per household (Table 2.20). The English regions did not vary much from this figure, with the West Midlands having the highest average household size (2.41) and the South West having the lowest (2.31). At the local level there is far more variation. According to the 2001 Census, the London Borough of Newham had the highest average household size (2.64) among local and unitary authorities in England, while the City of London had the lowest (1.58).

Northern Ireland had a much higher average household size than other parts of the UK, with 2.65 people per household in 2001. This is partly because a smaller proportion of households in Northern Ireland – 27.4 per cent – consist of only one person, compared with the rest of the UK, for example, 30.1

Table **2.20**

Households: by country and Government Office Region, 2001

United Kingdom   Numbers and percentages

	Households 2001[1]		
	Number of households (thousands)	Average household size (number of people)	One-person households as a percentage of all households
England	20,451	2.36	30.1
North East	1,066	2.32	30.7
North West	2,813	2.35	30.9
Yorkshire and the Humber	2,065	2.36	29.5
East Midlands	1,732	2.36	28.2
West Midlands	2,154	2.41	28.8
East	2,232	2.37	28.3
London	3,016	2.35	34.7
South East	3,287	2.38	28.5
South West	2,086	2.31	29.6
Wales	1,209	2.37	29.1
Scotland	2,192	2.27	32.9
Northern Ireland	627	2.65	27.4

1 *2001 Census data are used in this table. Household estimates and projections based on 2003 data and produced by the Office for the Deputy Prime Minster are available at www.statistics.gov.uk.*

Source: Office for National Statistics; General Register Office for Scotland; Northern Ireland Statistics and Research Agency

per cent in England and 32.9 per cent in Scotland. Within England, Londoners were most likely to be living alone, with 34.7 per cent of households being one-person households. The East Midlands had the lowest proportion of households containing one person among the English regions (28.2 per cent).

According to the 2001 Census, the proportion of one-person households differed far more dramatically at a local level. The City of London had the highest proportion of one-person households in England and Wales in 2001 (60.5 per cent), which is consistent with its low average household size. Eight of the ten highest proportions of one-person households were found in London boroughs. Hart in the South East had the lowest proportion of one-person households in 2001 (22.2 per cent).

The London GOR also stands out when housing tenure is considered. In the UK as a whole in 2004, 71 per cent of dwellings were owner-occupied, and the remainder were rented: 11 per cent from local authorities, 10 per cent privately and 8 per cent from registered social landlords (Table 2.21). However, London had the lowest proportion of owner-occupied dwellings among the countries and regions of the UK (59 per cent) and by far the highest proportion of privately rented accommodation (17 per cent). This may reflect London's high proportion of relatively mobile young adults, who tend to see rented accommodation as more suitable for their needs, as well as the above-average house prices in the region, which may deter homebuyers.

The proportion of homes that are rented from local authorities illustrates the varying nature of housing provision in different parts of the UK. In the South East and South West of England, only 6 per cent of dwellings were rented from local authorities in 2004. In the North East this was 17 per cent. As with other housing indicators, the proportion of local authority rented dwellings varies considerably more at the local level. For example, the local authority with the highest proportion in England in 2001 was Southwark. According to the 2001 Census, over 42 per cent of homes in Southwark were rented from the local authority. In contrast, two authorities in the South East (Hart, and Epsom and Ewell) each had less than 0.5 per cent of their housing rented from this source.

The availability of different types of housing will clearly have an impact on where people choose to live. Tenure is one way of assessing affordability and availability but does not necessarily imply that sufficient numbers of dwellings are available. Table 2.22 provides details of the number of new completions – houses built by private enterprises, registered social landlords

Table **2.21**

Dwelling stock by tenure: by country and Government Office Region, 2004[1,2]

United Kingdom

	Percentages[3]				
	Owner occupied	Rented privately or with a job or business	Rented from registered social landlords	Rented from local authorities	All dwellings (thousands)[4]
United Kingdom	71	10	8	11	25,953
England	71	11	8	11	21,613
North East	65	9	9	17	1,126
North West	72	8	10	10	2,989
Yorkshire and the Humber	70	10	5	15	2,190
East Midlands	75	8	5	12	1,843
West Midlands	72	8	10	11	2,259
East	75	9	6	10	2,361
London	59	17	9	15	3,146
South East	75	12	7	6	3,466
South West	74	13	7	6	2,236
Wales	74	9	5	13	1,296
Scotland	65	7	11	16	2,366
Northern Ireland	77	5	3	14	679

1 Data are provisional.
2 Figures refer to 31 March 2004 for England, Wales and Northern Ireland and 31 December 2003 for Scotland. The UK figures are derived from England and Wales data as at 31 March 2004 and Scotland and Northern Ireland data as at 31 December 2003.
3 Percentages may not add exactly to 100 due to rounding.
4 Stock estimates are expressed to the nearest thousand but should not be regarded as accurate to the last digit.

Source: Office of the Deputy Prime Minister; National Assembly for Wales; Scottish Executive; Department for Social Development (Northern Ireland).

and local authorities[30] – to provide a further indication of growth and demand for housing in these areas.

From April 2004 to March 2005, almost 206,000 new homes were built in the UK. The majority (89 per cent) were built by private enterprises. Only 11 per cent were built by registered social landlords and a very small number by local authorities. Regionally, Scotland saw the greatest number of new completions (26,831), followed by the South East (25,692). In contrast, the North East (7,060) had the lowest number, followed by Wales (8,492). The regional pattern for housing built by private enterprise is similar to that for all new completions. However, London had the highest number of completions by registered social landlords in 2004/05 and over half of local authority completions took place in the South East.

Across local districts in 2003/04, new completions were greatest in Leeds at just under 3,000, followed by Tower Hamlets with just over 2,000. Manchester and Birmingham also had high numbers of newly-built homes. At the opposite end of the scale, Berwick-upon-Tweed (North East) saw only one new completion during 2003/04, the Isles of Scilly, six and Chester-le-Street, nine. These figures probably reflect the fairly small populations in these authorities.

Finally, some UK residents are classified as homeless and have very little choice about where they live. In England, 135,430 households were accepted by local authorities as unintentionally homeless and in priority need in 2003/04. Of the GORs, London had the highest number of households accepted as homeless (30,080), followed by the North West (18,030).[31] Similarly, 9,147 Welsh households were accepted as

Table 2.22

Housing completions:[1] by country and Government Office Region, 2004/05[2]

United Kingdom

	Housing completions (numbers) 2004/05			
	Private enterprise	Registered social landlords	Local authorities	All dwellings
United Kingdom	183,138	22,692	131	205,961
England	138,133	16,637	100	154,870
North East	6,567	493	0	7,060
North West	17,290	642	0	17,932
Yorkshire and the Humber	13,814	373	0	14,187
East Midlands	14,737	778	0	15,515
West Midlands	12,997	1,156	0	14,153
East	17,846	2,106	2	19,954
London	17,937	6,175	0	24,112
South East	22,200	3,400	92	25,692
South West	14,745	1,514	6	16,265
Wales	7,986	475	31	8,492
Scotland	22,079	4,752	0	26,831
Northern Ireland	14,940	828	0	15,768

1 Housing completions data refer to new homes built during the period. In principle, a dwelling is regarded as completed when it becomes ready for occupation whether it is in fact occupied or not. In practice, there are instances where the timing could be delayed and some completions are missed, for example as no completion certificate was requested by the owner.
2 Data are for April 2004 to March 2005. Data for Scotland, Northern Ireland and the UK are provisional.

Source: Office of the Deputy Prime Minister; National Assembly for Wales; Scottish Executive; Department of the Environment, Northern Ireland

homeless in the same period.[32] Homelessness legislation is slightly different in Scotland and Northern Ireland from that of England and Wales. In 2003/04 in Scotland, 24,979 households were accepted as unintentionally homeless and in priority need,[33] while 8,594 households in Northern Ireland were awarded priority status.[34]

Summary

This chapter has illustrated the diversity of the countries, regions and local districts of the UK in terms of population and related characteristics. Some districts have among the highest or lowest scores for several different characteristics,

highlighting how these factors can be inter-related. For example, Christchurch and Rother local authorities on the south coast of England had the highest proportions of residents of pensionable age in the UK in 2004. As a result, these two districts also had notably high proportions of females compared with the UK average and low proportions of young adults aged 16 to 24.

In contrast, the London Borough of Newham had the second lowest proportion of people of retirement age in the UK and correspondingly the fifth highest proportion of children in 2004. Newham also had the highest average household size in England in 2001 and the largest proportion of residents from an ethnic group other than White in 2001. These factors are extremely likely to be linked. For example, the 2001 Census showed that Asians had the largest average household sizes in Great Britain,[35] hence the high average household size in Newham is likely to be related to the fact that one-third of the population is of an Asian ethnic origin. Since most non-White ethnic groups also have younger age structures than the White population,[36] reflecting past in-migration and fertility patterns, the high proportion of children in Newham is probably partly related to its ethnic composition.

While this chapter has outlined where people live, it has also explored some of the issues that determine where people choose to live. Factors such as employment or housing availability may have some influence on residential choices. Population characteristics such as the age or ethnic group breakdown of an area's residents may be both a result and a determinant of people's choices about where to live. In addition to easily quantifiable factors, there are many personal influences involved in people's decisions about where to live, such as the proximity of family and friends, and personal preferences about different locations. Such factors can be extremely difficult to measure objectively.

Finally, the role of choice in where people live is not clear-cut. While in some cases, people make conscious decisions about where to live, in other cases, people may live where they were born and never move away. Others may be restricted by economic or other constraints and be unable to live where they would choose.

Further information on the characteristics of people living in different parts of the UK can be found on the National Statistics website and among the titles published by ONS. These sources provide a wide range of information on different topics for a variety of geographical areas. For example, Regional Trends[37] provides statistics covering a number of themes for Scotland, Wales, Northern Ireland and the GORs within England, while the Region in Figures series provides similar data for each region in England. *Key Population and Vital Statistics*[38] provides detailed population data for local administrative areas of the UK. *The Neighbourhood Statistics* website[39] provides detailed information on smaller areas of England and Wales. More information on Scotland, Wales and Northern Ireland is available from the websites and publications issued by those countries' governments.[40]

Notes and references

1. Population estimates for government office regions, local authorities and unitary authorities in England, and unitary authorities in Wales, can be found at: www.statistics.gov.uk/statbase/Product.asp?vlnk=601&More=N
Population estimates for Scotland can be accessed at: www.gro-scotland.gov.uk/statistics/library/index.html
Population estimates for Northern Ireland are available from: www.nisra.gov.uk/statistics/financeandpersonnel/DMB/datavault.html
All UK estimates refer to the population as at 30 June of the year specified.

2. 2001 Census data from Theme Tables T02 (England and Wales), T17 (Scotland) and T43 (Northern Ireland).

3. Department for Education and Skills (2004) *Education and Training Statistics UK 2004*, Tables 3.6 and 3.10: www.dfes.gov.uk/rsgateway/DB/VOL/v000538/index.shtml

4. Higher Education and Research Opportunities in the United Kingdom (HERO): www.hero.ac.uk/uk/universities__colleges/index.cfm

5. Simpson L (2004) Statistics of racial segregation: measures, evidence and policy in *Urban Studies* **41**.

6. See reference 5.

7. Office for National Statistics (2004) *Focus on Ethnicity and Identity*: www.statistics.gov.uk/focuson/ethnicity/

8. Dorling D and Thomas B (2004) *People and Places: a Census Atlas*. Policy Press: Bristol.

9. The term community background refers to a person's current religion or if no current religion was stated, the religion that the person was brought up in. Protestant includes 'Other Christian' and 'Christian related', and those brought up as Protestants. Catholic includes those respondents who gave their religion as Catholic or Roman Catholic, and those brought up as Catholics.

10. Office for National Statistics (2004) *Focus on Religion*: www.statistics.gov.uk/focuson/religion/

11. Office for National Statistics Guide to Questions on Religion: www.statistics.gov.uk/cci/nugget.asp?id=984

12. The English Indices of Multiple Deprivation 2004: www.odpm.gov.uk/stellent/groups/odpm_urbanpolicy/documents/page/odpm_urbpol_029534.pdf

13. See reference 11.

14. Welsh Index of Multiple Deprivation 2005: www.lgdu-wales.gov.uk/eng/Project.asp?id=SXAB37-A77FB4C0

15. Scotland Indices of Multiple Deprivation 2004: www.scotland.gov.uk/stats/simd2004/

16. Northern Ireland Multiple Deprivation Measure 2005: www.ninis.nisra.gov.uk/

17. Office for National Statistics (2005) *Focus on Social Inequalities*: www.statistics.gov.uk/focuson/socialinequalities/

18. The employment rate refers to the percentage of working-age people who are employed. All employment and unemployment rates in this section are from the Annual Population Survey and cover the period January to December 2004.

19. The working-age population consists of men aged 16 to 64 years and women aged 16 to 59 years.

20. The unemployment rate is the percentage of economically active people aged 16+ who are unemployed, using the International Labour Organisation (ILO) measure of unemployment.

21. Data for the Isles of Scilly are unavailable. Data for local districts in Northern Ireland are not available in order to protect respondent confidentiality.

22. Unemployment rates are shown by county and unitary authority for England and Wales as counts of unemployed people are very small in some local authorities within counties and would provide estimates with a low level of reliability.

23. The average used here is the median (the middle value if all employee incomes were ordered from highest to lowest).

24. Office for National Statistics (2004) *Focus on Gender*: www.statistics.gov.uk/focuson/gender/

25. Office for National Statistics Annual Survey of Hours and Earnings. Data for some local authorities are unavailable in order to protect respondent confidentiality.

26. Dixon S (2003) Migration within Britain for job reasons in *Labour Market Trends* **111(4)**, 191–201.

27. See reference 26.

28. The data shown here come from the Annual Business Inquiry 2003 and refer to districts within Great Britain only.

29. See reference 26.

30. Please see appendix for a description of different types of housing completion.

31. Office of the Deputy Prime Minister: www.odpm.gov.uk/stellent/ groups/odpm_control/documents/contentservertemplate/odpm_ index.hcst?n=5516&l=3 Data for 2003/04 are provisional.

32. National Assembly for Wales: www.wales.gov.uk/ keypubstatisticsforwales/content/publication/housing/2004/sb85-2004/sb85-2004.htm

33. Scottish Executive: www.scotland.gov.uk/stats/bulletins/00363-06.asp

34. Northern Ireland Department for Social Development: www.dsdni.gov.uk/publications-results?docid=56&pageid=44&title=Northern%20Ireland%20Housing%20Statistics

35. Office for National Statistics (2004) *Focus on Ethnicity and Identity:* www.statistics.gov.uk/focuson/ethnicity/

36. See reference 35.

37. Office for National Statistics (2004) *Regional Trends:* www.statistics.gov.uk/StatBase/Product.asp?vlnk=836&Pos=&ColRank=1&Rank=422

38. Office for National Statistics (2005) *Key Population and Vital Statistics:* www.statistics.gov.uk/StatBase/Product.asp?vlnk=539&Pos=&ColRank=1&Rank=272

39. Neighbourhood Statistics: www.neighbourhood.statistics.gov.uk/ dissemination/

40. General Register Office for Scotland: www.gro-scotland.gov.uk
Northern Ireland Statistics and Research Agency: www.nisra.gov.uk/
National Assembly for Wales: www.wales.gov.uk/keypubstatisticsforwales/

The UK's major urban areas

Graham Pointer

Chapter 3

Introduction

Nearly eight of every ten people in the United Kingdom lived in an urban area in 2001, according to the most recent definition of the term. Urban areas covered 8.9 per cent of the UK's land mass at that time.

Nearly 41 per cent of urban dwellers lived in one of the ten most populous urban areas. They accounted for 19,024,665 people or 32.4 per cent of the UK's population.

The ten most populous urban areas in the UK are:

- Greater London Urban Area
- West Midlands Urban Area
- Greater Manchester Urban Area
- West Yorkshire Urban Area
- Greater Glasgow
- Tyneside
- Liverpool Urban Area
- Nottingham Urban Area
- Sheffield Urban Area
- Bristol Urban Area.

These covered over a fifth of all urban land in the UK in 2001, or 4,375.9 km^2 with a population density of 4,347.6 people per km^2 compared to a density of 241.9 people per km^2 in the UK as a whole. Between the 1991 and 2001 Censuses the ten most populous urban areas grew by 660,060 people and 66.6 km^2.

Given that nearly one-third of the population lives in these ten most populous urban areas, an understanding of the characteristics of these populations is very important. This chapter begins by defining an urban area, before describing the size and location of the United Kingdom's most populous places. Census data are used to examine changes in the population and expanse of some urban areas between 1991 and 2001.

Finally, the chapter uses census data to compare some of the population characteristics of 2001's most heavily populated urban areas to see what, if anything, they have in common. This will enable conclusions to be drawn as to whether the people living in these places exhibit homogenous or heterogeneous traits. A more detailed analysis, accounting for variations between smaller areas within these urban areas, is beyond the scope of this chapter.

The 2001 Census is the most suitable data source for urban areas.[1] Urban areas do not stick to administrative boundaries. This makes more recent sources, such as the Labour Force Survey and the mid-year population estimates, less useful. Greater London Urban Area, for example, doesn't share a border with the administrative boundary of the Government Office Region for London.

Key strengths of 2001 Census data are that they can be used to examine almost any geographic area and cover a wide range of variables based on information for the whole population. 2001 Census data include adjustments for undercoverage in the census, but they lack the smaller adjustments that were subsequently made to the mid-year population estimates.[2] Most of the analyses in this chapter are based on proportions, so the impact of the adjustments would be slight.

What is an urban area?

An area that is described as urban has a minimum population density and number of people. Such spaces are normally relatively built-up, with housing and industrial buildings or both. The people who live in urban areas also tend to be regarded as town or city dwellers. Outside the boundaries, housing, offices or factories become more thinly distributed and open spaces more common. Some houses or industrial buildings might be in areas not classified as urban.

Urban areas do not adhere to administrative boundaries; for example Greater Manchester Urban Area is 4.8 times larger than the local authority district of Manchester and the urban area's boundaries do not follow those of the former metropolitan county of Greater Manchester. Because boundaries are not static, the land area and urban population may change over time. Changes in land use can lead to a boundary change of an urban area. New houses built at the edge, changing the land use from non-urban to urban, would increase the size of that urban area. But an urban area can decrease in size if housing or industrial buildings at the edge of the area fall into disuse.

The definition of an urban area depends on the circumstance and experience of the wider area in which it is set. It is perfectly reasonable for different countries to have differing definitions of what makes an area urban and this is the case in the UK. The latest definition in England and Wales[3] is an area with 10,000 people or more; in Scotland[4] this is 3,000 people or more; while in Northern Ireland[5] it is 4,500 people or more. These apparent differences do not prevent comparisons between the largest urban areas across the countries of the UK. But definitional issues need to be considered when discussing all the UK's urban areas.

For the Belfast area, Northern Ireland Statistics and Research Agency (NISRA) use a broad definition of urban areas such that Belfast Metropolitan Urban Area includes nearby non-connected settlements. For comparability with the rest of the UK, these non-connected settlements have been excluded from the definition of the urban area of Belfast and connected settlements which is used in this report.[6]

Data referring to urban areas in Scotland and England and Wales are aggregations of a best fit of Census Output Areas, the smallest building block of census data. The ways in which Census Output Areas were configured differed between Scotland, England and Wales. If made up of Census Output Areas subject to the England and Wales specification, it is likely that a Scottish urban area would comprise a smaller area and population than is currently the case. In any event, an urban area's definition depends upon the circumstance and

experience in the wider area. Urban areas in Northern Ireland are based on 100 metre grid blocks. NISRA argues that these more closely represent urban area boundaries, and so provide more accurate data. For more information see the appendix: Definitions of an urban area - differences within the UK.

The UK's most populous urban areas

Table 3.1 shows the 25 urban areas with the largest populations, according to results reported from the 2001 Census. They are spread throughout the UK.

Table **3.1**

The 25 most populous urban areas in the United Kingdom: resident population and population density, 2001 Census

		All people	Area (km^2)	Density (number of people per km^2)
1	Greater London Urban Area	8,278,251	1,623.37	5,099.4
2	West Midlands Urban Area	2,284,093	599.72	3,808.6
3	Greater Manchester Urban Area	2,240,230	556.72	4,024.0
4	West Yorkshire Urban Area	1,499,465	370.02	4,052.4
5	Greater Glasgow	1,168,270	368.47	3,171.0
6	Tyneside	879,996	210.91	4,172.4
7	Liverpool Urban Area	816,216	186.17	4,384.3
8	Nottingham Urban Area	666,358	158.52	4,203.6
9	Sheffield Urban Area	640,720	162.24	3,949.2
10	Bristol Urban Area	551,066	139.78	3,942.4
11	Urban area of Belfast and connected settlements	483,418	161.67	2,990.2
12	Brighton/Worthing/Littlehampton	461,181	94.09	4,901.5
13	Edinburgh	452,194	120.11	3,765.0
14	Portsmouth Urban Area	442,252	94.52	4,678.9
15	Leicester Urban Area	441,213	101.64	4,340.9
16	Bournemouth Urban Area	383,713	108.15	3,548.0
17	Reading/Wokingham	369,804	93.17	3,969.1
18	Teesside	365,323	113.99	3,204.9
19	The Potteries	362,403	96.62	3,750.8
20	Coventry/Bedworth	336,452	75.56	4,452.8
21	Cardiff Urban Area	327,706	75.72	4,328.0
22	Birkenhead Urban Area	319,675	89.11	3,587.4
23	Southampton Urban Area	304,400	72.80	4,181.3
24	Kingston upon Hull	301,416	80.44	3,747.1
25	Swansea Urban Area	270,506	79.81	3,389.0

Source: 2001 Census – Office for National Statistics, General Register Office for Scotland and Northern Ireland Statistics and Research Agency

The areas have been ranked according to population size. Greater London Urban Area dwarfs the others. It has the highest population, greatest area and highest population density of all urban areas in the United Kingdom. Its population is over 3.6 times and its area over 2.7 times that of West Midlands Urban Area – the second most populous and largest. There are five urban areas with a population greater than one million people and a further five urban areas with a population between 500,000 and one million.

Northern Ireland is represented in the list of 25 most populous urban areas by the urban area of Belfast and connected settlements, which is ranked eleventh. Greater Glasgow, fifth, and Edinburgh, thirteenth, represent Scotland. Cardiff Urban Area, ranked twenty-first, and Swansea Urban Area, twenty-fifth, represent Wales. The remaining urban areas are in England.

Table 3.1 shows that the order of the ten most populous urban areas would have the same ranking if based on area rather than population, except that Nottingham Urban Area and Sheffield Urban Area would swap places. There is a relationship between the population size and the area of the ten most populous – as the population increases so does the area. This is not so among the urban areas ranked 11 to 25. Their population size does not relate directly to their area. This may be a consequence of these urban areas having relatively similar population sizes. As there is little variation in population between urban areas, there is little variation in area.

The population density of the 25 largest urban areas follows no discernible pattern, when compared in terms of either population or area. Greater London Urban Area has the highest population density, 5,099.4 people per km^2, and the urban area of Belfast and connected settlements the lowest with 2,990.2 people per km^2. The second lowest population density is in Greater Glasgow, 3,171.0 people per km^2.

The urban areas with the largest populations are not necessarily the most densely populated. Of the 25 most populous urban areas, the second most densely populated is Brighton/Worthing/Littlehampton, which has the twelfth-largest population. Greater Glasgow is fifth in terms of population but twenty-fourth by population density. A contributing factor to this disparity is the differing definitions used between the Office for National Statistics (ONS) and the General Register Office for Scotland (GROS) to construct Census Output Areas, which make up the urban area. Under the ONS definition, Greater Glasgow would include a reduction in area disproportionate to a reduction in population, increasing density.

Map 3.2 shows the location and boundaries of the 25 most populous urban areas in the UK. The boundaries do not keep to any administrative areas. At this large scale, urban areas appear to consist of a main body with arms shooting outward, for example Greater London Urban Area and Nottingham Urban Area. Urban areas are also interspersed with non-urban areas, appearing as holes in the wider urban area. The term 'urban conglomeration' seems particularly fitting to describe these places. Conglomeration means combining many different parts into a whole – bringing cities and towns into a larger urban area. Of the ten most populous urban areas: Greater London Urban Area dominates the south and south east of the United Kingdom; Liverpool Urban Area, Greater Manchester Urban Area, West Yorkshire Urban Area, Sheffield Urban Area and Nottingham Urban Area form a belt across the middle of the United Kingdom; while Bristol Urban Area, West Midlands Urban Area, Tyneside and Greater Glasgow are presented as regional centres. The remaining urban areas are loosely concentrated in the southern half of the UK.

Changes since 1991

Urban areas, especially the larger ones discussed here, change over time in both their population and the area they cover. They expand when people occupy new developments on the fringes and decline when people move away. If population density declines, the land may cease to be urban. The population may change due to rates of births and deaths and migration into and out of the area. These dynamics can be explored by comparing a snapshot of the urban area and population as recorded by the 1991 Census with another as recorded by the 2001 Census.

Data are reported from the census for sub-divisions of major urban areas. These provide recognisable areas within larger urban areas that often follow the boundaries of local authorities existing before the 1974 re-organisation in 1974, current authority boundaries, well-defined localities, or previously separate urban areas. (Prior to 1974, there were two-tiered administrations based on counties and a mixture of sub-administrations including municipal boroughs, county boroughs, rural districts and urban districts with Greater London separate.) The boundaries of the sub-divisions are broadly adhered to between censuses, making it possible to make comparisons with previously published census results.

One should be careful when making comparisons between the 1991 and 2001 Censuses. They operated under different definitions and assumptions. The principal impact on this analysis relates to the comparison of urban area sub-divisions that can have quite small populations. The identification of small urban areas in the 1991 Census was less precise than in

Map **3.2**

The 25 most populous urban areas in the United Kingdom, 2001

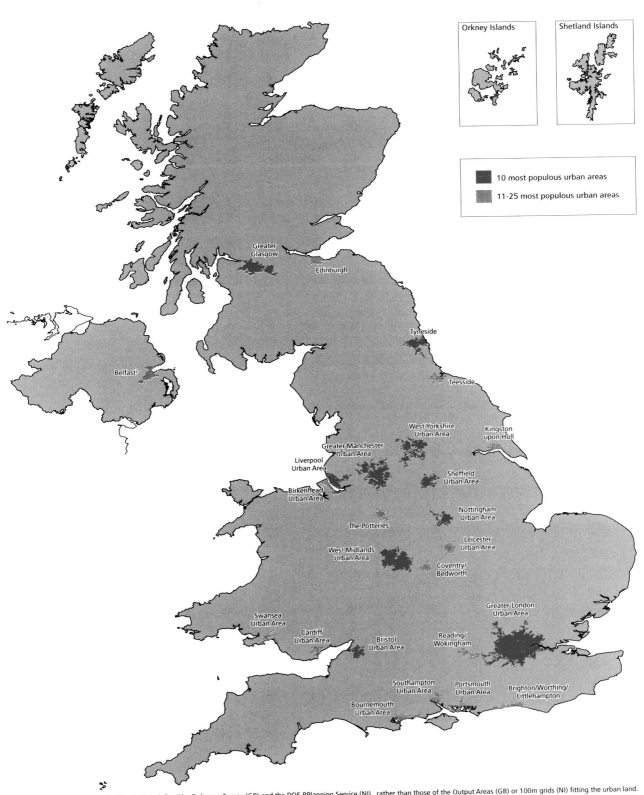

Orkney Islands

Shetland Islands

■ (dark)	10 most populous urban areas
■ (light)	11-25 most populous urban areas

Greater
Glasgow

Edinburgh

Tyneside

Belfast[2]

Teesside

West Yorkshire
Urban Area

Kingston
upon Hull

Greater Manchester
Urban Area

Liverpool
Urban Area

Sheffield
Urban Area

Birkenhead
Urban Area

Nottingham
Urban Area

The Potteries

Leicester
Urban Area

West Midlands
Urban Area

Coventry/
Bedworth

Greater London
Urban Area

Swansea
Urban Area

Cardiff
Urban Area

Bristol
Urban Area

Reading/
Wokingham

Southampton
Urban Area

Portsmouth
Urban Area

Brighton/Worthing/
Littlehampton

Bournemouth
Urban Area

1   The boundaries shown are for the extent of urban land as defined by Ordnance Survey (GB) and the DOE PPlanning Service (NI), rather than those of the Output Areas (GB) or 100m grids (NI) fitting the urban land.

2   Urban area of Belfast and connected settlements used in this report includes the connected areas of Belfast Urban Area, Castlereagh Urban Area, Greenisland Urban Area, Holywood Urban Area, Lisburn Urban Area, Newtownabbey Urban Area and Milltown (Lisburn LGD).

Source: 2001 Census - Office for National Statistics, General Register Office for Scotland and Northern Ireland Statistics and Research Agency

the 2001 Census. The biggest difference in method is that the distance for merger of areas of urban land increased from 50 to 200 metres. So a gap between two urban areas of 150 metres would be deemed as two separate urban areas in 1991 and as one in 2001. When considering sub-divisions, comparisons for areas with a population fewer than 2,000 people are not advisable and comparisons of areas of fewer than 5,000 should be made with caution. Census data for urban areas are reported on a best fit of Census Output Areas in 2001 and 1991's Enumeration Districts. There are more Census Output Areas than Enumeration Districts, meaning that 2001 data are likely to be more closely aligned to the boundary of the urban area. Another point to keep in mind is that the 2001 Census was designed to allow for people who didn't return the census form, while the 1991 Census was not. This means that if the 2001 methodology was used in 1991, the counts would have been higher.

Figure 3.3 portrays the population change of the ten most populous urban areas between the 1991 and 2001 Censuses. The top ten are the same; the only difference is that Nottingham Urban Area moved up one place, to eighth in 2001, at the expense of Sheffield Urban Area which fell to ninth.

Nottingham Urban Area experienced the largest proportional increase in population (8.6 per cent). This was primarily due to the inclusion of Ilkeston (a separate urban area in 1991) and growth in West Bridgford. The second largest proportional increase in population was in Greater London Urban Area at 8.2 per cent, a result of population growth in existing areas and the envelopment of urban areas that were separate in

Figure **3.3**

Population change between the 1991 and 2001 Censuses, 2001

Percentages

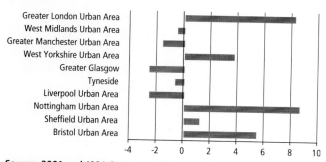

Source: 2001 and 1991 Census – Office for National Statistics, General Register Office for Scotland

1991. The third largest was Bristol Urban Area with a 5.4 per cent increase mainly due to the annexation of Almondsbury, a separate urban area in 1991.

The Greater Glasgow population fell by 2.6 per cent – the largest proportional decline. Definitional differences mean that 1991 Census data for Greater Glasgow reported here are based on the 2001 geographic boundaries, while the 1991 England and Wales Census data are based on 1991 boundaries. The area of Greater Glasgow is therefore represented as constant between censuses in Table 3.4. The population of Scotland has declined by 0.80 per cent between 1991 and 2001. The population decline in Greater Glasgow is greater than that of Scotland as a whole.

Along with Greater Glasgow there were four more urban areas that experienced a decrease in population. They were:

- Liverpool Urban Area
  (2.6 per cent fewer people)
- Greater Manchester Urban Area (1.6 per cent fewer)
- Tyneside (0.7 per cent fewer)
- West Midlands Urban Area (0.5 per cent fewer).

Of the ten, only West Yorkshire Urban Area and Greater London Urban Area increased in population, area and population density between the 1991 and 2001 Censuses. Population density tells us how concentrated the population is in each area. If the population of an area increases at a greater rate than its size, the population density increases. Conversely, if the size of the urban area increases at a greater rate, then the population the population density falls. Table 3.4 provides a snapshot of the population, area and population density as at Census day 1991 compared to Census day 2001. Of the ten urban areas, only Greater London Urban Area, Sheffield Urban Area and West Yorkshire Urban Area saw an increase in population density between censuses. West Midlands Urban Area was the only one to record a decrease in area, population and population density. Sheffield Urban Area also registered a decrease in area but experienced an increase in population size and, by extension, population density. Five urban areas recorded a decrease in population size.

Greater London Urban Area experienced the highest proportional increase in population density between the censuses, with Sheffield Urban Area the second highest. Both the population and area of West Midlands Urban Area decreased by a similar proportion, meaning that the population density has remained fairly constant between censuses.

Table **3.4**

Population, area and density change between the 1991 and 2001 Censuses

		Population (people)			Area (km²)			Density (people per km²)		
		1991	2001	Percentage change	1991	2001	Percentage change	1991	2001	Percentage change
1	Greater London Urban Area	7,651,634	8,278,251	8.2	1,617.2	1,623.4	0.4	4,731.3	5,099.4	7.8
2	West Midlands Urban Area	2,296,180	2,284,093	−0.5	602.3	599.7	−0.4	3,812.4	3,808.6	−0.1
3	Greater Manchester Urban Area	2,277,330	2,240,230	−1.6	531.4	556.7	4.8	4,285.3	4,024.0	−6.1
4	West Yorkshire Urban Area	1,445,981	1,499,465	3.7	360.6	370.0	2.6	4,009.7	4,052.4	1.1
5	Greater Glasgow¹	1,199,629	1,168,270	−2.6	368.5	368.5	0.0	3,255.7	3,171.0	−2.6
6	Tyneside	885,981	879,996	−0.7	206.8	210.9	2.0	4,285.1	4,172.4	−2.6
7	Liverpool Urban Area	837,998	816,216	−2.6	185.4	186.2	0.4	4,520.4	4,384.3	−3.0
8	Nottingham Urban Area	613,726	666,358	8.6	145.5	158.5	9.0	4,218.6	4,203.6	−0.4
9	Sheffield Urban Area	633,362	640,720	1.2	163.3	162.2	−0.6	3,879.7	3,949.2	1.8
10	Bristol Urban Area	522,784	551,066	5.4	128.4	139.8	8.9	4,072.5	3,942.4	−3.2

1 1991 Greater Glasgow data are based on 2001 boundaries; as such, there is no change in area shown between censuses.

Source: 2001 and 1991 Census – Office for National Statistics, General Register Office for Scotland

Case Studies: Change in size and population of three urban areas over time

Commentaries follow on how Greater Manchester Urban Area, Nottingham Urban Area and Bristol Urban Area have changed between the 1991 and 2001 Censuses. Maps depicting the change in urban area boundaries between 1991 and 2001 for the three urban areas are provided. The 2001 sub-division names can be seen at the centre of each sub-division and should not be confused with place names that share the title. Sub-divisions are referred to where possible, as these allow a rough comparison of areas within the larger urban area between censuses.

Three colours are discernible on the maps. These refer to land which was part of the urban area; in:

- 1991 and 2001
- 1991 and not in 2001
- 2001 and not in 1991

Only urban areas that were part of the larger urban area are shown in each map. For example an urban area close to but separate to Greater Manchester Urban Area in both 1991 and 2001 does not appear. The 1991 and 2001 boundaries refer to the extent of urban land, as defined by Ordnance Survey. The census data in this chapter are based on best fit Enumeration Districts (1991) and Census Output Areas (2001) which may be smaller in area but more likely larger than the boundaries depicted in the maps.

Greater Manchester Urban Area

Greater Manchester Urban Area extends from Whitworth in Lancashire to the north, Longdendale in Tameside to the east, Wilmslow/Alderley Edge in Cheshire to the south, and Hindley, near Bolton, to the west. Greater Manchester Urban Areas includes the centres of Bolton, Bury, Rochdale, Oldham, Stockport and Sale.

Sub-divisions of the larger urban area do not adhere to existing administrative boundaries; for example the sub-divisions of Manchester, Bolton and Stockport do not equate to the local authority districts of Manchester, Bolton and Stockport. Sub-divisions are broadly adhered to between censuses, making it possible to make comparisons with previously published census results.

The most populous sub-division of Manchester forms the centre of the wider urban area. It extends to Middleton in the north and includes Manchester Airport to the south. The population decreased by 2.1 per cent between censuses and the area increased by 2.2 per cent. The increase in area was primarily due to the development of a spur of urban land south west of Manchester Airport. The second most populous sub-division was Bolton and the third was Stockport near to the centre of the wider urban area. Bolton and Stockport have similar populations with a difference of only 3,321 people, 1.2 per cent of their combined populations. The population and area of Stockport remained fairly constant between 1991 and 2001. The population increased by 2.5 per cent and the area increased by 1.5 per cent resulting in a 0.9 per cent increase in density to 4,612.9 people per km^2.

The population density of Greater Manchester Urban Area decreased from 4,285.3 people per km^2 in 1991 to 4,024.0 in 2001, the largest decrease of the ten most populous urban areas. The primary driver of this decrease was the increase in area of Bolton, up 48.6 per cent between 1991 and 2001, with little increase in population, up 0.3 per cent. The extra area was primarily the result of the industrial use of land at Cutacre for mining purposes.

Two sub-divisions of Greater Manchester Urban Area in 1991 were independent urban areas in 2001. They were Mossley and Buckton Vale situated to the east of Greater Manchester Urban Area.

The smattering of pale pink and, in particular, grey throughout Map 3.5 portrays the non-uniform change of urban land area over a period of time. There are no concentrated areas of

urban land expansion or reduction; rather these can be found throughout Greater Manchester Urban Area.

Nottingham Urban Area

Nottingham Urban Area is dominated by the sub-division Nottingham at its centre. A swathe of urban land extends from the north west of Nottingham including the sub-divisions of Kimberley and Eastwood in Nottinghamshire, to Heanor and on to Ripley in Derbyshire. The outermost points of Nottingham Urban Area are found in the sub-divisions of Carlton to the east, Ruddington to the south east, Long Eaton to the south west, and Ripley to the north west. Sub-divisions do not correspond with administrative geographic boundaries; the subdivision of Nottingham does not equate to Nottingham Unitary Authority.

The proportional increases in population (8.6 per cent) and area (9.0 per cent) in Nottingham Urban Area between the 1991 and 2001 Censuses were the largest of the ten most populous urban areas.

Map **3.5**

Greater Manchester Urban Area, 1991 and 2001

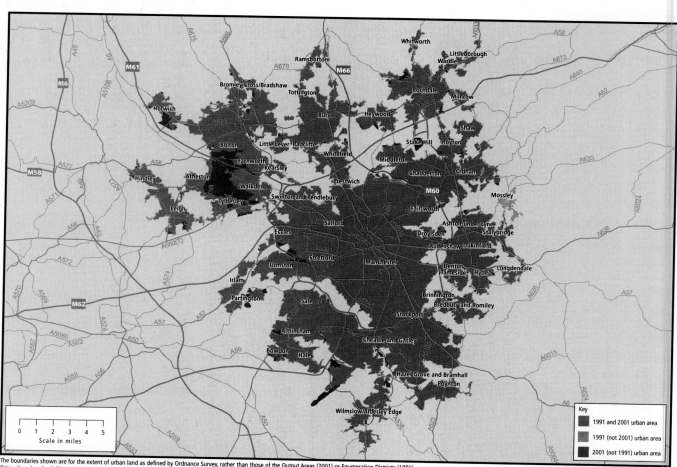

Key

■ 1991 and 2001 urban area
▨ 1991 (not 2001) urban area
■ 2001 (not 1991) urban area

The boundaries shown are for the extent of urban land as defined by Ordnance Survey, rather than those of the Output Areas (2001) or Enumeration Districts (1991) fitting the urban land. Place names shown refer to the centre of each sub-division of the urban area. Sub-divisions are areas within larger urban areas that often follow the boundaries of local authorities existing before the re-organisation in 1974, current authority boundaries, well-defined localities, or previously separate urban areas.

Map **3.6**

Nottingham Urban Area, 1991 and 2001

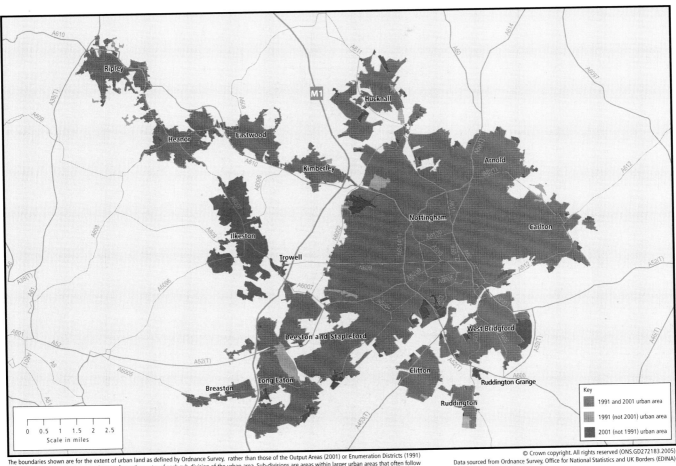

Key
- 1991 and 2001 urban area
- 1991 (not 2001) urban area
- 2001 (not 1991) urban area

The boundaries shown are for the extent of urban land as defined by Ordnance Survey, rather than those of the Output Areas (2001) or Enumeration Districts (1991) fitting the urban land. Place names shown refer to the centre of each sub-division of the urban area. Sub-divisions are areas within larger urban areas that often follow the boundaries of local authorities existing before the re-organisation in 1974, current authority boundaries, well-defined localities, or previously separate urban areas.

The only change in the top ten urban areas based on population between the 1991 and 2001 Censuses was Nottingham Urban Area, moving up one place to eighth whilst Sheffield Urban Area dropped to ninth.

The main source of the population and area increase in Nottingham Urban Area was the inclusion of the sub-division of Ilkeston, which had a population of 37,270 people and an area of 9.1km^2 in 2001. Ilkeston was reported in the 1991 Census results as an independent urban area. It has since been subsumed by Nottingham Urban Area through a bridge of urban land stretching from Nottingham to Beeston and Stapleford, and through Trowell.

West Bridgford experienced large proportional growth in population and area between the 1991 and 2001 Censuses. The population rose by 28.2 per cent to 43,395 people and the area rose by 28.7 per cent to 10.5km^2. The small settlement of Ruddington Grange between Ruddington and West Bridgford was not referred to in 1991 and consisted of 117 people in 2001.

Bristol Urban Area

Bristol Urban Area extends from the sub-division of Almondsbury in the north, Kingswood to the east, Bristol to the south and Easton-in-Gordano in the west. The sub-division Bristol, which does not equate to the City of Bristol Unitary Authority, includes more than three out of every four Bristol Urban Area residents and a similar proportion of the area.

The population increase in Bristol Urban Area between the 1991 and 2001 Censuses did not keep pace with its expansion in terms of size. The sub-division Easton-in-Gordano contributed greatly to the expansion of area between censuses. This area can be seen coloured in grey on Map 3.7 in western Bristol Urban Area. It is important to remember that there are small definitional differences between the 1991 and 2001 Censuses. The industrial area that is home to The Royal Portbury Dock and now part of Easton-in-Gordano would have been separate in 1991. The inclusion of this large area of industrial land means that the population density of Bristol Urban Area as a whole decreased between 1991 and 2001.

Map 3.7

Bristol Urban Area, 1991 and 2001

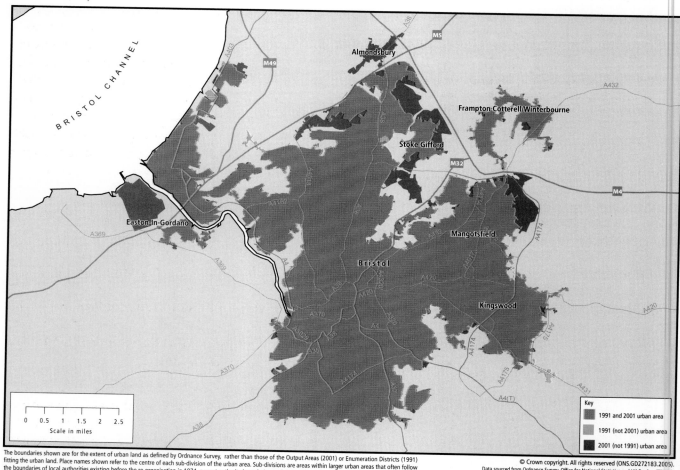

The boundaries shown are for the extent of urban land as defined by Ordnance Survey, rather than those of the Output Areas (2001) or Enumeration Districts (1991) fitting the urban land. Place names shown refer to the centre of each sub-division of the urban area. Sub-divisions are areas within larger urban areas that often follow the boundaries of local authorities existing before the re-organisation in 1974, current authority boundaries, well-defined localities, or previously separate urban areas.

Contributing to the increase in the physical size of Bristol Urban Area was the annexation of a previously separate urban area, together with the expansion of existing urban areas, mainly in the north. Almondsbury, situated to the north of the M5 motorway, was a separate urban area in 1991. The area of Mangotsfield increased by 35.4 per cent and the population by 21.2 per cent. Pockets of new urban land can be seen in northern Mangotsfield and a large area of new urban land in the north-west.

The area of Stoke Gifford increased significantly between the 1991 and 2001 Censuses, by 78.5 per cent, and the population by 72.4 per cent. Map 3.7 shows that the nearby part of Bristol also increased in area. Small areas of land which were urban in 1991 and not in 2001 can also be seen, particularly offshoots of land from south eastern Kingswood and north western Bristol.

For more information about the urban areas not included as a case study, see the appendix.

Top ten urban areas compared

The fundamental characteristics of a group of people include their age, sex, recent migration and their ethnic group – how they identify themselves. A comparison of these four characteristics provides the opportunity to observe differences between groups of people based on their place of residence. Analysis of these four variables will allow us to examine whether the populations of large urban areas, or conglomerations, are homogenous. We will ascertain whether the populations of these burgeoning swathes of urban land are interchangeable, or whether these populations are distinct.

Age

Five urban areas contained higher proportions of people under 16 years than the UK as a whole (20.2 per cent). The urban area with the largest proportion of people under 16 years was West Midlands Urban Area with 22.0 per cent. The second largest proportion was in West Yorkshire Urban Area with 21.6 per cent. The lowest proportion was found in Greater Glasgow,

Figure **3.8**

Percentage of the population aged 0 to 15 years, 2001

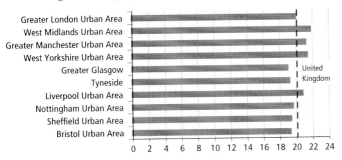

Source: 2001 Census – Office for National Statistics, General Register Office for Scotland and Northern Ireland Statistics and Research Agency

19.2 per cent, and the second lowest in Tyneside with 19.4 per cent. Figure 3.8 portrays the range of experience amongst the ten most populous urban areas.

Three urban areas had higher proportions of the population of pensionable age (65 years and above for males and 60 years and above for females) than the UK as a whole (18.4 per cent). They are Greater Glasgow, Tyneside and Sheffield Urban Area. Greater London Urban Area was home to the lowest proportion of people of pensionable age (15.0 per cent) of the ten most populous urban areas. Tyneside had the highest proportion with 19.2 per cent. Sheffield Urban Area was second largest at 18.7 per cent. The urban area with the second lowest proportion of people of pensionable age was West Yorkshire Urban Area with 17.0 per cent. Figure 3.9 reveals the varied experience amongst the ten most populous urban areas in the UK.

Greater London Urban Area includes the highest proportion of people of working age, 64.8 per cent. This corresponds to 5,368,165 people. West Midlands Urban Area includes the smallest proportion at 59.8 per cent. The working age population includes all people aged between 16 and pensionable age.

The dependency ratio is the number of people in dependent age groups, zero to fifteen years and those of pensionable age, divided by the number of people of working age (16 to pensionable age).[7] West Midlands Urban Area was home to the population with the highest dependency ratio of the top ten urban areas. There were 672 dependants per 1,000 people of working age. Greater London Urban Area had the lowest ratio with 542. The urban areas ranked three to six in terms of the magnitude of the dependency ratio were closely grouped with between 622 and 633 dependants per 1,000 people of working age. A difference of 130 between the urban area with the highest dependency ratio compared to the lowest indicates a variety of experience amongst the urban areas, shown in Figure 3.10.

The proportion of the population of working age is higher than the UK average for six of the ten most populous urban areas. This indicates that the population structure of these largest of urban areas is not consistent. The four urban areas with a dependency ratio higher than that of the UK overall were West Midlands Urban Area, Greater Manchester Urban Area, Tyneside and Liverpool Urban Area. Tyneside was the only one of these where the proportion of the population aged 0 to 15 years was lower than that of the UK.

Greater London Urban Area and West Yorkshire Urban Area had relatively low proportions of pensionable-age population. These areas had a dependency ratio below that of the UK, while the proportion of the population aged 0 to 15 years was higher.

A common characteristic of the largest urban areas is a relatively large proportion of the population aged 16 to 24, but there is a large variation between urban areas. All of the ten most populous urban areas contained a higher proportion of 16 to 24-year-olds than the UK as a whole. This age group accounted for 12.0 per cent of the total population of the ten most populous urban areas combined and 11.0 per cent of the

Figure **3.9**

Percentage of the population of pensionable age, 2001

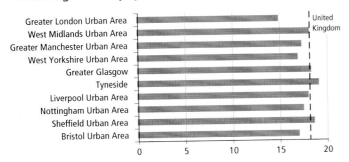

Source: 2001 Census – Office for National Statistics, General Register Office for Scotland and Northern Ireland Statistics and Research Agency

Figure **3.10**

Dependency ratio, 2001

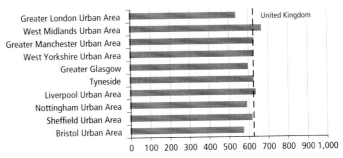

Source: 2001 Census – Office for National Statistics, General Register Office for Scotland and Northern Ireland Statistics and Research Agency

UK population. Figure 3.11 portrays the proportion of each urban area's population that was aged 16 to 24. This population group includes university-age people and represents a significant portion of the current and future workforce. The lowest proportion was in Greater Manchester Urban Area – 11.7 per cent of the population. The highest proportion was in Nottingham Urban Area – 13.2 per cent.

Figure **3.11**

Percentage of the population aged 16 to 24, 2001

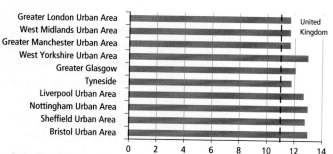

Source: 2001 Census – Office for National Statistics, General Register Office for Scotland and Northern Ireland Statistics and Research Agency

Sex

According to the 2001 Census, females made up 51.4 per cent of the United Kingdom population. There are more females than males in each of the ten most populous urban areas, shown in Table 3.12.

The population of Nottingham Urban Area was 50.8 per cent female; the lowest proportion of the ten most populous urban areas and lower than the United Kingdom as a whole. The populations of Bristol Urban Area and Sheffield Urban Area also had a smaller proportion of females than that of the United Kingdom, 51.1 per cent and 51.2 per cent respectively. Greater Glasgow included the largest proportion of females with 52.7 per cent. The second highest proportion of females could be found in Liverpool Urban Area, 52.3 per cent. Greater London Urban Area was home to the fifth highest proportion of females at 51.6 per cent of total population.

Migration

A fundamental characteristic of an area is the extent to which it experiences population movement. Analysis of migration to, from or within each of the top ten urban areas during the year before the census reveals that the populations of the ten most populous urban areas are heterogeneous, both when

Table **3.12**

Proportion of the population by sex, 2001

		Male		Female	
		Count	Per cent	Count	Per cent
1	Greater London Urban Area	4,007,297	48.4	4,270,954	51.6
2	West Midlands Urban Area	1,109,397	48.6	1,174,696	51.4
3	Greater Manchester Urban Area	1,088,658	48.6	1,151,572	51.4
4	West Yorkshire Urban Area	724,818	48.3	774,647	51.7
5	Greater Glasgow	552,037	47.3	616,233	52.7
6	Tyneside	425,119	48.3	454,877	51.7
7	Liverpool Urban Area	389,119	47.7	427,097	52.3
8	Nottingham Urban Area	327,851	49.2	338,507	50.8
9	Sheffield Urban Area	312,619	48.8	328,101	51.2
10	Bristol Urban Area	269,689	48.9	281,377	51.1
	United Kingdom	28,579,869	48.6	30,209,325	51.4

Source: 2001 Census – Office for National Statistics, General Register Office for Scotland and Northern Ireland Statistics and Research Agency

considering the scale and type of migration. The census definition, from which the data are obtained, of a migrant is: someone now resident in an area who either moved into or within the area during the year before the census or, had no usual address the year before the census.

Bristol Urban Area included the highest proportion of migrants with 14.6 per cent of the resident population on Census day 2001, 80,264 people, having changed address during the previous year. Over six out of ten of these migrants moved within Bristol Urban Area during the year before the census, and over a quarter moved into the area from within the UK. The second largest proportion of migrants was in Nottingham Urban Area with 13.9 per cent of the population. Nottingham Urban Area, home to a smaller population than Liverpool Urban Area, included 3,555 more migrants. Table 3.13 shows the types of migrants as a proportion of the population of each urban area.

West Midlands Urban Area recorded the smallest proportion of migrants with 10.2 per cent of the resident population having changed address during the previous year. More than seven out of every ten migrants in this area moved within the area during the year before the census. A fairly low 1.6 per cent of West Midlands Urban Area residents moved from inside the

United Kingdom, the next smallest proportion was in Greater London Urban Area with 2.0 per cent of residents.

The highest proportion of the resident population with no usual address one year before the census was 1.6 per cent, in Greater London Urban Area. The second highest proportion was in Bristol Urban Area at 0.94 per cent. The lowest proportion was Tyneside with 0.74 per cent.

Greater London Urban Area included the highest proportion of people who moved within the area, 8.9 per cent. Bristol Urban Area and West Yorkshire Urban Area included 8.8 per cent. The lowest proportion was in Greater Glasgow with 6.6 per cent.

Of the migrants in Greater London Urban Area, 11.5 per cent moved into the area from outside the UK, representing 1.6 per cent of the total population. This proportion is nearly double that of the next urban area – 5.9 per cent of migrants living in Bristol Urban Area moved into the area from outside the UK during the year before the census. The smallest proportion of migrants who moved into the area from outside the United Kingdom was Liverpool Urban Area with 0.37 per cent of the total population or 3.4 per cent of migrants. Nearly three in ten migrants in Greater Glasgow lived in a different UK area during the year before the census.

Table **3.13**

Migrants as a percentage of all people in each urban area, 2001

			Percentage[1] of all people				
		Migrants (number)	Migrants	Moved within area	No usual address one year ago	Moved into the area from within the UK	Moved into the area from outside UK
1	Greater London Urban Area	1,140,662	13.8	8.9	1.60	2.0	1.60
2	West Midlands Urban Area	233,108	10.2	7.4	0.81	1.6	0.47
3	Greater Manchester Urban Area[2]	266,571	11.9	8.4	0.89	2.1	0.52
4	West Yorkshire Urban Area	196,959	13.1	8.8	0.92	2.8	0.58
5	Greater Glasgow	130,066	11.1	6.6	0.88	3.1	0.54
6	Tyneside	104,942	11.9	8.1	0.74	2.5	0.55
7	Liverpool Urban Area	89,061	10.9	7.6	0.82	2.1	0.37
8	Nottingham Urban Area	92,616	13.9	8.6	0.87	3.7	0.71
9	Sheffield Urban Area	84,040	13.1	8.5	0.80	3.2	0.63
10	Bristol Urban Area	80,264	14.6	8.8	0.94	4.0	0.86

1 Percentages may not add exactly to totals due to rounding.
2 Migration data for the separate urban area of Helsby is included for the Greater Manchester Urban Area. These data were included in previously published material in error.

Source: 2001 Census – Office for National Statistics, General Register Office for Scotland

Identity

A fundamental feature of a person's identity is their ethnicity. Bulmer (1996) was cited in the ONS publication *Ethnic Group Statistics* (2003)[8] as describing an ethnic group as a:

'...collectivity within a larger population having real or putative common ancestry, memories of a shared past, and a cultural focus upon one or more symbolic elements which define the group's identity, such as kinship, religion, language, shared territory, nationality or physical appearance.'

It is important to note that an individual can have many layers of identity and hence ethnic groups. For example, an individual may identify strongly with the area of York in Yorkshire on the lowest layer, Yorkshire as a whole on the next, as a Northerner on the next and as a White Briton on the next. The census results provide us with information on this highest layer of identity.

Table 3.14 shows the percentage of population in each urban area by ethnic group. Greater London Urban Area included the lowest proportion of people identifying as White British and the highest proportions for all thirteen ethnic groups except for White British, Indian and Pakistani. The highest proportion of people identifying as Indian resided in West Midlands Urban Area, 5.8 per cent, compared to 5.6 per cent of the Greater London Urban Area population – the second largest proportion, and 0.3 per cent of Liverpool Urban Area, the smallest proportion. While the highest proportion of Indians can be found resident in West Midlands Urban Area there were 327,703 more people identifying as Indian in Greater London Urban Area.

Table 3.14

Percentage of population by ethnic group, 2001

		White			Mixed	Asian or Asian British				Black or Black British			Chinese or Other ethnic group	
	All people	British	Irish	Other White	Any Mixed Groups	Indian	Paki-stani	Bangla-deshi	Other Asian	Caribbean	African	Other Black	Chinese	Other
1 Greater London Urban Area	8,278,251	63.5	2.9	7.7	2.9	5.6	1.9	1.9	1.7	4.2	4.6	0.7	1.0	1.4
2 West Midlands Urban Area	2,284,093	76.6	1.9	1.2	2.2	5.8	5.8	1.2	0.7	3.2	0.4	0.4	0.4	0.4
3 Greater Manchester Urban Area	2,240,226	86.9	1.8	1.5	1.4	1.6	3.3	0.9	0.4	0.7	0.4	0.1	0.5	0.3
4 West Yorkshire Urban Area	1,499,465	83.1	1.0	1.4	1.5	2.7	7.5	0.5	0.4	0.9	0.3	0.1	0.3	0.3
5 Greater Glasgow	1,168,270	93.4	1.6	1.3	0.3	0.6	1.7	0.0	0.2	0.0	0.1	0.0	0.5	0.2
6 Tyneside	879,996	95.2	0.4	1.1	0.6	0.6	0.7	0.5	0.2	0.0	0.2	0.0	0.4	0.3
7 Liverpool Urban Area	816,216	94.4	1.0	0.9	1.2	0.3	0.2	0.1	0.2	0.2	0.4	0.2	0.8	0.2
8 Nottingham Urban Area	666,358	89.0	1.0	1.8	1.8	1.5	1.7	0.1	0.2	1.7	0.3	0.2	0.5	0.3
9 Sheffield Urban Area	640,720	90.1	0.6	1.2	1.4	0.5	3.2	0.3	0.4	0.8	0.5	0.1	0.4	0.4
10 Bristol Urban Area	551,066	90.4	1.0	2.2	1.7	1.0	0.8	0.2	0.2	1.1	0.5	0.2	0.5	0.3

Note: Results from the 2001 Census in England and Wales are reported using 16 ethnic groups, Scotland census data are reported using 14 groups. The differing groupings have been harmonised into 13 ethnic groups. The Scotland groupings of White Scottish and Other White have been merged with White British, Other South Asian with Other Asian, Other Black with Black Scottish and Other Black, and African with Black African. The England and Wales mixed ethnic categories have been combined into one group.

Source: 2001 Census – Office for National Statistics, General Register Office for Scotland

The largest proportion of people identifying as Pakistani existed in West Yorkshire Urban Area with 7.5 per cent; the smallest proportion was in Liverpool Urban Area, 0.2 per cent. Both Greater London Urban Area (153,479 people) and West Midlands Urban Area (131,844) included a higher number of people identifying as Pakistani than West Yorkshire Urban Area (111,949).

Of the ten urban areas, Greater Glasgow had the smallest proportion of people identifying as Bangladeshi, African, Mixed and Other ethnic groups. Tyneside had the smallest proportion of people identifying as White Irish, Other Asian, Caribbean and Other Black. Liverpool Urban Area had the smallest proportion of Other White, Indian and Pakistani.

Throughout this report, the term 'ethnic minority' refers to those people who identify with an ethnic group other than White. The differences between the proportions of residents in ethnic minority populations among the urban areas are noteworthy. The identity of the population of these urban areas is heterogeneous, ranging from 25.9 per cent of the Greater London Urban Area population identifying as part of the ethnic minority and 20.4 per cent of West Midlands Urban Area to 3.4 per cent of the Tyneside population. The range across the ten urban areas is shown in Figure 3.15.

Census data provide clues as to whether people of similar or differing identities/ethnic groups choose to live together in households. Most UK-household members are of the same ethnic group or identity. There are large differences between urban areas in the proportion of households that include people of differing ethnic groups.

Greater London Urban Area differs to the other nine urban areas. Of households consisting of more than one person, 21.9 per cent in Greater London Urban Area were made up of

people not of the same ethnic group. The smallest proportion was 4.1 per cent in Tyneside.

Conclusion

The urban areas that are home to nearly a third of the UK population have been found to consist of heterogeneous populations. Comparisons of age, sex, migration and identity using 2001 Census data have borne this out. The population of one of the ten most populous urban areas would not be interchangeable with the population of another.

The populations of the ten major urban areas in the United Kingdom exhibit a diverse range of characteristics. Population change between 1991 and 2001 ranged from an increase of 8.6 per cent in Nottingham Urban Area to a decrease of 2.6 per cent in Greater Glasgow. There were 672 dependents per 1,000 people of working age in West Midlands Urban Area compared to 542 in Greater London Urban Area. The Bristol Urban Area population included 14.6 per cent migrants compared to 10.2 per cent in West Midlands Urban Area. Tyneside had the highest proportion identifying as White British, 95.2 per cent, compared to 76.6 per cent in West Midlands Urban Area and 63.5 per cent in Greater London Urban Area.

The population of Greater London Urban Area was found to exhibit an extreme set of characteristics across a number of variables compared to the other urban areas. The population included the largest proportion identifying as other than White British, the lowest dependency ratio, the lowest proportion of pensionable age, and the lowest proportion of households where all members share the same ethnic identity.

Boundaries of urban land are not static. Nottingham Urban Area expanded between 1991 and 2001 to include Ilkeston. Bristol Urban Area increased through the inclusion of a predominantly industrial area in Easton-in-Gordano and the previously separate residential area of Almondsbury. Greater Manchester Urban Area no longer included the urban areas of Mossley and Buckton Vale in 2001 compared to 1991, while Bolton almost doubled in area without a commensurate increase in population.

Figure **3.15**

Ethnic minority population, as a percentage of all people in each urban area, 2001

Percentage

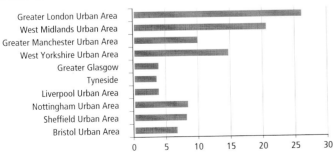

Source 2001 Census – Office for National Statistics, General Register Office for Scotland

Notes and references

1. Census data reported here are derived or reported from data included in publications released by the UK's statistical offices: General Register Office for Scotland, Northern Ireland Statistics and Research Agency and Office for National Statistics.

2. The adjustments made to the mid-year population estimates were a result of the Local Authority Population Studies and were made following an extensive review of census results and processes. This showed that, for a small number of authorities, there was evidence which provided a basis for making a better estimate of the population. More information can be accessed here: www.statistics.gov.uk/about/Methodology_by_theme/LAStudies.asp

3. Countryside agency *et al.* (2004) *Rural and Urban Area Classification 2004*, An Introductory Guide. www.statistics.gov.uk/geography/downloads/Rural_Urban_Introductory_Guidev2.pdf

4. General Register Office for Scotland (2004) *Scottish Executive Rural Urban Classification* 2003–2004. www.scotland.gov.uk/library5/rural/seurc-00.asp

5. Northern Ireland Statistics and Research Agency (2005) *Report of the Inter-Departmental Urban-Rural Definition Group, Statistical Classification and Delineation of Settlements*, February 2005. www.nisra.gov.uk/statistics/financeandpersonnel/DMB/urban_rural.html

6. The urban area of Belfast and connected settlements used in this report includes the connected areas of: Belfast Urban Area, Castlereagh Urban Area, Greenisland Urban Area, Holywood Urban Area, Lisburn Urban Area, Newtownabbey Urban Area and Milltown (Lisburn LGD). The nearby non-connected settlements of Bangor, Carrickfergus, Carryduff, Crawfordsburn, Groomsport, Helen's Bay, and Seahill, which are used by NISRA in the definition of Belfast Metropolitan Urban Area, have been excluded from the definition of the urban area of Belfast and connected settlements for this report.

7. Griffiths C (2001) Demographic Backgrounds, 2, 6–9, in Griffiths C (ed.) and Fitzpatrick J (ed.) *Geographic Variation in Health*. London: The Stationery Office; www.statistics.gov.uk/downloads/theme_health/DS16/DS16_cap02.pdf

8. Office for National Statistics (2003) *Ethnic Group Statistics, A guide for collection and classification of ethnicity data*. www.statistics.gov.uk/about/ethnic_group_statistics/downloads/ethnic_group_statistics.pdf

The changing age structure of the UK population

Chris Smith, Cecilia Tomassini,
Steve Smallwood and Mike Hawkins

Chapter 4

Introduction

This chapter explores changes in the age structure of the UK population over the last three decades. The ways in which the age profile of the population might change in the future are also discussed. Mid-year population estimates for 2004 are compared with those for selected years back to 1971, using changes in the median age and in the population age structure. Country patterns within the UK are examined, and this chapter includes a comparison with changes that have occurred in the age structure of Japan, where the population is ageing rapidly. As well as age distribution, this chapter analyses the changing distribution of the UK population by legal marital status.

Current and recent trends in the age structure of the UK population

The UK population reached 59.8 million in 2004, its highest level ever. It has increased in size by 7 per cent in the three decades since 1971, when the figure was 55.9 million. But this population growth has not occurred at all ages. In fact, some age groups have shrunk and so become a smaller proportion of the whole population.

This chapter considers three broad age groups, together with some more detailed age breakdowns. The three groups are:

- children (those aged 0 to 15 years)

- the working age population (females aged 16 to 59 and males aged 16 to 64)

- those above state pension age (females aged 60 and above and males aged 65 and above).

The exception to this is in the section on future projections where the age groups 0 to 15, 16 to 64 and 65 and over have been used. This gives consistency over time, since the pension age for women is expected to change from 60 to 65 between 2010 and 2020.

The changes that have occurred in the proportion that these groups represent of the total population are shown in Figures 4.1 a–c.

Figure 4.1a illustrates the number of children aged under 16, a segment of the population that decreased by 18 per cent from 14.3 million to 11.7 million between 1971 and 2004. The working-age population increased by 13 per cent in the same period, from 32.6 million to 37.0 million (Figure 4.1b). The greatest proportional rise was in the size of the population above state pension age. This older population increased by 22 per cent from 9.1 million in 1971 to 11.1 million in 2004 (Figure 4.1c). The changing numbers of people in the different age

groups have led to a progressive transformation of the age profile of the UK population, a structural change that may have significant social, health and economic consequences.

Figure 4.2 shows the percentage age composition of the population for 1971 to 2004. The proportion of children declined from a quarter to a fifth between 1971 and 2004. This decline reflects a sustained pattern of fertility at or below replacement level (the minimum fertility level required to ensure a population continues to replace itself, usually around 2.1 children per woman in developed societies[1]). This pattern is

Figure 4.1

Population[1] by age group[2], 1971 to 2004

United Kingdom

4.1a Population aged 0 to 15

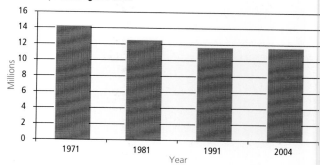

4.1b Population aged 16 to state pension age

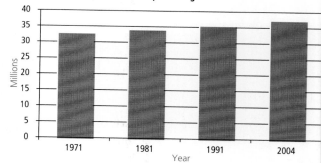

4.1c Population above state pension age

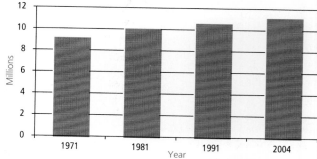

1 Population estimates refer to mid-year point (30 June).
2 State pension age is defined here as ages 65 and above for men and 60 and above for women.

Source: Population estimates – Office for National Statistics; General Register Office for Scotland; Northern Ireland Statistics and Research Agency

typical of much of western Europe and, within the last decade, of Europe as a whole. But current UK fertility levels are not as low as Italy or Spain and are very similar to the Netherlands and Sweden (see Chapter 10 for more European comparisons).

Figure 4.2

Percentage of population[1] by age group[2], 1971 to 2004

United Kingdom

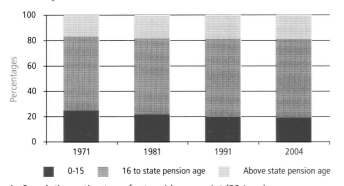

1 Population estimates refer to mid-year point (30 June).
2 State pension age is defined here as ages 65 and above for men and 60 and above for women.

Source: Population estimates – Office for National Statistics; General Register Office for Scotland; Northern Ireland Statistics and Research Agency

The working age population has grown from 58.2 per cent to 61.9 per cent of the total population between 1971 and 2004. This rise is partly due to ageing of people born in the early to mid-1960s, when birth rates were relatively high. 'Baby boomer' generations affect the age structure of the population as they grow older. People born in the late 1940s and 1960s reached working age between the early 1960s and 1980s and will leave it between 2006 and 2029.

The population of working age is growing older. The median age of this group has increased, for men from 37.4 in 1991 to 39.6 in 2004, and for women from 35.7 to 38.4. Those aged between 16 and 24 represented 20.8 per cent of the male and 21.8 of the female working population in 1991, but they comprised only 18.4 and 19.1 per cent respectively in 2004. Conversely, older male workers (those aged 50 to 64) increased their share in the working population from 23.9 in 1991 to 27.2 per cent in 2004, while for women the proportion aged 50 to 59 rose from 17.8 in 1991 to 21.5 per cent in 2004.

Between 1971 and 2004, the proportion of people above state pension age increased from over 16 per cent to more than 18 per cent. Within the older population, the more substantial growth occurred among the oldest old (those aged 85 and over). There were around a half million oldest old in 1971, comprising 0.9 per cent of the total population. By 2004, the

oldest old had more than doubled to 1.1 million, representing 1.9 per cent of the UK population. This rise is the result of the relatively high number of births that occurred in the first two decades of the 20th century, combined with increased longevity at older ages. The consequences of the increase of the oldest old may have significant implications in terms of welfare, health and social support.[2]

It is useful to relate these population groups in terms of dependency of the old and young on the working age population. Table 4.3 shows the trends in four age structure indicators for the period between 1971 and 2004. The total dependency ratio (that is the number of people aged 0 to 15 plus the number aged above state pension age, relative to the number of people of working age) shows a decrease from 72 to 61 per hundred over the last 30 years. This is due to the fall in the child dependency ratio (number of people aged 0 to 15 relative to the size of the working population), which has declined from 44 to 31 per hundred population of working age. In contrast, the old-age dependency ratio (number of people above state pension age relative to the size of the working population) has risen slightly from 28 to 30 per hundred.

Another useful age structure indicator is the ageing index (population above state pension age per hundred children aged 0 to 15). A large change occurred in the ageing index, between 1971 and 2004, when it increased from 64 to 96. In the past, children outnumbered older people and provided a buoyant pool for the future population of working age. By 2004 there were almost the same number of people above state pension age as children below age 16. The implications for future ageing trends are considered later in this chapter.

Table 4.3

Age structure indicators[1], 1971 to 2004

United Kingdom

	1971	1981	1991	2004
Total Dependency Ratio	71.8	66.8	63.2	61.4
Child dependency ratio	43.8	37.1	33.2	31.4
Old-age dependency ratio	28.0	29.7	30.0	30.0
Ageing Index	64.0	80.0	90.4	95.5

1 Indicators are calculated from population estimates referring to the mid-year point (30 June). See text for explanation of indicators.

Source: Population estimates – Office for National Statistics; General Register Office for Scotland; Northern Ireland Statistics and Research Agency

Note that neither dependency ratios nor the ageing index, based as they are on age alone, take account of economic dependence. For example, students aged 16 and above are included in the working age population, even though many are not actually economically active. Conversely older people still in the paid or unpaid workforce are not included even though many are still actually working.

Table 4.4

Median age of population, 1971 to 2004

	United Kingdom
1971	34.1
1981	34.5
1991	35.8
2004	38.6

Source: Population estimates – Office for National Statistics; General Register Office for Scotland; Northern Ireland Statistics and Research Agency

Table 4.5

Marital status distribution, by age and sex, 2001

United Kingdom

Percentages[1]

The median (average) age of the population summarises the age of a population in a single measure. Table 4.4 shows the median age of the UK population during the period 1971 to 2004. The median age has increased by 4.5 years (from 34.1 to 38.6) over the three decades from 1971 to 2004.

This section has clearly shown that the UK population has aged between 1971 and 2004. This ageing is due to:

- sustained low fertility – and thus a decline in the proportion of children in the population

- a rising proportion of older people in the population (especially at the oldest old ages).

These trends are reflected in the overall dependency ratio, which has fallen over the last three decades as the decreasing number of children has exceeded the rise in the number of older people. Future ageing patterns are considered later in this chapter.

Men	Total	Single (never married)	Married (first marriage)	Re-married	Separated (but still legally married)	Divorced	Widowed
16–24	100	97	2	0	0	0	0
25–34	100	59	34	2	2	4	0
35–44	100	24	53	8	4	10	0
45–54	100	12	57	13	3	13	1
55–64	100	8	63	13	2	11	3
65–74	100	8	65	10	1	6	9
75–84	100	7	57	8	1	3	24
85+	100	7	38	7	1	2	47

Women	Total	Single (never married)	Married (first marriage)	Re-married	Separated (but still legally married)	Divorced	Widowed
16–24	100	93	6	0	1	0	0
25–34	100	47	41	3	4	6	0
35–44	100	17	53	9	5	14	1
45–54	100	7	57	13	4	16	3
55–64	100	5	59	11	2	12	11
65–74	100	6	49	6	1	7	31
75–84	100	7	27	3	0	4	58
85+	100	10	8	1	0	2	79

1 Percentages may not add exactly to 100 due to rounding.

Source: 2001 Census – Office for National Statistics; General Register Office for Scotland; Northern Ireland Statistics and Research Agency

The changes in the UK's age structure, though significant, are less striking than those in some countries in Southern and Eastern Europe, as well as Japan. In these countries, changes in the age structure of the population are occurring faster than in the UK. This presents challenges from a pensions and healthcare perspective, both now and over the next few decades.

UK adult population by legal marital status

The marital status of the UK population varies both by age and sex. Table 4.5 presents 2001 Census data on marital status for men and women by age group.

A number of factors account for the gender differences in the marital status distributions. First, women tend to marry earlier than men and, on average, wives are younger than their husbands.[3,4] Second, men are more likely to remarry after a divorce. Another third important factor, especially at older ages, is the difference in survival between men and women.

At younger ages, a higher proportion of women than men are married, reflecting the general tendency of women to marry at younger ages. Between 35 and 54 the proportions married are very similar for both sexes. At older ages, gender differences in marital distribution are more remarkable, with men more likely to be married or remarried than women.

At ages 65 and above, seven men out of ten were married in 2001 compared with only four women. Five out of ten women above age 64 were widowed. Since women tend to marry older husbands, the pattern of longer life expectancy for women (making widowhood more common than widowerhood) accentuates this pattern. Among those aged 85 and over, while 44 per cent of men were still married, only 10 per cent of women had a surviving husband. Nearly 80 per cent of women aged 85 or over were widowed. Around 6 per cent of both sexes aged 65 and over were divorced.

Figures 4.6a and 4.6b illustrate changes in the proportion of married people in 1971 and 2001 in different age groups for men and women. The marital status categories used in 1971 data did not include remarriage or separation; so for comparison, the 2001 figures combine married, remarried and separated people.

The proportion of married men aged 16 and over declined from more than 70 per cent in 1971 to around 50 per cent by 2001. Over the same period, the proportion of single people rose from just over a quarter to just over a third, while the divorced increased from around 1 per cent to more than 7 per cent. Among women aged 16 and over, 65 per cent were married in 1971, but only 56 per cent in 2001. Divorced women

represented 2 per cent of the population in 1971, but this had increased to 10 per cent by 2001.

Despite these general trends of decreasing proportions of married people and an increase in divorce, there are substantial differences between age groups. The proportion of married people has declined consistently at young adult ages. Among men aged 16 to 24 the married represented 22 per cent of the total population in 1971, but only 3 per cent in 2001; for women the proportions are 39 and 7 per cent respectively. For adults aged 25 to 34 the decline has been considerable as well. In 1971, 79 per cent of men and 87 per cent of women were married against, respectively, 37 and 47 per cent in 2001.

The decline over last three decades in the proportion of young adults married is not only due to postponement of marriage (a phenomenon common in most Western countries), but also to the increased popularity of cohabitation. Data from the General Household Survey show that 28 per cent of people aged 25 to 29 were living together in 2001.[5]

Other reasons may explain the rise of marriage among older people, especially older women. The composition by marital

Figure **4.6**

Proportion married[1] by age and sex, 1971 and 2001

United Kingdom

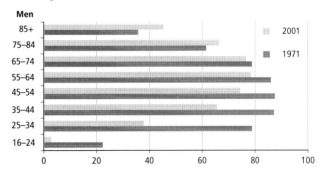

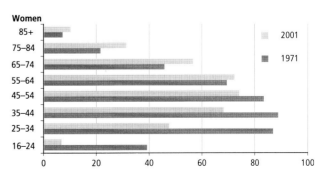

1   Data refer to the proportion married on Census day (not the proportion ever married).

Source: 1971 and 2001 Censuses – Office for National Statistics; General Register Office for Scotland; Northern Ireland Statistics and Research Agency

status of older people is largely determined by past marriage patterns and the incidence and duration of widowhood and divorce. High proportions of women born at the beginning of the 20th century never married due to high male mortality (both general and wartime) and emigration. This can be partly seen in the low proportion of women married at older ages in 1971.

Improvements in life expectancy (especially among men), which have made it more likely that spouses will survive together into old age, are also partly responsible for the increase in the proportion married for women aged 65 and over; but higher rates of ever-marrying, particularly for cohorts who did so in the 1960s, also played a part. The more modest increase in the proportion of married men at older ages can be explained to some extent by the consistent increase in the proportions divorced; among those aged 65 and over the proportion of those who were divorced increased from 1 per cent in 1971 to 5 per cent in 2001.

Being without a spouse may have important consequences on living arrangements and support in later life. In 2001, 23 per cent of men and 46 per cent of women aged 65 and above were living alone.[6] Never-married older people are more likely than the married to live either alone or in a communal establishment due to their lack of a spouse to care for them and high level of childlessness among them. For example, 24 per cent of men aged 65 and over living in communal establishments were never-married, compared to only 7 per cent among all men of that age, according to the 2001 Census. Previously married older people were also more likely to be living alone than older people with a living spouse. Future plans for the provision of housing and services to older people will therefore need to take into account the changing marital status distribution in this age group.

Future trends

The national population projections for the UK, produced by the Government Actuary's Department (GAD), show the size and age structure of the population for the next seventy years. These projections are based on assumptions for changes in mortality, and fertility rates, as well as numbers and age distributions of migrants. Trends in the main components of population change (growth due to births and immigration, decrease due to deaths and emigration) will determine the population's future ageing trends. The further into the future that projections are made, the more uncertain the ageing pattern becomes. But the pattern over the next couple of decades is largely determined by the size and age distribution of the population today, which is a known factor not subject to assumptions.

The Government Actuary's Department produce a main, or 'principal', projection but, to acknowledge the inherent uncertainty of looking into the future, they also produce 'variant' projections, with different assumptions for fertility, mortality and migration. For each of the three population-change components, a plausible alternative high and low assumption is produced. Combinations of these variants can be used to produce the largest, smallest, oldest or youngest population given the variant assumptions (Box 1).

Box 1 Population projection assumptions

In order to make assumptions about future population the Government Actuary's Department makes assumptions about fertility, mortality and migration. The table below summarises the assumptions used in the 2004-based principal projections and the variant assumptions used to create the scenarios shown in the article. Note that the variant assumptions are plausible alternative scenarios and are not formal limits or confidence intervals.

Summary measures of long-term assumptions

	Principal	High	Low
Fertility (completed family size cohorts born from 1990 onwards)	1.74	1.94	1.54
Migration (net per year)	145,000	205,000	85,000
Life expectancy (period life expectancy at birth 2031)			
Males	81.4	83.5	79.2
Females	85.0	86.5	83.6

The following table shows the combinations of the above assumptions used to create the scenarios discussed in the chapter.

Combinations of long-term assumptions used to create projection scenarios

	Fertility	Life expectancy	Migration
'Large' population	High	High	High
'Small' population	Low	Low	Low
'Young' population	High	Low	High
'Old' population	Low	High	Low

Figure 4.7 summarises the results of these projections. The 2004-based principal projection shows that the UK population will continue to rise over the next seven decades from 59.8 million in 2004 to around 70.7 million by 2074 (Figure 4.7a). This continued rise is not inevitable. Plausible alternative fertility, mortality and migration assumptions could indicate population decline within 70 years.

While age distributions will vary under the different scenarios it is clear that the population will continue to age. For ease of comparison the groups used here are: under 16, 16 to 64 and 65 and over. It is assumed that the latter group can be

Figure **4.7**

Projected population (principal and variants¹), selected age groups, 2004 to 2074

United Kingdom

4.7a Total population (millions)

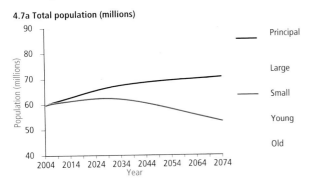

4.7b Percentage of population aged 0 to 15

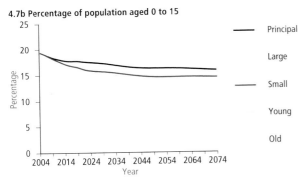

4.7c Percentage of population aged 65+

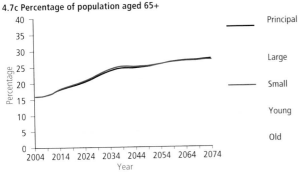

1 See Box 1 for explanation of different variants.

Source: 2004-based population projections – Government Actuary's Department

described as the retirement age group, as the female retirement age will increase from age 60 to age 65 between 2010 and 2020.

Figure 4.7b shows the percentage aged under 16 in the principal and variant populations. Even under the 'young' variant, the percentage under 16 does not change much from the current proportion of a little under 20 per cent. The principal projection shows the proportion aged 0 to 15 falling to just over 16 per cent in 2050.

Figure 4.7c indicates that the proportion of the population aged 65-plus rises in all the scenarios shown. For the principal projection, the rise is from 16 per cent in 2004 to over 25 per cent in 2050. Even under the 'young' variant the proportion rises to over 21 per cent.

Figure 4.8 shows the trend in the median age for each of the projections. All suggest the median age will rise above 40, with the principal projection suggesting a median age of a little under 45 by the middle of the century, and the 'old' scenario suggesting it will approach 49 by then.

The ageing process will occur at different speeds in the UK's four component countries, due to different patterns of fertility and varying improvements in mortality at older ages. In 2004, the median age of the population was 38.5 in England, 40.2 in Wales, 39.8 in Scotland and 35.8 in Northern Ireland. By 2050, these median ages are projected to increase to 44.2, 47.2, 47.9 and 46.4 respectively.[7]

Northern Ireland is the component country that is ageing, and will continue to age, the fastest. The proportion of people aged 65 and over will increase most in Northern Ireland; between 2004 and 2050 it will almost double from 13.6 to 26.9 per cent. But the proportion of older people will be higher

Figure **4.8**

Projected median age of UK population (principal and variant projections¹), 2004 to 2074

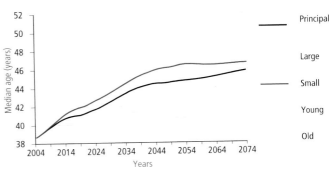

1 See Box 1 for explanation of different variants.

Source: 2004-based population projections – Government Actuary's Department

in Scotland, where 28.6 per cent of the whole population will be over 65 in 2050, compared with 16.3 in 2004. England and Wales will age as well; between 2004 and 2050 the proportion aged 65 and above will increase from 16.0 to 24.8 in England and from 17.5 to 27.5 in Wales.

Changes in the population of England and Wales, by marital status, have been projected by GAD.[8] The proportion of older people who are divorced is expected to rise from 6 to 14 per cent for males and 6 to 17 per cent for females between 2003 and 2031. But the proportion of females over 65 who are widowed is expected to fall from 46 per cent in 2003 to 28 per cent by 2031, with a fall from 16 to 12 per cent for males. GAD also produces projections by partnership status. These show that the proportion of people aged 65 and over who are cohabiting will rise from 1 to 5 per cent for men and 1 to 3 per cent for women by 2031. Recent work[9] has demonstrated that a higher proportion of older people are likely to have a surviving child than for any generation ever born in Britain. In the next quarter century the proportion of women aged 80 with at least one surviving child will rise from two-thirds to three-quarters.

Ageing populations: a comparison with Japan

The ageing process of the UK population has followed some patterns that have been experienced by other developed countries; for example postponement of childbearing, higher levels of childlessness and growing longevity. But the timing and the intensity of these trends have been different.

The example of Japan provides an excellent case study of a non-European population whose ageing process has been quite different from the UK. In 1950 the median age of UK population was 34.6, while the Japanese figure was 22.3. By 2004, the UK median age had increased by four years to 38.6 while the median age of Japan's population had risen by 20.4 years to 42.7.[10]

The time it took for the UK population aged 65 and over to double from being 7 per cent of the total population to 14 per cent was 45 years (between 1930 and 1975). The same increase was achieved by the Japanese population in only 26 years (between 1970 and 1996). The doubling time of the older population is an important indicator for the debate on financing health care and the pension system; the more rapid the ageing process, the faster the political response has to be.[11]

Figure 4.9 shows the changes in the proportion of people aged 65 and over in Japan and the UK over the period 1971 to 2004. In 1971, the older population in Japan comprised just over 7 per cent of its total population, almost half that of the UK (just over 13 per cent). But by 2004 the Japanese level had reached 19.5 per cent, compared to 16.0 per cent in the UK.

Japan's faster ageing process has only partly been due to differential declines in fertility. In fact the total fertility rate in 1971 was 2.4 in the UK and 2.2 in Japan, while in 2003 the rates were 1.6 and 1.3 respectively (the Japanese total fertility rate now being similar to those in southern Europe).

Apart from the fertility differences, there has been a dramatic difference between the two countries in improvements in survival at older ages. Mortality rates in 1970 gave a 65-year old British woman an expected 16.0 years of life compared with 15.3 years for her Japanese counterpart (Table 4.10), showing very little difference between the two countries with a slightly longer survival for UK women. In 2002, the life expectations were 19.1 in the UK and 23.0 in Japan, showing

Figure **4.9**

Percentage of population aged 65 and above, 1971 to 2004

Japan and UK[1]

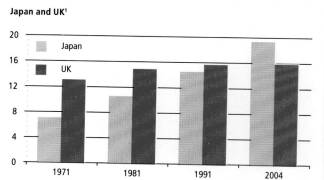

1   Population estimates for the UK refer to 30 June. Population estimates for Japan refer to 1 October.

Source: UK population estimates – Office for National Statistics; General Register Office for Scotland; Northern Ireland Statistics and Research Agency. Japan population estimates – Statistics Bureau (Japan), Ministry of Internal Affairs and Communication

Table **4.10**

Life expectancy at older ages, 1970 to 2002

Japan and UK

	Men		Women	
	Japan	UK	Japan	UK
1970				
Life expectancy at age 65	12.5	12.1	15.3	16.0
Life expectancy at age 85	3.8	4.1	4.5	5.1
2002				
Life expectancy at age 65	18.0	16.1	23.0	19.1
Life expectancy at age 85	6.0	5.1	7.9	6.1

Source: UK – Office for National Statistics; General Register Office for Scotland; Northern Ireland Statistics and Research Agency. Japan – Statistics Bureau (Japan), Ministry of Internal Affairs and Communication

the striking improvement in Japanese later-life survival of almost eight years in only three decades. The figures for men are slightly less impressive; Japanese men aged 65 and over have gained 5.5 years between 1971 and 2002 compared with 4.0 years for British men.

Analysis and conclusion

The changes in fertility, mortality and migration trends that have shaped the ageing of the population over the last three decades have developed against a backdrop of huge technological, economic, and political change for the entire developed world, including all of the European nations. In parallel to these changes have been major social readjustments, including: the rising participation of women in the workforce and the wider use of part-time employment and job sharing; changing trends in partnership formation, such as delay and decline in marriage, and the rise in divorce, remarriage and cohabitation. Undoubtedly these changes have had, and will continue to have, profound effects on the demographic trends of fertility, mortality and migration which shape the population's age distribution.

While changes in society are difficult to predict, and their effects on demographic trends even more difficult to interpret, it is clear that to a greater or lesser extent the population of the UK will age, because a key component of population ageing is the age distribution of the population alive today. There will continue to be variation in ageing at country and subnational level within the UK as there is variation in the current age structure. In the south west and Wales there is a higher proportion of people of pensionable age, while in London the proportion is lower (these patterns are shown in more detail in Chapter 2).

While the example of the UK is valuable as a case study of a developed European (or European-type) country, it is by no means solely within Europe, North America and Australasia that major shifts in demographic structures have occurred in recent decades. Common to all nations experiencing such changes are the profound adjustments in prevailing social and economic values. The Japanese example illustrates how much and how fast Japanese age structure has changed as a result of declining fertility and rising life expectation. The Japanese example is one where immigration is closely controlled, but recent work demonstrates that migration is not the way to stop the population ageing, since migrants age too.[12]

While the 'greying' of population has major implications for health, pension and welfare planners everywhere, it is in nations that have experienced very speedy and relatively abrupt adjustments where the full impact of these changes will be

most keenly felt. Finally, it is worth saying that not all the consequences of ageing are ones that need to invoke concern. An ageing society has many positive aspects, as death is postponed and couples are able to spend more years together.

Notes and references

1. Smallwood S and Chamberlain J (2003) Replacement fertility, what has it been and what does it mean? *Population Trends* **119**, 16–27.

2. Tomassini C (2005) The demographic characteristics of the oldest old in the United Kingdom. *Population Trends* **120**, 15–22.

3. Hancock R, Stuchbury R and Tomassini C (2003) Changes in the distribution of marital age differences in England and Wales 1963 to 1998. *Population Trends* **114**, 19–25.

4. Ní Bhrolcháin M (2005) The age difference at marriage in England and Wales: a century of patterns and trends. *Population Trends* **120**, 7–14.

5. Office for National Statistics (2003) *Living in Britain: Results from the 2002 General Household Survey.* TSO: London.

6. Tomassini C *et al* (2004) Living arrangements among older people: an overview of trends in Europe and the USA. *Population Trends* **115**, 24–34.

7. Figures for 2050 are from the principal projection. Further information on UK population projections can be found at: www.gad.gov.uk.

8. Office for National Statistics (2005) Report: 2003-based marital status and cohabitation projections for England and Wales. *Population Trends* **121**.

9. Murphy M, Grundy E (2003) Mothers with living children and children with living mothers: the role of fertility and mortality in the period 1911–2050. *Population Trends* **112**, 36–44.

10. Population estimates for Japan are from the Japanese Statistics Bureau: www.stat.go.jp/english/data/jinsui/2.htm.

11. Kinsella K, Velkoff VA (2001) *An Aging World.* US Census Bureau, Series P95/01-1, US Government Printing Office: Washington DC.

12. Shaw C (2002) United Kingdom population trends in the 21st century. *Population Trends* **103**, 37–46.

Fertility and mortality

Jessica Chamberlain, Baljit Gill

Chapter 5

Introduction

The population of the UK has experienced natural growth for almost all of the last century, with births exceeding deaths. However, all UK countries are projected to experience natural decrease in the future. This chapter begins by describing natural change in the population and how births and deaths shape the population's structure. The numbers of births and deaths that take place are themselves influenced by the size and age distribution of the population.

The rest of the chapter examines trends in fertility and mortality in the UK. These trends are important in understanding and projecting the size and age structure of the population. They are also useful in their own right, as they can inform policy and planning needs.

Fertility refers to reproductive behaviour (the number of children born to women) rather than the actual ability to reproduce, which is called fecundity. This section explores changing age patterns of fertility for men and women, together with changes in family size and childlessness over different generations of women. It also looks at births in relation to mothers' country of birth and parents' marital status.

Mortality refers to the deaths occurring in a population. The chapter focuses on the decline in mortality during the 20th century in the UK and how this varied for different age groups, and by sex. It also compares the mortality experiences of different generations of men and women in terms of their survival rates and life expectancy.

Data used in this chapter are based largely on the registration of births and deaths, and are described in Box 1. Period and cohort analyses are used to illustrate different aspects of fertility and mortality trends. These show how fertility and mortality levels in the population have changed over time, and how the experiences of different generations, or cohorts, of people have differed from one another (see Box 2 for more information).

Box 1

Data sources

In England and Wales it has been compulsory to register a birth or death since 1837, in Scotland since 1855 and Northern Ireland since 1864. Because of this, there are high quality registration data available for births and deaths, giving good coverage of the UK. Over the years there have been changes to the information collected. For example, when the Population (Statistics) Act of 1938 came into force, mother's age began to be collected in England, Wales and Scotland, and later in Northern Ireland. During the 1960s and 1970s electronic data sets began to be kept. Analyses in this chapter have been carried out to different time periods and geographies, according to the availability of data.

Births and deaths statistics are based on registrations collected by the General Register Offices of the UK countries. The data are compiled by the General Register Office for Scotland (GROS), the Northern Ireland Statistics and Research Agency (NISRA) and, for England and Wales, the Office for National Statistics (ONS). Statistics for the UK in this chapter were produced by aggregating data from each of these sources. There are however differences in the way the data are collected or compiled by each agency. These are described in the appendix.

All data presented in this chapter are shown on a calendar-year basis. All fertility analyses are based on live births and exclude stillbirths and miscarriages. Mortality analyses are based on data for all causes of death combined.

Projected numbers of births and deaths are produced by the Government Actuary's Department (GAD) as part of the national population projections. The period for the 2004-based projections for the UK countries runs from 2005 to 2074. GAD also provided historical databases of mortality in England and Wales. These were used to calculate life expectancy and chances of survival.

Box 2

Period and cohort analyses

Period and cohort analyses are used in demography to gain insights into fertility and mortality trends and compensate for the limitations of each perspective. Both period and cohort effects on births and deaths influence the size and age structure of the population; it is important to understand trends from both perspectives.

Period analysis uses data from a specific time or period to provide a snapshot of trends and existing conditions. It has been used here to estimate levels of, and trends in, fertility and mortality at particular times in the UK population.

Because fertility and mortality can vary from year to year, period measures in isolation may not accurately represent what happens to people during the whole of their lifetime. Cohort analysis can be used to look at what happens to a generation (or cohort) of people over their lifetime. By relating events to a group of people born at a specified time (for example, all women born in 1920) it reflects the actual experience of a generation over a specific period of time.

Complete cohort data take a long time to collect and so lack the immediacy of period data. Full cohort data are available only at age 45 (considered to be the end of childbearing years) for fertility or when the entire cohort has died for mortality (now taken as age 110). Thus the trends shown using cohort analysis may not reflect the current experiences of the population. However, incomplete cohort data can be used to look at the experiences of current generations to date, for example by comparing the experiences of different cohorts when they were at a particular age.

Births, deaths and population change

Natural change

The difference between the numbers of births and deaths, natural change, is a key determinant of population size and growth. If there are more births than deaths a population will experience natural increase. Conversely, if more deaths occur than births, a population will experience natural decrease. Migration has replaced natural change as the largest element of population growth in the UK. Migration is covered further in Chapter 7, and this section focuses on natural change.

Over the last century there were more births than deaths in the UK as a whole every year, except in 1976. With the exception of that year natural change has always been positive. England,

Wales and Scotland each experienced some natural decrease in the population in the mid-1970s. There have been more deaths than births in Scotland in every year since 1995. Similarly there has been natural decline in Wales since 1997, although there were more births than deaths in 2004. In contrast, Northern Ireland did not experience natural decrease at any point during the 20th century.

The annual number of births in UK countries fluctuated significantly over the last century, while there was much less variation in the number of deaths (Figure 5.1). There were three main peaks in births or 'baby booms': one after each of the two World Wars and another, more sustained boom throughout the 1960s. The large generations born during the 1960s' baby boom produced an 'echo' of the original boom in the 1980s when they reached their peak childbearing years. This echo was small in Scotland, where fertility levels in the 1980s were lower than in the rest of the UK.

The number of deaths each year in the UK remained fairly constant during the 20th century. This is due firstly to the large increase in the size of the UK population over this period, and secondly to the decline in mortality and its increasing concentration at older ages. These two factors have resulted in the number of deaths remaining stable.

All UK countries have been projected to experience a natural decrease in their future populations (Figure 5.2). 2004-based projections suggest that the natural decrease already taking place in Scotland is likely to continue until the end of the projection period (2074). The current small natural decrease in Wales is likely to end at around 2007 but resume at around 2022. England and Northern Ireland are both projected to experience natural decrease, from around 2039 and 2034 respectively.

In the UK, the numbers of births and deaths are projected from the existing population size and age structure, and from assumptions made about fertility and mortality trends. The assumptions are based on existing trends, knowledge of determinants of fertility and mortality, and judgements about possible future trends. The 2004-based projections assume that average completed family size will level off for cohorts (generations) born at the start of the 1990s, at 1.75 children per woman in both England and Wales, 1.80 in Northern Ireland and 1.60 in Scotland. According to the mortality assumptions, there will be generally higher rates of improvement in life expectancy for all ages in the early years of the projection, tailing to a constant rate after 2029.[1]

Figure **5.1**

Births, deaths and natural change: UK countries, 1901 to 2004

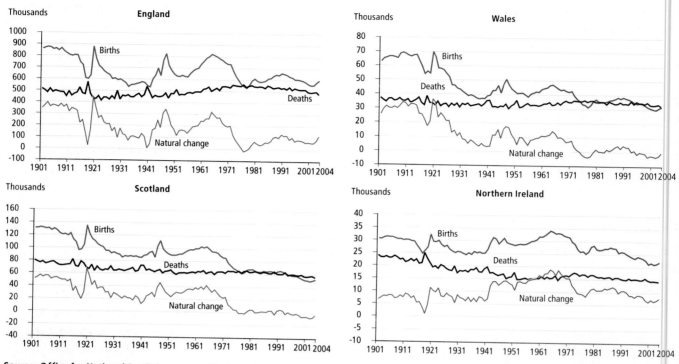

Source: Office for National Statistics; General Register Office for Scotland; Northern Ireland Statistics and Research Agency

Figure **5.2**

Projected births, deaths and natural change: UK countries, 2005 to 2043[1]

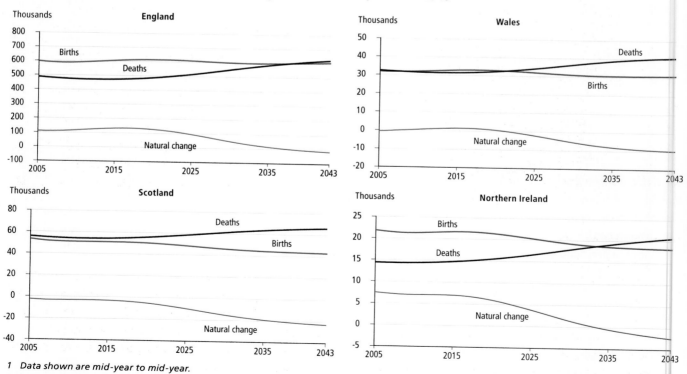

1 Data shown are mid-year to mid-year.

Source: United Kingdom 2004 – based national population projections – Government Actuary's Department

The changing population structure

Births, deaths and migration each shape the age structure of a population. The key determinant of the existing population's age distribution is the annual number of births over the last 90 years (Figure 5.3). The correlation between births and the age structure of the population is strong up to around age 70. From this age onwards deaths have an increasing effect on the age structure and the close relationship is lost. This happens because members of a birth cohort do not all die at the same age. Their deaths are spread out, mainly over older ages. For example, in 2004 there were 58,600 men aged 85 alive in England and Wales, but these men were just a small part of the 1919 birth cohort of 356,200 male births.

Figure **5.3**

Births 1915 to 2004 and 2004 population by age and sex

England and Wales

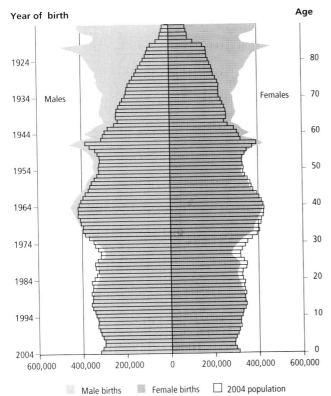

Source: Office for National Statistics

The age structure of a population also affects the numbers of births and deaths that occur. For example, in an ageing population the number of deaths may increase in spite of falling mortality rates. This is because there are growing numbers of older people and they are the age group with the highest risk of dying. A population with high numbers of women aged 15 to 44 would be expected to have more live births than one of the same size but with fewer women in this

age group, even if the women of childbearing age in the two populations had the same fertility rates.

The future growth of the population will be influenced by its present age distribution. This effect is known as population momentum.[2] There are projected to be more births than deaths at the start of the projection period (2005) in England and Northern Ireland, even though fertility rates are projected to remain below the level required to replace the population (Box 3). High fertility in the past means that current cohorts of women are sufficiently large that the births they have exceed the number of deaths, even though fertility rates are below replacement level. But, as the population ages, the large cohorts of men and women at older ages will slow this effect and eventually stop it.

Box 3

Replacement fertility

Replacement fertility is the level of fertility required to ensure a population continues to replace itself in size. To replace themselves women, on average, need to have one female child who survives long enough for a female grandchild to be born, and so on for succeeding generations.[3] An average of two children will 'replace' all mothers and fathers, but only if the same number of boys as girls are born and all female children survive to the end of their reproductive age. However, because of mortality and the fact that in most populations around 105 boys are born for every 100 girls, fertility needs to be a little higher than a rate of 2.0 children per woman to achieve replacement.

In the UK, as in all developed countries, a fertility rate of 2.1 is usually taken as roughly approximate to the level of replacement fertility, although the precise level will vary between countries. It is important to remember that the level of 2.1 children is an average across all women. To ensure replacement fertility, a substantial proportion of women must have three or more children in order to compensate for those who remain childless or have only one child.[4]

Fertility

This section examines trends in fertility and how it varies, for example, between the UK countries, and in relation to the ages of mothers and fathers. It also looks at changes in family size and levels of childlessness over generations. It describes differences in fertility trends according to the mothers' country of birth, and investigates whether there are fertility patterns associated with the act of migration itself. Finally, it looks at births with regard to the marital or cohabitation status of parents.

Trends in fertility

The total fertility rate (TFR) is the average number of children a group of women would have if they experienced the age-specific fertility rates of a particular year throughout their childbearing life (Box 4). It is the most commonly used period measure of fertility as it gives a single rate of fertility for a population for a specific period, usually a year. (See Box 2 for more information on period and cohort analyses.) The TFR is an age-standardised measure. It allows fertility trends to be separated out from the effects of changes in the population's age structure over time. It also allows fertility patterns to be compared across population subgroups with different age distributions.

Box 4

Glossary of fertility terms

Age-specific fertility rate (ASFR) – the number of births in a year to women aged x, per thousand women aged x in the mid-year population.

$$\text{Age-specific fertility rate} = \frac{\text{Births to women aged } x}{\text{Mid-year population of women aged } x} \times 1,000$$

Childbearing years – defined as being ages 15 to 44.

Completed family size (CFS) – the average number of live births a woman (in a cohort) has had by the end of her childbearing years. Completed family size can be calculated for all women or only for those who have had children.

Total fertility rate (TFR) – the average number of children a woman would have if she experienced the age-specific fertility rates for a particular year throughout her childbearing life. For example, a TFR of 1.78 in 2004 means that, on average, a woman would have 1.78 children during her lifetime based solely on 2004's age-specific fertility rates. It is calculated as the sum of the age-specific fertility rates in one year.

Since 1938 (when official data were first available) the TFR in England and Wales has varied considerably. There was a short baby boom after the Second World War, which was followed by a period of lower fertility in the 1950s (Figure 5.4). A more sustained baby boom occurred during the 1960s and resulted in the TFR reaching its peak of 2.93 children per woman in 1964. The late 1960s and 1970s saw a rapid decline in fertility.

Figure **5.4**

Total fertility rate, 1938 to 2004

England and Wales

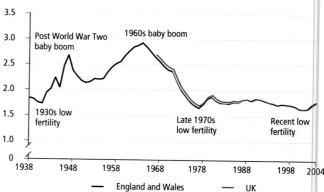

Children per women

Source: Office for National Statistics, General Register Office for Scotland, Northern Ireland Statistics and Research Agency

In 1973 the TFR fell below the level needed to replace the population (2.1 children per woman).[5] It continued to decrease until 1977, when it fell to 1.66. There was a slight recovery from this trough, but fertility remained at low levels throughout the 1980s and 1990s. It fell to its lowest point in 2001, reaching a TFR of 1.63 children per woman.

Since 2001 there has been a rise in fertility each year, and in 2004 the TFR was 1.78 children per woman. It is too early to predict whether this represents the start of a sustained rise in fertility. The previous short upturn in fertility, after the 1977 trough, was followed by two decades of gradual decline.

Fertility trends in the UK countries

Fertility has been below the level required to replace the population since 1973 in England and since 1974 in Wales and Scotland (Figure 5.5). Northern Ireland has had a higher TFR than the other UK countries for at least 30 years. In 1967 the TFR in Northern Ireland was 3.28 children per woman compared with 2.69 for the UK as a whole. However, since the late 1980s this difference has substantially declined. In 1993 the Northern Ireland TFR also fell to below replacement level and, by 2004, it had declined to 1.87 children per woman, compared with 1.77 children for the UK.

The longest time series available for fertility rates is for England and Wales. Figure 5.4 demonstrates that this is likely to be a good indicator of trends for the UK as a whole, even though the constituent countries have had their own distinct trends over time. This is because England and Wales make up a large proportion of the UK population. In 2004 approximately 85 per cent of births in the UK were in England, 7.5 per cent in Scotland, 4.5 per cent in Wales and 3.1 per cent in Northern Ireland.

Figure **5.5**

Total fertility rate: by UK country 1967 to 2004

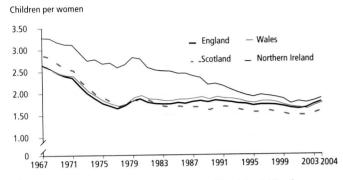

Children per women

Source: Office for National Statistics, General Register Office for Scotland, Northern Ireland Statistics and Research Agency

Factors associated with low fertility

TFRs have declined and, at the start of the 21st century, were at low levels across nearly all countries in the developed world (see Chapter 10 for fertility in the countries of the European Union). For almost all the previous 25 years, TFRs in most western European countries have been stable at low levels (below replacement level).

There is plentiful academic debate about the reasons for these low TFRs. Many factors affect childbearing behaviour, and hence fertility levels. These include increased education and economic independence among females. High and rising aspirations have created a need for a second income and also encouraged women's participation in the labour force. This has led to both sexes investing more in their careers. There have been important changes in society's attitudes and people are increasingly less constrained by social norms. There has been a rise in the importance attached to the individual and freedom of choice, and a greater emphasis is placed on quality of life and leisure. People have also retreated from permanent commitments and are more cautious about investing their identity in family because of the increased probability of separation and divorce.[6]

There will also be country-specific factors that impact on fertility levels, including the cost and availability of housing, and flexibility of the labour market.[6] The effect of all of these factors is difficult to quantify, and there is no agreement on which of them are more important in determining fertility trends.[7] Their impact will vary between countries and between different groups within countries, and will also change over time.

There have been two notable changes in childbearing in the UK associated with such factors. Firstly, there has been a reduction in the size of family that women desire or intend to have. In

England and Wales, women's childbearing intentions are slightly lower now than in the previous 20 years, with a greater proportion of women in 2000–01 intending to have a smaller family or to remain childless than in 1979–81.[8] This is associated with changing attitudes to ideal family sizes[9] and greater acceptability of voluntary childlessness. Secondly, women are postponing childbearing to later ages. Age of marriage and age of cohabitation leading to marriage have increased and, since the majority of childbearing takes place in a married or cohabiting environment, delayed entry into this will delay childbearing.[10] Higher levels of education are also associated with a later average age of entry into motherhood.[11] These changes in family size, childlessness and the age at which women become mothers are discussed further in the next two parts of this chapter.

Age patterns of fertility

Women in the UK are increasingly bearing their children at older ages. Since records began in 1938 women in their 20s in England and Wales have generally had the highest fertility rates (Figure 5.6). But, since the start of the 1980s, the fertility of women in their 20s has fallen, while that of women in their 30s has risen. In 1992 the fertility of women in their early 30s overtook that of women in their early 20s. In 2004, for the first time, women in their early 30s had the highest fertility rate of all age groups, with marginally higher fertility than 25 to 29 year olds.

Fertility among women in their 40s has increased since the early 1980s but has remained below 21 births per 1,000 women since 1938. The current trend for women to delay the start of childbearing has contributed to this rise. In 2004 there were 10.4 births per 1,000 women aged 40 to 44. The fertility rate among women in their 40s peaked in the mid-1940s at around 20 births per 1,000 women. These women had larger families than later generations and their childbearing was spread over more years. Three-quarters of their births were to women who already had at least two children. In 2004 just over half of births to women in their 40s were first or second children.

The fertility rate of the 15 to 19-year-old group increased between 1938 and 2004, from 14.7 to 26.9 births per 1,000 women. It peaked in 1971, at 50.6 births per 1,000 women.

From 2002 onwards fertility rates have increased for women in all age groups, except those under 20. It is too early to say whether this is the start of a new trend. The rise in fertility among women in their 20s is a reversal of a long-term decline, but the reasons behind this change are not yet understood.

Figure **5.6**

Age-specific fertility rates: females, 1938 to 2004

England and Wales

Births per 1,000 women

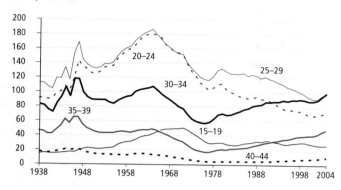

Age-specific fertility rates: males, 1964 to 2004

England and Wales

Births per 1,000 men

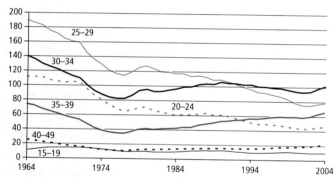

Age of fathers for sole-registered births were estimated - see appendix for more details.

Source: Office for National Statistics

Men, like women, are having children later. As for women, the fertility rates of men in their 20s has declined from the 1980s onwards, and those of men in their 30s has generally increased (Figure 5.6). In 2004 the highest fertility rate for men was for those aged 30 to 34 (at 101.9 children per 1,000 men).

The age distribution of fertility for men leans more towards older age groups compared with that of women. In 2004, 61 per cent of the male TFR could be attributed to men aged 30 and over fathering children. The comparable figure for women was 44 per cent (Figure 5.7). In particular, the fertility of men aged 40 and over contributed 12 per cent of the TFR compared with only 3 per cent for women. The fertility rate of 15 to 19-year-old men has always been lower than for women of the same age and has remained below 15 children per 1,000 men, except in 1971 (Figure 5.6).

Figure **5.7**

Percentage contribution to total fertility rate by age group, 2004

England and Wales

Percentage

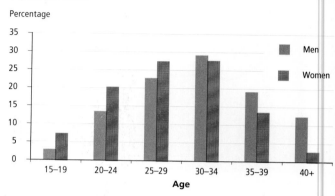

Source: Office for National Statistics

Because women are having their children at older ages, over the last 30 years there has been a steady increase in their average (age-standardised mean) age at childbirth (Figure 5.8). The average age declined throughout the second half of the 1960s and early 1970s, reflecting the early childbearing that contributed to the 1960s' baby boom, and reached a low in 1974 of 26.4 years. Subsequently, every year there was an increase in women's mean age at childbirth, and in 2004 it reached 28.9 years.

Men have followed the same trend for mean age at childbearing as women over the last 40 years, but their mean age at childbirth has always been around three years higher. This reflects the fact that the majority of births occur to married or cohabiting couples. Within marriage, the man is, on average, two years older than the woman, and cohabiting partners typically have a greater age difference than marital partners.[12]

Figure **5.8**

Standardised mean age at birth: by sex, 1964 to 2004

England and Wales

Age (years)

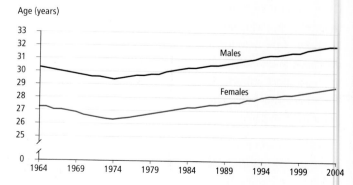

Source: Office for National Statistics

The average age at which women *commence* childbearing has also increased. From the 1946 cohort onwards, each successive generation of women postponed the start of their childbearing to older ages (Figure 5.9). The age-standardised mean age at first birth was 25.6 years for women born in 1920, the first cohort for which data are available, and fell for subsequent cohorts, reaching a low of 23.8 years for women born in the years 1941 to 1943. Women born in the first half of the 1940s would have started childbearing during the 1960s' baby boom. Thus the boom, in part, resulted from women starting childbearing earlier than previous cohorts. The mean age at first birth for the cohort who have most recently completed childbearing (those born in 1959) was 25.7 years, a return to the level of the 1920 cohort.

Figure 5.9

Standardised mean age of mother at first birth, 1920 to 1959 cohorts

England and Wales

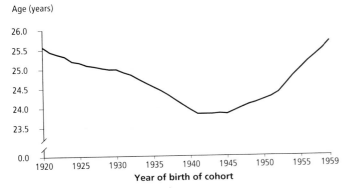

Source: Office for National Statistics

Changes in family size and childlessness

Completed family size (CFS) is the average number of children born to a woman by the end of her childbearing years, and is a cohort measure of fertility. The average CFS in the UK declined from 2.45 children for women born in 1935 to 1.99 children for those born in 1959, the cohort to have most recently reached the end of their childbearing years. (See Box 5 for more information on CFS and how it compares to the TFR.)

In Northern Ireland the decline in CFS started later than in the other UK countries, occurring from the 1947-born generation onwards (Figure 5.10). Cohorts in Northern Ireland have also had larger families on average than women in other UK countries. In contrast, there has been little difference in CFS between England, Wales, and Scotland from the 1935-born generation to the most recent generation to complete childbearing.

The CFS of women who have most recently completed childbearing was below replacement level in the UK as a whole

Box 5

Completed family size and total fertility rate

Completed family size (CFS) is the average number of children born to a woman by the end of her childbearing years. The total fertility rate (TFR) is sometimes mistakenly used as a measure of family size. However, changes in the timing of childbearing between generations can distort the TFR. It will then not reflect the average number of children a cohort of women will have had by the end of childbearing (family size).

Currently, the TFR is likely to underestimate the average family size because women are delaying childbearing. It can also overestimate the average family size if women have children earlier in their childbearing years compared with previous generations, as happened during the 1960s' baby boom. However, the TFR is not actually intended to reflect completed family size but the current intensity of childbearing and the rate at which the population is replacing itself.

The disadvantage of CFS is that it may not reflect the family size of women still in their childbearing years because it is based on women who have completed childbearing. Therefore CFS does not provide a timely measure of family size.

Figure 5.10

Completed family size: by UK country 1935 to 1959 cohorts

UK countries

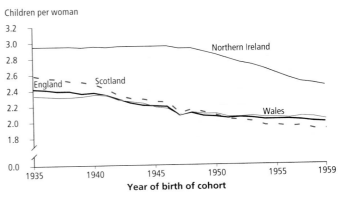

Source: Office for National Statistics

and in every constituent country, except Northern Ireland. Replacement level is the level of fertility required to replace the population. It is approximately equal to a CFS of 2.1 children per woman. Below-replacement fertility leads to population ageing and, in the absence of net in-migration, eventually to a decrease in population size.[5] (Replacement fertility is explained in Box 3.)

This measure of family size includes women who remained childless but it is also useful to assess family size for only those women who have had a child. Completed family size for women who have had children has remained stable for women born since the Second World War, at around 2.4 children per woman, it having declined from 2.70 for those born in 1930 (Table 5.11). Thus the common perception of an average family size of 2.4 children is true for women born from 1945 onwards who have had children.

Table 5.11

Completed family size: 1920 to 1959, selected cohorts

England and Wales

Year of birth	Completed family size of all women	Completed family size of women who had children
1920	2.00	2.53
1925	2.12	2.55
1930	2.35	2.70
1935	2.42	2.73
1940	2.36	2.66
1945	2.19	2.42
1950	2.07	2.39
1955	2.02	2.39
1959	1.98	2.42

Source: Office for National Statistics

The increase in the number of childless women is a notable recent trend in fertility. The proportion who were childless at the end of their childbearing years has increased from one in ten for women in England and Wales born in the 1940s to almost one in five for those born in 1959 (Table 5.12). This is the same level as for the 1920s-born cohort. The decline in the size of the families of women born from the mid-1930s onwards began because women were having fewer children, but has continued because the proportion of women remaining childless has increased.

Women born between 1930 and the early 1940s were less likely than those in previous and later cohorts to have remained childless, and more likely to have had larger families of four or more children. This is part of a set of childbearing behaviours shown by these cohorts. For example, they started childbearing at younger ages compared with previous cohorts. They were the cohorts that produced the 1960s' baby boom.

Data from the General Household Survey show that the proportion of women in their 20s intending to have fewer than two children increased slightly between 1978 to 1981 and the period 1998 to 2001. The result of this was a slight reduction in

Table 5.12

Distribution of women by number of children born, 1920 to 1959, selected cohorts

England and Wales   Percentages

Year of birth	Number of children				
	0	1	2	3	4 or more
1920	21	21	27	16	15
1925	17	22	28	17	16
1930	13	18	30	19	20
1935	12	15	32	21	20
1940	11	13	36	22	18
1945	9	14	43	21	12
1950	14	13	44	20	11
1955	15	13	41	20	10
1959	18	13	38	20	11

Source: Office for National Statistics

intended average family size.[8] Women are also delaying starting their childbearing to later ages. This can affect their ability to achieve their desired family size and may result in further declines in the average size of families.

Because delayed entry into motherhood is associated with a lower likelihood of going on to have another child, women who postpone childbearing may not be able to achieve the family size they intend. Other women may end up 'involuntarily' childless because their fecundity has declined before they can start a family. Analysis of British Household Panel Study data found that among childless women in their 30s who intended to start a family, only around a half had managed to do so in the subsequent six years.[13]

Fertility and country of birth

Recently the percentage of births to women born outside the UK has increased. In the 1980s and 1990s, around 12 to 13 per cent of births in England and Wales were to mothers born outside the UK. From 1998 onwards this percentage rose, and in 2004 almost 20 per cent of births were to non-UK born mothers.

This increase is likely to be due to changes in both population structure and fertility levels. The number of women living in England and Wales who were born outside the UK has grown, and this has largely been among women of childbearing age. In addition, these women have higher fertility than UK-born women and, as found among migrants in other countries, their fertility may be particularly high in the years immediately after arrival.

Since 1994 there has been net migration into the UK. Although some migrants stay for a few years only,[14] others come with their families, or form families after arrival, and settle. The proportion of women of childbearing age living in England and Wales who were born outside the UK rose from 6.9 per cent in 1971 to 11.5 per cent in 2001.

Women who are resident in England and Wales but were born outside the UK have higher average fertility than UK-born women (Table 5.13). The TFR for non-UK born women was 2.2 children per woman in 2001 compared with 1.6 for UK-born women. Women born outside the UK are a heterogeneous group and their fertility will vary over a range, with some groups having fertility above and some below their combined TFR. In 2001, women born in Pakistan had the highest TFR (4.7), followed by women born in Bangladesh (3.9).

Migrant women tend to commence childbearing at an earlier age than UK-born mothers.[15] They can also have a distinctive pattern of fertility, which can lead to their fertility being overestimated. Studies in several countries indicate that

Table **5.13**

Total fertility rate: by country of birth of mother, 1991 and 2001

England and Wales

Country of birth of mother	1991	2001
Total	1.8	1.6
United Kingdom[1]	1.8	1.6
Total Outside UK	2.3	2.2
including:		
New Commonwealth	2.8	2.8
India	2.5	2.3
Pakistan	4.8	4.7
Bangladesh	5.3	3.9
East Africa	1.9	1.6
Rest of Africa[2]	2.7	2.0
Rest of New Commonwealth[3]	1.9	2.2
Rest of the World	1.9	1.8

1 *Including Isle of Man and Channel Islands.*
2 *Includes countries listed under Southern Africa and Rest of Africa in Table A of Birth Statistics, series FM1 No. 32.*
3 *Includes countries listed under Far East, Mediterranean, Caribbean and Rest of New Commonwealth in Table A of Birth Statistics, series FM1 No. 32.*

Source: Office for National Statistics, FM1 Table 9.5

migrants often have lower fertility before they migrate than the women in their destination country. After migration, they often show a steep rise and peak in their fertility, followed by a decline. Their fertility may later become similar to that of native-born women.[16, 17, 18] This pattern may indicate a disruption effect whereby migrants compensate for births, and possibly the formation of partnerships, they postponed due to migration. It may also reflect a lower likelihood of women with already established or larger families to migrate compared with those with fewer or no children. Younger childbearing and the timing of births in relation to migration, combined with changes to immigration levels, can exaggerate the differences in TFRs between UK-born women and those from other countries.

Therefore the difference in family size at the end of childbearing for UK-born and non-UK born women may not be as large as indicated by period measures such as TFR. However, a French study found that, even after adjusting for the migrant fertility pattern described above, women born outside France still had a higher TFR than French-born women.[16] This suggests that there may be some residual difference between the fertility of UK-born and non-UK born women that cannot be explained by the timing of births around migration.

As well as differences in fertility between UK-born and non-UK born women, there are likely to be variations in TFR between ethnic groups. However, investigations are limited to analyses by parents' country of birth because ethnicity is not collected at registration. Further information on ethnicity and country birth in fertility analysis is available in the appendix.

Childbearing and marital status

In 2004 the majority (58 per cent) of all births in the UK took place inside marriage, 35 per cent were registered outside marriage by both parents and 7 per cent were registered outside marriage by the mother alone.

The proportion of births taking place outside marriage in England and Wales was relatively low, at between 4 and 7 per cent until the 1960s (Figure 5.14). This is with the exception of a spike around the Second World War. From the 1960s onwards the proportion of births taking place outside marriage has risen and there have been rapid increases from the late 1970s. This has been due to shifting social norms, including the greater acceptability of cohabitation, for both men and women, and having children outside marriage. Even though most births still take place within marriage, childbearing has continued to become less strongly associated with marriage over the last three decades.

Figure **5.14**

Births occurring outside marriage: 1845 to 2004

England and Wales

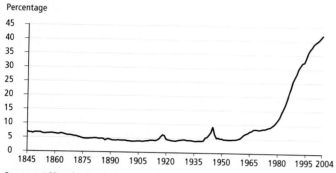

Source: Office for National Statistics

In 2004 Wales had the highest proportion (51 per cent) of births outside marriage, having seen a steep rise throughout the 1980s (Figure 5.15). In 2004, 47 and 42 per cent of births in Scotland and England respectively happened outside marriage. The difference between Scotland and England largely reflects the steeper increase in the percentage of births outside marriage in Scotland since 1994. Northern Ireland has had the lowest proportion of births outside marriage of the four UK countries throughout the last three decades (35 per cent in 2004).

Most of the rise in births outside marriage has been due to births to cohabiting couples rather than lone mothers. Over three-quarters (76 per cent) of births outside marriage that were jointly registered in the UK in 2004 were to parents living at the same address. This is taken as a proxy indicator of cohabitation because neither cohabitation nor lone parenthood are recorded in the birth registration process. Births to lone

Figure **5.15**

Births occurring outside marriage: 1974 to 2004

UK countries

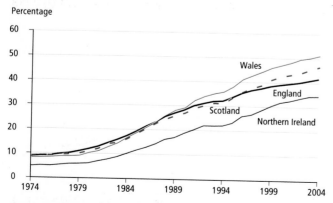

Source: Office for National Statistics

mothers may be registered solely by the mother but they may also be registered by both parents. Sole-registered and jointly registered births where the parents are living at separate addresses are taken as an indicator of lone parenthood at birth.

As discussed, the age at which people marry or start a cohabitation that leads to marriage has risen. In 1966 the average (mean) age at which women in England and Wales first married was 22.5 years. In 2003 it had risen to 28.9 years. This shift to later ages at marriage has implications for the age at which women begin to form families and the size of family they are able to achieve.

Mortality

This section examines the fall in mortality that occurred over the 20th century and how it varied between the UK countries and different age groups. It also looks at how differences between male and female mortality rates have changed over time, and compares the survival rates and life expectancy of different generations. The analysis is based on mortality from all causes. There is a more detailed analysis, showing the different causes of death, in *Focus on Health*.[19]

Because the age distribution of a population affects its overall mortality, age-specific and age-standardised mortality rates are used here (Box 6). This allows comparisons of mortality over time and between countries without the results being affected by the populations' differing age structures.

Changes in mortality rates over time

Mortality has been declining in the UK since the 18th century but the greatest decline occurred in the 20th century, especially for infants.[20] Mortality rates fell for all age groups during the 20th century. This means that people alive at the start of the 21st century are much more likely to survive to older ages than those alive around the turn of the previous century.

In the first half of the 20th century, the fall in mortality occurred predominantly among babies and children. In the second half, mortality also fell for adults, with deaths occurring at increasingly later ages for successive generations.

This fall in mortality is associated with the decline of infectious diseases, such as tuberculosis, as the leading causes of death and reflects improvements in both medicine and living conditions. Prior to this the main reasons for declining mortality were improved living conditions, including advances in nutrition, sanitation, housing and working conditions.[21]

There were notable annual fluctuations in the decline in mortality during the 20th century in England and Wales, but these have been diminishing since the 1950s (Figure 5.16). The

Box 6

Glossary of mortality terms

Age-specific mortality rate – the number of deaths in a year of males or females aged x, per thousand males or females aged x in the mid-year population. It is calculated as:

$$\text{Age-specific mortality rate} = \frac{\text{deaths in age/sex group}}{\text{mid-year population of age/sex group}} \times 100,000$$

Age-standardised mortality rate – the expected mortality rate when the observed age-specific mortality rates are applied to a given standard population.

A comparison of crude mortality rates may present a misleading picture when comparing populations because of differences in their respective sex and age structures. Age-standardised rates make allowances for differences in the age structure of a population over time and between sexes. The age-standardised mortality rate is the number of deaths (per 100,000 people) that would have occurred if the observed age-specific mortality rates had applied in a given standard population.

In this chapter the European Standard Population was used for standardisation. This is a hypothetical population standard, which is the same for both males and females, allowing standardised rates to be compared for each sex and between sexes.

Infant mortality rate – the number of deaths of infants aged between 0 and 1 in a year per 1,000 live-births in the same year. It is calculated as:

$$\text{Infant mortality rate} = \frac{\text{deaths of infants aged under 1}}{\text{number of live-births}} \times 1,000$$

Life expectancy – the average number of additional years a person would live under a given set of mortality conditions. This can be calculated on a period or cohort basis (see Box 7).

peak in mortality in 1918, which interrupted the general declining trend, was due to an influenza outbreak that occurred after the end of the First World War.

There were spikes in the mortality rate around the time of both World Wars, but these must be interpreted with caution. Deaths in the armed forces occurring in England and Wales were included in the figures for the years of the First World War but not the Second. And the deaths in the armed forces that happened overseas were not included in the figures for

Figure **5.16**

Age-standardised annual mortality rate: by sex, 1901 to 2003

England and Wales

Age-standardised rate per 100,000

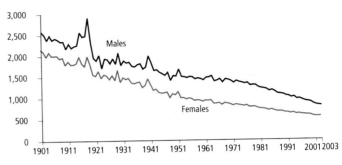

Source: Office for National Statistics

either war.[20] Therefore wartime rates refer, on the whole, to the civilian population. The spikes partly reflect that the population was depleted of healthy individuals.[22]

Over the last 30 years mortality has declined for all UK countries but there have been differences between them. Since 1981 the highest mortality rate has been in Scotland (Figure 5.17). In the 1970s, Northern Ireland had a similar level of mortality to Scotland. But mortality in Northern Ireland declined more steeply than in Scotland during the early 1980s. In 2003 Northern Ireland's age-standardised mortality rate was similar to that of England and Wales.

One factor that has been linked to Scotland's poor mortality status is deprivation.[23] However, deprivation explains less of the gap in mortality between Scotland and England and Wales now than it did in the early 1980s. The excess of deaths in Scotland that is not accounted for by deprivation has been referred to as the 'Scottish effect'.[23]

Figure **5.17**

Age-standardised annual mortality rate, 1974 to 2003

UK countries

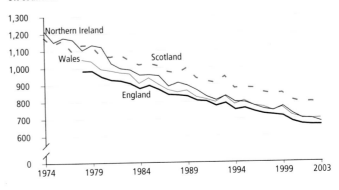

Source: Office for National Statistics

Age patterns of mortality

The overall decline in mortality during the 20th century in England and Wales (Figure 5.16) was accompanied by large changes in the age distribution of deaths. The decline in infectious diseases meant that mortality at young ages decreased hugely and became increasingly concentrated at older ages. This was associated with a rise of chronic diseases (for example, coronary heart disease) as the main cause of death. These diseases take a lifetime of exposure to different risk factors to manifest themselves so mainly occur at older ages.

Whatever the prevailing mortality rate, the first year of life is one of high risks. This is particularly true at the time of birth and immediately following it. Infants aged less than a year old have a higher risk of dying than other children. Therefore, infant mortality is often examined separately from overall and child mortality.

The infant mortality rate (IMR, see Box 6) has declined dramatically over the course of the last century in England and Wales (Figure 5.18). The decline began abruptly around the early 1900s, with rates having been stable before this.[20] In 1901 the IMR for boys was 165.6 infant deaths per 1,000 live births. By 1950 the male IMR had declined to 33.6 deaths per 1,000 live births. In 2003 it was 5.7 deaths per 1,000 live births. The female IMR has followed the same trend, but has always been slightly lower. As the IMR has declined, the difference between male and female infant mortality rates have narrowed.

The peaks in infant mortality in the early part of the 20th century coincided with hot summers when diarrhoeal disease played a part in many deaths.[20] There was a period of accelerated decline in IMR immediately after the Second World War. This could have been due to the national food policy, which concentrated on the health of expectant mothers, infants

and children.[20] It may also have been associated with the use of antibiotics or other improvements in social conditions.[22] Since the 1970s, there have been further marked improvements.

The reduction in the infant mortality rate has been a major factor in the overall increase in life expectancy of the last century. The rate gives an indication of child-rearing behaviour, sanitation, health and communities at risk, as well as overall levels of social and economic development.[24] As such, it is often used as a measure of the level of 'development' of a country. Chapter 10 discusses infant mortality rates and life expectancy in the countries of the European Union.

Mortality has fallen in both sexes and across all age groups over the 20th century. In particular, there was a large and steady decrease in the 1 to 14-year-old mortality rate (Figure 5.19). The age-standardised rate for this age group declined from 883 deaths per 100,000 males in 1901 to 16 deaths per 100,000 in 2003. Over the same period, the age-standardised rate for females declined from 863 deaths per 100,000 females to 15 deaths per 100,000.

Figure **5.19**

Age-standardised age-specific mortality rates: by sex and age group, 1901 to 2003

England and Wales

Age standardised rate per 100,000 (log scales)

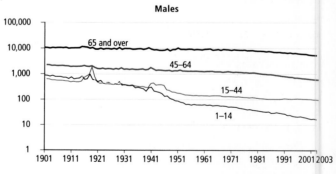

England and Wales

Age standardised rate per 100,000 (log scales)

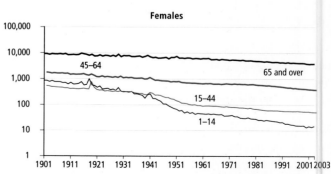

The age-specific mortality rates have been presented on a log scale because the data cover a large range of values and the log scale reduces this to a more manageable range.

Source: Office for National Statistics

Figure **5.18**

Infant mortality rate: by sex, 1901 to 2003

England and Wales

Deaths of under ones, per 1,000 live births

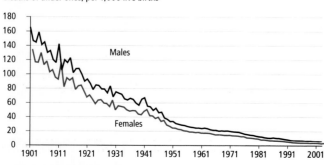

Source: Office for National Statistics

The mortality rate for 15 to 44-year-olds was similar to the mortality rate for children in 1901 and, until the 1940s, both were declining at a similar rate. The decrease in 15 to 44-year-old mortality slowed during the 1940s, compared with child mortality and, over the last 20 years, has levelled off. In 2003 the mortality rate for 15 to 44-year-olds was 103 deaths per 100,000 for males and 55 deaths per 100,000 for females.

Falls in the mortality of adults aged 45 to 64 happened throughout the 20th century for women, but began only in the second half of the century for men. The decline in the mortality rates of men and women aged 65 and over followed the same pattern.

Since the early 1970s, the mortality rate at very old ages (aged 85 and over) has also been declining, for both men and women. Between 1970 and 2003 it fell from 25,110 deaths per 100,000 to 19,042 for men and from 20,038 deaths per 100,000 to 16,576 for women. However, because mortality rates at younger ages have declined to low levels, deaths have become more concentrated at very old ages. Consequently, the contribution of deaths at very old ages to the overall mortality rate has increased. Between 1983 and 2003 deaths at age 85 and over increased from 19 to 24 per cent of all deaths for males and from 24 to 30 per cent for females. (Because death counts have been standardised, these findings reflect changes in mortality at older ages, excluding the effects of the ageing of the population).

Sex differences in mortality

Females had a lower overall mortality rate than males throughout the 20th century (Figure 5.16). The sex differential started widening after the Second World War but narrowed from the mid-1970s onwards. This may be due to changes in smoking trends among men and women. Smoking influenced many of the major causes of death in the UK after the Second World War, for example, heart disease, lung cancer and respiratory diseases.[20] Since 1900 a larger proportion of men than women have smoked cigarettes, which has elevated men's risk of death and contributed to the sex differential in mortality.[26] Women, however, increased their cigarette smoking after the Second World War, which may account for the decreased sex differential from the mid-1970s onwards.

Smoking patterns do not account for the whole gender gap, since non-smoking males still have lower life expectancies than non-smoking females.[26] Other lifestyle differences between men and women, such as alcohol consumption and dietary patterns,[27] are also likely to contribute to the sex differential. Biological differences, for example the role of sex hormones in the risk of heart disease and degenerative diseases, may also play a part.[27, 28, 29]

The difference between male and female mortality rates is explored further in Figure 5.20, which looks at the sex ratio of mortality rates for different age groups. For example, a ratio of 1.5 indicates that male mortality rates are 1.5 times, or 50 per cent higher than, female rates.

Females had lower mortality than males in every age group throughout the 20th century, with the exception of 1 to 14-year-olds in 1918. The sex ratio for the mortality rate of infants has stayed around the same over the last century but, for those aged 1 to 14, it has increased since 1901. For both age groups, the fluctuation in the sex ratio increased over the 20th century as the number of deaths in each group fell to low levels.

After the Second World War, the sex difference in mortality of 15 to 44-year-olds increased. In 2003 male mortality was 1.9 times, or 90 per cent higher than, female mortality for this age group. Some of this is due to differences in male and female mortality resulting from accidents.[27] The decline in maternal mortality (deaths of mothers up to a year after childbirth) since the mid-1930s onwards in England and Wales might also have played a role in widening the sex gap at reproductive ages.[27] However, the level of mortality among 15 to 44-year-olds is low and so the sex difference does not represent a large number of excess male deaths over female deaths.

Figure **5.20**

Sex ratio of mortality rates by age groups, 1901 to 2003

England and Wales

Ratio of male to female death rates

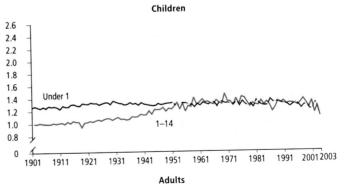

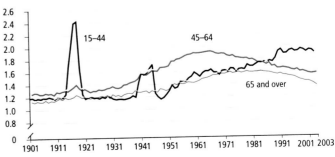

Source: Office for National Statistics

The sex difference for the 45 to 64-year-old group rose between the early 1930s and mid-1960s, before falling. This is likely to be due to the effect of the changes in smoking trends on different cohorts of men and women. The ratio of mortality rates for men and women aged 65 and over followed a similar pattern of an increase followed by fall, in part due to the same cohort effect.

Cohort survival

Changes in mortality rates throughout the 20th century have meant that people's chances of survival to any age have improved. This also means that their life expectancy has increased. The analysis of survival and life expectancy here has been done on a cohort basis, that is, for different generations of men and women. The calculations were based on mortality data up to age 110. Thus for the cohorts born from 1893 onwards, the data include an increasing element of projection for survival beyond their current ages.

Changes in survival between different ages have led to the changes in the age distribution of mortality described in the previous section. As infant mortality has declined, so the chance of survival to age 1 has increased over generations. The chance of surviving to one's first birthday was unchanged between 1851 and 1901 (at 83 per cent for males and 86 per cent for females) (Table 5.21). For those born in 1951 the chance of surviving to age 1 had increased to 97 per cent for both males and females. The increased chance of survival for women between ages 65 and 85 has been particularly marked, rising 48 percentage points between the 1851 and 1951 cohorts.

Table 5.21

Percentage chance of survival between selected ages: selected birth cohorts

England and Wales

	Male			Female		
	1851	1901	1951	1851	1901	1951
0–1	83	83	97	86	86	97
1–15	81	89	99	79	89	99
15–65	45	64	86	53	77	91
65–85	11	17	55	18	37	66
65–100	0	0	6	0	1	9

Areas of the table that are shaded are based on projected mortality.

Source: Government Actuary's Department Mortality Database (Author's own calculations)

Figure 5.22 shows the percentage chance of survival to each exact age for a cohort. For example, the age to which males born in 1851 had a 50 per cent chance of survival was 45. This increased for the 1901 cohort to approaching age 64 and is projected to be around age 83 for men born in 1951. For females the age to which there was a 50 per cent chance of survival increased from 50, to 72 and to over 87 for the 1851-, 1901- and 1951-born generations respectively.

Figure 5.22 also illustrates how mortality has become concentrated at older ages over the last two centuries. This reflects the tendency over time, as a country develops, for the chance of survival to younger and middle ages to approach 100 per cent and to decline only in the oldest ages. The decline in infant mortality is apparent from the absence of the sharp drop between age 0 and age 1 for the 1951 cohort compared with the 1851- and 1901-born generations. A comparison of the survival curves for each of the 1951, 1901 and 1951 cohorts shows the move from a curved shape to a more rectangular one, as survival to early middle age is now almost certain.[21]

Figure 5.22

Percentage chance of survival to exact age: selected cohorts, by sex

England and Wales

Number alive out of each 100 born

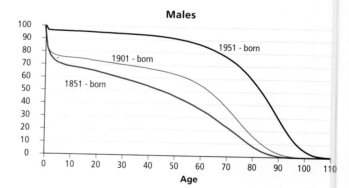

England and Wales

Number alive out of each 100 born

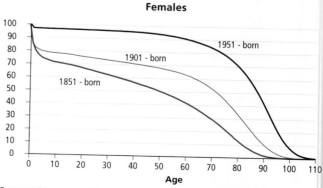

Source: Government Actuary's Department Mortality Database (Author's own calculations)

Cohort life expectancy

Life expectancy at birth in England and Wales increased substantially from generations born in the mid-19th century to the 1951-born cohort (Figure 5.23). For people born in 1851 expectation of life at birth was years 40.2 for males and 43.6 years for females. This is projected to increase to 77.3 years for males and 82.1 years for females born in 1951.

Cohort life expectancy is the average number of additional years a member of a cohort would live based on the mortality rates the cohort has experienced or is projected to experience. (See Box 7 for more information on cohort and period life expectancy.) Life expectancy at *birth* is not a guide to the remaining expectancy of life at any given age, so it is informative to look at the expectation of life at other ages.

For generations born during the 19th century when infant and childhood mortality was high, the differences between life expectancy at birth and life expectancy at ages 15 or 65 were very wide (Figure 5.23). As infant and childhood mortality declined, the gap between life expectancy at birth and life expectancy at older ages narrowed. For the 1851-born generation life expectancy at age 65 (including years lived) was 76.0 years for males. For males born in 1951 it is projected to be 85.7 years. The gap between life expectancy at birth and life expectancy at age 65 (including years lived) is therefore projected to narrow from around 36 years for males born in 1851 to eight years for those born in 1951. Female life expectancy is projected to follow a similar pattern to this.

Box 7

Period and cohort life expectancy

The expectation of life at birth is a commonly used summary measure of mortality rates. Life expectancy can be presented on a period or cohort basis. Period life expectancy is the average number of additional years a person would live if they experienced the age-specific mortality rates of a particular year throughout their life.

Cohort life expectancy is the average number of additional years a member of a cohort would live based on the mortality rates the cohort has experienced or is projected to experience. Because improvements in mortality happen over the life of a cohort, period life expectancy at birth cannot be taken as an estimated average age at death for the generation born in that year.

Life expectancy at birth represents the average of the individual life expectancies of all people born in the same year. It is therefore an average of all their ages at death. Consequently, life expectancy at birth is not a guide to the remaining expectancy of life at any given age. For example, if male life expectancy at birth for a population is 80 years, the life expectancy of men aged exactly 80 would not be zero. Similarly, remaining life expectancy for those aged 75 would exceed five years. This reflects the fact that survival from a particular age depends only on the mortality rates beyond that age, whereas survival from birth is based on mortality rates for all ages.[31]

For the generations born up to and at the start of the 20th century the main increases in life expectancy at birth were due to the decline of infant mortality, and to some extent child mortality, rather than increased survival at older ages. This can be inferred from the shallow rates of increase in life expectancy for men and women who survived to age 65. For later cohorts, it is worth noting that, although life expectancy at age 65 has not increased greatly, the number of men and women surviving to age 65 has (Figure 5.22).

Further analysis of life expectancy at birth by social class and by local authority is presented in *Focus on Social Inequalities*.[30] This also features standardised death rates and infant mortality by social class.

Summary

Throughout the last century there have been large changes in fertility and mortality in the UK. Fertility trends have been more variable than mortality trends. There have been several periods

Figure **5.23**

Life expectancy by sex: at selected ages and selected birth cohorts

England and Wales

Years (including years lived)

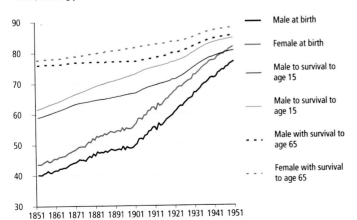

Legend:
— Male at birth
— Female at birth
— Male to survival to age 15
— Male to survival to age 15
- - - Male with survival to age 65
- - - Female with survival to age 65

Source: Government Actuary's Department Mortality Database (Author's own calculations)

of high fertility (baby booms) but also of low fertility. The last 30 years have seen low fertility rates and notable changes in childbearing behaviour. These include a decrease in average completed family size; an increase in childlessness; postponement of childbearing to older ages; and an increase in the percentage of births occurring outside marriage. Migration has also played an increasingly important role in fertility. The percentage of births occurring to women born outside the UK has grown, reflecting the rise in the number of women of childbearing age born overseas and their higher fertility rates.

There has been an increase in longevity, with falls in mortality at every age. As a result, mortality has become concentrated at (ever) older ages. Infant mortality has declined steeply and is now at a very low level. Childhood mortality has also fallen, and continues to do so, while the decline in young adult mortality has levelled off. Since the 1950s there have been improvements in survival to pensionable age and to very old ages.

The shift to mortality at older ages combined with the decline in fertility has caused the UK population to age. This has led to rises in the median age of the population and in the proportion of the population aged 65 or over, as noted in Chapter 4. Currently, population momentum means that there are still more births than deaths each year, and so natural increase occurs. But it is likely that current and future fertility and mortality trends will result in the UK experiencing natural decrease in the 21st century.

Notes and references

1. Shaw C.(2005) 2004-based national population projections for the United Kingdom and constituent countries. *Population Trends* forthcoming.

2. Knodel J (1999) Deconstructing population momentum. *Population Today* **27(3).** 1–2.

3. Craig J (1994) Replacement level fertility and future population growth. Population Trends **78**, 20–22.

4. Cliquet R (1991) *Desirabilities and possibilities of a fertility recovery at replacement level in Europe.* Netherlands Interuniversity Demographic Institute and Population Family Study Centre Vol. 21.

5. Smallwood S and Chamberlain J (2005) Replacement fertility, what has it been and what does it mean? *Population Trends* **119**, 16–27.

6. Lesthaeghe R (2001) Postponement and recuperation: Recent fertility trends and forecasts in six Western European countries. Paper presented at the IUSSP Seminar, International perspectives on low fertility: Trends, theories, and policies. 21–23 March: Tokyo.

7. Bongaarts J (2002). The end of fertility transition in the developed world. *Population and Development Review* **28(3)**, 419–443.

8. Smallwood S and Jefferies J (2003) Family building intentions in England and Wales: trends, outcomes and interpretations. *Population Trends* **112**, 15–28.

9. Goldstein J, Lutz W and Tests M (2003) The emergence of sub-replacement family size ideals in Europe. *Population research and policy review* **22**, 479–496.

10. Haskey J (2001) Cohabitation in Great Britain: past, present and future trends – and attitudes. *Population Trends* **103**, 4–25.

11. Rendall M and Smallwood S (2003) Higher qualifications, first-birth timing, and further childbearing in England and Wales. *Population Trends* **111**, 18–26.

12. Hancock R, Stuchbury R and Tomassini C (2003) Changes in the distribution of martial age differences in England and Wales, 1963 to 1988. *Population Trends* **114**, 19–25.

13. Berrington A (2004) Perpetual postponers? Women's, men's and couple's fertility intentions and subsequent fertility behaviour. *Population Trends* **117**, 9–19.

14. Rendall M and Ball D (2004) Immigration, emigration and the ageing of the overseas-born population in the United Kingdom. *Population Trends* **116**, 18–27.

15. Collingwood Bakeo A (2004) Trends in live births by mother's country of birth and other factors affecting low birthweight in England and Wales, 1983–2001. *Health Statistics Quarterly* **23**, 25–33.

16. Toulemon L (2004) Fertility among immigrant women: new data, a new approach. *Population & Societies* **400**.

17. Ford K (1990) Duration of residence in the United States and the fertility of US immigrants. *International migration review* **24(1)**, 34–68.

18. Østby L (2002) Fertility patterns of foreign women in Norway. *The demographic characteristics of immigrant population in Norway.* Statistics Norway.

19. Office for National Statistics (2005) www.statistics.gov.uk/focuson/health

20. Griffiths C and Brock A (2003) Twentieth century mortality trends in England and Wales. *Health Statistics Quarterly* **18**, 5–17.

21. Coleman D and Salt J (1992) *The British population: patterns, trends and processes.* Oxford University Press: Oxford.

22. Charlton J (1997) Trends in all-cause mortality: 1841–1994 in Charlton J and Murphy M (eds) The health of adult Britain 1841–1994, Office for National Statistics series DS No. 13. The Stationery Office: London.

23. Hanlon P *et al.* (2001) *Chasing the Scottish effect*, Public Health Institute of Scotland: NHS Scotland.

24. http://web.idrc.ca/en/ev-2669-201-1-DO_TOPIC.html

25. Weeks J (1999) *Population: an introduction to concepts and issues.* Wadsworth Publishing Company: Belmont

26. Rogers R and Powell-Griner E (1991) Life expectancies of cigarette smokers and nonsmokers in the United States. *Social Science and Medicine* **32**, 1151–59.

27. Gronjca A, Tomassini C, Toson B and Smallwood S (2005) Sex differences in mortality, a comparison of the United Kingdom and other developed countries. *Population Trends* **26**, 6–16.

28. Waldron I (1995) Contributions of biological and behavioral factors to changing sex differences in ischaemic heart disease mortality', in Lopez A, Caselli G and Volkonen T (eds), *Adult mortality in developed countries: from description to explanation.* Clarendon Press: Oxford, 161–78.

29. Waldron I (1993) Recent trends in mortality ratios for adults in developed countries. *Social Science and Medicine* **36(4)**, 451–462.

30. Office for National Statistics (2004) www.statistics.gov.uk/downloads/theme_compendia/fosi2004/SocialInequalities_full.pdf

31. www.nchod.nhs.uk

Population movement within the UK

Tony Champion

Chapter 6

Introduction

This chapter and Chapter 7 deal with the movement of people, both within the UK and between the UK and other countries. Internal migration refers to people changing address within the UK and is the focus of this chapter.[1] International migration refers to the movement of people into and out of the UK and is covered in Chapter 7.

Internal migration is a very important component of population change for local areas within the UK, both because it changes the total numbers of people resident in each area and because it may alter the composition of the population. Internal migration is a 'zero-sum game': any net migration gain in one area can take place only through a net loss somewhere else, with consequences for labour supply and the need for housing, schools, shops and other services. The biggest social policy issues in recent years have been the 'North-South drift' (the movement of people from the northern areas of the UK to southern areas) and the 'urban-rural shift' (the movement of people from inner cities to the suburbs and more rural areas).

Even where internal migration is having little effect on the size of populations, it may still be altering population composition. The characteristics of the people moving into an area can be substantially different from those of the people moving out. For example, London normally gains many more young adults than it loses through migration to and from other parts of the UK. At the same time, London usually has a large net outflow of older adults to the rest of the UK.[2]

There are two main sources of data on internal migration used in this chapter. The first is the 2001 Census, which asked where people had been living one year previously and compared this with their Census-day address. The second source uses administrative records produced when people re-register with a new NHS general practitioner (GP) after moving house. Further information on these sources is provided in the box 'Sources of data on internal migration'.

This chapter has five main sections. The first looks at how many people in the UK change address in a year and what proportion of these moves takes place over short distances. The second section identifies which types of people are most prone to change address and which tend to move over longer rather than shorter distances.

The third section examines the degree of variation around the country in the extent of address changing. It highlights the regions, districts and census wards with the highest and lowest proportions of residents moving to their census address from somewhere else in the UK during the previous 12 months. Fourth, the chapter describes the overall patterns of population

redistribution produced by this within-UK migration, focusing primarily on the shifts between the North and South and between the more urban and more rural parts of the country. Finally, examples are given of distinctive geographical patterns of migration, looking at different age groups, ethnic groups and occupations.

Sources of data on internal migration

The two main sources of internal migration data used in this chapter differ considerably in nature, even in their definition of a migrant.

The migration data from the 2001 Census are based on a comparison of each individual's address on Census day (29 April 2001) with the address they stated they were living at one year previously (29 April 2000). An individual's 'address' in the census is the place that they consider to be their 'usual residence', that is, where they live most of the time.

An internal migrant in the 2001 Census is defined as a person resident in the UK on Census day who was living at a different address in the UK 12 months previously.

Therefore the census counts a maximum of one move per person during the twelve month period, does not cover any intermediate moves made during that year and excludes moves by people who moved away but then returned to the original address within the one-year window. Census data are only available every ten years.

In contrast, the National Health Service Central Register (NHSCR) provides a continuous monitoring of migration, but does not record all types of move. It is restricted to changes of address being made between former health authorities by patients registered with NHS general practitioners (GPs). In this context, a person's address is the address registered with their GP and a migrant is defined as a person who re-registers with a GP in a different former health authority from their previous GP.

The NHSCR is generally regarded as providing the best available proxy data on internal migration but it is known that people who move quite frequently and only rarely need a medical consultation (most notably young adult men) may be slow to re-register with a GP or may not re-register after every move.

The census migration data used in this chapter include moves of armed forces personnel, whereas the NHSCR data do not. Both the NHSCR data and 2001 Census migration data include the movements of students to and from places of higher education. The 1991 Census did not measure the migration of students, since students were counted as resident at their family home, but the 2001 Census enumerated students at their term-time address, bringing the census migration data into line with the NHSCR data.

Further information on these two data sources can be found in the appendix.

How many move?

According to the 2001 Census, over seven million UK residents were migrants in the sense that they were living at a different usual address from that of 12 months earlier. As 407,000 of these had been living outside the UK, the total number of residents who had moved from one address in the UK to another during the pre-census year was just under 6.7 million. This figure includes 467,000 people who indicated that they had 'no usual address one year ago' (see the appendix for further information on this group).

The 6.7 million internal migrants represent 11.4 per cent of the population living in the UK, meaning that roughly one in nine people had moved. This 11.4 per cent figure for 2001 ('2001' is used here, and below, as a shorthand for the 12 months to Census day) was relatively high by UK standards and reflects the fact that migration rates vary over time, principally in response to the prevailing economic climate. The rate of internal migration recorded by both the 1991 and 1981 Censuses was significantly lower. This is likely to reflect the fact that the country was in the grips of economic recession in 1991 and 1981, with people finding it harder to get new jobs or sell their houses.[3]

Direct comparisons of migration rates recorded by the 2001 Census and those from the 1991 and 1981 Censuses are problematic. The earlier censuses excluded both moves of students to and from university and moves of infants aged under one, while the 2001 Census migration data includes these moves. However, an idea of the degree of volatility of migration over time can be obtained from the NHSCR. As shown in Figure 6.1, the total level of movement between 'health areas' in England and Wales has fluctuated between 30 and 39 per 1,000 residents since 1975. The level of migration has been almost one-third higher at the peak of an economic cycle (as in 1987 to 1989 and 2000 to 2002) than in the depths of recession (as in 1990 to 1991). A similar pattern of variation over time is found for moves between Government Office Regions and moves within them, but the relative degree of fluctuation is slightly greater for the latter.

The majority of moves are over short distances. Though the standard area tables from the 2001 Census do not provide breakdowns by full type of move or by distance of move, these can be calculated from the data contained in the Individual Sample of Anonymised Records (ISAR). The results show that, of those who are known to have changed address in the UK in the pre-census year (that is, excluding those moving from outside the UK and those with no usual address one year previously), almost three out of every five (59.6 per cent) stayed within the same local authority district. Roughly another one in five (21.6 per cent) changed district but did not cross a

Government Office Region or country boundary, while 18.8 per cent did cross a regional or country boundary. The latter includes those who moved in or out of London.

In terms of distance moved, again according to the ISAR, over two in five (43.0 per cent) of those within-UK migrants had moved no further than 2 km. Another 10.6 per cent had moved between addresses that were 3 to 4 km apart, while 12.1 per cent were 5 to 9 km from their previous address. Thus for almost two-thirds (65.7 per cent) of these migrants, less than 10 km separated their current and previous addresses. At the other extreme, just one in 15 (6.7 per cent) had moved 200 km or more. Altogether only 18.5 per cent had moved at least 50 km.

Who moves and how far?

It is well known that some types of people move home more frequently than others and some tend to move more locally than others.[4] The ISAR can be used to illustrate some of the differentials in migration behaviour within the UK.

Gender is one of the most fundamental of demographic characteristics, but it is not a major discriminator of migration behaviour except in certain contexts such as the movement of armed forces personnel. Males were the slightly more migratory in 2001, with 11.7 per cent at a different address from one year previously compared with 11.2 per cent of females. Males also tended to move slightly further, with 19.1 per cent moving 50 km or more compared with 18.0 per cent of females. While 42.2 per cent of males moved no more than 2 km, the comparable figure for females was 43.7 per cent.

Figure **6.1**

Rates of migration[1] between NHSCR[2] areas of England and Wales, per 1,000 people rolling annual averages: by quarter, 1975 to 2004

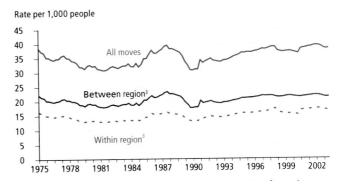

Rate per 1,000 people

1. Data are rolling annual averages by quarter, starting from the year ending 31 December 1975.
2. NHSCR areas refer to Family Health Service Areas (FHSAs) up to 1999 and former Health Authorities (HAs) from 2000 onwards. Estimates of internal migration within regions between quarter one 1999 and quarter one 2001 were slightly affected by this changeover.
3. Region refers to Wales and the Government Office Regions of England.

Source: Data from National Health Service Central Register

Part of these differences is likely to arise from the fact that women, living longer on average than men, tend to account for more of the higher age groups, which have below-average migration rates and distances.

Turning to *age*, there is a marked contrast between the migration of younger adults and people aged 45 and over at the Census (Figure 6.2). For the latter, the propensity to move house falls with increasing age up to around age 75. Above this age, the percentage migrating rises again, reflecting the greater incidence of 'defensive moves' prompted by loss of partner or increasing frailty and involving getting closer to relatives or moving into smaller dwellings or special accommodation.[5] Although longer-distance retirement migration takes place among people in their 60s, the increasing spread of age of retirement means that the official retirement ages of 60 for women and 65 for men produce barely perceptible blips in the profile.

The highest levels of residential mobility are for those in their late teens and early 20s,[6] as seen in the peak in Figure 6.2. This peak represents people starting and leaving university, as well as those leaving school and entering the labour market. It also includes people leaving the parental home to set up by themselves or with partners and others. The higher rate for women in their early 20s partly reflects the general age difference in partnerships, though women are also more likely to move into a dwelling already occupied by their boyfriend than the other way round. (This higher rate for women is consistent with the earlier observation that the all-age migration rate for men is slightly higher than for women because the former outnumber the latter at these more mobile ages.) The higher rate for men in their 30s and early 40s

Figure **6.2**

Percentage of residents[1] known to have changed address within the UK: by age and sex, 2001[2]

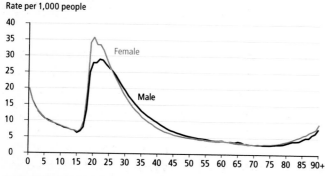

Rate per 1,000 people

1 *Excludes residents living outside the UK one year ago and those with no known address one year ago.*
2 *Data refer to moves during the 12 months prior to the 2001 Census.*

Source: Data from 2001 Census special tabulation – Office for National Statistics; General Register Office for Scotland; Northern Ireland Statistics and Research Agency

probably arises from divorce or separation more often involving the departure from the family home of the father than the mother.[7]

Evidently, the vast majority of people moving home within the UK are from the younger half of the age span. Data on absolute numbers of migrants by age (not shown here) reveal that people aged 45 and over made up only one in six (16.6 per cent) of all migrants despite constituting 40 per cent of all UK residents in 2001. The 16- to 29-year-olds accounted for just under two in five (38.9 per cent) of all people changing address, 30- to 44-year-olds for nearly a quarter (24.6 per cent) and the under 16s for almost one in five (19.8 per cent). Inevitably, the higher migration rates of young adults will be reflected in the variations between people for other characteristics, as – all other things being equal – migration rates will be highest for those characteristics most associated with younger members of the population.

As regards age differences in distance of move, the most distinctive group is the under 16s, of whom fully half (50.9 per cent) relocate within 2 km of their previous address, almost three-quarters (74.2 per cent) move less than 10 km, and only 4.9 per cent move 200 km or more. While this reflects migration decisions made by their parents, one important consideration for the latter is minimising the disruption to their children's schooling. The age group with the next highest proportion of the shortest moves is 75 and over, with 68.7 per cent moving under 10 km and reflecting the 'defensive' nature of most moves at this age mentioned above. Long distance moves are undertaken most commonly among 16- to 29-year-olds, with 8.2 per cent of their moves being of at least 200 km. The only other broad age group with a proportion of such moves that is higher than the national figure of 6.7 per cent is the 55- to 64-year-olds, with their 7.4 per cent probably reflecting the long distances moved by some people at retirement.[8]

In the remainder of this section, only the more extreme cases are noted, so as to indicate the range of migration behaviour in 2001 and build up an overall picture of the factors influencing the propensity to change address and the distance moved.

Marital status

- Single never-married people had the highest propensity to change address (16.4 per cent had moved in the year before the census), while the widowed had the lowest (5.8 per cent).

- Among those who did move, the widowed were also the group that moved most locally (69.3 per cent moving less than 10 km), closely followed by the divorced and the separated. The remarried were the longest-distance movers (20.7 per cent moving at least 50 km), followed by the single never-married.

Family type

- Cohabiting couples with no children had by far the highest propensity to migrate, with 30.5 per cent moving in the previous year. At the other extreme were married couples with no children living in the household, with only 5.6 per cent moving – presumably mainly older families whose children had already left home.

- Lone mothers were the shortest-distance movers (79.1 per cent moved less than 10 km), followed by cohabiting couples. Married couples with no children were the longest-distance movers (with 22.6 per cent moving at least 50 km). Individuals not in a family moved the next furthest.

Health

- More healthy people change address more often and move over longer distances. In terms of general health over the previous 12 months, 12.5 per cent of people describing their health as 'good' had moved, compared with 8.6 per cent saying 'not good'. However, there were large numbers of 'health-related' moves among the very old.

- The proportion of movers who remained within 10 km of their previous address rose from 64.8 per cent for those describing their health as 'good' to 67.4 per cent for 'fairly good' and 70.8 per cent for 'not good'. The pattern for those with or without limiting long-term illness was very similar.

Housing tenure

- Private renting was the sector with the highest turnover of population, with 33.7 per cent of its residents having moved into their accommodation within the 12 months prior to the census. This is more than twice the level of the next highest sector – renting from housing associations, co-operatives and other voluntary and charitable bodies, at 13.7 per cent.

- Owner-occupying residents were the least migratory, especially those who were outright owners (only 4.9 per cent of whom had lived at their present address for less than 12 months). This is because they are predominantly older people who have had time to pay off their mortgages.

- Distance of move also varies greatly by tenure.[9] People moving into accommodation rented from councils in England and Wales and equivalent bodies in Scotland and Northern Ireland were much more likely to come from the local area, with only 15.6 per cent moving 10 km or more. By contrast, 43.4 per cent of outright owners and 31.9 per cent of owners with a mortgage or loan had moved from at least 10 km away.

Economic activity of people aged 16 to 74

- By far the most migratory group at the time of the census was students. Of the economically inactive students (both part-time and full-time students aged 16 to 74), 27.0 per cent were living at a different address from that of one year before. This percentage is lower than might be expected since students aged 16 and above in schools and further education institutions are included and this group is likely to be less migratory than higher education students. The economic group next most likely to have moved was those unemployed and seeking work, where 19.0 per cent had been living at a different address twelve months earlier.

- The least migratory were the retired, of whom only 3.8 per cent moved in the year before the census, followed by part-time self-employed people without employees, at 7.8 per cent.

- The group moving over the longest distances was the economically inactive students. One-third (33.1 per cent) of those who moved were at least 50 km from their previous address. A quarter (25.0 per cent) of the relatively small proportion of retired people who had moved in the year before the census had moved 50 km or more, as had almost 23 per cent of those who were unemployed and seeking work in the week before the census.

- Those groups whose migrants were least likely to move over a long distance comprised the self-employed with employees (only 12.3 per cent moving at least 50 km) and the permanently sick or disabled (12.5 per cent).

Industry

- Those employed in the week before the 2001 Census were classified into 17 categories according to the business of their employer (further details of this industrial classification can be found in the appendix.

- The two industrial classes with the highest proportion of employees making within-UK moves in the pre-census year were people working in hotels and restaurants and those working for international organisations such as the United Nations, with 18.8 per cent and 18.5 per cent moving respectively. Least migratory were those working in agriculture, hunting and forestry (9.0 per cent), education, manufacturing, and mining and quarrying.

- In terms of the distance moved by those changing address, those working in construction had the highest proportion of people moving less than 10 km, at 72.4 per cent, followed by workers in manufacturing and fishing. The highest proportions moving 50 km or more were for public administration and defence (32.2 per cent) and hotels and restaurants (24.3 per cent).

Occupation

- Several alternative classifications are available in the ISAR, including the Standard Occupational Classification 2000, the International Standard Classification of Occupations and the NS Socio-economic Classification (see the appendix for further details). Drawing selectively from all three, it is found that that the highest mobility is for members of the armed forces, 31.5 per cent of whom were at a different address at the census from that of 12 months earlier and with fully two out of three (67.0 per cent) of these having moved at least 50 km.

- Full-time students come close to this migration rate (25.2 per cent of the group), with almost one-third of these moving 50 km or more.

- Higher professionals (excluding self-employed) saw one in five of their number moving in the pre-census year, over a quarter of whom had moved 50 km or more.

- Health professionals, those in culture, media and sport occupations, those in customer service occupations and those in protective service occupations such as security staff all had migration rates of at least 18 per cent. The proportions moving 50 km or more were particularly high for protective services (42.1 per cent) and health professionals (36.0 per cent).

- At the other extreme, migration rates were lowest for people in agricultural occupations, for people in skilled metal and electrical trades and for transport and mobile machine drivers and operators. These latter two groups also had the lowest proportions of migrants moving 50 km or more, along with skilled construction and building trades and process/plant/machine operatives – all with under 12.5 per cent moving 50 km or more.

Qualifications

- People who changed address the least were those with no qualifications at all.

- Generally, the higher the qualification level, the higher was the proportion moving long distances.

Ethnicity

- Across the UK as a whole, 14.1 per cent of people in non-White ethnic groups changed address within the UK in the pre-census year, a rather higher proportion than for the White population (11.2 per cent). This difference probably arises from the younger average age of the former.

- Out of the four generic ethnic minority groups in England and Wales, Asians were least migratory (11.9 per cent changing address), followed by those of Black and Mixed ethnic origins. Those from Chinese and other ethnic groups were the most migratory (18.8 per cent).

- The proportion of migrants moving under 10 km in Scotland was slightly higher for Whites than non-Whites, the reverse of the situation in Northern Ireland and England and Wales. Among non-Whites, the Black group had the highest proportion of these short-distance moves, and the Chinese the lowest.

Geographical differences in migration behaviour

People's propensity to change address varies not only between types of people but also between places, though the two may well be connected in the sense that places differ in the make-up of their populations by age, ethnicity and the other dimensions associated with migration behaviour (as outlined in the previous section). This section examines variation across the UK between places defined at three different geographical levels:

- regional/country level, defined in terms of England's Government Office Regions and the countries of Wales, Scotland and Northern Ireland;

- district level, defined in terms of the local and unitary authorities of England and Wales, the council areas of Scotland, and the local government districts of Northern Ireland; and

- ward level, using the 2001 Census standard wards.

Attention is focused on known within-UK moves in the pre-census year. However, at the regional/country level, a broader context is provided by also considering moves made by people who had no usual address one year prior to the census and by people who are known to have been living outside the UK then.

Region/country level

The migration experience of each region/country is shown in Table 6.3. It can be seen that there are some quite substantial regional differences across the UK. In relative terms, the most marked is for the proportion of residents who are known to have been living outside the UK one year before the census. This ranges from 0.3 per cent of residents in Wales to 1.7 per cent for London. Only the latter, together with the adjacent South East and East regions of England, have proportions at or above the national figure, indicating the degree of concentration of international arrivals in this corner of the UK (see Chapter 7). The proportion declaring that they had no usual address one year ago was also highest in London at 1.4 per cent, but otherwise the inter-regional range is much smaller, with values of 0.6 to 0.8 per cent.

The proportion of residents who are known to have moved within the UK is highest for the South West, at 11.6 per cent. Also with rates of at least 11.0 per cent of residents are London, the South East, and Yorkshire and the Humber. Northern Ireland's population contains the smallest proportion of within-UK migrants, at 8.3 per cent, followed by the West Midlands.

These differences in within-UK migration rates are partly driven by the level of within-region movement (shown in the penultimate column of Table 6.3). Thus Yorkshire and the Humber and the South West had within-region migration rates of over 9 per cent, while Northern Ireland's rate of internal movement was 7.6 per cent.

The degree to which migrants have moved across regional and country boundaries within the UK also plays a part. Northern Ireland recorded by far the lowest rate, as is understandable in view of its physical separation from the rest of the UK. The North West and North East also appear to have been weak attractors in the year to 2001. The highest presence of migrants from elsewhere in the UK are shown by the 3.2 per cent figures for Wales and Scotland. Rates of in-migration of 2.4 per cent or more were also registered by the South West, the South East, the East Midlands and the East, probably reflecting their attraction to migrants from London and the West Midlands.

The distances moved by people changing address within the UK can be calculated by country and region from the ISAR (Table 6.4). The North East and North West had the highest

Table **6.3**

Residents by address 12 months prior to the 2001 Census: by UK country and Government Office Region, 2001[1]

Numbers and percentages

Country, Government Office Region	Total number of residents	Same address	Address outside the UK one year ago	No usual address one year ago	At known UK address	In region/ country of current residence	In different region/ country
North East	2,515,442	88.7	0.4	0.7	10.2	8.8	1.4
North West	6,729,764	88.8	0.4	0.8	10.1	8.7	1.3
Yorkshire and the Humber	4,964,833	87.7	0.5	0.7	11.1	9.3	1.8
East Midlands	4,172,174	88.0	0.5	0.7	10.9	8.5	2.5
West Midlands	5,267,308	89.2	0.5	0.7	9.6	8.0	1.6
East	5,388,140	88.4	0.7	0.7	10.2	7.9	2.4
London	7,172,091	85.8	1.7	1.4	11.1	9.0	2.2
South East	8,000,645	87.3	0.9	0.7	11.1	8.5	2.6
South West	4,928,434	87.1	0.6	0.7	11.6	9.1	2.6
Wales	2,903,085	88.8	0.3	0.7	10.1	7.0	3.2
Scotland	5,062,011	88.4	0.6	0.7	10.3	7.1	3.2
Northern Ireland	1,685,267	90.7	0.4	0.6	8.3	7.6	0.7
United Kingdom	58,789,194	88.0	0.7	0.8	10.6	10.6	0.0

1 Data refer to moves during the 12 months prior to the 2001 Census.

Source: Data from 2001 Census Key Statistics – Office for National Statistics; General Register Office for Scotland; Northern Ireland Statistics and Research Agency

Table **6.4**

Distance moved by people changing address within the UK in the year prior to the 2001 Census: by UK country and Government Office Region of usual residence in 2001[1]

Percentages

Country, Government Office Region	0–2 km	3–9 km	10–49 km	50–199 km	200 km and over	All
North East	53.8	20.8	11.3	6.5	7.5	100
North West	50.4	22.8	12.2	8.0	6.6	100
Yorkshire and the Humber	46.8	22.6	13.4	10.2	7.0	100
East Midlands	42.9	21.2	15.4	16.2	4.2	100
West Midlands	45.0	24.7	14.3	12.6	3.4	100
East	37.3	21.0	21.9	14.3	5.4	100
London	38.0	30.2	16.9	9.0	6.0	100
South East	37.5	21.3	18.8	16.1	6.4	100
South West	38.9	20.5	14.4	15.6	10.6	100
Wales	46.2	20.2	14.8	11.1	7.7	100
Scotland	46.7	19.8	15.7	8.7	9.1	100
Northern Ireland	47.2	21.1	17.1	6.7	8.0	100
United Kingdom	43.0	22.7	15.8	11.8	6.7	100

1 Excludes those with no usual address one year ago.

Source: 2001 Census Individual SAR – Office for National Statistics; General Register Office for Scotland; Northern Ireland Statistics and Research Agency

Table **6.5**

Percentage of residents at 2001 Census known to have changed address within the UK in the previous 12 months: highest and lowest ten districts in the UK[1,2]

Percentages

Rank	District	Percentage	Rank	District	Percentage
1	Oxford	20.1	434	Cookstown	5.9
2	Cambridge	19.5	433	Strabane	6.0
3	City of London	17.0	432	Dungannon	6.2
4	Southampton	16.9	431	Fermanagh	6.3
5	Exeter	16.9	430	Magherafelt	6.3
6	Wandsworth	16.9	429	Newry and Mourne	6.3
7	Ceredigion	16.6	428	Castlereagh	6.6
8	Nottingham	16.6	427	East Dunbartonshire	6.6
9	Manchester	16.3	426	Armagh	6.8
10	Lancaster	15.9	425	Omagh	6.8

1 Excludes those with no usual address one year ago.
2 Includes both residents who have moved from outside the district and residents who have moved within the district.

Source: Data from 2001 Census Key Statistics – Office for National Statistics; General Register Office for Scotland; Northern Ireland Statistics and Research Agency

proportions moving very short distances (over half of migrants moved less than 2 km), whereas the smallest proportions of very short distance migrants were among those moving within and into the South East and East. London has a particularly high proportion of migrants moving 3 to 9 km, possibly reflecting its situation as a large densely-populated urban area. At the other extreme, the South West and Scotland had the highest proportions of migrants who had moved at least 200 km, reflecting their positions at the two extremities of the mainland.

District level

Table 6.5 lists the top and bottom ten districts in the UK for the proportion of their 2001 Census residents who one year earlier were living at a different address in the UK.

The highest proportion is for Oxford, at 20.1 per cent – nearly double the national figure of 10.6 per cent (see Table 6.3). Cambridge comes a close second, suggesting the importance of students moving to these university towns or moving within them during their time there. Southampton, Exeter, Ceredigion (containing Aberystwyth), Nottingham, Manchester and Lancaster also have a substantial university presence. The City of London – the 'Square Mile' – contains a very small population and one that clearly has a high turnover, while the presence of Wandsworth in the list may similarly reflect the degree of local churn at the centre of a major city like London. Three other London boroughs not shown here (Westminster, Camden and Hammersmith and Fulham) appear among the twenty districts with the highest proportions of residents changing address within the UK.

At the other extreme, some districts have little more than half the national within-UK migration rate. All but one of the lowest ten are in Northern Ireland, primarily reflecting the low turnover of population within the province (Table 6.3). The exception is East Dunbartonshire on the edge of the Clydeside conurbation in Scotland.

Map 6.6 presents the picture for the whole of the UK. This confirms the importance of students in the proportion of residents who changed address in the year before the census. In Scotland, for instance, Aberdeen, Dundee, Edinburgh, Glasgow and Stirling are the only areas with the top rate shown, similarly Durham and Newcastle in the North East of England. Other areas with high scores include districts with a military presence such as Forest Heath (Suffolk) and Richmondshire (North Yorkshire), coastal and rural retirement areas especially in the South West, and Central and Inner West London.

At the other end of the scale are places that contain low-turnover populations or are attracting fewest incomers from the rest of the UK. Besides the case of Northern Ireland already noted, these districts fall into two main categories. A considerable number are suburban districts around the larger cities, as around Glasgow, Liverpool, Birmingham/ Wolverhampton and some inner parts of the Home Counties. A second group comprises areas with an above-average proportion of blue-collar workers or a previous history of such work, such as some of the South Wales valley districts and Outer East London Boroughs (Map 6.6).

Ward level

Table 6.7 shows the wards with the highest and lowest proportions of residents who had changed address within the UK in the year prior to the 2001 Census. Keele ward tops the list, with nearly two out of every three residents having moved from another address in the UK in the previous year. This is due to a large proportion of housing in this ward being student accommodation. The other nine wards in the top ten also contain student accommodation such as halls of residence.

At the other extreme, in Lissan ward in Cookstown barely one in 40 residents was new to their census-time address. Not surprisingly, given the district-level results, all but one of these lowest ten were in Northern Ireland. The exception was in East Dunbartonshire, Scotland.

Population redistribution produced by within-UK migration

With around one in ten people changing address each year, migration has the potential to cause big shifts in population distribution. To a large extent, people moving in to areas replace the people leaving. In many cases, the types of people moving in are similar to those moving out or, at least, have similar characteristics to those of the previous residents when they originally moved in to the area. Nevertheless there are also some important cases where migration is producing shifts in the geographical distribution of the population or is altering the population profiles of certain areas in the short or longer term. This section focuses primarily on the two main spatial dimensions of net within-UK migration (that is, inflow minus outflow), namely what have long been dubbed the 'North-South drift' and the 'urban-rural shift'.

Migration between North and South

Southward net migration dates back at least to the Great Depression era of the early 1930s and has been continuing in recent decades. As shown in Figure 6.8, however, the level of

Map **6.6**

Percentage of residents known to have moved within the UK during the year prior to the 2001 Census: by unitary authority or local authority, 2001[1]

United Kingdom

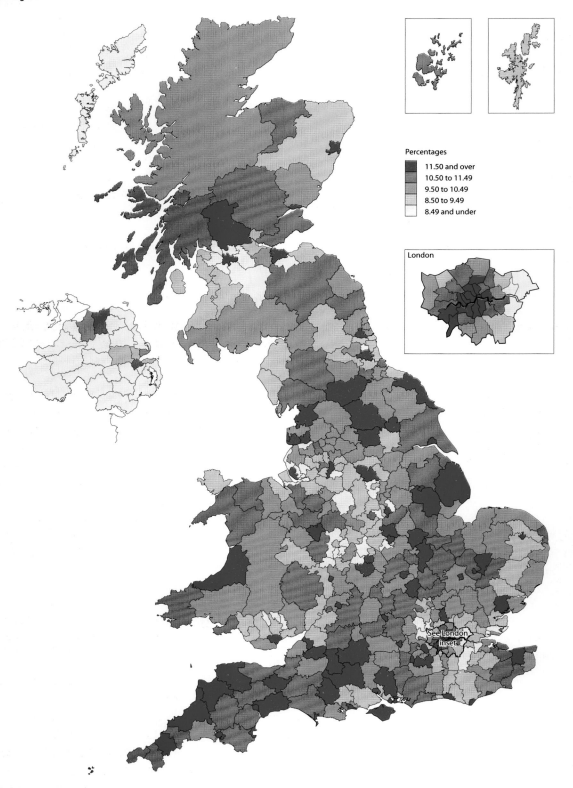

Percentages

- 11.50 and over
- 10.50 to 11.49
- 9.50 to 10.49
- 8.50 to 9.49
- 8.49 and under

London

See London inset

1   *Data refer to persons changing their address of usual residence between April 2000 and April 2001.*

Source: 2001 Census – Office for National Statistics; General Register Office for Scotland; and Northern Ireland Statistics and Research Agency

Table **6.7**

Percentage of residents at 2001 Census known to have changed address within the UK in the previous 12 months, highest and lowest ten wards in the UK[1,2]

Rank	Ward	Percentage	Rank	Ward	Percentage
1	Keele, Newcastle-under-Lyme	63.7	10,626	Lissan, Cookstown	2.7
2	Llanbadarn Fawr, Ceredigion	58.6	10,625	Termon, Omagh	3.1
3	Heslington, York	58.0	10,624	Shantallow East, Derry	3.1
4	Headingley, Leeds	52.6	10,623	Ardboe, Cookstown	3.3
5	Menai, Gwynedd	52.1	10,622	Dunnamore, Cookstown	3.5
6	Elvet, Durham	52.0	10,621	Balmuildy and Park, East Dunbartonshire	3.6
7	St Nicholas, Durham	51.5	10,620	Lisnasharragh, Castlereagh	3.6
8	Logie, Stirling	49.7	10,619	Ladybrook, Belfast	3.6
9	Aberystwyth Central, Ceredigion	49.4	10,618	Lasnacree, Newry & Mourne	3.6
10	Cathays, Cardiff	47.6	10,617	Silver Bridge, Newry & Mourne	3.7

1 *Excludes those with no usual address one year ago.*
2 *Includes both residents who have moved from outside the district and residents who have moved within the district.*

Source: 2001 Census Key Statistics – Office for National Statistics; General Register Office for Scotland; Northern Ireland Statistics and Research Agency

Figure **6.8**

Net migration between North and South[1] of the UK: 1971 to 2003[2]

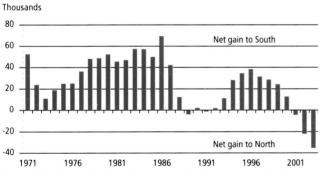

1 *The South comprises the Government Office Regions of London, South East, South West, East and East Midlands; 'the North' is the remainder of the UK.*
2 *Data refer to calendar years.*

Source: Data from National Health Service Central Register; General Register Office for Scotland; Northern Ireland Statistics and Research Agency

population redistribution resulting from this process fluctuates considerably in the short term and has, on average, reduced since the 1980s. The average for the three decades to the year 2000 was an annual gain of 31,000 people for the South (defined as the Government Office Regions of London, South East, South West, East and East Midlands). The figures for 1971 to 1980 and 1981 to 1990 were higher than this, at 34,300 and 38,000 respectively, but for 1991 to 2000 it was down to 21,200.

Figure **6.9**

Net within-UK migration by Government Office Region and country: annual average: 1991–1994 to 2000–2003

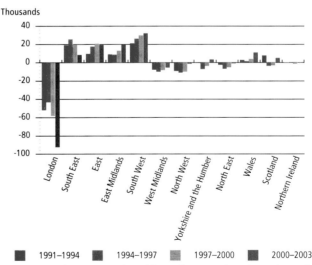

| ■ 1991–1994 | ■ 1994–1997 | ■ 1997–2000 | ■ 2000–2003 |

Source: Data from National Health Service Central Register; General Register Office for Scotland; Northern Ireland Statistics and Research Agency

Moreover, while the level had been running at around twice its long-term average in the mid 1980s, there have been two periods since then when either the flows between North and South have been roughly in balance (1989 to 1992) or there has been a significant reversal of flow (2001 to 2003). The North's net gain of just over 35,000 people from the South in 2003 is unprecedented, at least as far as can be judged from the NHSCR records which began in 1971 and from the migration data provided by the census from 1961 onwards.

Figure 6.9 shows the separate contributions to the North-South net shifts made by the nine Government Office Regions of England and the other three countries of the UK between 1991 and 2003. The single most impressive feature is the scale of net migration loss from London and the massive acceleration in this since the mid-1990s. In 1994 to 1997 London's net migration loss to the rest of the UK averaged 43,400 a year, but it had moved up to nearly 60,000 by 1997 to 2000 and to 92,400 in 2000 to 2003. Indeed, by 2002 to 2003 (not shown separately), the figure had risen to just over 110,000.

Throughout this period the main recipients of London's exodus were the other four regions of the South. Over most of the period shown in Figure 6.9, the latter absorbed not only all London's net losses but also the net losses from the North, notably from the other four regions of England. In the last few years shown, however, this was no longer the case. While the East Midlands and the South West saw a further acceleration in their net gains, the rate of net inflow to the East and the South East reduced, particularly so the latter. As a result, the extra losses from London since 1999 are paralleled by upward shifts in net migration balance in the North. All seven areas there were affected, but Wales, the North West and Yorkshire and the Humber saw the greatest absolute change over this period and Northern Ireland the least.

Various factors are likely to be responsible for these recent changes in London's migration balance. One is the marked acceleration in the UK's net migration gains from overseas since the early 1990s and London's predominant role in accommodating this (see Chapter 7). This, however, has perhaps served only to accentuate a well-established tendency for London to see its out-migration to other parts of the UK rise during the later years of a national economic boom. Regularly, as the nation emerges from a recession, London drives the process of recovery. Initially, this draws in extra migrants from other parts of the UK, but as the recovery leads

to inflationary pressures in London, its residents take advantage of the higher value of their homes to move out, first mainly to the two adjacent regions but later on further out, including to the North. Meanwhile, potential migrants from the North become increasingly deterred by London's rising house prices and eventually by the narrowing of the job gap as the recovery spreads out across the UK.

Urban-rural migration

London's role as a driver of the UK's regional migration patterns can also be associated with the process of urban out-migration. Starting in the 19th century, the growth of suburbs around the cores of the cities led to the latter becoming home to an increasing proportion of the country's urban dwellers. Later on, partly as a result of government policies aimed at reducing densities in the original cores of the larger cities, notably the post-war New and Expanded Towns programme, there was an absolute population loss from many of these areas and faster growth in the suburbs and the separate cities and towns further away. Despite the official abandonment of the urban dispersal programme in the 1970s, the urban-rural shift remains a major element of internal migration.[10]

The scale, persistence and pervasiveness of the urban exodus can be illustrated in a number of ways. First, Figure 6.10 shows net migration out of 'metropolitan England', defined as Greater London and the six former metropolitan counties of Greater Manchester, Merseyside, South Yorkshire, Tyne and Wear, West Midlands and West Yorkshire. In all, since 1981 metropolitan England has lost 2.25 million people as a result of net migration exchanges with the rest of the UK, an average of 97,800 a year. Like the North-South dimension shown in Figure 6.8, the scale varies over time, most notably dropping from 125,100 in 1987 to barely half this in 1989 and 1990 before moving upwards again fairly steadily through the 1990s and then accelerating markedly to reach almost 143,500 in 2003.

Figure **6.10**

Greater London and six metropolitan counties:[1] net out-migration to the rest of the UK, 1981 to 2003

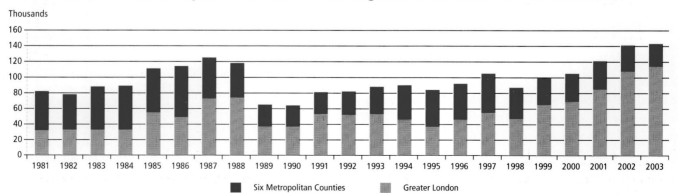

1   The six metropolitan counties are Tyne and Wear, Greater Manchester, Merseyside, South Yorkshire, West Yorkshire and West Midlands.
Source: Data from National Health Service Central Register

Unlike the North-South dimension, the net metropolitan exodus is very persistent: there is no recorded year with a reversal of flow, nor any time where this has seemed even a remote possibility. This is particularly true of London (as shown in Figure 6.9 from 1991 onwards), but is also the case for the rest of metropolitan England. Since the end of the 1980s the scale of net loss from the six metropolitan counties has remained below the level of the mid 1980s. More recently,

Figure **6.11**

Net within-UK migration in the year prior to the 2001 Census: as a percentage of 2001 residents, for a district classification of Great Britain[1]

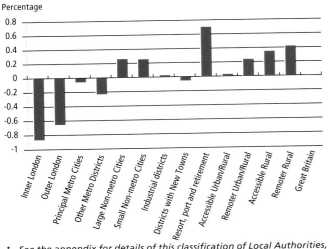

Percentage

1 See the appendix for details of this classification of Local Authorities, Unitary Authorities and Council Areas.

Source: Data from 2001 Census Key Statistics – Office for National Statistics; General Register Office for Scotland

while it has fallen from its 1997 peak, its level in 2003 was still above that of the early 1990s (Figure 6.10).

The pervasiveness of net urban-rural migration across the whole country is shown in Figure 6.11. This uses a classification of local and unitary authorities based on urban status, function and distance from metropolitan England (see the appendix for further details). All four metro types of district recorded net migration loss in the year before the 2001 Census, whereas net gains are found for eight of the other nine types, the exception being the districts with New Towns and reflecting the winding down of the New Towns programme since the 1970s.

Moreover, there is a pretty regular association between 'urbanness' and net migration rate (Figure 6.11). The highest rates of net loss are recorded for Inner and Outer London, with the lower figure for the latter signifying a degree of outward population movement within the capital. At the rural end of the scale, the two types of rural district recorded a stronger rate of net gain than the mixed urban/rural districts, with remoteness conveying a clear premium in both cases. Resorts and retirement districts, however, gained migration at an even higher rate than these, greatly out of line with what would be expected from their intermediate position in the urban hierarchy. Both types of non-metro city also recorded stronger migration balances than their urban status would have predicted.

The importance of the urban-rural dimension can also be gauged from the pattern of net migration gains at district level (Table 6.12). Rural areas and resorts feature strongly in the list

Table **6.12**

Ten UK districts with the highest and lowest rates of net within-UK migration: as a percentage of total population, in the year prior to the 2001 Census

Rank	Highest	Percentage		Rank	Lowest	Percentage
1	Isles of Scilly	2.55		434	Newham	−1.68
2	North Kesteven	1.72		433	Shetland Islands	−1.52
3	East Northamptonshire	1.71		432	Ealing	−1.46
4	Forest Heath	1.70		431	Surrey Heath	−1.44
5	East Devon	1.55		430	Hounslow	−1.41
6	Warwick	1.50		429	Harrow	−1.35
7	Eastbourne	1.49		428	Kensington and Chelsea	−1.30
8	Torbay UA	1.41		427	Brent	−1.30
9	Torridge	1.40		426	Haringey	−1.26
10	North Dorset	1.35		425	Islington	−1.22

1 The percentage for the Isles of Scilly is based on a small number of residents, hence a small absolute number of migrants may have a disproportionate effect in percentage terms.

Source: Data from 2001 Census Key Statistics – Office for National Statistics; General Register Office for Scotland; Northern Ireland Statistics and Research Agency

Map 6.13

Net within-UK migration as a percentage of all residents: by unitary authority or local authority, 2001[1]

United Kingdom

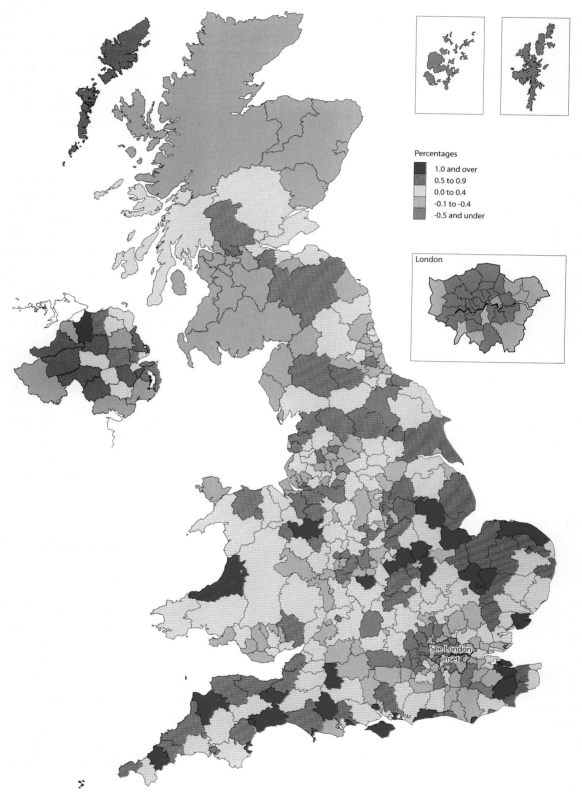

Percentages

- 1.0 and over
- 0.5 to 0.9
- 0.0 to 0.4
- -0.1 to -0.4
- -0.5 and under

London

See London inset

1   Data refer to persons changing their address of usual residence between April 2000 and April 2001.

Source: 2001 Census – Office for National Statistics; General Register Office for Scotland; Northern Ireland Statistics and Research Agency

of districts with the highest rate of net within-UK migration gains during the year before the 2001 Census. At the other extreme, London boroughs dominate the list of top ten areas losing population due to net within-UK migration.

Map 6.13 amplifies this picture. Particularly clear for the two highest categories is the coastal strip of districts around the South West peninsula and extending along the south coast. Here, net migration gains from the rest of the UK are equivalent to at least 0.5 per cent of Census populations. The fast-gaining areas also include much of East Anglia and Lincolnshire, together with areas that fringe the main urban centres of the Midlands and North of England.

There are also some familiar features among the two categories of areas losing population through migration exchanges with the rest of the UK in 2000 to 2001 (Map 6.13). These include much of Northern Ireland (especially the more rural west), northern Scotland (especially the Shetlands and Eilean Siar), the Glasgow area and south-west Scotland, several of the larger English cities (including Liverpool and Birmingham) and many of the older industrial towns. Rather less expected is the way in which London's overwhelming picture of net migration loss (all except the City of London, Kingston upon Thames, and Lambeth) extends out deep into the Home Counties and indeed south into East Sussex and west into Wiltshire. This must be due largely to the tightness of the housing market in this broad zone, especially around that time as the 'house price ripple' of the late 1990s economic boom moved further out from London. The high net-loss outliers in rural West Oxfordshire and North Yorkshire are likely due to movements of military personnel.

Geographical patterns of migration for selected types of people

As shown earlier, migration can be a very selective process, involving some types of people much more than others. Differences in the characteristics of those moving in and those moving out can have a significant impact on the population composition of individual places. Chapter 2 describes many of the geographical variations in population characteristics that arise from internal migration and other factors. This chapter describes in further detail the geographical patterns of internal migration relating to four selected characteristics.

Age

One of the most important features of migration patterns by age is the difference by settlement size. Migration data from the 2001 Census support the assertion that young adults seek out the 'bright city lights' and show that families with children and older people are more likely to move out of large cities than to move to them. This is demonstrated in Table 6.14, which shows net migration by age group for seven categories of settlement ranging from London to 'other' (comprising urban areas of under 10,000 residents and rural areas).

London and the next three size categories down (places of 100,000 or more residents) recorded net losses of 0- to 15-year-olds and of all groups aged 30 and over, except for 75 and over, in the 100,000 to 250,000 category. By contrast, the three smallest size categories registered net gains of these ages, but net losses of young adults. Moreover, within these three size categories the severity of the losses increases regularly down the size hierarchy, both in terms of total

Table 6.14

Net within-UK migration in the year prior to the 2001 Census: by size of urban area and age group[1]

England

Population size of urban area	Age group							
	0–15	16–19	20–24	25–29	30–44	45–59	60–74	75 and over
Over 3 million[2]	**−24,846**	**−3,649**	27,956	4,458	**−30,608**	**−13,820**	**−10,227**	**−4,147**
750,000 to 3 million[3]	**−6,342**	10,290	961	**−3,971**	**−9,788**	**−5,625**	**−3,486**	**−1,947**
250,000 to 750,000	**−2,726**	19,003	3,582	**−837**	**−4,448**	**−1,915**	**−617**	**−1,060**
100,000 to 250,000	**−545**	7,489	551	469	**−2,790**	**−888**	**−450**	498
25,000 to 100,000	3,849	**−2,877**	723	2,738	4,564	1,369	2,816	2,044
10,000 to 25,000	5,765	**−8,382**	**−3,254**	1,273	5,933	2,820	3,937	3,122
Under 10,000[4]	22,745	**−21,612**	**−23,752**	**−1,744**	33,567	13,733	5,696	1,146

1 Bolding denotes net outflows.
2 This category refers to the Greater London conurbation.
3 This category refers to five conurbations: West Midlands, Greater Manchester, West Yorkshire, Tyneside and Merseyside.
4 This category includes rural areas.

Source: Data from 2001 Census Standard Tables – Office for National Statistics

Map **6.15**

Net within-UK migration of full-time students as a percentage of all residents aged 16 to 74: by unitary authority or local authority, 2001[1]

United Kingdom

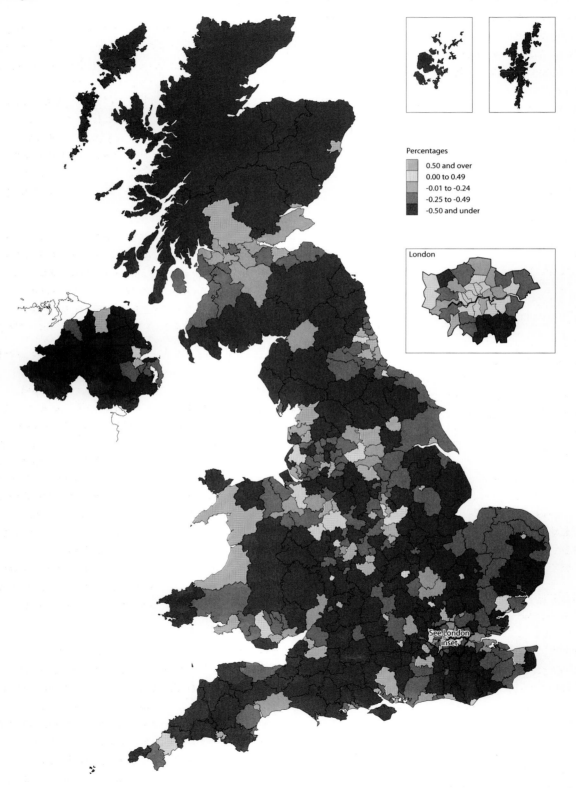

Percentages

0.50 and over
0.00 to 0.49
-0.01 to -0.24
-0.25 to -0.49
-0.50 and under

London

See London inset

1   Data refer to persons changing their address of usual residence between April 2000 and April 2001.

Source: 2001 Census – Office for National Statistics; General Register Office for Scotland; Northern Ireland Statistics and Research Agency

numbers and the width of age band affected – just 16 to 19 for urban areas of 25,000 to 100,000, 16 to 24 for those of 10,000 to 25,000 and 16 to 29 for those of under 10,000 residents.

For most of the largest types of place, it is only for the 16- to 19-year-olds that substantial net gains occurred. The exception is London, which experienced a small net loss of 16- to 19-year-olds in 2001 but gained very large numbers of people aged 20 to 24. London's net loss of 16- to 19-year-olds arises from more of its school leavers going to university elsewhere in the UK than there are places taken up in London by students from elsewhere. London's gain of 20- to 24-year-olds probably reflects the capital's great attraction to university graduates from all over the UK, including returning Londoners.

Student migration

As mentioned earlier, the 2001 Census was the first census in the UK that has enumerated students at their term-time address (rather than their home address as in previous censuses) and therefore includes the movements to and from places of higher education in its migration statistics. Only the moves to and at university can, however, be identified, as those leaving university were no longer students at the time of the census. Map 6.15 shows the net effect on local populations of full-time students migrating to their place of study or changing residence at their place of study. The category also includes secondary-level students aged 16 and over moving home with their families, though this group rarely engages in long-distance moves because of the likely disruption caused to preparation for exams.

Not surprisingly, the districts gaining students on balance are those containing places of higher education. Oxford and Cambridge led the way in 2001, with their net migration gains of full-time students from elsewhere in the UK being equivalent to 3.5 and 3.3 per cent respectively of their total populations aged 16 to 74.

The majority of districts around the UK are net suppliers of students. The largest proportionate losses of students in 2001 – besides the two small special cases of Eilean Siar (the Western Isles) and the Shetlands – were recorded by Dungannon (Northern Ireland), Hambleton (North Yorkshire) and Malvern Hills. All these lost at least 1.2 per cent of their 16- to 74-year-olds through the movement of people aged 16 and over and in full-time education.

In London (see inset on Map 6.15) there is a striking contrast between the inner and outer boroughs. Most of the latter generated large numbers leaving for university elsewhere but contained no university places, Kingston and Hillingdon being

the main exceptions. Inner London boroughs generated fewer university students and at the same time gained students moving out of university accommodation in central London at the end of their first year.

Ethnic origin

Maps 6.16 and 6.17 show the 2001 net migration balances for White and non-White people respectively. Both are presented in terms of percentages of all residents (White and non-White together), but the class intervals differ because of the much smaller migration balances for non-Whites in most districts. Because of this latter point, the picture for Whites shown in Map 6.16 is very similar to that for all people in Map 6.13. Probably the most notable difference is in London, where within-UK migration produced a net gain of Whites for Wandsworth and Southwark as well as an even stronger gain for Lambeth than for all persons.

For non-White migration exchanges with the rest of the UK (Map 6.17), however, the picture is substantially different from those in Maps 6.13 and 6.16. This is especially the case for London, within which migration has produced a clear decentralisation, with the majority of inner boroughs registering a net loss and the majority of outer ones a net gain.

Indeed, of all UK districts, it was many in London that saw the largest absolute increases and decreases in non-White population due to within-UK migration. Hillingdon and Redbridge both gained at least 1,500 non-White residents in this way, while Brent, Lambeth and Ealing each lost over 1,700. In percentage terms, the national extremes are provided by the borough of Barking and Dagenham, with its net migration gain of non-Whites boosting its total population by 0.78 per cent, and by Haringey, which saw a 0.78 per cent net loss of total population because of its non-White migration. Clearly, London's non-White population – traditionally concentrated in its inner parts, with a few exceptions such as Brent – is following the well-trodden path of inner London residents in moving to the outer boroughs and adjacent suburbs as they prosper and their family requirements call for different housing.[11]

Beyond London's boundaries, evidence of similar decentralisation is found for a number of other cities. In particular, Birmingham, Cambridge, Glasgow and Newcastle recorded net migration losses of non-Whites, while adjacent districts saw net gains. In some other cases, including Reading, Bristol and Leicester, there were gains of non-Whites, but these represented a smaller proportionate increase in total population than was the case for adjacent districts, signifying a degree of relative decentralisation.

Map **6.16**

Net within-UK migration of White people as a percentage of all residents: by unitary authority or local authority, 2001[1]

United Kingdom

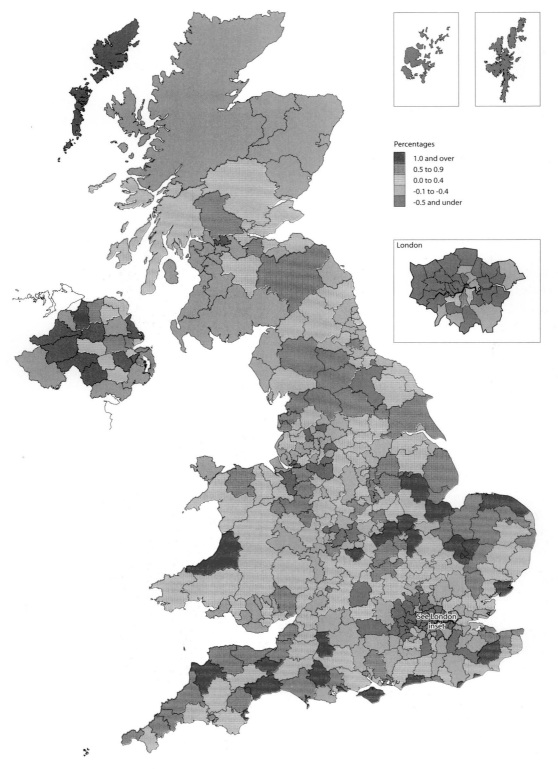

Percentages

- 1.0 and over
- 0.5 to 0.9
- 0.0 to 0.4
- -0.1 to -0.4
- -0.5 and under

London

See London inset

1 Data refer to persons changing their address of usual residence between April 2000 and April 2001.

Source: 2001 Census – Office for National Statistics; General Register Office for Scotland; Northern Ireland Statistics and Research Agency

Map **6.17**

Net within-UK migration of non-White people as a percentage of all residents: by unitary authority or local authority, 2001[1]

United Kingdom

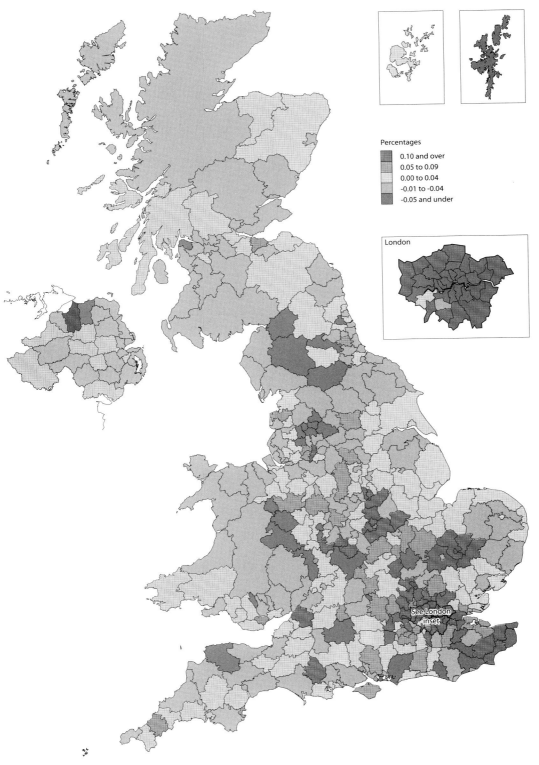

Percentages

- 0.10 and over
- 0.05 to 0.09
- 0.00 to 0.04
- -0.01 to -0.04
- -0.05 and under

London

See London inset

1   *Data refer to persons changing their address of usual residence between April 2000 and April 2001.*

Source: 2001 Census – Office for National Statistics; General Register Office for Scotland; Northern Ireland Statistics and Research Agency

Across the UK as a whole, 244 of the 434 districts registered an increase in non-White population due to within-UK migration. The overall picture of net gains and losses thus presents a considerably more complex picture than the image of 'White flight' from certain areas that is frequently conveyed by the media. On the one hand, it is clear that many of these 244 districts also had net inflows of White people (compare Map 6.17 with Map 6.16). On the other, as just shown, a fair number of districts – but especially London boroughs – that lost White population through their migration exchanges with the rest of the UK during this one-year period were also losing non-Whites through this process. This, however, does not necessarily mean that these latter districts were seeing an overall decline in their non-White populations, as in-migration from overseas and natural increase (the surplus of births over deaths) may have more than offset the effect of their within-UK migration losses.

Higher managerial and professional occupations

The attraction and retention of more skilled elements of the workforce is seen as vital to regional growth and urban regeneration.[12] Figure 6.18 reveals a very unbalanced regional situation, with only the four most southerly regions of Great Britain making net gains through within-UK migration of people who were classified in higher managerial and professional occupations in the 2001 Census. The length of the columns is in proportion to the impact of this net migration on the total population aged 16 to 74. It can be seen that London performed most strongly on this indicator, with the other three

most southern regions also recording considerable net gains. These four regions are markedly different from the rest of Great Britain. At the other extreme, the North East stands out with an especially high net loss of this group relative to its population size, followed by Yorkshire and the Humber.

Map 6.19 focuses on the inflow element of the migration of this group at district level across Great Britain and expresses it as a proportion of the total inflow of people classified by occupation. The strong attraction for this group of an arc extending from central and west London out through south central England and round to Cambridge is clearly apparent from the map. In addition, this group features strongly in the inflows to a number of other cities and/or their more salubrious suburbs across the rest of the country. The highest proportions of higher managerial and professional in-migrants were for the City of London, Cambridge, Westminster, Camden and Tower Hamlets, all with at least 33 per cent of classified in-migrants being in this group. At the other extreme, besides the special case of the Isles of Scilly, it is Easington (Co Durham), East Lindsey (Lincolnshire), Blackpool (Lancashire) and West Somerset that recorded the smallest proportion of in-migrants in higher managerial and professional occupations.

Conclusion

Both census and NHS-derived data have shown that the year leading up to the 2001 Census was characterised by relatively high levels of residential mobility in comparison with that at the time of the two previous censuses.

Among the main findings from this mainly census-based review is that some types of people change address much more often than others. This is especially so for young adults, including people moving to, at and from university (treated as migrants by the 2001 Census unlike previously). Second, some areas have a much higher population turnover than others. Third, changing address is very largely a short-distance process. Only students moving to and from higher education institutions and members of the armed forces are strongly associated with long-distance moves. Other groups moving above-average distances include people who at the census (that is, after their move) were married couples with no children at home, outright owner-occupiers, the retired, the unemployed and higher professionals. These are all patterns that have been observed in previous work, allowing confidence in the quality of the 2001 Census migration data, as well as suggesting that there have been no major changes in individual people's migration behaviour in recent years.

The net impact of this within-UK migration on the distribution of the population between areas has varied rather more over time. In particular, the 'North-South drift' has not only

Figure **6.18**

Net within-UK migration of people in higher managerial and professional occupations: by Government Office Region and country of Great Britain, 2001[1]

Per 10,000 people aged 16–74

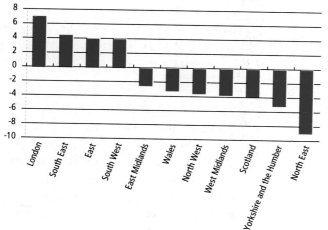

1   *Data refer to moves during the 12 months prior to the 2001 Census.*

Source: Data from 2001 Census Special Tabulation – Office for National Statistics; General Register Office for Scotland

Map **6.19**

Higher managerial and professional in-migrants as a percentage of all in-migrants aged 16 to 74 from the rest of the UK: by unitary authority or local authority, 2001[1]

Great Britain

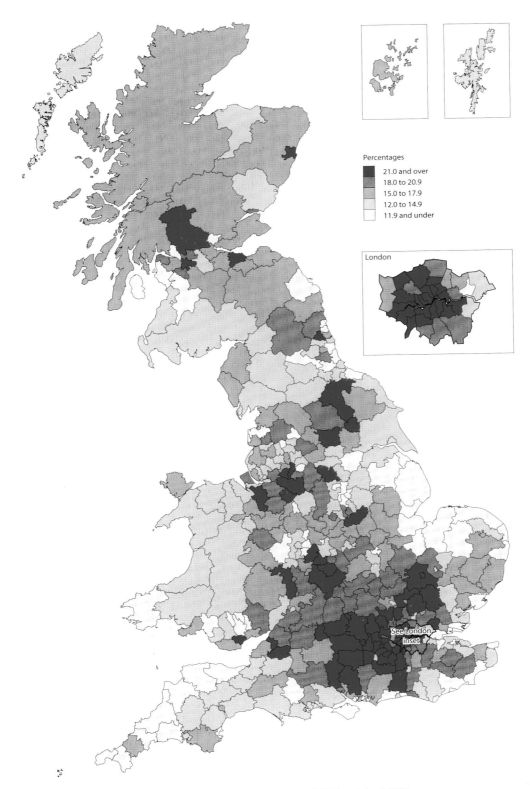

Percentages

- 21.0 and over
- 18.0 to 20.9
- 15.0 to 17.9
- 12.0 to 14.9
- 11.9 and under

London

See London inset

1   Data refer to persons changing their address of usual residence between April 2000 and April 2001.

Source: 2001 Census – Office for National Statistics; General Register Office for Scotland

fluctuated considerably in volume in response to economic cycles and other factors, but has also been running at a considerably lower average rate since the end of the 1980s. Indeed, the unusually large scale of net migration from South to North recorded in the first three years of the new century is unprecedented as far as can be judged from available records.

On the other hand, the pace of the urban-rural shift of population resulting from within-UK migration – while fluctuating somewhat over time – appears to be continuing at roughly the same overall rate. Though there are signs that the net migration losses of the large northern conurbations are diminishing, London's net loss has increased in recent years, resulting in substantial population gains for most other types of place. While traditional resort and retirement areas are the most affected, shire-county cities, smaller towns and more rural areas also gained population from the metropolitan losses in the year leading up to the 2001 Census. Moreover, this exodus from the cities included members of ethnic minority groups as well as White people.

The widespread nature of this dispersal process is underlined in the 2001 Census results by the great extent of the more heavily populated areas that were losing more people to the rest of the UK than they were gaining from them. Not just the main conurbations but also extensive areas around them are shaded grey in Map 6.13, signifying net loss of migrants. This is most marked for the large zone of net loss centred on London but stretches out a great distance, especially to the south and west. Only part of this can be attributed to the stage reached in the national economic cycle in 2001, when the house-price gradient between South and North was at its steepest. It would also seem that the growth of population pressures in south-eastern England arising from higher levels of both natural increase and net in-migration from overseas has led to a more permanent reduction in North-to-South migration.

Notes and references

1. For annual updates of internal migration for England and Wales, see *Population Trends*. For example: ONS (2005) Report: Internal migration estimates for local and unitary authorities in England and Wales, health authorities in England and former health authorities in Wales, year to mid-2004. *Population Trends* **121**, 90–103. Migration in Scotland is described in *Scotland's Population 2004: The Registrar General's Annual Review of Demographic Trends* (2005) and *Scotland's Census 2001 – Statistics on Migration*, Occasional Paper 15 (2005), both General Register Office for Scotland. A study of earlier patterns and trends in migration can be found in Tony Champion (1996) Population review; Migration to, from and within the United Kingdom. *Population Trends* **83**, 5–16.

2. Fielding A (1993) Migration and the metropolis: an empirical study of inter-regional migration to and from South East England. *Progress in Planning* **39**, 70–166. Ford T and Champion T (2000) Who moves into, out of and within London? An analysis based on the 1991 Census 2% Sample of Anonymised Records' *Area* **32**, 259–270.

3. Stillwell J C H (1994) Monitoring intercensal migration in the United Kingdom. *Environment and Planning A* **26**, 1711–1730.

4. Owen D W and Green A E (1992) Migration patterns and trends, in Champion T and Fielding T (eds), *Migration Processes and Patterns Volume 1 Research Progress and Prospects*, Belhaven Press: London.

5. Warnes T (1992) Migration and the life course, in Champion T and Fielding T (eds), *Migration Processes and Patterns Volume 1 Research Progress and Prospects*, Belhaven Press: London. Grundy E (1992) The household dimension in migration research, in Champion T and Fielding T (eds), *Migration Processes and Patterns Volume 1 Research Progress and Prospects*, Belhaven Press: London.

6. Stillwell J, Rees P and Boden P (1992) Internal migration trends: an overview, in Stillwell J, Rees P and Boden P (eds), *Migration Processes and Patterns Volume 2 Population Redistribution in the United Kingdom*, Belhaven Press: London.

7. Flowerdew R, Al Hamad A and Hayes L (1999) The residential mobility of divorced people, in Macrae S (ed), *Changing Britain: Families and Households in the 1990s*, Oxford University Press: Oxford.

8. Rees P H (1992) Elderly migration and population redistribution in the United Kingdom, in Rogers A (ed), *Elderly Migration and Population Redistribution* Belhaven: London.

9. Boyle P J (1995) Public housing as a barrier to long-distance migration. *International Journal of Population Geography* **1**, 147–164.

10. Champion T (2000) Flight from the cities? In Bate A, Best R and Holmans A (eds), *On the Move: The Housing Consequences of Migration*, York Publishing Service: York. Champion T and Atkins D (2000) Migration between metropolitan and non-metropolitan areas in England and Wales, in Creeser R and Gleave S (eds), *Migration within England and Wales using the ONS Longitudinal Study*. ONS Series LS No. 9, TSO: London.

11. See also Simpson L (2004) Statistics of racial segregation: measures, evidence and policy. *Urban Studies* **41**, 661–681. Champion T (1996) Internal migration and ethnicity, in Ratcliffe P (ed), *Ethnicity in the 1991 Census Volume 3*, HMSO: London.

12. For more detail on the social composition of migration, see
Champion T and Fisher T (2003) The social selectivity of migration
flows affecting Britain's larger conurbations: an analysis of the
1991 Census Regional Migration Tables. *Scottish Geographical
Journal* **119**, 229–246. Champion T and Fisher T (2004) Migration,
residential preferences and the changing environment of cities, in
Boddy M and Parkinson M (eds), *City Matters*, Policy Press: Bristol.

International migration

Giles Horsfield

Chapter 7

Introduction

International migration statistics tell us about people who have left one country to go and live in another. This chapter deals with people who migrate to the UK and people who migrate from the UK to live in another country.

An international migrant is defined in this chapter as someone who changes their country of usual residence for a period of at least a year so that the country of destination effectively becomes the country of usual residence. This is the internationally agreed, UN-recommended definition of a long-term migrant,[1] and is also the standard definition of an international migrant used by the Office for National Statistics (ONS). Under this definition, migration does not necessarily mean a permanent move from one country to another: a person may migrate between countries several times over a number of years. When someone moves from one country to another for a period of less than one year, this is not considered to be migration for the purposes of this chapter.

We need to know about the UK's international migration for a number of reasons. One of the most important is that the numbers of people entering and leaving the country are needed in order to work out the total number of people living in the country, and their characteristics. This population information is required by central government to allocate resources to local and health authorities so that they can provide efficient services such as schools and healthcare.

Migration is also interesting in its own right. Historically, it has been important for spreading people and technologies across the world. Levels of international migration have increased over recent years, both for the UK and many other countries. For example, substantial increases in migration to the USA were observed during the 1990s;[2] in Europe, the picture has been more varied over the last ten years,[3] with some countries experiencing increases in net inflows of migrants (excluding citizens of the receiving country) and others experiencing decreases. In many cases, cheaper travel and better work and other opportunities have promoted higher levels of migration.

This chapter examines the following aspects of the UK's international migration over recent years:

- the total numbers of people who migrate

- the characteristics of these people in terms of their age, gender and their usual occupation

- where migrants arrive from, and where they go to

- why people migrate

- how long people go to live in a different country for

- where in the UK migrants go to live.

All data presented in this chapter have been rounded.

Trends in international migration

Trends in the UK's international migration have changed substantially over the last 30 years. Both migration into the country and out of the country have increased. This pattern is reflected in many countries, including most of those in the European Union (EU).

Figure 7.1 shows the UK's migration over the years 1975 to 2004. The chart shows migration into and out of the UK. Net migration is the difference between in-migration and out-migration. Net migration can be seen on the chart as the gap between in-migration and out-migration. When more migrants enter the UK than leave, there is a net inflow; when more migrants leave than enter, there is a net outflow.

Most of the information about migration between the UK and other countries comes from the International Passenger Survey (IPS).[4] However, the IPS does not cover all types of migrant, such as most asylum seekers and people who initially intend to stay in or leave the UK for less than a year but subsequently extend that period. For each year from 1991 adjustments have been made to account for migrants not covered in the IPS, to produce estimates of Total International Migration (TIM). For earlier years the IPS alone has been used. Estimated migration is shown here using both old and new methodologies for 1991, which is why there is a discontinuity on the graph at this point.

Figure **7.1**

International migration flows, 1975 to 2004

United Kingdom

Thousands

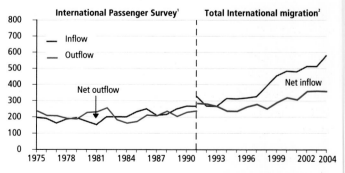

1 *International Passenger Survey data alone were used to estimate international migration prior to 1991.*
2 *Total International Migration data are produced using the latest methodology for estimating international migration and include adjustments for migrants who were not previously counted.*

Source: International migration, Office for National Statistics

The effect of introducing the new methodology was, generally, to increase estimated inflows and outflows of migration. This is because the new methodology introduced adjustments to account for migrants who were not previously counted. The method used to estimate international migration is explained in more detail in the appendix.

The rest of this section considers migration over the years 1975 to 2004, broken down into three main periods, in which different patterns can be observed.

Net out-migration: 1975 to 1982

There was a net outflow of migrants in all but one of the years from 1975 to 1982. Inflows fluctuated between 153,000 and 201,000 per year, while outflows fluctuated between 189,000 and 257,000. Over the eight years, 1.8 million migrants left the UK and 1.5 million entered, giving a net outflow of 300,000 people.

Similar sized inflows and outflows: 1983 to 1993

Numbers of in-migrants and out-migrants were broadly similar over this period. Both inflows and outflows fluctuated, and both experienced some growth overall: in-migration increased from 202,000 in 1983 to 265,000 in 1993, while out-migration increased from 184,000 in 1984 to 266,000 in 1993.

There were net inflows of international migrants in most years from 1983 to 1993. However, there were small net outflows in 1988 (21,000), 1992 (14,000) and 1993 (1,000). 1993 was the last year for which a net outflow of migrants was recorded. Over the 11 years from 1983 to 1993, 2.7 million migrants entered the UK and more than 2.4 million left, giving a net inflow of 240,000.

Net in-migration: 1994 to 2004

Over the 11 years from 1994 to 2004, 4.7 million people entered the country as migrants and 3.3 million left, giving a net inflow of more than 1.4 million people.

Both inflows and outflows of international migrants were higher than during the previous two decades. However, some of this increase can be attributed to the change in methodology that was introduced for the years from 1991 onwards. Prior to this, only IPS data were used.

Both in-migration and out-migration increased over the decade. Migration into the UK increased from 314,000 in 1994 to 582,000 in 2004; the inflow in 2004 was the highest since the present method of estimation began in 1991. Out-migration also increased over the period, but to a much lesser extent, from 238,000 in 1994 to 360,000 in 2004; the outflows were similar in 2004 to each of the two preceding years.

In-migration increased more than out-migration between 1994 and 2004 and, as a result, net migration into the country increased. The UK experienced a net inflow for each year from 1994 onwards. Net in-migration was 77,000 in 1994, and increased in the late 1990s to 172,000 in 2001. There was a slight fall to around 150,000 in 2002 and 2003, before a further increase to 223,000 in 2004.

Trends in migration inflows and outflows can change quite quickly. The relatively large net inflows into the UK observed during the period between 1994 and 2004 had not been seen in the previous two decades.

The most recently available data on the UK's international migration are the summary figures for 2004,[5] which show inflows and outflows by broad citizenship. However, 2003 is the most recent year for which full detailed information is available. More information about the publication of international migration data is given in the appendix. Later sections of this chapter will consider in more detail the people who migrated to and from the UK over the ten years between 1994 and 2003 and where they came from and went to.

The contribution of migration to population change

The recent past

Net migration is one of the three main components of population change; the other components are births and deaths.

As net international migration to the UK has increased, migration has become much more important in determining the UK's population change. In the early 1990s the contribution of migration to population change varied as net migration fluctuated on a year-by-year basis. In none of these years did migration contribute more than half of the country's population increase, and generally the figure was much lower than this.

In the year to mid-2004 international migration contributed approximately two-thirds of the UK's annual population increase; this is slightly less than each of the previous five years. More information on migration and population change is presented in Table 1.9 in Chapter 1.

The future

Population projections,[6] based on projecting current fertility, mortality and net migration trends, suggest that migration will remain an important element of UK population change in the future.

The number of births each year is projected to change little in the years to 2031. This is because the average numbers of children born per woman is assumed to remain roughly the same, and the numbers of women of key childbearing ages are projected also to remain roughly the same

The number of deaths each year is expected to start rising in about ten years' time, reflecting the ageing of the large generation born in the years of high fertility following the Second World War. These changes mean that, in the longer-term, population growth due to the difference between births and deaths (natural change) will decline. In the years up to 2020, natural change is projected to add between 120,000 and 145,000 people to the population each year, but this figure is projected to fall in subsequent years to only 40,000 by 2031. By contrast, international migration is assumed to remain at similar levels to those experienced in the last ten years, adding 145,000 people to the population each year in the long-term. Higher net inflows are assumed for each of the first three years of the projection.

If the assumed net international migration inflow of 145,000 people each year were to be realised, migration would be the major determinant of population change in the future.

However, future levels of international migration are particularly difficult to predict and the assumptions used to produce population projections may not be borne out. This is increasingly so, the further into the future a projection goes.

Variant projections use different assumptions to those used in the principal projection, which allow different scenarios to be explored. The variant population projection with zero net international migration is a special-case scenario. It is extremely unlikely to occur, but can be compared with the principal projection to show the contribution of international migration to the future population, under the assumptions of the principal projection. In Table 7.2 the UK's population projections, and projected components of change, are shown for both the principal projection and zero-net-migration variant for the years 2004 to 2031.

If net migration into the UK were to average 145,000 per year in the long-term, following three years of higher inflows, as assumed in the principal projection, the net number of migrants entering the UK over the years 2004 to 2031 would be 4.1 million. However, migration also increases the numbers of women of childbearing age in the country, and hence the numbers of births. This effect is made significant, even in the

Table 7.2

Projected population change by scenario, 2004 to 2031[1]

United Kingdom, principal projection

Thousands

	2004–2009	2009–2014	2014–2019	2019–2024	2024–2031	2004–2031
Population at start	59,835	61,351	62,731	64,166	65,519	59,835
Births	3,531	3,520	3,595	3,613	4,960	19,219
Deaths	2,926	2,865	2,884	2,985	4,481	16,141
Natural change	+606	+655	+711	+628	+479	16,141
Net migration	+910	+725	+725	+725	+1,015	+4,100
Total change	+1,516	+1,380	+1,436	+1,353	+1,494	+7,178
Population at end	61,351	62,731	64,166	65,519	67,013	67,013

United Kingdom, zero-net-migration scenario

Thousands

	2004–2009	2009–2014	2014–2019	2019–2024	2024–2031	2004–2031
Population at start	59,835	60,350	60,765	61,107	61,287	59,835
Births	3,438	3,274	3,217	3,153	4,237	17,320
Deaths	2,923	2,859	2,875	2,974	4,462	16,093
Natural change	+515	+415	+342	+179	-225	16,093
Net migration	0	0	0	0	0	0
Total change	+515	+415	+342	+179	-225	+1,226
Population at end	60,350	60,765	61,107	61,287	61,061	61,061

1 Data refer to mid-year (30th June).

Source: 2004-based population projections, Government Actuary's Department

short-term, by the fact that migrants tend to belong to younger age groups. There's also a slight increase in the projected number of deaths, because of the overall increase in the number of people in the population.

Under the principal projection, with assumed net in-migration of 145,000 per year, the UK's projected population increases by 7.2 million between 2004 and 2031, to 67 million; under the zero-net-migration variant projection, the population increases by 1.2 million over the same period. Both use the same underlying assumptions about fertility and mortality.

Comparing the figures from these two projections allows the 7.2 million population change in the principal projection to be divided up as follows:

1. 4.1 million assumed net in-migration

2. approximately 3.1 million natural change, of which:

   • approximately 1.2 million would take place in the absence of migration

   • approximately 1.9 million would be additional, as a result of the net effect of migration on births and deaths.

This analysis highlights the contribution of international migration to projected future population change under the assumptions of migration, fertility and mortality used to produce the principal projection

Migration is driven by many different factors, and the overall international migration totals hide complex patterns in terms of the characteristics of migrants. These characteristics are investigated in the following sections.

The origins and destinations of the UK's migrants

The origins of people migrating to the UK, and the destinations of out-migrants, are considered here: first for all migrants (Table 7.3), and then separately for British citizens and citizens of other countries.

Over the decade to 2003, there was consistently high migration between the UK and the rest of the EU as it was constituted before May 2004, when the accession countries joined (see glossary). The annual inflows from EU countries fluctuated between 85,000 and 110,000. However, migration from the UK to the EU increased, from 75,000 in 1994 to a record high of 125,000 in 2002 and to a similar level of 122,000 in 2003. The EU, along with the USA and Australia, was among the few areas that received a net outflow of migrants from the UK during this period.

Flows between the USA and the UK remained relatively constant over the decade. Inflows fluctuated between 23,000 and 37,000, while outflows fluctuated between 26,000 and 37,000. This resulted in a net outflow of migrants to the USA for six of the last ten years.

Migration to the UK from the Middle East increased substantially over the decade, from 12,000 in 1994 to 27,000 in 2003. Over the same period, outflows to the Middle East changed little, fluctuating between 7,000 and 15,000. These patterns resulted in a net outflow of 1,000 in 1994 changing to a net inflow of 20,000 in 2003 and each of the two preceding years.

Much of the UK's migration is to and from the Commonwealth. This can be divided into the Old and New Commonwealth:

Table 7.3

International migration by country of last or next residence, 1994 to 1998 and 1999 to 2003[1]

United Kingdom

Thousands

	1994–98			1999–2003		
	Inflow	Outflow	Net	Inflow	Outflow	Net
European Union	491	421	+70	471	546	75
Remainder of Europe	125	84	+42	225	124	+101
United States of America	148	137	+10	134	159	25
Remainder of America	22	18	+4	41	24	+17
Middle East	67	54	+14	133	53	+80
Old Commonwealth	268	297	29	461	452	+9
New Commonwealth	334	143	+192	499	129	+370
Other Foreign	205	115	+90	478	154	+325

1 The figures in this table include all categories of migrants and therefore represent Total International Migration.

Source: International migration, Office for National Statistics

Old Commonwealth is defined as Australia, Canada, New Zealand and South Africa; New Commonwealth is defined as all other Commonwealth countries (see glossary). In the years 1994 to 1998, there was an overall net outflow to Old Commonwealth countries, but this changed to a net inflow in the second half of the decade. Of the Old Commonwealth countries, Australia contributed the most to UK inflows. However, the large inflow from Australia was often exceeded by a larger outflow from the UK, with Australia receiving a net outflow of migrants from the UK for all but two years between 1994 and 2003.

In-migration from the New Commonwealth increased over the decade from 1994 to 2003. Inflows from Bangladesh, India, Sri Lanka and African New Commonwealth countries contributed to this increase. Nigeria, Kenya, Ghana and Zimbabwe accounted for the majority of in-migrants to the UK from New Commonwealth countries in Africa. In particular, inflows from Zimbabwe more than tripled between 1994 and 2003. Outflows to these countries remained relatively stable over the decade. These trends led to a substantial increase in the net inflow from New Commonwealth countries, from 40,000 in 1994 to around 84,000 in 2003.

Inflows from countries not included in any of the other categories also increased, with a net inflow of 90,000 in the years 1994 to 1998 increasing to a net inflow of 325,000 from 1999 to 2003. These inflows came from a wide range of countries, but the Asian countries China, the Philippines and Hong Kong were among the most prominent.

The citizenship of migrants

The most recently available information gives TIM by broad citizenship for 2004, so these figures are included in this section.

The migration of British citizens: totals

As already noted in the introduction, a migrant is defined as someone who changes their country of residence for at least a year. This means that people who enter the country, and later leave, are counted as both in-migrants and out-migrants, as long as they have lived in the UK for at least one year. The same is true of people leaving the country: if they live in another country for one year or more, they are counted as out-migrants, even if they later return to the UK. This means we can talk about British citizens migrating to the UK, as well as away from the UK. In most cases, British citizens migrating to the UK are people returning to the country after living abroad for a year or more. However, some may never before have lived in the UK, for example, those British citizens who were born in another country and arrive to live in the UK for the first time.

Table 7.4 shows that over the years from 1994 to 2004, the migration of British citizens to the UK has been relatively stable, fluctuating around 100,000 per year throughout the period.

Table 7.4

International migration by citizenship, 1994 to 2004[1]

United Kingdom			Thousands[2]
	British	Non-British	Total
Inflow			
1994	108	206	314
1995	84	228	312
1996	94	224	318
1997	89	237	326
1998	103	287	390
1999	116	337	454
2000	104	379	483
2001	106	373	480
2002	95	418	513
2003	106	407	513
2004	88	494	582
Outflow			
1994	125	113	238
1995	136	101	237
1996	156	108	264
1997	149	131	279
1998	126	126	252
1999	139	152	291
2000	161	160	321
2001	159	149	308
2002	186	174	359
2003	191	171	362
2004	208	152	360
Balance			
1994	−17	94	77
1995	−52	127	75
1996	−62	116	54
1997	−60	107	47
1998	−23	162	139
1999	−23	186	163
2000	−57	220	163
2001	−53	225	172
2002	−91	245	153
2003	−85	236	151
2004	−120	342	223

1 The figures in this table include all categories of migrants and therefore represent Total International Migration.
2 Figures may not add exactly due to rounding.

Source: International migration, Office for National Statistics

Migration of British citizens out of the UK also fluctuated between 1994 and 2001, but increased in the last three years, rising from 125,000 in 1994 to 208,000 in 2004. This most recent figure is the highest recorded since the current method of estimation was introduced.

These figures show that, for each of these years, there has been a net outflow of British citizens from the UK to other countries. The highest net outflow of British citizens during this period was 120,000 in 2004, which was a substantial rise from 85,000 in 2003.

The migration of British citizens: where they come from and go to

Data from the IPS can be used to investigate where British citizens have migrated to and from. The IPS alone does not capture all migrants (see appendix), but it is nonetheless a valuable source for these kinds of detailed analyses, for which estimates of TIM are not available.

As shown in Figure 7.5, 38 per cent (40,000) of British citizens migrating to the UK in 2003 had previously been living in other EU countries. Of British citizens migrating out of the UK, 42 per cent (71,000) were destined for EU countries.

After Europe, Australia was the most common country from which British citizens migrated to the UK, accounting for 15 per

Figure **7.5**

International migration of British citizens: by country of last or next residence, 2003[1]

United Kingdom

Thousands

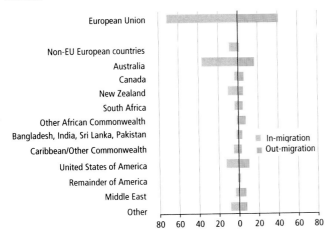

1 *The figures in this chart are from the International Passenger Survey only.*

Source: International migration, Office for National Statistics

cent of the total (16,000). Overall, 38 per cent of the incoming British citizens had been living in Commonwealth countries, while 37 per cent of outgoing British citizens were destined for Commonwealth countries. In addition to Australia, Commonwealth countries that were frequent destinations for outgoing British citizens included Canada, New Zealand and South Africa.

Nine per cent of the inflows of British citizens came from the USA, and 7 per cent of outflows were destined for the USA.

The migration of citizens of other countries

Less coverage is given here to the citizenship of non-British migrants than to British migrants. Most of the UK's in-migrants are not British and, for such people, country of citizenship is often the same as country of last or next residence, which has already been covered in this chapter.

In-migration to the UK by non-British citizens increased substantially, from 206,000 in 1994 to 494,000 in 2004. Out-migration by non-British citizens also increased over the same time, but by much less, from 113,000 in 1994 to 152,000 in 2004. As a result, net inflows of non-British citizens increased from 94,000 in 1994 to 342,000 in 2004. Much of this increase over this period is attributable to people who are citizens of countries outside both the Commonwealth and the EU. These people are citizens of a wide range of countries, with non-EU European countries and the USA among the most prominent.

The composition of the EU changed in May 2004 when the accession countries joined. Citizens of these countries were first included as EU citizens in the international migration figures for 2004. The number of non-British EU citizens who migrated to the UK increased from 64,000 in 2003 to 117,000 in 2004. The net inflow of non-British EU citizens increased from 14,000 in 2003 to 74,000 in 2004, of which an estimated 48,000 was attributable to citizens of the accession countries.

How long do migrants intend to stay or leave for?

On average, people leaving the UK as migrants intend to stay in their destination country for longer than in-migrants intend to stay in the UK.

In 2003, 42 per cent of migrants entering the UK intended to stay for between one and two years (an increase from 30 per cent in 1994), while 31 per cent intended to stay for more than four years (a decrease from 43 per cent in 1994). It is interesting to compare these figures on the intended length of stay of migrants on arrival to the UK with the findings of Rendall and Ball.[7] They estimated that, of overseas-born migrants arriving in the UK in the 1980s and 1990s, 29 per cent departed again within two years and 54 per cent stayed for five years or longer.

Among people migrating out of the UK, two-thirds intended to live outside the country for at least four years in 2003, while only 17 per cent intended to return in less than two years.

Over the ten years to 2003, there was a substantial increase in the number of migrants intending to stay in the UK for relatively short periods of time, as shown in Figure 7.6. Those intending to stay between one and two years rose from 95,000 in 1994 to 215,000 in 2003, while the numbers of those intending to stay for between two and four years increased from 53,000 to 103,000. There was a much smaller increase in the numbers of migrants who intended to stay in the country for more than four years: from 136,000 in 1994 to 160,000 in 2003.

The trend in intended length of stay for migrants leaving the country over the 10 years to 2003 was different from the trend for people entering. The numbers of people intending to leave for more than four years increased by 86 per cent, from 132,000 in 1994 to 245,000 in 2003. However, the numbers who intended to leave for relatively short periods of time – less than four years – remained fairly constant at around 100,000 each year.

Where do in-migrants go to live in the UK?

The most detailed source of information about where in the UK migrants go to live is the 2001 Census.[8] Unless stated otherwise, the data in this section come from the census. Migration estimates are derived from the question that asked people where they were living one year prior to Census day (29 April 2001). The Census can provide this information at much finer geographic levels than those published in ONS's annual migration estimates. However, the census can only provide data on in-migrants. The appendix provides more information about migration estimates derived from the Census.

A large majority of migrants arriving in the UK in the year prior to the 2001 Census went to live in England: nearly 90 per cent of the total. Seven per cent were destined for Scotland, and around 2 per cent each for Wales and Northern Ireland. Overall, the Census showed that 0.7 per cent of the UK's population had migrated into the country within the previous year.

London

London was the most common destination in the UK for international migrants: nearly 30 per cent of migrants arriving in the year preceding April 2001 were living in the capital at the time of the Census. This was much higher than for any other area. The next most common destination was the South East of England, where 18 per cent of the migrants who entered the country in the previous year were living. Each of the other Government Office Regions of England received less than 10 per cent of the total migrants entering the country.

Figure **7.6**

International migration: by intended length of stay, 1994 to 2003[1]

United Kingdom

Thousands

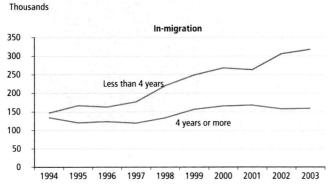
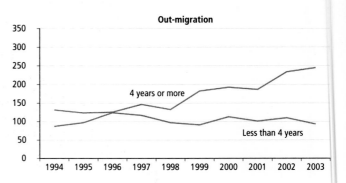

1 *The figures in this chart include all categories of migrants and therefore represent Total International Migration.*

Source: International migration, Office for National Statistics

Map **7.7**

People living outside the UK 12 months before Census day as a percentage of all residents,[1] by local or unitary authority, 2001

United Kingdom

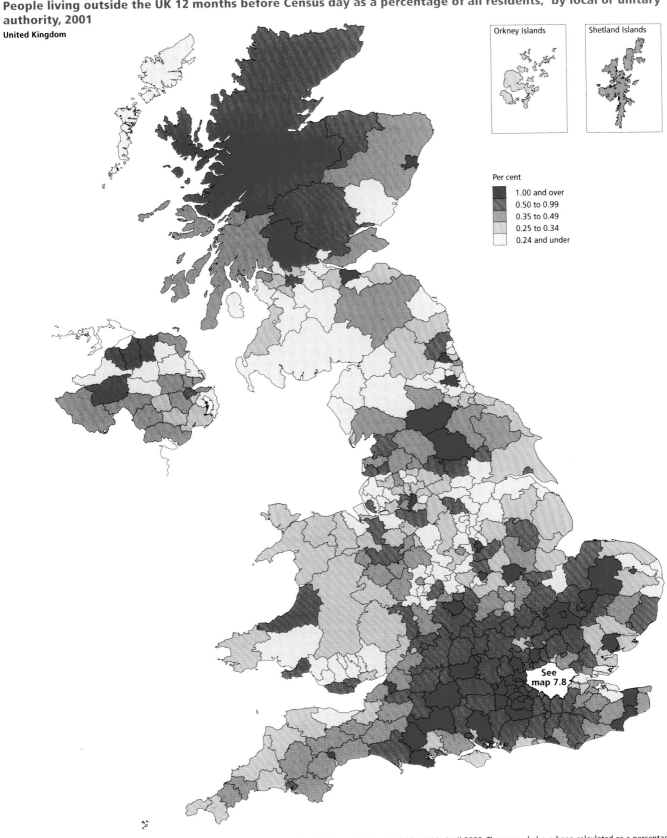

Orkney Islands

Shetland Islands

Per cent

- 1.00 and over
- 0.50 to 0.99
- 0.35 to 0.49
- 0.25 to 0.34
- 0.24 and under

See map 7.8

1 The data refer to UK residents in April 2001 who stated in the Census that they had been resident outside the UK in April 2000. These people have been calculated as a percentage of the total population of each area, using population numbers obtained from the Census.

Source: 2001 Census – Office for National Statistics, General Register Office for Scotland and Northern Ireland Statistics and Research Agency

Map **7.8**

People living outside the UK 12 months before Census day as a percentage of all residents,[1] by London borough, 2001

Greater London

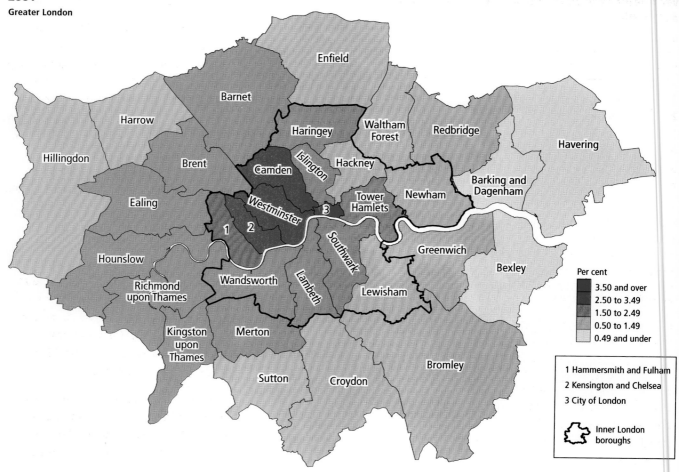

1 The data refer to UK residents in April 2001 who stated in the Census that they had been resident outside the UK in April 2000. These people have been calculated as a percentage of the total population of each area, using population numbers obtained from the Census.

Source: 2001 Census – Office for National Statistics

While London is the region that attracts the most international migrants, the numbers vary widely among the city's boroughs. The City of Westminster attracted 10,000 international migrants who entered the UK in the year before the census: more went to live in Westminster than any other local authority in the UK. After Westminster, the London boroughs that received the most international migrants were Kensington and Chelsea (9,000) and Camden (7,000). As can be seen in Table 7.9, of the ten local authorities in the UK that received the most international migrants, eight were London boroughs.

Not all London boroughs were the destination for large numbers of international migrants: fewer than 1,000 moved into each of Bexley, Havering, Barking and Dagenham, and the City of London (although the last has a very small resident population).

The high levels of international migration to these areas are reflected in the proportions of their populations who migrated to the UK in the year prior to the 2001 Census, as can be seen in Map 7.8. Six per cent of the Census day populations both of Westminster and of Kensington and Chelsea were living outside the UK one year previously.

Other areas

Some Northern and Midland areas of England are important destination areas for international migrants. Although each region's overall share of the total UK in-migration is relatively modest (between 2 per cent and 7 per cent of the total), some of their cities attract many migrants. For example, 7,000 of Birmingham's residents in April 2001 had been living outside the UK one year previously, making the city the most common

Table **7.9**

Numbers of people who migrated to the UK in the year before the 2001 Census: the top ten local authorities

United Kingdom   Thousands

Rank	Local Authority	
1	Westminster	10
2	Kensington and Chelsea	9
3	Camden	8
4	Birmingham	7
5	Wandsworth	6
6	Ealing	6
7	Brent	6
8	Hammersmith and Fulham	6
9	Barnet	6
10	Manchester	5

Source: 2001 Census – Office for National Statistics; General Register Office for Scotland; Northern Ireland Statistics and Research Agency

destination in England outside London. Birmingham was followed by the local authorities of Manchester, Leeds and Oxford, each of which received 5,000 in-migrants.

The importance – in certain areas – of students from overseas to the international migration figures is illustrated by the high numbers of international migrants moving to Oxford, and the slightly fewer (4,000) who went to live in Cambridge. (The reasons people have for migrating to the UK are discussed in the next section). When the numbers of migrants moving in over the previous year is presented as a proportion of the total population, these two relatively small cities with large universities ranked among the highest in the UK: 4 per cent of the population of each had migrated to the UK in the year preceding the census. This figure was only surpassed by the London boroughs of Westminster, Kensington and Chelsea, and the small City of London.

In general, the local authorities with the most residents who lived outside the UK one year before April 2001 were urban. However, urban areas generally have large populations, and when the numbers of migrants are worked out as percentages of the total populations, these percentages are relatively low for areas outside London (Map 7.7). Less than 1.5 per cent of Manchester's population, and less than 1 per cent of the populations of Birmingham and Leeds, had been resident outside the UK one year before April 2001.

Conversely, there are local authorities in rural areas where relatively small numbers of migrants go to live, but because the populations are small, migrants make up relatively high

proportions of the populations. One example is Rutland, where the 2001 Census showed that, while fewer than 1,000 residents lived outside the UK one year before Census day, these people made up around 2 per cent of the population.

Relatively few international migrants arrived in Scotland and Northern Ireland. In Scotland, areas that attracted the most international migrants were the largest cities, with 8,000 going to Edinburgh and 5,000 to Glasgow. The more remote Scottish areas were the destination for particularly few international migrants, with fewer than 100 adding to the small populations of each of the Orkney Islands, the Shetland Islands and Eilean Siar (Western Isles). The most common destination for Northern Ireland's international migrants was Belfast, where 2,000 of the residents lived outside the UK one year before the Census.

Migration by ethnic group

The census also gives us information about the ethnicity of people who lived outside the UK one year previously. Overall, the 2001 Census showed that around 70 per cent of the people who migrated to the UK were White and 30 per cent belonged to non-White ethnic groups. This was slightly different from the 1991 Census, which showed that 75 per cent of in-migrants to Great Britain were White.[9]

The West Midlands was the English region with the highest proportion of its in-migrants from non-White ethnic groups (40 per cent), followed by Yorkshire and the Humber, the North East, and London (around 35 per cent). There were lower proportions of in-migrants from non-White ethnic groups in other areas: around 25 per cent in Wales, the East of England and the South East of England, and only around 20 per cent in the South West of England.

Net migration by Government Office Region

Although the census provides data only on inflows of international migrants, data on net flows of international migration by region are available from ONS's published annual migration estimates.

All regions of England experienced a net inflow of international migrants in 2003. London had both the largest inflows and outflows of any area, with 173,000 in-migrants and 102,000 out-migrants. Its net inflow, 71,000, was also the highest by a large margin. The other English regions experienced net inflows of between 2,000 in the East Midlands and 22,000 in the North West. Both inflows and outflows were higher in the South East than any other area outside London (69,000 and 53,000, respectively). There were net inflows to each of Wales and Scotland in 2003, and a net outflow from Northern Ireland.

When geographical areas within the UK are considered, the components of population change (described in The contribution of migration to population change, above) become slightly more complicated. Internal migration (migration within the UK) must also be taken into account. For example, the effect of high levels of international migration on London's population is countered by migration out of London to other areas of the UK: there were net outflows from the capital to the rest of the UK of more than 100,000 people in each of 2002 and 2003. Internal migration is discussed fully in Chapter 6 (Population movement within the UK).

Why do people migrate?

Economic factors are important in driving international migration. The 2001 Census showed that more than half of people of working age who migrated to the UK in the year before the Census were economically active at the time of the Census. ONS's annual migration data showed that 114,000 migrants to the UK, in 2003, came for 'work-related' reasons, meaning that they had a specific job to go to. These numbers rose from 57,000 in 1994 to 114,000 in 2003 (Figure 7.10). This increase was in step with the overall increase in in-migration, and the proportion of in-migrants who came to the UK to do a specific job remained at around 20 per cent over the years 1994 to 2003.

The number of people leaving the UK for a specific job in 2003 (91,000) was lower than the number entering. Over the years 1994 to 2003, between 25 per cent and 36 per cent of those migrating out of the UK did so to go to a specific job: a slightly higher proportion than for those entering. However, because more people migrated into the UK than out of the UK in total, there was a small net inflow of people migrating to the UK for this reason. In addition, some people migrated in order to look for work.

Many people migrate to the UK in order to study, and the numbers have increased in recent years, from 50,000 in 1994, when students accounted for 16 per cent of inflows, to 135,000 in 2003, when they accounted for 25 per cent of inflows. Far fewer people leave the UK to study than enter: 11,000 in 2003, which was lower than in the preceding years. Students account for less than 5 per cent of migrant outflows. However, it should be noted that people who migrate to the UK to study may subsequently leave for other reasons, for example to take up a job.

Another important reason for people to migrate is to accompany or join another person, for example, as the partner or a dependent of someone who has a specific job to go to. People accompanying or joining another person accounted for about 15 per cent of migrants in 2003, both among those entering the UK and among those leaving.

Other reasons for migrating to the UK include seeking asylum and looking for work. Also, small numbers migrate to visit friends and family or take extended holidays.

Figure **7.10**

International migration: by main reasons for migration, 1994 to 2003[1]

United Kingdom

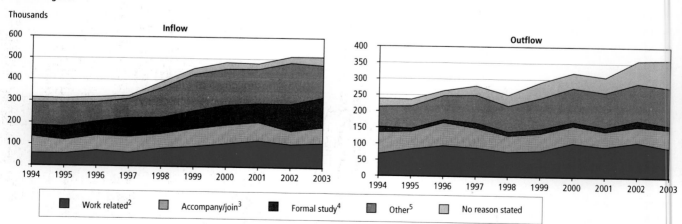

1 The figures in this chart include all categories of migrants and therefore represent Total International Migration.
2 `Work related' refers to those with a definite job to go to.
3 `Accompany/join' refers to those migrating to accompany or join a partner/immediate family. This includes foreign residents arriving in the UK to get married.
4 `Formal study' includes those migrating to attend a formal study course.
5 `Other' includes those looking for work, working holidaymakers, asylum seekers, visiting friends and family or taking an extended holiday.

Source: International migration, Office for National Statistics

Figure **7.11**

International migration: by usual occupation before migration, 1994 to 2003[1]

United Kingdom

Thousands

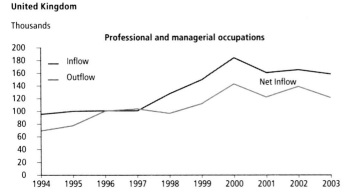

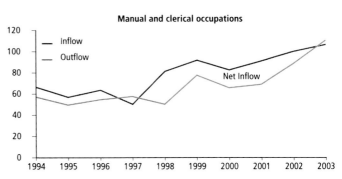

1 The figures in these charts include all categories of migrants and therefore represent Total International Migration.

Source: International migration, Office for National Statistics

The usual occupations of people before they migrate do not necessarily reflect their reasons for migrating but in many cases do. Just over half of migrants of all ages entering the UK in 2003 were employed before migrating. Of these, 60 per cent were in professional or managerial occupations, and 40 per cent were in manual or clerical occupations. The proportion of the UK's in-migrants who were previously employed remained fairly constant over the years 1994 to 2003; the proportions in professional or managerial occupations, and in manual or clerical occupations, also changed little. In both cases, inflows rose in line with the overall increase in in-migration.

In 2003 migration added a net inflow of 37,000 professional or managerial workers to the UK population, while there was a small outflow of 4,000 people in manual or clerical occupations. These figures fluctuated over the years 1994 to 2003 (Figure 7.11) but, in eight of these ten years, there were net gains of workers in both these categories.

The age and sex of migrants

Migration is generally most common among younger adult age groups, as Figure 7.12 shows. In 2003 the 15 to 24 and 25 to 44 age groups combined accounted for the great majority of both in-migrants (84 per cent) and out-migrants (75 per cent).

However, the age profile of in-migrants showed that they tended to belong to younger age groups than out-migrants. In 2003, 41 per cent of in-migrants were aged 15 to 24, compared with 23 per cent of out-migrants, while 43 per cent of in-migrants were aged 25 to 44, compared with 52 per cent of out-migrants. The 2003 figures show a shift in the age profile of in-migrants, compared with the 2002 figures, to the 15 to 24 age group. The age profile of out-migrants in 2003 was similar to the profile in 2002 (and earlier years). Smaller

Figure **7.12**

International migration: by age and sex, 2003[1]

United Kingdom

Thousands

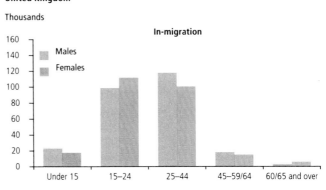

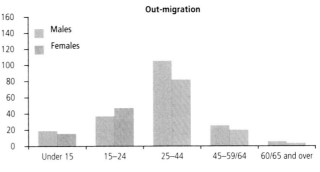

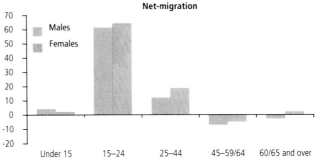

1 The figures in these charts include all categories of migrants and therefore represent Total International Migration.

Source: International migration, Office for National Statistics

numbers of people migrate at ages 45 to pensionable age, but in 2003 this age group was represented more among in-migrants (13 per cent of the total) than among out-migrants (6 per cent of the total).

Overall there were more in-migrants than out-migrants. This, combined with the high proportion of in-migrants aged 15 to 24, meant that there was a large net inflow of 126,000 people in this age group in 2003. There was a smaller net inflow of 31,000 migrants aged 25 to 44.

The pattern of inflows and outflows was different for the age group from 45 to pensionable age. Among this group there was a net outflow of 12,000 migrants, representing an inflow of 33,000 and an outflow of 45,000. The net outflows observed for this age group are a recent phenomenon, which has been driven by increases in out-migration since 1999. Numbers of migrants over retirement age were lower – fewer than 10,000 – for both inflows and outflows.

The prominence of younger adult age groups in the migration figures can easily be understood in the light of the main reasons for migration: work and study (discussed above). Data from the IPS show that, in 2003, 58 per cent of those who migrated to the UK for work-related reasons were in the 25 to 44 age group, while 74 per cent of those who migrated to the UK for formal study were in the 15 to 24 age group. (Note that IPS data do not include all migrants. See the appendix for further details.)

Males outnumbered females slightly among both in-migrants and out-migrants in 2003, making up 51 per cent of the total inflows and 53 per cent of total outflows. There was little change in these proportions over the previous decade. IPS data show that, in 2003, males were more likely than females to migrate to the UK for work-related reasons or for formal study, but less likely to migrate to accompany or join another person. There were slightly more male than female in-migrants in professional and managerial occupations, but slightly more females than males in manual or clerical occupations. Those who declared themselves to be 'housewives' were all female in 2003, although small numbers of male 'housewives' were recorded in previous years.

Summary

This chapter first described the trends in migration since the mid-1970s, moving through periods of net out-migration, of similar levels of in-migration and out-migration, and into the most recent decade for which data exist, which has been characterised by net in-migration. Most of the chapter's analysis concentrated on this recent decade from 1994 to 2003. Migration has increased over this period, most notably

for inflows but also for outflows. However, the overall numbers of international migrants who enter and leave the UK conceal a much more complex picture. Closer examination of the data reveals many different facets of the story.

Both inflows and outflows of international migrants have been relatively high in recent years, but comparisons with previous decades show how these trends can change over relatively short periods of time. There has been a trend, among people migrating to the UK, to intend to leave the country again fairly shortly. Migrants – both to and from the UK – represent citizens of many different countries, and British citizens form an important part of these flows in both directions. People migrate for a variety of reasons, and taking up a specific job is among the most frequently given.

Currently, as historically, international migration is an important and complex feature of the UK's demography.

Notes and references

1. United Nations Statistics Division, (1998) *Recommendations on Statistics of International Migration,* Series M No. 58, Rev.1. New York.

2. Hill K and Wong R (2005) Mexico-US migration: Views from both sides of the border. *Population and Development Review* **11(1)** 1–18.

3. Salt J (2005) *Current Trends in International Migration in Europe.* Council of Europe: Strasbourg.

4. More information about migration data, and the methods used to measure it, can be found in a methodology document on the National Statistics website: www.statistics.gov.uk/downloads/ theme_population/Methodology_for_Revised_International_ Migration_Estimates.doc

5. The 2003 international migration reference volume contains detailed breakdowns of the data by a number of different variables, plus extensive background information. The first release of 2004 data gives total inflows and outflows broken down by broad citizenship. Both these documents can be accessed from the following address on the National Statistics website: www.statistics.gov.uk/STATBASE/Product.asp?vlnk=507 The annual reference volume for 2004 will be published in spring 2006.

6. Population projections for the UK and its constituent countries are produced by the Government Actuary's Department (GAD). More information about national population projections is available on GAD's website: www.gad.gov.uk/Population_Projections/ Population_projections_background.htm

7. Rendall M S and Ball D J (2004) Immigration, emigration, and the ageing of the overseas-born population in the United Kingdom. *Population Trends* **116**, 18–27.

8. Information on the 2001 Census can be found from the following web links: England and Wales – www.statistics.gov.uk/census2001/default.asp; Scotland – www.gro-scotland.gov.uk/statistics/census/index.html; Northern Ireland – www.nisra.gov.uk/census/start.html

9. Coleman D and Salt J (1996) *Ethnicity in the 1991 Census, Volume One: Demographic Characteristics of the Ethnic Minority Population.* Office of Population Censuses and Surveys. HMSO: London.

The foreign-born population

Michael Rendall and John Salt

Chapter 8

Introduction

At the 2001 Census, there were 4.9 million people living in the UK who had been born overseas. They represented a snapshot of an ongoing migration process. Both the timing of immigration and the prevalence of emigration (return or onward) will affect the profile of the foreign-born population and, in particular, the balance between those foreign-born people who are very recent immigrants and those who have been in the country for many years.

A foreign-born population is defined by birthplace and not nationality or ethnicity. Birthplace, nationality and ethnicity are related, but to varying degrees. The UK's foreign-born population will include people who have been British citizens since birth and others who have become British citizens since their arrival in the UK. Because other countries also have multi-ethnic populations, as a result of their own international migration histories, country of birth correlates with, but does not equate to, ethnic group.

The first purpose of this chapter is to provide a demographic overview that accounts for the diversity and complexity of migrant origins and processes of the foreign-born population of the UK. Features described include country of birth, age, family status and where they live in the UK. Also examined is how strongly 'attached' those born overseas are to the UK: how many have a parent born in Britain; how many have become British citizens; and how many settle for long periods in the UK.

The second purpose of this chapter is to compare the 2001 labour market characteristics of the foreign-born population with those of the UK-born population. This is of particular interest because a high proportion of the foreign-born population are of working age. Some of the analyses are of all people of working age, while others are restricted to those either in employment or in the labour force (including the currently unemployed). Differences between the labour market characteristics of all foreign-born immigrants (the 'stock') and those who have arrived in the UK in the last year (the 'flow') are also described. One of the purposes here is to understand better the relationship between the characteristics of immigrants as they enter the UK (as described in Chapter 7) and the characteristics of the stock of immigrants resident in the UK.

A theme that runs through this review is comparison between immigrants from higher-income and lower-income countries. Previous analysis has indicated patterns of migration from higher-income countries that involve relatively short stays in the UK.[1] Some of this migration occurs as a system of labour

movement that includes the overall global circulation of staff.[2] Migration between the UK and other higher-income countries happens also frequently as a response to reciprocal arrangements (such as EU free mobility or Australasian working holidaymakers).

Although some of these processes of international migration apply as well to people born in lower-income countries, these people are also implicated in other, different processes, for example those involving less-skilled seasonal or service workers and asylum seekers.[3] For this reason, their overall characteristics and outcomes are expected to differ from those of migrants from higher-income countries.

In the demographic overview that forms the first part of this chapter, specific countries or geo-political groups of countries of birth are identified.[4] The main groups of higher-income countries are the European Union (EU), North America (USA and Canada) and Oceania (Australia and New Zealand). Because the main source of data used is the 2001 Census, the EU is defined as the 15 member states at that time. Among the lower-income countries, those that represent 'older' sources of immigrants – notably countries in the Caribbean and South Asia – are identified separately from 'newer' sources, including countries in Africa and the Far East. This follows previous analysis using similar geographic distinctions that are based on migration patterns to the UK over recent decades.[5]

The demographic overview includes analyses that rely primarily on sample survey data. For these, and the analyses used in the discussion of labour market characteristics, a simple 'high-income' and 'low-income' categorisation of migrant source countries has been achieved by distinguishing between those migrants born in OECD (Organisation for Economic Co-operation and Development) countries and those born in non-OECD countries. The former include migrants from most of Europe, North America, Australia, New Zealand, Japan and South Korea.[6] Non-OECD countries include some high-income countries (such as Singapore) but the lower-income countries of Asia, Africa and Latin America predominate. The OECD/non-OECD breakdown also allows for this chapter's findings to be seen in the context of other analyses from around 2001 of the foreign-born labour forces of other high-income countries.[7]

Demographic overview

Growth of the foreign-born population, 1951 to 2001

The second half of the 20th century saw the foreign-born population of the UK more than double, from 2.1 million in

Table **8.1**

Growth of the foreign-born population 1951 to 2001

United Kingdom

	Total foreign born (thousands)	Percentage increase over the previous decade	Percentage of total population
1951	2,118.6		4.2
1961	2,573.5	21.5	4.9
1971	3,190.3	24.0	5.8
1981	3,429.1	7.5	6.2
1991	3,835.4	11.8	6.7
2001	4,896.6	27.7	8.3

Source: Census – Office for National Statistics; General Register Office for Scotland; Northern Ireland Statistics and Research Agency

1951 to 4.9 million in 2001 (Table 8.1). As a proportion of the total UK population, too, the foreign-born population almost doubled over this period, from 4.2 per cent in 1951 to 8.3 per cent in 2001. This puts the UK slightly above the OECD average of 7.8 per cent foreign-born, though still substantially below that of major immigration countries such as the USA (12.3 per cent), Canada (19.3 per cent) and Australia (23.0 per cent).[8]

The decades of the 1950s, 1960s and 1990s stand out as those in which the strongest growth in the UK's foreign-born population occurred. Each of these decades experienced more than 20 per cent growth (21.5, 24.0 and 27.7 per cent respectively). In terms of absolute numbers, the decade of 1991 to 2001 stands out with its increase of almost 1.1 million foreign-born people. This is substantially more than the increase of 600,000 between 1961 and 1971, the decade that saw the next largest absolute increase.

The rate of growth of the foreign-born population over the 1970s and 1980s was much lower, at 7.5 per cent and 11.8 per cent respectively. Part of the explanation given for these hiatuses is the introduction of legislation that restricted immigration channels which had previously been open to residents of the former British colonies of South Asia and the Caribbean (the 'New Commonwealth' countries).[9] While this is undoubtedly part of the explanation, people born in these two regions accounted for only one in four foreign-born people living in Britain in 1971 (see immediately below). Therefore, a broader explanation must be sought involving changes in immigration from other geographical regions as well as emigration and death among the various foreign-born sub-populations over this period.

Changes in the geographical and ethnic origins of the UK's foreign-born population

Comparison between 1971 and 2001 is particularly informative. It sheds light on the changes that have taken place in the patterns of geographical origin of the UK's foreign-born population since the major waves of immigration from South Asia and the Caribbean that occurred in the 1950s and 1960s. This comparison is shown in Table 8.2, where census data on the UK in 2001 are compared to data for Great Britain in 1971. Great Britain rather than the UK is used in 1971, as detailed country-of-birth tabulations are not available for Northern Ireland in 1971. Northern Ireland, however, contributed only 1.4 per cent of the UK's foreign-born population in 2001. Other issues affecting comparisons between 1971 and 2001 are the change in country boundaries and formation of new countries. The creation of Bangladesh and break-up of the Soviet Union are two examples. To deal with such change, standard census country groupings of 2001[10] are applied as closely as possible to 1971. The notes to Table 8.2 indicate where changes have occurred either in the countries themselves or in the census groupings of countries between 1971 and 2001.

A major increase in diversity of the foreign-born population of the UK by geographical origin is apparent in this 1971 to 2001 comparison. In both 1971 and 2001, Europe was the largest contributing continent of birth, and the Republic of Ireland the largest single country of birth, among the foreign-born respectively of Great Britain and the UK. Europe's dominance as a migrant source region was much greater, however, in 1971 than in 2001. Europe accounted for half (50.9 per cent) of all foreign-born people in Great Britain in 1971, with the Republic of Ireland alone accounting for almost one in four (23.8 per cent). By 2001 Europe's proportion had fallen to one in three (33.1 per cent), while Ireland's share had halved to 11.0 per cent.

The absolute number of European-born people changed little over these 30 years, however, as declines in the number born in Ireland were offset mainly by increases in numbers born elsewhere in western Europe. Thus, in 2001, as many as 1.6 million people in the UK were born elsewhere in Europe. North America and Oceania together contributed 400,000 people to UK's foreign-born population in 2001, up from 250,000 in 1971. These countries of mainly European-origin settlement contributed a further 8 per cent of the total foreign-born populations in both 1971 and 2001.

Asia was the second largest contributor to the foreign-born population in both 1971 and 2001, but saw large growth in this 30-year period. In absolute terms, Asia's contribution more

Table **8.2**

Countries of birth of the foreign-born population in 1971 and 2001

Country of birth	United Kingdom 2001				Great Britain 1971			
	Number (thousands)	Per cent	Number (thousands)	Per cent	Number (thousands)	Per cent	Number (thousands)	Per cent
Europe	1,620.0	33.1			1,516.9	50.9		
Republic of Ireland[1]			537.1	11.0			709.2	23.8
Other Western Europe[2]			834.9	17.1			632.8	21.2
Eastern Europe[3]			248.0	5.1			174.9	5.9
North America and Oceania	397.1	8.1			253.4	8.5		
USA			158.4	3.2			110.6	3.7
Canada			72.5	1.5			64.7	2.2
Australia			107.9	2.2			57.0	1.9
New Zealand			58.3	1.2			21.2	0.7
South Asia	1,032.4	21.1			479.0	16.1		
India			467.6	9.6			322.0	10.8
Pakistan[4]			321.2	6.6			139.9	4.7
Bangladesh			154.4	3.2				
Other South Asia			89.2	1.8			17.0	0.6
Caribbean	255.0	5.2			237.0	7.9		
Africa	834.1	17.0			210.0	7.0		
South Africa			141.4	2.9			45.8	1.5
Kenya			129.6	2.6			59.5	2.0
Other Africa			563.1	11.5			104.7	3.5
Far East	398.2	8.1			108.9	3.7		
China			52.5	1.1			13.5	0.5
Hong Kong			96.4	2.0			29.5	1.0
Other Far East[5]			249.2	5.1			65.9	2.2
All other countries	359.9	7.3			177.8	6.0		
Total	4,896.6	100.0			2,983.1	100.0		

Notes:
1 *includes 'Ireland, part not stated'.*
2 *In 1971, Other Western Europe excludes Ireland and identified Eastern European countries.*
3 *Poland, Hungary, USSR only in 1971.*
4 *In 1971 includes East Pakistan (now Bangladesh).*
5 *Burma, Malaysia and Singapore only in 1971.*

Source: Census 1971 – OPCS (1974) Great Britain, Country of Birth Tables. 2001 Census – Office for National Statistics; General Register Office for Scotland, Northern Ireland Statistics and Research Agency

than doubled from 600,000 in 1971 to 1.4 million in 2001 (counting together the South Asia and Far East groupings). In terms of proportions of the total foreign-born population, Asia's contribution increased from 19.8 per cent in 1971 to 29.2 per cent in 2001. The number of people born in either Pakistan or Bangladesh more than tripled from only 140,000 in 1971 to 475,000 in 2001. India, however, remained the largest single contributing country in Asia, with its number increasing from 320,000 in 1971 to 470,000 in 2001. People born in the

Far East contributed a total of 400,000 (8.1 per cent) to the UK's foreign-born population in 2001, increasing by four-fold in absolute numbers since 1971 and more than doubling its proportionate share.

Apart from Europe, the Caribbean was the other major region with a declining share of the total foreign-born population. Its quarter of a million people in the UK in 2001 constituted 5.2 per cent of the total foreign-born population, down from its

7.9 per cent share in 1971. In absolute terms, though, the number of Caribbean-born people was stable at around 250,000 in both years. Africa contributed 830,000 foreign-born people to the UK in 2001, after having contributed only 210,000 in 1971. Accordingly, Africa's share of the total foreign-born population increased from 7.0 per cent to 17.0 per cent over these three decades. Previously published results from the 2001 Census have shown that the people born in Africa and resident in the UK in 2001 were from a broad range of ethnic origins, 20 per cent identifying themselves as Indian, 31 per cent as White and only two-fifths (38 per cent) as Black.[11] This reinforces the earlier observation that country of birth correlates with, but does not equate to, ethnic group. An alternative presentation of the foreign-born population of the UK in 2001 by ethnicity is provided in Table 8.3.

Just over half (52.6 per cent) the foreign-born population in the UK in 2001 was from a White ethnic group, substantially more than the two-fifths share born in Europe, North America or Oceania. Another quarter (25.1 per cent) was Asian or Asian British, and 3.6 per cent Chinese. Indian was the largest ethnic group among foreign-born Asians, at 11.6 per cent, exceeding the 9.6 per cent of the total foreign-born population made up of people born in India. The higher representation of people of Indian ethnicity than of Indian country of birth is due to the

substantial numbers of Indian immigrants born in Africa, as noted above. Black or Black British people made up another 11.9 per cent of the 2001 foreign-born population. This is much lower, however, than the 22.2 per cent of the 2001 foreign-born population who were born in the Caribbean or Africa. The Mixed and Other ethnic groups together account for the remaining 6.9 per cent of the foreign-born population.

UK destinations: geographical distribution

The geographical distribution of the UK's foreign-born population in 2001 is summarised in Map 8.4. In broad terms, the major concentration of the foreign-born population occurs roughly south of a line linking the Humber and Severn estuaries, with a secondary band across the southern Pennines, extending into north east England. Between these there is a zone of relatively low concentration of foreign-born people, which includes rural Yorkshire, parts of the East and West Midlands and parts of Wales. Another zone of low concentration extends from northern England, through the Scottish borders and includes much of the central lowlands. To the north of this there is another large contiguous zone of higher concentration, albeit in a context of low total population numbers. Northern Ireland shows a mixed picture, mainly because most of the foreign-born residents of Northern Ireland are from the Republic of Ireland and their location in part reflects sectarian settlement patterns.

Within this general pattern there are particular concentrations that reflect historical as well as contemporary immigration trends. Both these trends explain the high levels of foreign-born in London, which contains the 22 local authorities with the highest concentrations of foreign-born people: Brent (46.6 per cent), Kensington and Chelsea (44.5 per cent) and Westminster (44.2 per cent) being the leaders. In general, London north of the Thames has higher concentrations of foreign-born people than areas to the south (Map 8.5), which is due in part to affordable housing and associated patterns of networked migration.

The more urban places around London, such as Slough (24 per cent), Luton (19.7 per cent) and Reading (14 per cent), as well as the leafier suburbs such as Elmbridge (16 per cent) and Woking (13.7 per cent) have attracted large numbers of foreign-born people at various occupational levels because of the jobs and housing they have been able to offer. Further afield, in southern England, relatively high proportions of foreign-born people in the populations in Oxford (19.3 per cent) and Cambridge (19.2 per cent) reflect the attraction of these towns to students from overseas, while the high proportion in Forest Heath in Suffolk (23.0 per cent) may be ascribed to the presence of American military bases.

Table **8.3**

Ethnicity of the foreign-born population, 2001

United Kingdom

Ethnic group	Number (thousands)	Per cent	Number (thousands)	Per cent
White	2,575.1	52.6		
Mixed	140.8	2.9		
Asian or Asian British	1,229.3	25.1		
Indian			569.8	11.6
Pakistani			336.4	6.9
Bangladeshi			151.6	3.1
Other Asian			171.4	3.5
Black or Black British	580.5	11.9		
Black Caribbean			238.5	4.9
Black African			321.5	6.6
Other Black			20.5	0.4
Chinese	176.2	3.6		
Other Ethnic Group	194.7	4.0		
Total	4,896.6	100.0		

Source: 2001 Census – Office for National Statistics; General Register Office for Scotland (GROS); Northern Ireland Statistics and Research Agency (NISRA)

Map **8.4**

Foreign-born population as a percentage of all residents,[1] by local or unitary authority, 2001
United Kingdom

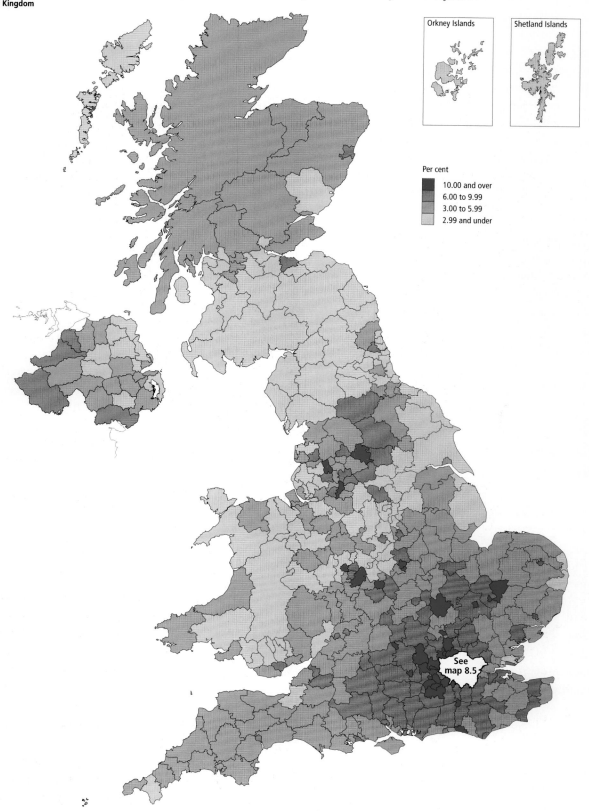

Orkney Islands

Shetland Islands

Per cent

10.00 and over
6.00 to 9.99
3.00 to 5.99
2.99 and under

See
map 8.5

1 The data refer to UK residents in April 2001 who stated in the Census that their country of birth was outside the UK. The foreign-born population has been calculated as a percentage of the total population of each area.

Source: 2001 Census – Office for National Statistics; General Register Office for Scotland; Northern Ireland Statistics and Research Agency

Map **8.5**

Foreign-born population as a percentage of all residents,¹ by London borough, 2001

United Kingdom

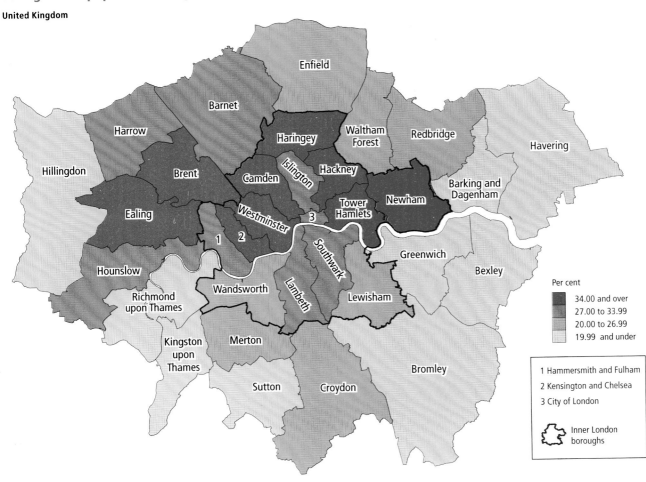

Per cent

- 34.00 and over
- 27.00 to 33.99
- 20.00 to 26.99
- 19.99 and under

1 Hammersmith and Fulham
2 Kensington and Chelsea
3 City of London

Inner London boroughs

1 The data refer to UK residents in April 2001 who stated in the Census that their country of birth was outside the UK. The foreign-born population has been calculated as a percentage of the total population of each area.

Source: 2001 Census – Office for National Statistics

Further north, the high proportions of foreign-born people in Leicester (23.1 per cent) and in several places on the flanks of the Pennines, such as Bradford (11.8 per cent) and Blackburn (10.9 per cent), have been caused by historical migration. From the 1960s onwards, people have migrated to the area from overseas to work in the textile industries The first generations have been followed by members of their home communities with whom they have family and other ties.

In Scotland, the relatively high proportion of foreign-born people in Aberdeen (6.3 per cent) is due to the inflow of oil industry workers. Capital cities often have a higher proportion of foreign-born people. Both Edinburgh (8.4 per cent) and Cardiff (7.6 per cent) seem to be showing such an effect that is giving them a higher proportion of foreign-born people than many other authorities in Scotland and Wales.

Indicators of attachment: nationality, parents' countries of birth and lengths of stay

The foreign-born population of the UK exhibits great variation in its propensity to put down roots once in the UK. Also, as noted in the previous chapter, a trend towards migrants intending to stay in the UK for only relatively short periods has been observed. In this section, a range of indicators of attachment is considered from non-census data sources. British citizenship ('nationality') is the first such indicator analysed (Table 8.6). It is available in sample survey data in the annual Labour Force Survey (LFS). The 2001/02 year is used to match most closely to the period of the 2001 Census. Note that the coverage of sample surveys, including the LFS, is slightly less than that of the census, as only certain categories of communal establishments (for example, nurses' group accommodation) are surveyed.

Nationality and country of birth are cross-classified for the foreign-born population in three country groupings. There are two higher-income groups consisting of (1) the EU and (2) North America and Oceania. The third is the residual (All Other) group that consists mainly of lower income countries. The table shows the proportions of people in each country grouping who are of: British nationality; a nationality from the same country group (typically, that of their country of birth); and a nationality from another of the three non-UK country groups.

Overall, almost half (47.2 per cent) the UK's foreign-born population in 2001/02 were British citizens (Table 8.6, last column). For the two higher-income country groups, however, only about one-third were British citizens (36.5 per cent for those born in another EU country and 33.7 per cent among those born in North America or Oceania). For the All Other group, over half (54.2 per cent) were British citizens. Cases where nationality was neither that of the country of current residence (the UK) nor the person's country group of birth are rare.

Another indicator of attachment that relates closely to a foreign-born person's citizenship rights at birth is whether one or both parents were born in the UK (Table 8.7). Again, this information was not collected in the 2001 Census so sample survey data are used. The General Household Survey (GHS) includes this question but has a smaller sample size than the LFS. For this reason, two years (2001 and 2002) are aggregated and averaged. Coverage in the GHS is limited to the household

Table **8.6**

Nationality of the foreign-born population of the UK by country of birth[1], 2001/02

United Kingdom

Percentages

Nationality	Country of birth			
	European Union (non-UK)	North America and Oceania	Other non-UK birth-place	All foreign born
European Union (non-British)	62.4	1.5	1.9	19.9
North America and Oceania	0.2	63.7	0.3	5.5
Other nationality	0.9	1.1	43.6	27.4
British	36.5	33.7	54.2	47.2
Total	100.0	100.0	100.0	100.0

1 Cases with missing values on nationality or country of birth are excluded.

Source: Annual Labour Force Survey 2001/02 – Office for National Statistics

Table **8.7**

Parents' countries of birth of the foreign-born population[1], 1971 and 2001/02

Great Britain

Percentages

	2001/02	1971
Both parents born outside the UK and Ireland	73.5	58.3
One parent born in the UK or Ireland	7.0	6.4
Both parents born in the UK or Ireland	19.5	35.3
Total	100.0	100.0

1 Cases with missing values on own or parents' countries of birth are excluded.

Sources: General Household Surveys of 2001 and 2002 averaged – Office for National Statistics. 1971 Census, OPCS (1974) Great Britain, Country of Birth Tables

population of Great Britain only. Comparison is made to Great Britain in 1971. The 1971 Census asked for parents' countries of birth but compiled responses for residents of Great Britain according to countries of birth outside the UK and Republic of Ireland, as opposed to outside the UK. The same breakdown of countries of parents' births is, therefore, also used here for the GHS analyses.

The comparison between 1971 and 2001/02 reveals a sharp decline in the proportions of foreign-born people with a UK- or Irish-born parent. More than one in three (35.3 per cent) of the foreign-born population of Great Britain in 1971 had both parents born in the UK or Republic of Ireland, compared with 19.5 per cent in 2001/02. A further 6.4 per cent in 1971 had one parent only born in the UK or Ireland, similar to the 7.0 per cent seen in 2001/02. Only three-fifths (58.3 per cent) of the foreign-born population in 1971 had both parents born outside the UK and Republic of Ireland, compared with almost three-quarters (73.5 per cent) in 2001/02. Most of this change in the distribution of parents' countries of birth over the 30 years may be attributed to the large fall in Ireland's share of the foreign-born population, from 23.8 per cent in 1971 to 11.0 per cent in 2001 (see again Table 8.2). Thus, in neither 1971 nor 2001/02 are the foreign-born children of two British emigrants likely to have accounted for more than about one in ten of the total foreign-born population.

Perhaps the most direct indicator of attachment of the foreign-born population to the UK is how long they stay. Estimates of length of stay for foreign-born immigrants who arrived in the UK in the 1990s are given in Figure 8.8.[12] The measure used is the proportion of immigrants who leave again within six years

Figure **8.8**

Proportions of foreign-born immigrants, emigrating again within six years of arrival, 1991 to 2002

United Kingdom

Percentage emigrating

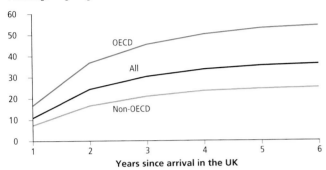

Source: International Passenger Survey data 1991 to 2002 Office for National Statistics. Asylum data – Home Office (see text for details)

of arrival. As in Table 8.6, countries are grouped into higher- and lower-income. A simple grouping into countries that are members of the Organisation for Economic Co-operation and Development (OECD) and non-member countries is used here, partly for reasons of sample size. This nevertheless reveals a similar pattern of contrast between foreign-born people from higher- and lower-income countries to that seen when British nationality is the measure of attachment: people born in higher-income countries stay on average for significantly shorter periods. Half the immigrants (50 per cent) born in OECD countries emigrate again within four years of arrival, compared with less than a quarter (23 per cent) of immigrants from lower-income (non-OECD) countries. Overall, as many as a third (34 per cent) of all foreign-born immigrants to the UK in the 1990s are estimated to have emigrated again within four years of arrival.

Age and family structure

One consequence of a shorter length of stay among immigrants is the greater youth of those who are resident (the stock of foreign-born people). This is because immigrants are typically young when they arrive. To have an older immigrant population requires both that immigrants settle and that they arrived a relatively long time ago. The old-age dependency ratios and proportions of foreign-born populations who are of pensionable age shown in Table 8.9 reflect the immigration and emigration processes (periods of arrival and how many subsequently leave) across a range of countries of birth in the 2001 Census population of the UK. The old-age dependency ratio presents the population above pensionable age (65 and over for men, 60 and over for women) as a ratio to those of working age: the higher the ratio, the 'older' the population.

Table **8.9**

Old-age dependency ratios and proportions of total foreign-born of pensionable age[1] by major groups of country of birth, 2001

United Kingdom

	Old-age dependency ratio[2]	Per cent of total foreign-born of pensionable age
Europe		
EU Countries	39.8	*39.9*
Republic of Ireland[3]	65.9	*24.8*
Other EU	24.6	*15.1*
Other Western Europe	24.1	*1.6*
Eastern Europe	41.2	*7.8*
Africa	8.4	*7.0*
Asia		
Middle East	15.6	*3.2*
Far East	10.2	*4.0*
South Asia	20.2	*19.5*
Americas		
Canada and USA	18.0	*3.5*
Caribbean	45.6	*9.2*
Latin America	18.8	*1.5*
Oceania	9.7	*1.7*
Other	32.9	*1.1*
Overseas-Born	23.1	*100.0*
UK-born[4]	30.7	
Total		

1 'Pensionable age' is 65 years old and over for men, and 60 years old and over for women.
2 Old-age dependency ratio = 100 * (pensionable-age population/ working age population).
3 Includes Ireland, part not stated.
4 Includes Channel Islands and Isle of Man.

Source: 2001 Census – Office for National Statistics; General Register Office for Scotland; Northern Ireland Statistics and Research Agency

Among the regions with the lowest old-age dependency ratios are those for which immigration to the UK has been more recent, notably Africa (8.4 older people per 100 of working age in 2001) and the Far East (10.2 older people per 100). Old-age dependency ratios are low, too, among regions characterised by shorter patterns of stay, notably Oceania (9.7 older people per 100 of working age in 2001) and, to a lesser extent, North America (18.0 per 100). These ratios contrast with the much higher UK-born old-age dependency ratio of 30.7 older people per 100 of working age in 2001 (Table 8.9).

People from Europe and the Caribbean, due to their earlier periods of large-scale immigration to the UK, have older populations on average than the UK-born population (with ratios of 39.8 and 45.6 older people per 100 of working age respectively in 2001). The Republic of Ireland had as many as 65.9 older people per 100 of working age in the UK in 2001, reflecting immigration from the 1950s and earlier. Thus, while Ireland's share of the total foreign-born population had fallen to 11.0 per cent (Table 8.2) by 2001, this one country still accounted for a quarter (24.8 per cent) of the UK's foreign-born people of pensionable age. High proportions of the total foreign-born population of pensionable age are also seen for the regions that generated large-scale immigration to the UK in the decades immediately after the Second World War: South Asia contributing 19.5 per cent and the Caribbean, 9.2 per cent in 2001.

The young ages of immigrants means that many arrive before they have formed a family. Additionally, the difficulties inherent in moving from one country to another often favour migration by single individuals. The result is a strong contrast between the family and household structures of foreign-born immigrants who have just arrived and those of all foreign-born immigrants. These contrasts are shown in Table 8.10 for England and Wales in 2001. To anticipate the analyses of labour market characteristics later in this chapter, OECD and non-OECD groupings are combined with breakdowns of flows and stocks, and comparisons are made with the UK-born population.

Overall, almost half of all immigrants arriving in 2001 consisted of individuals who were in non-family households (32 per cent, combining 'Not in family – pensioner' and 'Not in family – other') or not in a household (16 per cent). The high proportion of students among arriving immigrants, as noted in Chapter 7 (see also below), would have been an important factor here as many would have moved into halls of residence. In contrast, only about a quarter of the total immigrant stock was in a non-family household (23 per cent) or not in a household (3 per cent).

Only a third (33.5 per cent) of immigrant flows were individuals in a couple, compared with over half the immigrant stock (54.5 per cent). Dependent children in couple families, however, were more common in immigrant flows (12.6 per cent) than stocks (6.8 per cent). This should not be taken as an indicator of the higher fertility of recent migrants, but rather a greater likelihood that their children were born outside the UK (the only ways that a recent migrant's child could be born in the UK would be if the child were still under one year old or the parents were returning to the UK with a child born in the UK during an earlier stay). As shown in the right-hand column of Table 8.10, being a dependent child was accordingly much more common in the UK-born stock population than among the foreign-born stock population. Finally, and again emphasising the youth of arriving immigrants, only among the foreign-born immigrant stock (and not among the flows) were there significant proportions of individuals at pensionable age who were not in families (6.5 per cent).

Table **8.10**

Family status of total population, by country of birth and length of residence in the UK, 2001

England and Wales

Percentages

	OECD-born		Non-OECD-born		All foreign-born		UK-born	
	Resident for <1 year	All residents	Resident for <1 year	All residents	Resident for <1 year	All residents	Resident for <1 year	All residents
Not in a family – pensioner	0.4	8.7	0.9	5.1	0.7	6.5	1.5	6.9
Not in a family – other	33.3	18.3	28.4	15.8	31.0	16.8	21.4	9.7
In couple family – member of couple	32.3	51.7	34.7	56.1	33.5	54.5	38.5	46.6
In couple family – dependent child of couple	12.9	7.7	12.4	6.3	12.6	6.8	12.6	18.0
In couple family – other child of couple	1.2	1.8	2.0	2.8	1.6	2.5	9.5	5.2
In lone parent family – parent	0.8	4.5	1.9	6.9	1.3	6.0	2.7	4.4
In lone parent family – dependent child of parent	1.7	2.1	3.0	2.3	2.3	2.2	2.7	5.4
In lone parent family – other child of parent	0.6	1.0	1.2	1.7	0.9	1.5	3.4	2.1
Not in a household	16.7	4.2	15.5	2.8	16.1	3.3	7.7	1.6
Total	100.0	100.0	100.0	100.0	100.0	100.0	100.0	100.0

Source: 2001 Census – Office for National Statistics

The contrasts between family and household structures of immigrant stocks and immigrant flows are similar for people born in OECD and non-OECD countries (see the first four columns of Table 8.10). In both country groups, only approximately a third of recent migrants in 2001 were couple members in a couple family household, compared with over half the immigrant stock. In both country groups, people living not in a household were found in large proportions (16.7 and 15.5 per cent) only among recent migrants.

The main difference seen between the family and household structures of OECD-born and non-OECD born immigrants is the greater proportion of newly arrived OECD immigrants who were not in a family (34 per cent, as opposed to 29 per cent for non-OECD immigrants), and the smaller proportion of the stock of OECD immigrants who were either a lone parent or a member of a couple (56 per cent, compared with 63 per cent of non-OECD stock). If family migration and post-migration family formation are considered as further indicators of 'putting down roots' in the UK, this difference between the family structures of OECD and non-OECD immigrants is again consistent with greater attachment to the UK among immigrants from low-income countries than those from high-income countries.

Labour market characteristics

The labour market characteristics of the foreign-born population in 2001 are studied using census data for England and Wales only. In 2001, 95 per cent of the total UK foreign-born population lived in England and Wales. The labour market characteristics considered are labour force status (economic activity) and occupation, both overall and by age and sex. Country of birth is split throughout into two groups: OECD (higher-income) countries and non-OECD (lower-income) countries. As shown above, these two groups of countries generate distinct forms of migration flows and, therefore, are expected to differ in their contributions to the UK's foreign-born labour force. Migrants born in OECD countries are more likely to stay only a few years in the UK, while those born in non-OECD countries are more likely to settle permanently. Comparisons are also made between these two sets of foreign-born immigrants and the UK-born population, including UK-born people of working age who lived outside the country in the year before the census.

This analysis, using 2001 Census data, complements previous studies that have looked at the foreign-born population and the labour market using sample survey data from the GHS[13] and LFS[14], and at working age immigrants and emigrants using the International Passenger Survey.[15] The major advantages of the census over other data sources are that it is a single

instrument for collecting data on both stocks and flows, and its much larger numbers of respondents than any sample survey. These features have been important in realising one particular objective of this analysis, which is to differentiate between the characteristics of migrants measured as flows and as stocks. Doing this, using the question on place of residence one year prior to Census day, has allowed the analysis to look at social and economic issues around the transition of the foreign-born population from an immigration stream into a settled immigrant population.

Economic activity among the stock of foreign-born people of working age

Working age is taken to be from age 16 to 64 for men and 59 for women. The population of working age includes those who are employed, unemployed, inactive and students. The distribution of the foreign-born population of working age between these 'economic activity' statuses is shown in Table 8.11a. In 2001 there were 3.3 million foreign-born people of working age in England and Wales, of whom 61.4 per cent were employed and not students, 23.9 per cent were inactive, 9.6 per cent were students and 5.1 per cent were unemployed (see the column: Total, All Foreign born, Table 8.11a). Among those born in the UK, a higher proportion (71.1 per cent) were employed, and lower proportions were unemployed (3.8 per cent), inactive (17.7 per cent) or students (7.4 per cent).

Two major distinctions in economic activity are captured respectively by the labour force participation rate, which measures the proportion of the working-age population who are either employed or unemployed (the labour force), and by the unemployment rate, which measures the proportion of the labour force who are unemployed. These two rates are presented in the two bottom rows of Table 8.11a.

There were considerable differences in the labour force participation rates in 2001 between men and women and by birthplace. The overall labour force participation rate of foreign-born people of working age was 66.5 per cent but it was higher (71.3 per cent) for those born in an OECD country and lower (64.0 per cent) for those born in a non-OECD country. Both, however, were lower than rates for the UK-born population (74.9 per cent). Differences between men and women were marked, the participation rate for foreign-born men being 75.4 per cent, compared with 58.0 per cent for foreign-born women. Again there were differences between the OECD-born and non-OECD born groups, with the participation rate for both sexes being higher for the OECD-born, though only markedly so for women. Only just over half (53.8 per cent) of non-OECD born women were in the labour force, compared with two thirds of OECD-born and UK-born

Table 8.11a

Employment status of the total working-age population, by country of birth and sex, 2001

England and Wales

Percentages unless otherwise indicated

All resident in the UK	OECD-born (excluding UK)			Non-OECD-born			All foreign-born			UK-born		
	Male 16–64	Female 16–59	Total	Male 16–64	Female 16–59	Total	Male 16–64	Female 16–59	Total	Male 16–64	Female 16–59	Total
Employed and not students	73.3	62.4	67.5	67.1	49.3	58.2	69.2	54.0	61.4	75.8	66.1	71.1
Unemployed and not students	4.5	3.2	3.8	7.0	4.5	5.8	6.2	4.0	5.1	4.7	2.9	3.8
Inactive and not students	13.0	24.6	19.1	15.7	37.0	26.4	14.8	32.6	23.9	12.7	23.1	17.7
Full-time student	9.2	9.8	9.5	10.1	9.2	9.6	9.8	9.4	9.6	6.8	7.9	7.4
Total	100.0	100.0	100.0	100.0	100.0	100.0	100.0	100.0	100.0	100.0	100.0	100.0
Total number (thousands)	527.4	600.5	1,127.9	1,089.6	1,093.8	2,183.4	1,617.0	1,694.4	3,311.4	14,500.0	13,549.4	28,049.4
Labour Force participation rate[1]	77.8	65.6	71.3	74.2	53.8	64.0	75.4	58.0	66.5	80.5	69.0	74.9
Unemployment rate[2]	5.8	4.9	5.3	9.5	8.3	9.0	8.2	6.9	7.7	5.8	4.1	5.1

1 Labour Force participation rate is the proportion of the working-age population that is economically active.
2 Unemployment rate is the proportion of the economically active population that is unemployed. A person is defined unemployed if he or she is not in employment, wants a job, has actively sought work in the last 4 weeks and is available to start work within 2 weeks; or not in employment, but has found a job which will start within 2 weeks. This is consistent with the International Labour Office (ILO) standard classification.

Source: 2001 Census – Office for National Statistics

women of working age (65.6 and 69.0 per cent). The OECD-born and non-OECD born groups had similar proportions of students in the total population, but the proportion classified as inactive was higher for those born in non-OECD countries.

There were also differences in the unemployment rate. Overall, this was 7.7 per cent for all foreign–born people, higher than that for people born in the UK (5.1 per cent). The higher overall rate for the foreign-born population was due almost entirely to the much higher rate of unemployment among those born in non-OECD countries (9.0 per cent), the rate for people born in OECD countries (5.3 per cent) being almost the same as for those born in the UK.

Economic activity among the foreign-born immigrant flow

Of the 3.3 million foreign-born people of working age, 179,000 entered the UK in the 12 months leading up to the 2001 Census (see the column: Total, All Foreign born, Table 8.11b). These flows included slightly more OECD-born than non-OECD born people of working age (93,000 versus 86,000), in marked contrast to the two-to-one ratio of non-

OECD born to OECD-born in the total foreign-born stock of working age. These differences between flows and stocks reflect the greater turnover that occurs among the OECD-born migrants as large numbers of people from those countries enter the UK and subsequently leave again. Completing the picture of immigration's effects on the UK labour force, almost as many UK-born people of working age (76,000) entered the UK as did people from each of the two major foreign country groups (see far right column of Table 8.11b).

The profile of the foreign-born inflow was different from that of the foreign-born stock. In particular, only 52.9 per cent were employed, which is a considerably smaller proportion than among the foreign-born stock (61.4 per cent, see Table 8.11a). One reason for this is the number of students who comprised a larger proportion of recent entrants, around a fifth (21.1 per cent) compared with a 10th of all foreign-born immigrants. As might be expected from recent arrivals, a smaller proportion (19.8 per cent) were inactive, that is, were not in work or looking for work. A further 6.1 per cent were unemployed. The foreign-born new arrivals also differed from the UK-born newly-returned migrants. A higher proportion of the latter were employed (63.4 per cent) or unemployed (8.6 per cent), and a lower proportion were inactive (15.8 per cent) or were students (12.2 per cent).

The three groups – UK-born stocks, foreign-born stocks and recently arrived (foreign-born and UK-born) migrants – thus had significantly different profiles in their economic activity characteristics. The reasons for this are complex and have their genesis in the different migration streams that have at various times made up the in-migrant flow.

The labour force participation rate for recent arrivals was lower than that of the total foreign-born population (59.0 compared with 66.5 per cent, see respectively Tables 8.11b and 8.11a). The gap in participation rates between the total foreign-born population and people born in non-OECD countries was greater than it was for those born in OECD countries: of the former, only 53.0 per cent of the working-age immigrant inflow were in the labour force, whereas, of the latter, 64.6 per cent were in the labour force. Lower labour force participation rates are to be expected among the foreign-born migrant in-flow given the greater significance of students among those entering in the previous 12 months and their prevalence, especially among the non-OECD born inflows

(22.5 per cent). The proportions classified as 'inactive and not students', however, were also much higher among both men (13.2 per cent) and women (35.1 per cent) from non-OECD countries than they were among men and women from OECD countries (7.1 and 22.5 per cent respectively).

UK-born people who had been living outside the country but entered in the year prior to the 2001 Census tended to have higher labour force participation rates than foreign-born people but slightly lower ones than the total UK-born population of working age. The difference, however, was relatively small: 72.0 per cent for UK-born returning migrants, compared with 74.9 per cent of all UK-born people of working age. There are several reasons for this, for instance a proportion of the UK-born migrants are likely to have been returning to the country to retire.

A feature in many countries is that newly arrived in-migrants tend to have higher unemployment rates than the population as a whole. This can be because of the time it takes people to find a job due to mismatches of skills between labour demand and supply, and to various cultural adjustment factors. Higher unemployment among recent arrivals than among the foreign-born stock was prevalent for both OECD-born and non-OECD

Table **8.11b**

Employment status of the working-age population who arrived in the last year, by country of birth and sex, 2001

England and Wales

Percentages unless otherwise indicated

Resident in UK less than one year	OECD-born (excluding UK)			Non-OECD-born			All foreign-born			UK-born		
	Male 16–64	Female 16–59	Total	Male 16–64	Female 16–59	Total	Male 16–64	Female 16–59	Total	Male 16–64	Female 16–59	Total
Employed and not students	70.4	51.6	60.0	52.9	37.9	45.2	61.7	45.3	52.9	73.4	52.3	63.4
Unemployed and not students	4.1	4.9	4.6	8.0	7.6	7.8	6.1	6.2	6.1	8.9	8.3	8.6
Inactive and not students	7.1	22.5	15.6	13.2	35.1	24.5	10.1	28.3	19.8	8.4	24.0	15.8
Full-time student	18.4	21.0	19.9	25.9	19.4	22.5	22.1	20.3	21.1	9.3	15.4	12.2
Total	100.0	100.0	100.0	100.0	100.0	100.0	100.0	100.0	100.0	100.0	100.0	100.0
Total number (thousands)	41.9	51.4	93.3	41.5	44.0	85.5	83.4	95.4	178.7	39.8	35.9	75.7
Labour Force participation rate[1]	74.5	56.5	64.6	60.9	45.5	53.0	67.7	51.4	59.0	82.3	60.6	72.0
Unemployment rate[2]	5.5	8.7	7.1	13.2	16.7	14.8	9.0	12.0	10.4	10.8	13.6	12.0

1 Labour Force participation rate is the proportion of the working-age population that is economically active.
2 Unemployment rate is the proportion of the economically active population that is unemployed. A person is defined unemployed if he or she is not in employment, wants a job, has actively sought work in the last 4 weeks and is available to start work within 2 weeks; or not in employment, but has found a job which will start within 2 weeks. This is consistent with the International Labour Office (ILO) standard classification.

Source: 2001 Census – Office for National Statistics

born immigrants, but especially for the latter (14.8 per cent). The unemployment rate among OECD-born recent arrivals was lower, however, than that among the UK-born people who had arrived during the same period (7.1 per cent compared with 12.0 per cent). For all three newly arrived in-migrant groups (OECD-born, non-OECD born and UK-born), unemployment rates were higher among women than men. This phenomenon is not seen in the stocks, and is possibly related to the 'tied' nature of movements of married women.[16]

The foreign-born labour force by age and sex

There were 2.8 million foreign-born members of the UK labour force (those either employed or unemployed) in 2001, accounting for 10.5 per cent of the total UK labour force (see bottom row of Table 8.12). This is significantly higher than the 8.3 per cent that foreign-born people contribute to the overall UK population (Table 8.1). This is due to the preponderance of people of working age among the foreign-born population, and occurs despite their overall lower labour force participation rates, as already seen in this chapter.

The age and sex composition of the foreign-born labour force participants is described further in Table 8.12. Overall, they

were both younger and more likely to be female than were UK-born labour force participants. The total foreign-born component of the labour force was more or less evenly split between men and women, with the former accounting for 49.4 per cent. However, those from OECD countries were more likely to be female (52.1 per cent), while the non-OECD group had a slight predominance of males (50.2 per cent). Among the UK-born participants, 46.7 per cent were female; it can be seen that, overall, the foreign-born population has been making a contribution to the feminisation of the workforce.

The gender differences between immigrant groups were also age related. At younger ages (34 and under), women were proportionately more numerous but the reverse was the case among the over 50s. This applied to both OECD- and non-OECD born labour force participants, but the difference between genders was greater in the OECD-born group. Women aged 16 to 34 accounted for almost one in four (24.0 per cent) of the participants from OECD countries, while men aged 16 to 34 accounted for almost one in five (18.8 per cent). Among the UK-born group, the male and female numbers were similar at these younger ages, though men were predominant at older ages. Reasons for the high female

Table 8.12

Age and sex distribution of the labour force[1]: by country of birth and length of residence in the UK, 2001

England and Wales

Percentages

	OECD-born		Non-OECD-born		All foreign-born		UK-born	
	Resident for <1 year	All residents	Resident for <1 year	All residents	Resident for <1 year	All residents	Resident for <1 year	All residents
Men								
16–24	8.4	4.2	9.5	3.6	9.0	3.8	7.6	6.5
25–34	22.8	14.6	23.5	13.1	23.1	13.6	22.0	12.7
35–49	12.0	16.4	11.2	22.2	11.6	20.2	17.8	19.2
50–64	3.3	12.7	2.9	11.4	3.1	11.8	8.6	14.8
Total 16–64	46.5	47.9	47.2	50.2	46.8	49.4	55.9	53.3
Women								
16–24	16.5	5.8	14.0	4.4	15.3	4.9	7.8	6.2
25–34	25.6	18.2	25.0	13.9	25.3	15.4	19.9	12.4
35–49	9.3	17.6	11.5	22.5	10.4	20.8	12.3	18.0
50–59	2.0	10.5	2.4	8.9	2.2	9.5	4.1	10.1
Total 16–59	53.5	52.1	52.8	49.8	53.2	50.6	44.1	46.7
Total men and women	100.0	100.0	100.0	100.0	100.0	100.0	100.0	100.0
Total number (thousands)	73.9	953.0	66.4	1,853.2	140.3	2,806.2	64.1	24,017.4

1 Labour Force = Employed plus unemployed people aged 16 to 64 (males) or 16 to 59 (females).
Source: 2001 Census – Office for National Statistics

component of the foreign-born labour force are complex and include the attraction for female migrants of the range of service activities that now characterise the UK economy.

The age distribution of the non-OECD born stock reflects the historical pattern of immigration. It shows the signs of demographic ageing that would be expected given the prevalence of long-term migrants among the inflow from these countries, and contrasts with the younger OECD-born migrant age structure. One third (33.6 per cent) of the total non-OECD born labour force is made up of men aged over 35, which is similar to that for the UK-born labour force (34.0 per cent). Both men and women aged 35 to 49 make up a larger proportion of the labour force for the non-OECD born group than they do for either the UK- or OECD-born populations.

The age structure of the foreign-born population arriving in the year prior to the 2001 Census demonstrates the demographic potential of migration to revitalise the labour force. Among the 140,000 foreign-born new entrants who were in the labour force in 2001, about a quarter were aged 16 to 24, which was a considerably higher proportion than among the foreign-born stock. Just under half the foreign-born in-migrants were aged 25 to 34. Neither age group showed much difference when examined by country group of origin (see the column: < 1 year, Table 8.12). Only 5 per cent of foreign-born new arrivals in the labour force were aged over 50, compared with 21 per cent of the total foreign-born labour force. Thus, the recent arrivals had a considerably younger profile than the foreign-born population as a whole.

As for the total foreign-born population of working age, the composition of recent arrivals in the labour force by OECD and non-OECD country of birth is very different in the flow from in the 2001 stock. The foreign-born labour force of England and Wales in 2001 was approximately one-third OECD born (950,000) and two-thirds non-OECD born (1.85 million). In contrast, there were slightly *more* OECD-born migrants (74,000) than non-OECD born migrants (66,000) in the newly arrived foreign-born component of the labour force in 2001. If the 64,000 returning UK-born migrants who entered the labour force in 2001 are also considered as OECD-born immigrants, the UK saw a two-to-one ratio of additions to its labour force through immigrants born in high-income countries to those born in low-income countries. This was the reverse of the ratio seen in the immigrant stock profile of the labour force by foreign country of birth.

A longer term trend towards feminisation of the labour force through in-migration continued in 2001 with the new arrivals from both OECD (excluding the UK) and non-OECD countries.

There was a clear female predominance in the total population of foreign-born new arrivals (53.2 per cent). This was especially apparent among those aged 16 to 24 and, to a lesser extent, 25 to 34. Among those aged over 35, men were slightly more numerous in the newly arrived labour force. In contrast, among returning UK-born migrants in the labour force in 2001, there were higher proportions of men than women at all age groups from age 25 upwards.

Socio-economic category and occupation among the foreign-born stock

One of the drivers behind much contemporary labour migration policy in many countries today is the competition for skills to fuel economic growth and counteract skill shortages in the labour market. The skill profile of foreign-born migrants is thus of considerable interest. The objective of this section is to describe the skill levels of the foreign-born stocks and flows. To this end, the seven major socio-economic groups, based on the standard occupational classification (SOC2000),[17] together with those who have never worked or are long-term unemployed, are first collapsed into three groups describing their labour force positions: professional and managerial; intermediate; and routine and long-term unemployed. This is followed by more detailed occupational breakdowns of those members of the labour force who were employed at the time of the 2001 Census.

The data in Table 8.13a show the polarised nature of the labour force positions of the foreign-born population compared with the UK-born: they are more likely to be either higher or lower skilled than somewhere in the middle. About 38 per cent of the foreign-born labour force stock were highly skilled professional and managerial workers but almost as many (36 per cent) were in the routine/unemployed category. The equivalent figures for UK-born labour force participants were 36.5 per cent and 31.6 per cent. Foreign-born men were more likely to be highly skilled than foreign-born women (41.6 and 34.4 per cent), while the reverse was the case for the routine/unemployed group, where there were higher proportions of women (41.9 per cent) than of men (29.9 per cent).

Major differences are apparent when labour force participants are examined by birthplace that demonstrate the 'brain exchanges' that take place between high-income countries. Almost half those born in OECD countries were employed in professional and managerial occupations, compared with only a third of the non-OECD born participants. This pattern can be seen for both sexes. The situation was reversed for the routine/ unemployed group.

Table **8.13a**

Socio-economic classification of total labour-force participants, by country of birth, age and sex, 2001

England and Wales

Percentages

	OECD-born			Non-OECD-born			All foreign-born			UK-born		
	Male	Female	Total	Male	Female	Total	Male	Female	Total	Male	Female	Total
All ages (16–59/64)												
Professional/Managerial	49.4	45.2	47.2	37.8	28.6	33.2	41.6	34.4	38.0	38.8	33.8	36.5
Intermediate	27.5	26.1	26.8	29.0	22.4	25.7	28.5	23.7	26.1	32.9	30.8	31.9
Routine/Unemployed	23.1	28.7	26.0	33.2	49.0	41.1	29.9	41.9	36.0	28.2	35.5	31.6
Total	100.0	100.0	100.0	100.0	100.0	100.0	100.0	100.0	100.0	100.0	100.0	100.0
Ages 16–24												
Professional/Managerial	30.4	26.8	28.3	22.0	16.2	18.8	25.1	20.5	22.5	22.3	21.7	22.0
Intermediate	27.6	27.6	27.6	21.9	19.8	20.7	24.1	22.9	23.4	30.7	31.1	30.9
Routine/Unemployed	42.0	45.6	44.1	56.1	64.0	60.4	50.8	56.5	54.0	47.0	47.2	47.1
Total	100.0	100.0	100.0	100.0	100.0	100.0	100.0	100.0	100.0	100.0	100.0	100.0
Ages 25–34												
Professional/Managerial	59.3	53.8	56.3	40.5	32.2	36.2	47.4	40.9	43.9	42.5	39.5	41.0
Intermediate	22.8	24.6	23.8	24.3	19.9	22.0	23.7	21.8	22.7	31.1	29.6	30.3
Routine/Unemployed	17.9	21.6	19.9	35.2	47.9	41.8	28.9	37.3	33.4	26.4	31.0	28.7
Total	100.0	100.0	100.0	100.0	100.0	100.0	100.0	100.0	100.0	100.0	100.0	100.0
Ages 35–49												
Professional/Managerial	55.2	47.7	51.3	39.6	28.9	34.2	43.9	34.3	39.0	42.8	36.0	39.5
Intermediate	26.9	25.9	26.4	31.5	24.1	27.8	30.2	24.6	27.4	33.3	30.4	31.9
Routine/Unemployed	17.9	26.4	22.3	28.9	47.0	38.0	25.9	41.1	33.6	23.9	33.6	28.6
Total	100.0	100.0	100.0	100.0	100.0	100.0	100.0	100.0	100.0	100.0	100.0	100.0
Ages 50–59/64												
Professional/Managerial	36.8	36.5	36.7	36.1	28.1	32.6	36.4	31.3	34.1	37.8	30.0	34.6
Intermediate	33.7	28.0	31.1	31.6	23.3	28.0	32.4	25.1	29.1	35.0	32.6	34.1
Routine/Unemployed	29.5	35.5	32.2	32.3	48.6	39.5	31.3	43.7	36.8	27.2	37.3	31.3
Total	100.0	100.0	100.0	100.0	100.0	100.0	100.0	100.0	100.0	100.0	100.0	100.0

Source: 2001 Census – Office for National Statistics

As might be expected, the situation varies by age. The youngest group accounted for a low proportion of the highly skilled workers (22.5 per cent), while over half were in the least skilled group. The highest proportion of the highly skilled workforce were those aged 25 to 34, a group characterised by graduates and others who had completed their training. After this age group, the proportion of the workforce that was highly skilled falls, while the share accounted for by the routine/unemployed group rises. Thus, among the foreign-born labour force stock, people aged 24 and under, and those over 50 were more likely to be less skilled or long-term unemployed.

Table 8.13b provides a more detailed breakdown of the foreign-born workforce using the SOC2000 occupational classification and includes only those who were employed. The total number of employed foreign-born people included in the table is 2.1 million (number not shown), about a third of whom were from OECD countries. The analysis provides further confirmation that there are differences in skill levels according to birthplace. For example, those born in non-OECD countries were more likely to be classified as being in Sales and Customer Services, Plant and Machine Operatives or in Elementary Occupations than those born in OECD countries, while the

Table **8.13b**

Occupation of working-age population in employment, by country of birth and sex, 2001

England and Wales

Percentages

Occupation	OECD-born			Non-OECD-born			All foreign-born			UK-born		
	Male 16–64	Female 16–59	Total	Male 16–64	Female 16–59	Total	Male 16–64	Female 16–59	Total	Male 16–64	Female 16–59	Total
Managers and Senior Officials	23.7	13.9	18.9	19.1	11.0	15.7	20.7	12.2	16.9	18.3	11.1	15.0
Professional Occupations	17.9	16.4	17.1	17.3	12.7	15.3	17.5	14.2	16.0	11.6	9.7	10.7
Associate Professional and Technical Occupations	14.9	19.4	17.1	11.1	16.8	13.5	12.4	17.9	14.9	13.4	14.0	13.6
Adminstrative and Secretarial Occupations	4.8	18.5	11.6	6.0	19.3	11.7	5.6	19.0	11.6	5.4	23.2	13.4
Skilled Trades Occupations	14.0	2.0	8.0	13.4	2.7	8.8	13.6	2.4	8.5	20.2	2.3	12.1
Personal Service Occupations	2.5	11.1	6.8	2.4	11.1	6.1	2.4	11.1	6.3	2.0	12.9	6.9
Sales and Customer Service Occupations	3.0	7.7	5.3	5.3	9.8	7.2	4.5	8.9	6.5	4.0	12.3	7.8
Process; Plant And Machine Operatives	8.6	1.9	5.2	12.6	5.0	9.3	11.2	3.7	7.8	13.4	3.1	8.7
Elementary Occupations	10.6	9.1	9.9	12.9	11.7	12.3	12.1	10.6	11.4	11.8	11.6	11.7
Total (all employed)	100.0	100.0	100.0	100.0	100.0	100.0	100.0	100.0	100.0	100.0	100.0	100.0

Source: 2001 Census – Office for National Statistics

latter were more likely to be found in the Managers and Senior Officials group. The occupational distribution among people born in OECD countries was significantly more skewed towards higher-level occupations and away from lower-level occupations than the distribution of the UK-born workforce.

The occupational distribution of the employed, non-OECD born group, while not as favourable as that of the OECD-born group, was nevertheless as favourable as or more favourable than that of the UK-born workforce. The comparison is best seen when the occupational distributions are seen separately for men and women. Gender differences in occupation are found among the foreign-born population, as they are among the UK-born, although these are less marked for those born in OECD countries.

Both men and women born in OECD countries were more likely to be in the Managerial and Senior Official occupation category than were either non-OECD or UK-born employed people. Men born in non-OECD countries, however, were almost equally likely to be in professional occupations as men born in OECD countries (17.3 and 17.9 per cent respectively). Both were much more likely to be in professional occupations than were UK-born men (11.6 per cent).

Women born in OECD and non-OECD countries were also more likely to be in professional occupations than women born in the UK: 16.4 per cent and 12.7 per cent of those born in OECD and non-OECD countries respectively were in professional occupations compared with only 9.7 per cent of UK-born women. In addition, women born in both OECD and non-OECD countries were more likely to be in Associate Professional and Technical occupations (19.4 per cent of OECD-born and 16.8 per cent of non-OECD born women) than were UK-born women (14.0 per cent).

The pattern of differences between the occupations in which the UK-born participants were relatively more prevalent than the foreign-born is strongly gendered. UK-born men were much more likely than foreign-born men to be in the Skilled Trades category (20.2 per cent compared with 13.6 per cent), while UK-born women were more likely than either OECD-born or non-OECD born women to be in Administrative and Secretarial (23.2 per cent) and Sales and Customer Service (12.3 per cent) occupations.

Socio-economic category and occupation of the foreign-born flows

Turning to the newly arrived in-migrants, the foreign-born labour force was even more skewed towards the more skilled occupations than was seen for the foreign-born stock (Table 8.14a). Over half (52.1 per cent) of the foreign-born newly-arrived immigrants were professional and managerial compared with 38.0 per cent of the total foreign-born stock (see again Table 8.13a). A much lower proportion of the newly arrived were in intermediate occupations (18.4 per cent) than

was the case for the foreign-born stock, and the proportion in the routine/not working category was also lower. While this may be in part due to a shift over time towards more skilled foreign-born immigrants, a faster migrant turnover among the more highly skilled is probably the main explanation behind this phenomenon. Notable here is that the phenomenon of more highly skilled workers in the flows than in the stocks is also seen for the UK-born component of the labour force. This is again consistent with greater international mobility among the more skilled component of the workforce for both those born in the UK and those born abroad.

Table **8.14a**

Socio-economic classification of labour-force participants who arrived in the last year: by country of birth, age and sex, 2001

England and Wales

Percentages

	OECD-born			Non-OECD-born			All foreign-born			UK-born		
	Male	Female	Total	Male	Female	Total	Male	Female	Total	Male	Female	Total
All ages (16–59/64)												
Professional/Managerial	67.1	49.1	57.5	52.4	40.4	46.1	60.1	45.0	52.1	63.6	47.5	56.5
Intermediate	16.8	22.5	19.8	16.3	17.4	16.9	16.6	20.1	18.4	22.8	28.5	25.3
Routine/Unemployed	16.1	28.5	22.7	31.3	42.2	37.0	23.3	34.9	29.5	13.6	24.0	18.2
Total	100.0	100.0	100.0	100.0	100.0	100.0	100.0	100.0	100.0	100.0	100.0	100.0
Ages 16–24												
Professional/Managerial	36.3	24.8	28.6	27.8	19.1	22.6	32.0	22.3	25.9	32.4	29.5	30.9
Intermediate	24.6	24.9	24.8	16.6	17.1	16.9	20.6	21.5	21.2	35.7	34.3	35.0
Routine/Unemployed	39.1	50.3	46.6	55.5	63.9	60.5	47.4	56.2	52.9	31.9	36.2	34.1
Total	100.0	100.0	100.0	100.0	100.0	100.0	100.0	100.0	100.0	100.0	100.0	100.0
Ages 25–34												
Professional/Managerial	70.4	59.9	64.9	58.3	50.1	54.1	64.6	55.3	59.8	65.4	53.3	59.7
Intermediate	16.6	21.9	19.4	15.2	17.2	16.3	15.9	19.7	17.9	22.2	27.4	24.7
Routine/Unemployed	13.1	18.2	15.8	26.4	32.7	29.6	19.5	25.0	22.3	12.4	19.4	15.7
Total	100.0	100.0	100.0	100.0	100.0	100.0	100.0	100.0	100.0	100.0	100.0	100.0
Ages 35–49												
Professional/Managerial	79.6	60.7	71.3	59.6	45.6	52.5	70.5	52.8	62.1	72.8	51.1	64.0
Intermediate	12.8	20.1	16.0	17.6	18.1	17.8	14.9	19.0	16.9	18.4	25.8	21.4
Routine/Unemployed	7.6	19.2	12.7	22.9	36.3	29.7	14.6	28.2	21.0	8.8	23.0	14.6
Total	100.0	100.0	100.0	100.0	100.0	100.0	100.0	100.0	100.0	100.0	100.0	100.0
Ages 50–59/64												
Professional/Managerial	78.1	56.4	69.9	56.8	39.7	49.1	68.7	47.8	60.1	67.5	43.0	59.6
Intermediate	13.5	20.9	16.3	19.4	17.3	18.5	16.1	19.1	17.3	22.1	30.6	24.9
Routine/Unemployed	8.5	22.7	13.8	23.9	43.0	32.4	15.3	33.2	22.6	10.4	26.5	15.6
Total	100.0	100.0	100.0	100.0	100.0	100.0	100.0	100.0	100.0	100.0	100.0	100.0

Source: 2001 Census – Office for National Statistics

As with the stocks, there were differences between the sexes. Newly-arrived men were considerably more likely to be in the more skilled occupations than were newly-arrived women (60.1 and 45.0 per cent), although newly-arrived women were again more likely to be in the more skilled occupations than were women in the total foreign-born stock. Only the youngest age group had a relatively low proportion in the professional and managerial occupations, the figure for the other age groups being around 60 per cent. Differences according to country of birth were again manifest: 57.5 per cent of OECD-born migrants were in highly skilled occupations compared with 46.1 per cent of those born in a non-OECD country. Among the UK-born returning migrants, 56.5 per cent were in highly skilled occupations, which was almost identical to the level for the OECD-born group.

The older, newly - arrived, foreign-born migrants were more likely to enter highly skilled occupations than the younger (and especially the youngest) new migrants. The decline in proportions in the highly skilled occupations after the ages 25 to 34 that was seen in the stocks is not found in the flows. About 77 per cent of all entrants aged 50 and over were in either the professional and managerial or Intermediate groups.

The proportion was even higher for the OECD-born migrants (86 per cent). In contrast, 47 per cent of all foreign-born entrants aged 16 to 24 were in one of these two more skilled groups, though, again, with significant differences according to place of birth.

The occupational distribution of the newly - arrived employed migrant flows is shown in Table 8.14b. While the majority of new immigrants from the OECD-born and non-OECD born groups was employed in the higher-skilled occupations, including associate professional and technical occupations, significant numbers were initially employed in the lowest skilled, Elementary groups. This is especially so for men born in non-OECD countries, among whom, in 2001, 15.8 per cent had been employed in Elementary occupations in the year of their arrival, compared with 12.9 per cent of employed men born in non-OECD countries (see again Table 8.13b). Newly arrived foreign-born men were, in contrast, much less likely to be in occupations classified as Skilled Trades (7.0 per cent) than the stocks of all foreign-born men (13.6 per cent).

Table **8.14b**

Occupation of working-age population in employment who arrived in the last year: by country of birth, age and sex, 2001

England and Wales

Percentages

Occupation	OECD-born			Non-OECD-born			All foreign-born			UK-born		
	Male 16–64	Female 16–59	Total	Male 16–64	Female 16–59	Total	Male 16–64	Female 16–59	Total	Male 16–64	Female 16–59	Total
Managers and senior officials	25.7	10.8	18.6	14.5	6.5	11.0	20.8	9.1	15.4	24.7	11.6	19.4
Professional occupations	27.4	21.8	24.7	30.2	16.4	24.3	28.6	19.7	24.5	21.9	18.3	20.5
Associate professional and technical occupations	17.4	18.5	17.9	14.5	29.2	20.8	16.1	22.6	19.1	21.7	19.8	20.9
Adminstrative and secretarial occupations	6.2	15.9	10.8	5.7	16.3	10.3	6.0	16.0	10.6	6.0	20.8	11.9
Skilled trades occupations	6.9	1.4	4.3	7.1	1.2	4.5	7.0	1.3	4.4	10.3	1.4	6.7
Personal service occupations	2.5	15.3	8.6	2.1	9.7	5.4	2.3	13.1	7.3	1.6	9.7	4.8
Sales and customer service occupations	2.5	5.9	4.1	5.1	7.2	6.0	3.6	6.4	4.9	2.9	9.4	5.5
Process; plant and machine operatives	3.0	0.9	2.0	5.1	1.7	3.6	3.9	1.2	2.7	5.0	1.1	3.4
Elementary occupations	8.5	9.5	9.0	15.8	11.9	14.1	11.7	10.4	11.1	5.9	7.9	6.7
Total (all employed)	100.0	100.0	100.0	100.0	100.0	100.0	100.0	100.0	100.0	100.0	100.0	100.0

Source: 2001 Census – Office for National Statistics

Summary and conclusions

The aims of this chapter were to highlight the main features of the foreign-born population of the UK, both as a whole and among those of working age. Comparisons were made throughout between immigrants from higher-income and lower-income countries, sometimes by specific world region of origin and other times by a simple OECD/non-OECD split.

Demographically, immigrants to the UK from higher-income countries tended to be younger, were more likely to be single and were less likely to remain permanently in the UK. These are the typical characteristics of the temporary labour migrant streams that are increasingly part of the world economy.

The years that major immigration inflows took place are an additional factor affecting the ageing of the foreign-born population, and explain the very high old-age dependency ratios for the Irish-born residents of the UK, following much earlier migration streams. As many as one in four of all foreign-born people of pensionable age in the UK are from Ireland. The effect of the timing of major immigration inflows is also seen in the relative prominence of people born in the Caribbean and South Asia among the total foreign-born population of pensionable age. Conversely, very low old-age dependency ratios are seen among those born in the Far East and Africa. Large growth in the foreign-born populations from these latter regions also gave rise to a much greater diversity of country and ethnic origins within the overseas-born population in 2001 as compared with 30 years before.

Among the foreign-born population of working age, large distinctions in labour market characteristics were seen between those migrants who arrived in the year preceding the 2001 Census and the total foreign-born population. In particular, newly-arrived migrants were more likely to be either students or unemployed. This pattern was seen between migrants from both OECD and non-OECD countries and, indeed, between UK-born migrants who had been living abroad a year before the Census compared with the total foreign-born stock in the UK. Among those newly arrived migrants in the labour force or in employment, however, very high proportions were in the highly skilled occupations. This was true, too, for returning UK-born migrants of working age.

A very different labour-force breakdown by OECD/non-OECD country of birth was seen in the flows (those arrived in the previous year) as compared with the stocks (all those resident in the UK). While the non-OECD born component of the UK's foreign-born labour force exceeded the OECD-born component by a factor of two to one in the stocks, the number of labour-force participants born in OECD countries slightly exceeded the number born in non-OECD countries among those arriving in the year before the 2001 Census. This emphasises the need to understand the contribution of immigration to the labour force dynamically, as a result of both immigration and immigrants' lengths of stay in the UK. The picture provided here of large OECD-born inflows, with frequently short lengths of stay, is consistent with previous work showing that the UK plays a very active role in the international mobility of the highly qualified workforce of OECD countries.[18]

The foreign-born population from non-OECD countries had less favourable labour market characteristics than the OECD-born population, in terms of both employment and occupation. Gender gaps in labour market characteristics were also greater among the non-OECD born workforce than among the OECD-born. Compared with the UK-born population, however, the picture was more mixed. On one hand, both men and women from non-OECD countries were more likely to be either unemployed or economically inactive than UK-born men and women of working age. Among those employed, however, the non-OECD born population were overall as likely or more likely to be in highly skilled occupations compared with the UK-born. In particular, the proportion of employed non-OECD born workers in professional occupations was similar to that of workers born in OECD countries, and substantially higher than for those born in the UK. This difference, between the picture for entry to employment and that for outcomes among those in employment, is similar to that shown previously for the foreign-born and UK-born ethnic minorities in the early 1990s.[19]

Notes and references

1. Rendall M S and Ball D J (2004) Immigration, emigration and the ageing of the overseas-born population of the United Kingdom. *Population Trends* **116**, 18–27.

2. Salt J and McLaughlin G (2002) Global competition for skills: an evaluation of policies', 201–43 in Migration: Benefiting Australia, Department of Immigration and Multicultural and Indigenous Affairs: Canberra; Castles S and Miller M J (2003) *The Age of Migration: International Population Movements in the Modern World*, Guildford Press: New York.

3. Salt J (2005) *Current Trends in International Migration in Europe*, Council of Europe: Strasbourg.

4. The reader interested in individual countries of birth can consult the detailed 2001 Census output tables available on the National Statistics website: www.statistics.gov.uk/census, or refer to the country-by-country analyses (excluding Ireland) in the detailed

report of the UK's foreign-born population by Kyambi S (2005) *Beyond Black and White: Mapping New Immigrant Communities*, Institute for Public Policy Research, London.

5. See, for example, Haskey J (1997) Population review: (8) The ethnic minority and foreign-born populations of Great Britain. *Population Trends* **88**, 13–30.

6. Organisation for Economic Co-operation and Development (2005) *Society at a Glance: OECD Social Indicators – 2005 Edition*, OECD publishing: Paris.

7. Dumont J-C and Lemaitre G (2005) Counting immigrants and expatriates in OECD countries: A new perspective. OECD Social, Employment and Migration Working Paper 25, www.oed.org

8. Dumont J-C and Lemaitre G (2005) Table 1 (see note 7).

9. Owen D (1996) Size, structure and growth of the ethnic minority populations, 80–123 in Coleman D and Salt J (eds) *Ethnicity in the 1991 Census: Volume One, Demographic Characteristics of the Ethnic Minority Populations*. HMSO: London.

10. Office for National Statistics (2004) *Census 2001 Definitions*. TSO: London.

11. Office for National Statistics (2005) *Focus On People and Migration overviews: Overseas Born*, www.statistics.gov.uk/focuson/ migration

12. This has been estimated for the 1990s' period from out-migrants' responses in the International Passenger Survey to the question on what year they arrived in the UK. These data, when combined with immigrant numbers by country of birth and year as a denominator, allow for the estimation of the proportion of foreign-born immigrants emigrating again within a given number of years following arrival. The methodology is similar to that used in Rendall and Ball (2004: see note 1). The differences are that the immigrant denominator for non-OECD countries includes here total asylum seeker flows for each year (Home Office, various years, *Control of Immigration Command Paper series*), and that arrivals only in the 1990s are considered.

13. Bell B D (1997) The performance of immigrants in the United Kingdom: Evidence from the GHS. The Economic Journal **107(441)**, 333–44.

14. Wheatley Price S (2001) The employment adjustment of male immigrants in England. *Journal of Population Economics* **14**, 193–220; Dustmann C, Fabbri F, Preston I and Wadsworth J (2003) *The labour market performance of immigrants in the United Kingdom labour market*, Home Office Online Report 05/03.

15. Dobson J and McLaughlin G (2001) International migration to and from the United Kingdom, 1975-1999: consistency, change and implications for the labour market. *Population Trends* **106**, 29–38.

16. See, for example, Boyle P, Cooke T J, Halfacree K and D Smith (2001) A cross-national comparison of the impact of family migration on women's employment status. *Demography* **38(2)**, 201–13.

17. Office for National Statistics (2004) *Census 2001 Definitions*. TSO: London, 67–79.

18. Among OECD countries, for example, the UK has recently been shown to have simultaneously one of the largest numbers of its tertiary-qualified people resident in other OECD countries and one of the largest numbers of tertiary-qualified people from other OECD countries resident in the UK, see Chart 3 in Dumont and Lemaitre (2005: see note 7).

19. Leslie D, Drinkwater S, and O'Leary N (1998) Unemployment and earnings among Britain's ethnic minorities: some signs for optimism. *Journal of Ethnic and Migration Studies* **24(3)**, 489–506.

Special and communal populations

Gary Wainman, Francesca Ambrose
and Julie Jefferies

Chapter 9

Introduction

Consider a student hall of residence located near a university, where undergraduates are housed in their first year of study. A large proportion of the residents will be aged 18 or 19, with some being in their 20s and older. Each summer the majority of students leave the hall to live elsewhere and every autumn a new set of students comes to live in the accommodation.

The population of students living in the hall of residence is distinctive in several ways. First, it differs from the UK population as a whole in terms of demographic characteristics, such as age and marital status. Second, it has a high turnover as people regularly move in and out of the accommodation. Third, despite this high turnover, the population may be thought of as 'static' in terms of its age structure, which remains fairly constant over time. Similarly, its geographical location is 'static'.

This chapter deals with four populations that may be thought of as 'static' in this way: the armed forces, prisoners, students and those living in communal establishments. There is inevitably some overlap between the last group and the first three, because members of the armed forces, for example, are more likely than the general population to be living in a communal establishment.

Static populations are of interest for a variety of reasons:

- they have a different demographic profile from the rest of the UK population

- they tend to be geographically concentrated in certain areas, such as those containing prisons or universities

- the total numbers in each population may vary considerably from year to year at the national level as people join and leave the group

- at the local level, the opening or closing of an army base, prison or student residence may have a large impact on the population of that area

- some static population groups need to be considered separately when making population estimates.[1]

People joining or leaving static populations may be drawn either from the UK population or from overseas. In the case of prisons, inmates are generally UK residents on entering and leaving prison. As a result, changes in the size of the UK prison population do not have a significant impact on the size or structure of the UK population as a whole (although there will be an impact at the local level).

With students, some of the movement in and out of this static population will be to and from other countries, since many students from abroad choose to study in the UK and *vice versa*. Changes in the numbers of students entering and leaving the UK will therefore have an impact on the total number of people living in the UK.

This means that the size and structure of the UK population may be affected by changes in static populations, if some of those joining or leaving such populations are international migrants.

Information on static population groups comes from a variety of sources. Some government departments publish regular figures on groups within their remit. For example, the Home Office compiles data on prisoners in England and Wales. In addition, the 2001 Census provided a snapshot of the armed forces, prisoners, students and communal establishment residents as at April 2001.

Estimating the sizes of static populations presents particular challenges for census enumeration and population estimates in the years between censuses (see the appendix for more information). The following sections draw on both census and annual sources to investigate the characteristics of the UK's static populations.

Armed forces

The term 'armed forces' refers to a country's military forces, usually consisting of army, navy and air force personnel. The armed forces are generally considered to be a static population, which diverges from the general population in terms of demographic characteristics. It is usual to expect that a military population will be predominantly younger, have a higher proportion of men and be more geographically mobile than the population as a whole. This section discusses some of the characteristics of the armed forces employed by or resident in the UK and highlights how and why they differ from the UK population as a whole.

Armed forces that could be considered part of the UK population can be defined in several ways – according to which nation employs them, where they are permanently based or posted and where they are currently deployed. Figure 9.1 shows that, in the armed forces employed by the UK, who are often referred to as 'home armed forces', a distinction can be made between those currently posted in the UK and those based abroad. Similarly, among armed forces currently posted in the UK, the distinction can be made between those employed by the constituent countries of the UK (home armed

Figure **9.1**

Armed forces and the UK population

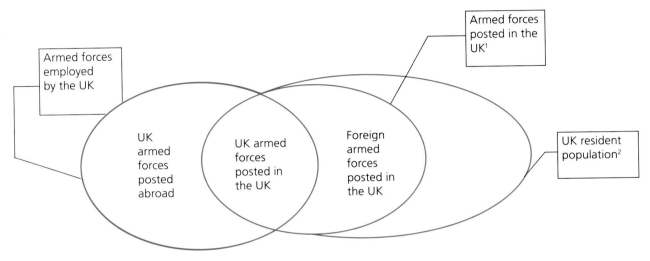

Armed forces
employed
by the UK

Armed forces
posted in the
UK[1]

UK
armed
forces
posted
abroad

UK armed
forces
posted in
the UK

Foreign
armed
forces
posted in
the UK

UK resident
population[2]

1 UK and foreign armed forces posted in the UK are considered to be usually resident in the UK and are included in the mid-year population estimates produced by ONS, GRO-Scotland and NISRA.
2 The size of the circles do not represent the size of the populations and hence are not to scale.

forces) and foreign armed forces employed by a nation outside the UK. These distinctions are critically important, especially when using armed forces data for other purposes, such as compiling the mid-year resident population estimates.[2]

This section starts by looking at the armed forces employed by the UK, then narrows its focus to examine where the home armed forces posted in the UK are based. Finally, it discusses the foreign armed forces based in the UK.

There are two main sources of data on home armed forces: the census and counts produced by the Defence Analytical Services Agency (DASA), a Ministry of Defence agency. The census provides a ten-yearly snapshot of the population, while the majority of DASA figures are produced quarterly and some even monthly. DASA data on UK regular armed forces[3] are used here as these provide the most up-to-date data on military personnel. The figures on foreign armed forces quoted in this chapter are collated by the United States Air Force, using data from RAF Mildenhall, the US Embassy and the US Navy HQ.

Armed forces employed by the UK

Changes in the number of UK armed forces over time

In 2004 the Ministry of Defence in the UK employed over 207,000 military personnel. This represents an overall decline of 15,000 from the 222,000 military personnel employed in 1996 (Figure 9.2). The reduction between 1996 and 2004 was seen mainly in the Naval Services[4] and Royal Air Force.

However, as Figure 9.3 shows, the numbers in the UK armed forces fluctuate from year to year. For example, there was an upwards trend between 2002 and 2004, with a 1.1 per cent increase in the number of UK armed forces. This increase was greater than for the UK population aged 16 to 55[5], which grew by only 0.15 per cent over the same period.

Gender

The proportion of UK regular forces who are female has been rising steadily over the last ten years, from 7.0 per cent in 1994 to 8.9 per cent in 2004. This shows that, despite the increased proportion of women, the armed forces population is still very male-dominated and does not reflect the gender split of the

Figure **9.2**

Number of UK regulars, by service, 1996 and 2004

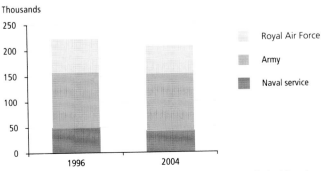

Thousands

Royal Air Force
Army
Naval service

Source: UK Defence Personnel in Figures – Defence Analytical Services Agency

Figure **9.3**

Number of UK regulars, 2001 to 2004[1]

Numbers

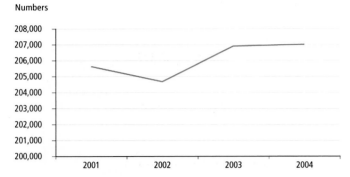

1   As at 1 April each year.
Source: TSP1 – Defence Analytical Services Agency

UK as a whole, which is more evenly balanced. In mid-2004, 50.4 per cent of the UK population aged between 16 and 55 was female.

Age

The age-sex profile of the armed forces is very different from that of the UK population (Figure 9.4). UK regular armed forces range mainly from ages 16 to 55, with a very small number over 55.

In 2004 the average (median) age of the UK armed forces was 29.6 years, which was considerably lower than the median age of 38.6 seen in the UK population as a whole. This is not surprising since the UK has a large population over the age of 55; they make up over a third (34.2 per cent) of the population aged 16 and over. In comparison, only 0.3 per cent of the armed forces are aged 55 and over. For the remainder of this section, the UK population aged 16 to 55 is used to enable meaningful comparisons with the armed forces population.

The largest numbers of UK regular armed forces are found at ages 19 to 25 (Figure 9.4). In 2004 this age group accounted for almost a third of the UK regular armed forces, a proportion that has changed little since 2000. In contrast, those aged 19 to 25 made up only 16.5 per cent of the UK population aged 16 to 55. Despite the large differences between the age distribution of the armed forces and the UK population, there are some similarities at certain ages, as shown in Figure 9.4. For example, both populations show a dip at around age 27 and 28, reflecting the low number of births in the late 1970s and, for the armed forces, a reduction in recruitment in the early 1990s.

For both sexes, the largest numbers of UK regular armed forces in 2004 occurred at age 23. This is younger than the largest single age group in the UK population, which was 39 for both

Figure **9.4**

Age distribution of UK regular armed forces[1] and UK population[2] aged 16 to 55, 2004[3]

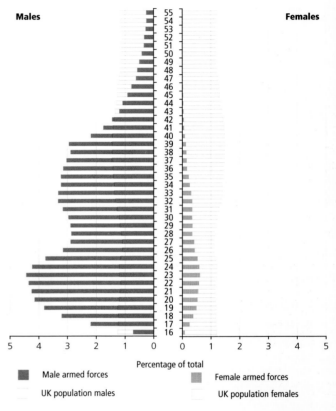

1   Ages 16 to 55+ shown for armed forces. The number aged 56 and above is very small.
2   Ages 16 to 55 shown for UK population.
3   Population estimates refer to 30 June, while armed forces data refer to 1 April.
Source: TSP 8 – Defence Analytical Services Agency. Population Estimates – Office for National Statistics, General Register Office for Scotland, Northern Ireland Statistics and Research Agency

males and females in 2004 (resulting from the mid-1960s' baby boom described in Chapter 5).

The age structure of the armed forces also varies by gender, with the female population younger than its male equivalent (Table 9.5). In 2004, 27.4 per cent of male, but only 11.0 per cent of female, personnel were aged over 35. In contrast, a greater proportion of females (45.5 per cent) than males (34.4 per cent) in the armed forces were aged between 16 and 24.

The lack of females in the older age groups in the armed forces reflects the fact that some areas of the military have only recently been opened to women. For example, women have only been able to serve at sea with the Royal Navy since 1991. Certain areas remain closed to women for reasons of health and safety or combat effectiveness. These include the infantry, submariners and Royal Marines (except the Band Service).

Table 9.5

The UK regular armed forces[1] and UK population,[2] by age and sex, 2004[3]

Percentages

Age	UK regular armed forces		UK population aged 16 to 55	
	Male	Female	Male	Female
16–20	15.5	19.2	12.4	11.6
21–25	23.1	32.3	11.7	11.6
26–30	16.2	20.9	11.4	11.3
31–35	17.9	16.5	13.5	13.7
36–40	15.6	7.5	14.4	14.6
41–45	7.0	2.5	13.4	13.6
46–50	3.1	0.7	11.8	12.0
51–54	1.3	0.2	9.0	9.2
55 +[4]	0.3	0.1	2.4	2.4
Total	100.0	100.0	100.0	100.0

1 UK regular forces data include Nursing services and exclude full time reserve service personnel, Gurkhas, the Home Service battalions of the Royal Irish Regiment, mobilised reservists and Naval Activated Reservists. Trained and untrained persons are included.
2 Population estimates include armed forces personnel.
3 Armed forces data are as at 1st April 2004. UK population estimates are taken at mid-year 2004.
4 Armed forces population aged 55+ and UK population aged 55 only.

Source: TSP 8 Defence Analytical Services Agency. 2004 population estimates – Office for National Statistics; General Register Office for Scotland; Northern Ireland Statistics and Research Agency

Ethnicity

Personnel declaring themselves to be from an ethnic minority group comprised 4.5 per cent of the UK regular armed forces in 2004. This is lower than the proportion of the total UK population describing themselves as from an ethnic group other than White in the 2001 Census (7.9 per cent[6]). However, this comparison may be affected by the different age distributions of the armed forces and the UK population, and the 7.6 per cent of armed forces who were of unknown ethnic group[7] in 2004.

Figure 9.6 shows the ethnic backgrounds of UK regular forces on 1 April 2004. The majority of UK regular armed forces declared themselves to be White (87.9 per cent). The Army had the greatest number of personnel declared to be from an ethnic minority, which amounted to 6.9 per cent of all Army personnel (3.8 per cent of UK regular forces). The Naval Services and Royal Air Force each had around 2.5 per cent of their personnel recorded as being from an ethnic minority background.

Marital status

Almost 97,000 armed forces personnel were classed as married[8]

Figure 9.6

Strength of UK regular forces by ethnic group and service, 1 April 2004

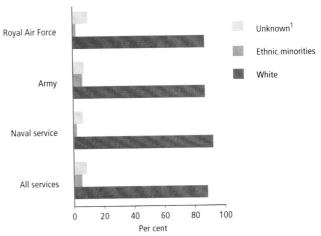

1 Includes those with an unrecorded ethnic origin and non-responses.

Source: Table 2.10 UK Defence Statistics 2004 – Defence Analytical Services Agency

in 2004. This was almost half of all UK armed forces. However, the majority (53.2 per cent) of personnel were not currently married; this contrasts with the UK population aged 16 and over, where the majority (53.3 per cent) were married in 2001. Although the armed forces data from DASA were captured in April 2004, the most recent data for the UK population on marital status are from the 2001 Census.[9]

Table 9.7 demonstrates that there is a greater difference between the marital status of service personnel and the UK population when looking at males and females separately. The UK population has fairly even proportions of married men and married women, with 55.3 per cent of men and 51.5 per cent of women married in 2001. Although this is true also for servicemen, nearly half of whom are married (48.8 per cent), it is not the case for servicewomen where only one in four are married (26.5 per cent). Armed forces personnel are often extremely transient, with personnel, and sometimes their families, being posted to different locations in the UK and abroad for varying periods. Married service personnel tend to have a greater number of social and family responsibilities that make moving difficult and this is especially the case for many married servicewomen. Single personnel are often free from such responsibilities and therefore have a greater propensity to move.

The proportion of servicewomen who are married is lower than for the UK female population in all age groups except those aged 16 to 24. In this age group, 9.2 per cent of females in the armed forces are married compared with only 6.6 per cent of females in the UK population. This is also true for servicemen,

Table **9.7**

Percentage currently married,[1] UK armed forces and UK population, by age and sex, April 2004[2]

Age	Armed forces			UK population[3]		
	Male	Female	Persons	Male	Female	Persons
16–24	8.9	9.2	9.0	2.6	6.6	4.6
25–29	38.9	27.1	37.5	24.3	36.0	30.3
30–34	71.2	47.5	69.1	49.0	56.8	53.0
35–39	83.2	56.4	81.9	62.0	65.9	64.0
40–44	87.0	60.0	86.0	68.6	70.3	69.5
45 and over[4]	91.8	47.8	90.9	73.9	58.7	65.7
16 and over	48.8	26.5	46.8	55.3	51.5	53.3

1 Married includes those separated who are still legally married. The definition of married varies between the services and is different from the census definition (see appendix).
2 The armed forces data are as at 1 April 2004. UK population data are taken from the 2001 Census and are the latest data available on marital status for the UK as a whole.
3 The 2001 Census population data include armed forces personnel.
4 The armed forces population spans the ages 16 to 55+, but the number aged over 55 is very small.

Source: TSP 11 – Defence Analytical Services Agency; 2001 Census – Office for National Statistics; General Register Office for Scotland; Northern Ireland Statistics and Research Agency

with a higher proportion (8.9 per cent) of 16 to 24-year-olds married than in the UK male population (2.6 per cent). But, for males, the proportion who are married is higher in the armed forces for every age group.

Table 9.7 illustrates that, overall, a member of the UK population is more likely to be married than a member of the armed forces, and that this is particularly the case for servicewomen. Conversely, in every age group, a member of the armed forces is more likely to be married than a member of the UK population. This paradox can be attributed to the difference in age structures: the armed forces have a younger age structure than the UK population and young people are less likely to be married.

UK armed forces posted in the UK

In 2004 almost 176,600 UK regular armed forces[10] were posted in the UK,[11] largely within England. Almost 86,000 of the UK regular forces posted in the UK were in the Army, almost as many as the Naval Services (just over 39,000) and Royal Air Force (almost 51,000) combined.

Armed forces location statistics may refer to either the posted location or deployed location. Posted location is where an individual is permanently based, while deployed location is where an individual is physically located at a given time. This part of the chapter uses figures on the number of armed forces personnel at the base that is their posted location.[12] Naval personnel on sea service are included in the local authority of the home port of their ship.

Over eight in ten of the UK regular armed forces posted in the UK were based in England. The remaining constituent countries of the UK contained a relatively small percentage of the UK total, reflecting the sizes of their populations. Scotland had 8 per cent, Northern Ireland 4 per cent and Wales 2 per cent. Within countries, the armed forces are not evenly distributed geographically and tend to be concentrated more in some areas than others.

Within England, the three Government Office Regions (GORs) where the greatest number of UK regular forces were based in 2004 were, in order: the South East, South West and East of England. The South East and South West were both home to over 40,000 regular forces (South East 49,000, South West 41,000). Combined, these two regions accounted for over 50 per cent of the UK total.

The South East was home to the greatest number of UK regular forces in both the Army (25,000) and the Royal Air Force (almost 11,000). The South West contained the greatest concentrations of personnel from the Naval Services, with just over 19,000 based in this GOR.

Reducing the geographical scale to the district level reveals an uneven distribution of UK regular forces. The local authority districts in the UK with the greatest numbers of UK regular forces in 2004 in order were: Portsmouth (South East), Plymouth (South West) and Richmondshire (Yorkshire and Humberside).

Portsmouth and Plymouth Unitary Authorities contained the greatest numbers of UK regular forces in 2004, with 9,300 and almost 8,000 regular forces respectively. These were almost entirely composed from members of the Naval Services: 9,200 in Portsmouth and 7,500 in Plymouth. The Naval Services comprised a little over 99 per cent of the UK regular forces within Portsmouth and almost 94 per cent of those within Plymouth. The armed forces based in these unitary authority districts contribute to the dynamics of these areas; in 2004 they made up 4.9 per cent of the population of Portsmouth and 3.3 per cent of that of Plymouth.

Richmondshire in Yorkshire and Humberside contained 50 per cent of the region's UK regular forces. All 7,110 of the UK regular service personnel based within Richmondshire were in the Army. The military presence in this local authority district has a greater impact than in Portsmouth and Plymouth; in 2004 they made up 14 per cent of the population.

Foreign armed forces

In mid-2004 there were over 9,800 foreign armed forces personnel based within the UK. These are members of another country's armed forces who are stationed on permanent bases within the UK. American armed forces are the only group from outside the UK to have bases within the UK. Foreign armed forces from countries other than America do enter the UK but usually on short-term postings, hence they are not normally included in the resident population.

This section focuses on England as, in 2004, virtually all members of the American armed forces in the UK were based in England.[13] Most often, when armed forces are stationed abroad for an extended period, their dependants, usually partners and children, are permitted to accompany them. There were just over 11,500 dependants of American armed forces resident in England in 2004, most located within the base or close by. In total, American armed forces and their dependants added over 21,300 people to England's resident population.

The majority of the American armed forces and their dependants are concentrated within the air force. In 2004, members of the United States Air Force and their dependants comprised almost 20,000 (92 per cent) of the American armed forces based in England. Members of the United States navy and their dependants comprised almost 1,000 (5 per cent) and the American army and their dependants made up the remainder.

In geographical terms, the American armed forces are heavily concentrated within the East GOR of England, with nearly 18,700 (87 per cent) of the foreign armed forces and dependants being based there in 2004. The concentration of American armed forces within the East of England is almost

15 times greater than in the South West, the GOR with the second highest number of such personnel. The North East and North West GORs contained no American armed forces or dependants and the remaining GORs fewer than 1,300 each.

In the East GOR, American armed forces are concentrated in a relatively small number of local authorities. The five local authorities where the highest numbers of personnel plus dependants were based accounted for 80 per cent of the total American armed forces within England in 2004. The largest numbers (nearly 10,000) were based in Forest Heath, where 46 per cent of the total American armed forces within England were stationed.

Summary

This section has highlighted how the characteristics and geographical distribution of the armed forces differ from the UK population as a whole and, most notably, the dramatic variations in age structure and gender composition. The vast majority of armed forces employed by the UK are men aged between 16 and 55, with large concentrations in the early 20s age groups.

Both the foreign and home armed forces are geographically concentrated in certain areas of the country. At the local authority level, Portsmouth (South East), Plymouth (South West) and Richmondshire (Yorkshire and Humberside) had the greatest concentration of home armed forces in 2004. The foreign armed forces were highly concentrated in a small number of areas, such as Forest Heath and East Cambridgeshire, both in the East GOR.

Prisoners

Prisons are the usual and eventual destination for offenders receiving custodial sentences. The prison population includes both sentenced and remand prisoners. Sentenced prisoners are those held in prison as a result of receiving a sentence in a criminal court. Remand prisoners are those awaiting commencement or continuation of trial prior to verdict and those awaiting sentence.

Sentenced prisoners are classified into different risk-level groups for security purposes and held in separate prisons or accommodation depending on their risk designation.

Men and women prisoners are held either in separate prisons or in separate accommodation within mixed prisons.

The UK prison population is a static population since it diverges from the general population in terms of demographic characteristics, it is geographically concentrated in certain areas and the numbers in prison can vary from year to year. The next sections of this chapter discuss the characteristics of the prison population and highlight why it differs from the UK population as a whole.

Prisons in the UK

In 2005 there were 158 prisons in the UK. Of the four constituent countries of the UK, England has the greatest number of prison establishments with 135. Scotland contains 16 prisons and Wales and Northern Ireland contain four and three respectively. Of the 158 prisons within the UK, 146 are public institutions, while a much smaller number (12) are run by the private sector in partnership with the public sector. This arrangement is called a Public Private Partnership (PPP). There are ten Public Private Partnership prisons in England, and one each in Wales and Scotland. Examples of prisons created as a result of Public Private Partnership initiatives include: HMP Rye Hill in England, HMP Parc in Wales and HMP Kilmarnock in Scotland.[14]

Trends in the UK prison population

In 2003 the prison population stood at almost 81,000. Figure 9.8 illustrates how the UK prison population has increased by almost 25,000 (44 per cent) over the last decade, from 56,000 in 1994. The number of prisoners, as a rate per 100,000 people living in the UK, has shown a similar increase, from 97 per 100,000 in 1994 to 140 per 100,000 in 2003. However, this increase in the prison population has been sporadic over the last decade and there was almost no growth at all between 1998 and 2000.

The majority of growth in the UK prison population was concentrated in England and Wales. Between 1994 and 2003, the prison population of these two countries increased by 50 per cent, while Scotland's rose by only 17 per cent. In contrast, the prison population of Northern Ireland declined by 52 per cent, from 1,900 in 1994 to 900 in 2001. From this point, the trend reversed and Northern Ireland's prison population increased to reach almost 1,200 by 2003.

Characteristics of the UK prison population

The demographics of prisoners are very different from those of the UK population as a whole. The starkest difference between the prison population and the general population is the asymmetric gender split of prisoners in the UK. Women prisoners are held in separate prisons or in separate accommodation in mixed prisons and are greatly outnumbered by men.

Table 9.9 shows the composition of the UK prison population by gender between 1994 and 2003. Men comprised 96 per cent of the UK prison population in 1994 and 94 per cent in

Figure **9.8**

UK prison population[1,2], 1994 to 2003

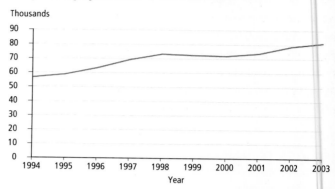

Thousands

1 England and Wales figures refer to the annual average population and exclude those held in police cells. Scottish figures refer to the average daily population in penal establishments. Northern Ireland figures are annual averages and include prisoners on remand, fine defaulters, immediate custody and non-criminal prisoners.
2 The total prison population includes both sentenced prisoners and those on remand.

Source: Home Office; Scottish Executive; Northern Ireland Office

2003. This asymmetric gender split has been narrowing throughout the decade, with a male to female ratio of 27 to one in 1994 gradually declining to 16 to one in 2003. The proportion of females in the UK prison population has been increasing, albeit gradually, over the last ten years, by an average of 0.2 per cent each year. This increase is due to the rising number of female prisoners rather than a decrease in the number of male prisoners.

Table **9.9**

The prison population[1,2] by sex, 1994 to 2003

United Kingdom

	Males	Females	Total[3]	Male to female ratio
1994	54,076	2,029	56,105	26.7
1995	56,161	2,189	58,350	25.7
1996	60,384	2,483	62,867	24.3
1997	65,941	2,889	68,830	22.8
1998	69,500	3,325	72,823	20.9
1999	68,563	3,480	72,044	19.7
2000	67,963	3,576	71,539	19.0
2001	69,343	4,005	73,348	17.3
2002	73,607	4,600	78,208	16.0
2003	75,977	4,744	80,722	16.0

1 England and Wales figures refer to the annual average population and exclude those held in police cells. Scottish figures refer to the average daily population in penal establishments. Northern Ireland figures are annual averages and include prisoners on remand, fine defaulters, immediate custody and non-criminal prisoners.
2 The total prison population includes both sentenced prisoners and those on remand.
3 Males and females may not add exactly to total due to rounding.

Source: Home Office; Scottish Executive; Northern Ireland Office

When considering the sentenced prison population,[15] the most common offence group differs by sex. In 2003 'violence against the person' was the most common reason for men to be in prison, accounting for 23 per cent of the male prison population. In contrast, 39 per cent of the female prison population were in prison for 'drug offences'. However, among those entering prison under an immediate custodial sentence in 2003, 'theft and handling' was the most commonly committed offence for both males and females. This is not reflected among the prison population as a whole because the length of sentences varies by type of offence. For example, theft and handling typically attracts a shorter sentence than violence against the person, hence there were nearly three times as many people in prison establishments for violence against the person than for theft and handling in 2003.

Figure 9.10 shows the age structure of the prison population and how it has changed between 2001 and 2003. The greatest concentrations of prisoners are aged between 21 and 39, with two-thirds in these age groups. Around 37 per cent of prisoners were in their 20s in 2003 and a further 29 per cent in their 30s. The proportions of the prison population within each age band have remained relatively stable between 2001 and 2003. The actual number of prisoners in each age group has increased annually between 2001 and 2003 with the exception of the age groups 15 to 17 and 18 to 20. Conversely, the UK population has seen a small increase in these younger age groups over the same period but a decrease in the numbers in the age groups 25 to 29 and 30 to 39.

Summary

This section has shown how the prison population differs from the UK population as a whole. In particular, the prison population is predominantly male and concentrated in the age group 20 to 39. In addition, the numbers in this static population have been increasing over the last decade at a faster rate than the UK population.

Students

The term 'student' encompasses a wide range of people studying for various types of qualification for different proportions of their time. For example, the following types of people could all be considered students and this list is by no means exhaustive:

● school pupils aged below 16

● young people aged 16 and above in schools, sixth form or further education colleges

● undergraduates and postgraduates in higher education institutions

● employees studying part-time for a qualification

● working-age or retired people taking evening classes.

From an educational standpoint, data on all types of students are essential for planning and monitoring. However, from a demographic perspective, there is one group that attracts the most interest. This is students aged 18 and over in higher education, whose decisions on when and where to study affect migration flows within the UK (Chapter 6). Many young adults also enter the UK to study while others leave to study abroad so higher education also contributes to international migration flows. In addition, becoming a higher education student and, to a lesser extent, staying in full-time education at age 16 or 17, has an impact on people's living arrangements and may delay partnership and family formation.[16] For these reasons, the following section of this chapter focuses on students aged 16 and above.

Various data sources provide numbers and demographic information on students in the UK (Box 1).

This chapter focuses on full-time students and looks at their demographic characteristics, for example age, sex and living arrangements. The student population is compared with the total UK population to highlight any differences between the two groups. The chapter also looks at how the student population has changed in size and structure since the 1991 Census.

Figure **9.10**

Sentenced prison population¹ by age, 2001 to 2003

United Kingdom

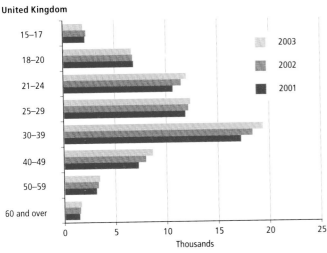

1 This chart shows sentenced prisoners only (and excludes those on remand).

Source: Home Office; Scottish Executive; Northern Ireland Office

Box 1

Data sources: students

Actual counts of students in further education are available from the Department for Education and Skills (DfES) in England, the National Assembly for Wales, the Scottish Executive and the Northern Ireland Department for Employment and Learning. Further education is defined as full- or part-time education for people over compulsory school age and is taught in a variety of settings, including further education colleges, schools and work-based training.

Similarly, numbers of higher education students enrolled in UK institutions are collected by the Higher Education Statistics Agency (HESA). Higher education includes study for degrees, higher national diplomas and postgraduate certificates of education.

All these sources provide annual data by academic year, enabling analysis of trends over time.

In contrast, the 2001 Census provides a snapshot of students at one point in time and is a useful addition as it can provide information on students' characteristics, such as the types of households they live in. There are two definitions for students used in 2001 Census outputs:

1. The narrower definition refers to full-time students[17] only (whether economically inactive or economically active[18]). There were 3.0 million full-time students aged 16 and over in the UK in April 2001.

2. The wider definition of a student includes an additional 80,000 economically inactive people aged 16 and over. These are people who are studying part-time and have been identified as a student for their main economic classification.[19]

Neither definition includes economically active part-time students, for whom the role of student may be thought of as secondary to their role in the labour market. It is not possible from the census to distinguish between students in further and higher education.

Census data used in this chapter focus on full-time students only, except for the analysis of ethnicity, which also includes economically inactive part-time students.

Age structure of the student population

The population of full-time students has a much younger age structure than the adult population as a whole. Of the 3.0 million students aged 16 and over in the UK according to the 2001 Census, nearly 60 per cent were aged under 20. Table 9.11 shows that there were over 1.1 million students aged 16 and 17 on Census day and nearly 0.7 million students aged 18 and 19.

Table **9.11**

Total[1] and full-time students by age, 2001

United Kingdom

	Total students	Full-time students
16	668,745	662,749
17	488,960	483,297
18	383,119	378,082
19	283,460	278,365
20–24	830,939	807,966
25–74	445,398	398,805
Total 16–74	3,100,621	3,009,264
Over 75	..	11,201
Total	..	3,020,465

1 'Total students' includes both full-time students and an additional 80,000 students classified as economically inactive part-time students.

Source: 2001 Census – Office for National Statistics; General Register Office for Scotland; Northern Ireland Statistics and Research Agency

Students are not exclusively young: 0.4 million full-time students identified by the 2001 Census were aged 25 and over.[20] More recent annual data published by the Department for Education and Skills (DfES) show that, for the academic year 2002/03, over one-fifth (20.9 per cent) of full-time higher education students were aged 25 and over.[21] Over one-quarter (27.4 per cent) of full-time further education students were in this age group. Full-time students are therefore predominantly young, but part-time students tend to be older because they are likely to be people with other commitments who fit their studies in by choosing part-time education. Of part-time students in further and higher education in 2002/03, around four-fifths were aged 25 and over.

Among the people starting full-time further education courses in the academic year 2001/02,[22] a large proportion (43.2 per cent) were aged 16 or 17. However, nearly one-quarter were aged 30 or above. Not surprisingly, the most common single age group for entering full-time higher education was 18 followed by 19, with 43.6 per cent of new entrants in these two age groups in 2002/03.[23] This proportion rises to nearly two-thirds when considering first degree courses only.

In 2001, the majority of those aged 16 to 18 were in full-time education, according to the census. Figure 9.12 shows that the proportion studying full-time declines with age, from 87.1 per cent at age 16[24] to 39.2 per cent by age 19. Only 1.1 per cent of the UK population in 2001 were studying full-time as 'mature students'.

Figure 9.12

Percentage of UK population that are full-time students by age, 2001

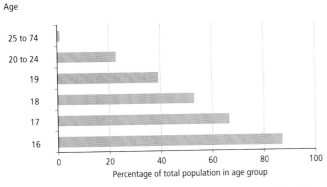

Age

Trends in the number of full-time students

The number of full-time students grew considerably between the 1991 and the 2001 Censuses.[25] The 1991 Census recorded 1,986,361 full-time students in the UK, representing 4.5 per cent of the population aged 16 and over. During the subsequent ten years, the number of full-time students increased by 52 per cent, to 3,020,465 in 2001. At the same time, the proportion of the population aged 16 and over studying full-time increased slightly to 6.4 per cent by 2001.

Table 9.13 shows that while the number of 16-year-old students increased by a quarter over the ten-year period,[26] the number of students aged 25 and over more than doubled. While students aged 16 and 17 combined outnumbered those aged 20 and over in 1991, this was no longer the case ten years later. By 2001, there were over 1.2 million full-time students aged 20 and over, which was more than the number aged 16 and 17.

While the student populations of all four countries of the UK increased between the two censuses, the greatest change took place in Scotland, where the number of students increased by 60 per cent, to 266,753 in 2001. In contrast, Northern Ireland had the smallest increase, with the number of students rising by 26 per cent, to 93,789 in 2001.

Table 9.13

Change in the numbers of full-time students, by age, 1991 to 2001

United Kingdom and constituent countries

	1991	2001	Percentage change 1991 to 2001
United Kingdom	1,986,361	3,020,465	+52
16	536,368	662,749	+24
17	354,175	483,297	+36
18	265,572	378,082	+42
19	183,666	278,365	+52
20–24	450,656	807,966	+79
25 and over	195,924	410,006	+109
England	1,644,775	2,509,027	+53
Wales	100,364	150,894	+50
Scotland	166,693	266,753	+60
Northern Ireland	74,529	93,789	+26

Male and female students

The proportion of full-time students that are female has increased between the 1991 and 2001 Censuses. According to the 1991 Census, the total numbers of male and female students were almost equal (50.5 per cent were female), while by 2001, 52.0 per cent of the full-time student population were female. In both 1991 and 2001, Northern Ireland had a slightly higher proportion of females among its full-time student population than the rest of the UK.

The balance of men and women studying full-time varies by age. Table 9.14 shows that at age 16, there were slightly more males in education than females in 2001, reflecting the gender split of UK population as a whole at this age. However for ages 17 to 19 and the 20 to 24 age group, female students outnumbered males. This is despite the fact that in 2001 there were more males than females in the UK population for all ages up to 22, at which point women became more predominant than men. For ages 25 and over, the ratio of females to males in the student population was even higher, with 56.0 per cent of full-time students being women.

Over the last decade, the proportion of UK full-time students that are women has increased only at ages 19 and over (Table 9.14). For example, among students aged 20 to 24 there were

Table 9.14

The percentage of full-time students that are female, by age, 1991 and 2001

United Kingdom and constituent countries — Percentage

	1991	2001
United Kingdom		
Total 16+	50.5	52.0
16	50.3	49.5
17	53.4	51.8
18	52.5	52.3
19	49.9	52.8
20–24	47.3	51.6
25 and over	51.3	56.0
Total 16+:		
England	50.3	51.6
Wales	51.1	53.2
Scotland	51.6	53.8
Northern Ireland	52.7	55.3

Source: 1991 Census and 2001 Census – Office for National Statistics; General Register Office for Scotland; Northern Ireland Statistics and Research Agency

more women than men recorded in the 2001 Census, but slightly more men than women studying full-time in the same age group ten years earlier. This trend is consistent with data on undergraduates and postgraduates by gender from the Higher Education Statistics Agency.[27]

Full-time students in higher education were more likely in 2002/03 to be female than their equivalents in further education[28] (Table 9.15). In that academic year, 53.9 per cent of full-time higher education students of all ages were female, compared with 50.4 per cent of those studying full-time in further education institutions.

Regional variations in the student population

In the 2001 Census, students were enumerated at their term-time address. This was a change from 1991, when students were counted as resident at their 'home' address. Table 9.16 shows that the proportion of the population (aged 16 and over) defined as full-time students in the 2001 Census was 6.0 per cent in England and slightly higher, at 6.5 per cent, in both Scotland and Wales. Among the constituent countries, Northern Ireland had the highest proportion of its population (7.3 per cent) counted as students. Differences between countries may result from differences in participation rates for post-16 education and in the age-sex structure of the populations, as well as migration of students into and between the constituent countries of the UK.

Table 9.15

Numbers of full-time students in further and higher education, all ages, 2002/03

United Kingdom — Thousands

	Post-compulsory further education	Higher education
Males	509.3	639.1
Females	517.5	747.6
Total	1,026.8	1,386.7

Source: Department for Education and Skills; National Assembly for Wales; Scottish Executive; Northern Ireland Department for Employment and Learning

Table 9.16

Full-time students as a proportion of the population aged 16 and over, 2001

United Kingdom, constituent countries and Government Office Regions

	Percentage of population who are full-time students	Total population aged 16 and over (thousands)
United Kingdom	6.1	46,930.3
England	6.0	39,237.3
North East	6.2	2,018.1
North West	6.3	5,337.6
Yorkshire and the Humber	6.6	3,949.3
East Midlands	6.2	3,335.4
West Midlands	6.2	4,171.4
East	5.2	4,305.4
London	8.4	5,723.9
South East	6.1	6,406.4
South West	5.6	3,989.9
Wales	6.5	2,315.9
Scotland	6.5	4,089.9
Northern Ireland	7.3	1,287.2

Source: 2001 Census – Office for National Statistics; General Register Office for Scotland; Northern Ireland Statistics and Research Agency

Within England, the London GOR had the highest proportion of its population in full-time education in 2001, with over 8 per cent of people aged 16 and over studying full-time. In comparison, less than 6 per cent of people in the East GOR were full-time students (Table 9.16).

Figure 9.17 shows that London had the highest proportion of its population in all age groups studying full-time. Both London and Northern Ireland had over 80 per cent of their 16–17 year olds studying full-time, while Scotland had less than 70 per cent. Looking at students aged 25 and over, London again had the highest proportion, with 2.1 per cent of people in this age group studying full-time. In contrast, the East GOR and the South West of England had only 0.7 per cent of their population aged 25 and over studying full-time, which could be due to the presence of fewer universities in these regions.

Figure **9.17**

Full-time students as a proportion of the population, by age group, 2001

Constituent countries and Government Office Regions of the United Kingdom

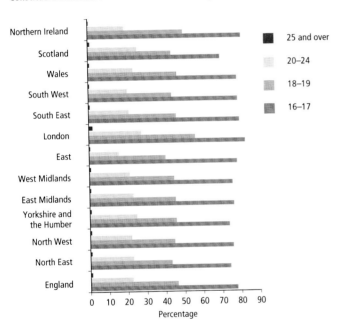

Source: 2001 Census – Office for National Statistics; General Register Office for Scotland; Northern Ireland Statistics and Research Agency

London's high proportion of students is due to the large number of educational establishments in the region and the accompanying migration of people from other parts of the UK and outside the UK to study there. The movement of students is discussed in more detail in Chapters 2, 6 and 7.

Ethnic group and country of origin

Nearly one-fifth (18.0 per cent) of all full- and part-time students aged 16 and over in the UK were from non-White ethnic groups, according to the 2001 Census (Table 9.18). This is considerably higher than the 7.5 per cent of the UK resident population aged 16 to 74 who defined themselves as belonging to an ethnic group other than White.

This difference can be partly explained by the fact that both the student population and ethnic minority populations have younger age structures than the UK resident population. The high proportion of students identifying with a non-White ethnic group could simply reflect the youthful age structure of the student population. However, the proportion of students defining themselves as belonging to an ethnic group other than White (18.0 per cent) is higher than the proportion of 16 to 24-year-olds in the population as a whole who defined themselves similarly in 2001 (12.0 per cent).

A further explanation for the high proportion of students identifying with a non-White ethnic group is that many students arrive from other countries to study in the UK and such in-migrants are less likely to be from a White ethnic group than the UK population as a whole.

According to the 2001 Census, 8.2 per cent of students in the UK classified themselves as Asian or Asian British, making this the largest group of non-White students. It included those who defined themselves as Indian, Pakistani, Bangladeshi or Other Asian. Students describing themselves as from Black or Black British ethnic groups made up 4.4 per cent of the total student population and those from the Mixed ethnic group, 2.2 per cent. The other students who classified themselves as non-White declared themselves to be either Chinese or of another ethnic origin not listed on the census form.

The ethnic origin of students varies throughout the UK, with Scotland having the highest proportion of students from White ethnic groups – 98.3 per cent. England has a much lower proportion of students from White ethnic groups (79.5 per cent) than the rest of the UK and the largest proportions of students from all other ethnic groups. While England, Wales and Scotland had larger proportions of Asian students than any other non-White ethnic group, Northern Ireland had a larger number of students of 'Chinese and other' backgrounds than any other non-White group. These patterns reflect the ethnic compositions of the resident adult populations of the four countries.

In the academic year 2002/03, 212,500 full-time higher education students in the UK were from overseas (15.3 per cent of all full-time higher education students).[29] Of these, 31 per cent were from EU countries and 6 per cent from elsewhere in Europe. One-quarter (25 per cent) had a Commonwealth country as their non-term time address, while the largest group (37 per cent) came from countries outside Europe and the Commonwealth to study.

Table **9.18**

Students[1] aged 16 to 74[2] by ethnic group, 2001

United Kingdom and constituent countries

Percentages[3]

Percentage of 16 to 74 year olds by ethnic group	Students in United Kingdom	Students in England	Students in Wales	Students in Scotland	Students in Northern Ireland	UK population aged 16 to 74
White	82.0	79.5	94.0	93.8	98.3	92.5
Mixed	2.2	2.5	1.2	0.7	0.3	0.8
Black or Black British	4.4	5.2	0.8	0.6	0.1	2.0
Asian or Asian British	8.2	9.4	2.3	2.7	0.2	3.8
Chinese and 'other'	3.2	3.5	1.7	2.2	0.2	3.8
Total	100.0	100.0	100.0	100.0	1.0	0.9

1   Includes both full-time and part-time economically inactive students. Figures are not available for full-time only.
2   Data are only available for 16 to 74 year olds rather than all students over 16.
3   Percentages may not add exactly to 100 due to rounding.

Source: 2001 Census – Office for National Statistics; General Register Office for Scotland; Northern Ireland Statistics and Research Agency

Around 31,200 students from China were enrolled on full-time higher education courses in the UK in 2002/03, the highest number from any country. In the same year, large numbers of students previously resident in Greece (20,500), India (10,900) and Malaysia (9,500) were studying full-time in UK higher education institutions. The Republic of Ireland, Germany, France, the USA and Hong Kong were also key countries from which people migrated to study in the UK.

Almost half the higher education students from overseas who were studying full-time in the UK in 2002/03 were studying at a postgraduate level. Overseas students made up 46.5 per cent of all full-time postgraduate students during that academic year, but only 9.8 per cent of full-time undergraduates. In the further education sector, the proportion was much lower, with the 13,900 students from overseas making up only 1.4 per cent of UK full-time further education students in 2002/03.[30]

Living arrangements of full-time students

The household and living arrangements of students vary considerably by age. Figure 9.19 shows the types of households in which full-time students were living during term-time in April 2001.

Virtually all 16 and 17-year-old students in full-time education were living in the parental home in 2001, as would be expected for students of this age in schools and further education colleges. The pattern at age 18 reflects both the living arrangements of those students still in schools and colleges and those starting higher education. At age 19 the distribution reflects living arrangements for first year undergraduates, with over one-quarter living in a communal establishment and 17 per cent living in a student-only

household. Even at age 19, nearly half of students were still living in the parental home. Students who remain in the parental home are likely to be either further education students who have not yet left or higher education students, who are increasingly choosing to live at home for financial and other reasons.

For older students, living arrangements are more diverse. Over one-third of 20 to 24-year-olds were living in a student household (36 per cent), 30 per cent in the parental home and only 14 per cent in a communal establishment in 2001. The different patterns for ages 18 to 24 reflect the experience of many undergraduates who live in a student hall in their first year and then move into private rented housing with other students. At ages 25 and above, living in the parental home or

Figure **9.19**

Living arrangements of full-time students by age, 2001

United Kingdom

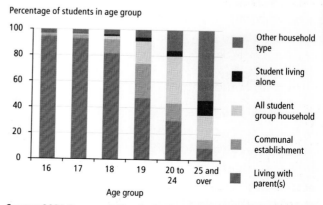

Source: 2001 Census – Office for National Statistics; General Register Office for Scotland; Northern Ireland Statistics and Research Agency

in a communal establishment is much less common. Over half of full-time students in this age group were living with non-students, either in owner-occupied or rented accommodation.

The living arrangements of students varied between the four constituent countries of the UK in 2001. For example, at age 19, students in Northern Ireland were most likely to live in the parental home (64 per cent) and students in Wales the least likely (43 per cent). Students aged 19 resident in Wales were nearly twice as likely to be living in a communal establishment (31 per cent) as those in Scotland (16 per cent) or Northern Ireland (18 per cent). These differences are likely to result from the varying availability and costs of types of accommodation in parts of the UK and the choices that students from different countries make about where to study in relation to their home address, as discussed in Chapter 2.

Summary

This section has described the population of full-time students and shown how this population differs from the UK population as a whole. For example, the full-time student population is relatively young and has a higher proportion who identify with a non-White ethnic group than the UK population of a similar age.

The numbers in this static population have increased between the 1991 and 2001 Censuses, with a 52 per cent rise in the number of full-time students aged 16 and over. Geographically, students are spread throughout the UK, with inevitable concentrations in areas containing universities and colleges. This section has also shown that there are regional variations in full-time students as a proportion of the population.

Communal establishments

While the majority of the UK population lives in private households, a minority lives in communal establishments, such as residential care homes, hostels and student halls of residence. In 2001, there were just over one million people living in communal establishments in the UK, according to the census. This figure includes staff and their families who were living in the establishments as well as the residents themselves,[31] who may, for example, be patients, students or prisoners depending on the type of establishment.

The census is a key source of data on people who are not living in private households. In the 2001 Census, a communal establishment was defined as an establishment providing managed residential accommodation. People were assumed to be 'resident' in a communal establishment if they had been living, or intended to live, there for six months or more. Usual residents absent on Census day were left a census form for completion on their return. Any person visiting or staying at the establishment on Census day who did not have a usual address elsewhere was also classified as a resident of the establishment.[32] Further information on communal establishment definitions and data quality can be found in the appendix.

Number of establishments

There were 52,600 communal establishments in the UK at the time of the 2001 Census (Table 9.20). Nearly 44,000 of these were in England, with smaller numbers in Scotland, Wales and Northern Ireland, reflecting the population sizes of these countries.

Table **9.20**

Number of communal establishments by type of establishment, 2001

United Kingdom and constituent countries

	Type of establishment					Total[1]
	Medical and care	Defence	Prison Service	Educational	Other	
England	22,167	285	145	2189	19,186	43,972
Wales	1,267	6	5	94	1,084	2,456
Scotland	1,925	39	17	224	2,885	5,090
Northern Ireland	624	11	4	66	324	1,029
United Kingdom	25,984	341	171	2,573	23,481	52,550

1 Some columns do not sum exactly to the UK total due to small cell adjustment in England and Wales.

Source: 2001 Census – Office for National Statistics; General Register Office for Scotland; Northern Ireland Statistics and Research Agency

Half the communal establishments in the UK in 2001 were medical and care establishments. The largest group of these was residential care homes, which made up 60 per cent of the 26,000 medical and care establishments. Nursing homes made up a further 20 per cent of this category, with the remaining establishments including psychiatric hospitals and children's homes.

In 2001, there were 2,600 educational establishments with residents, over 300 defence establishments with residents and fewer than 200 prison service establishments in the UK. The number of establishments accommodating these populations is much smaller than the number of medical and care establishments, since the former tend to accommodate larger numbers of people.

The remaining 23,500 communal establishments in the UK ranged from hotels and hostels for the homeless, to probation hostels and religious communities. A number of communal establishments (11,900) were not classified into a specific category – this group is discussed in the appendix.

Number of people living in communal establishments

There were 1.05 million people living in communal establishments in the UK on Census day in 2001. Nearly half (49 per cent) of these were living in medical and care establishments (Figure 9.21).

The second largest group resident in a communal establishment was those people living in educational establishments, such as student halls of residence (27 per cent).

Figure **9.21**

Residents¹ of communal establishments by type of establishment, 2001

United Kingdom

Type of establishment

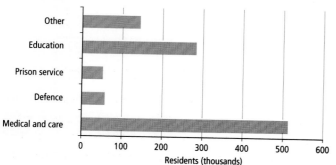

1 Includes residents, resident staff and their families.

Source: 2001 Census – Office for National Statistics; General Register Office for Scotland; Northern Ireland Statistics and Research Agency

Much smaller proportions were living in defence establishments (5 per cent) and prison service establishments (5 per cent). The remaining 14 per cent of people living in communal establishments in 2001 were resident in 'other' types of institution, such as guest houses and hostels.

In 2001, 1.8 per cent of the UK's total population was resident in a communal establishment (Table 9.22). The proportion was slightly lower in Wales, Scotland and Northern Ireland but differences between the constituent countries of the UK were small.

Since there is considerable overlap between those resident in communal establishments and the populations of prisoners, students and armed forces discussed earlier in this chapter, those in defence, prison service and education establishments are of less interest here. With these groups excluded, 1.1 per cent of the UK population was resident in other types of communal establishment in 2001 (Table 9.22).

Characteristics of the communal establishment population

The demographic characteristics of people resident in communal establishments are very different to those of the population as a whole and differ considerably between different types of establishment. This section looks first at the age-sex composition of the communal establishment population and then examines the results from the Census question on where communal establishment residents were living 12 months previously.

Residents of medical and care establishments are predominantly older people. In 2001, 78.4 per cent of those living in medical and care establishments were aged 65 or over, while 42.5 per cent were 85 or over. The population pyramid (Figure 9.23) clearly shows the top-heavy age distribution of this population.

Figure 9.23 also illustrates the fact that women outnumber men in the older age groups. In 2001, 76 per cent of residents aged 65 and over living in medical and care establishments were female, as were 83 per cent of those aged 85 and over. This reflects the higher life expectancy of females compared to males in the UK. However, there is still a higher proportion of women in the older population of medical and care establishments than there is in these age groups in the total UK population. Although women made up 76 per cent of those aged 65 and over living in medical and care establishments, they accounted for only 58 per cent of those aged 65 and over in the population as a whole on Census day.

Table **9.22**

Residents[1] in communal establishments, 2001

United Kingdom and constituent countries

	All communal establishments		Communal establishments (excluding defence, prison service and educational establishments)	
	Number of residents (thousands)	Residents of communal establishments as percentage of total resident population	Number of residents (thousands)	Residents of communal establishments as percentage of total resident population
United Kingdom	1,046.70	1.8	655.4	1.1
England	890.7	1.8	552.9	1.1
Wales	43.6	1.5	29.7	1.0
Scotland	86.0	1.7	55.5	1.1
Northern Ireland	26.5	1.6	17.3	1.0

1 Includes residents, resident staff and their families.

Source: 2001 Census – Office for National Statistics; General Register Office for Scotland; Northern Ireland Statistics and Research Agency

Figure **9.23**

Age-sex structure of people living in medical and care establishments[1,2], 2001

United Kingdom

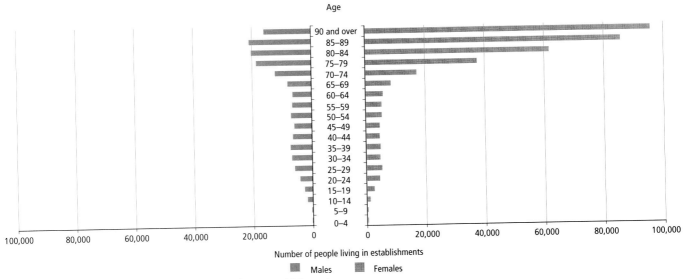

1 See appendix for a full list of types of medical and care establishments.
2 Includes residents, resident staff and their families.

Source: 2001 Census – Office for National Statistics; General Register Office for Scotland; Northern Ireland Statistics and Research Agency

The resident populations of defence, prison service and educational establishments have much younger age structures than those of medical and care establishments. Not surprisingly, school boarders and students were the youngest of these populations in 2001, with 89.6 per cent of residents of educational establishments being aged 10 to 24. Those living in defence establishments in 2001 were mainly young adults: 91.8 per cent were aged 15 to 34. Two-thirds of prison service establishment residents were also in this age group, with the remaining one-third being older. It is important to note that these figures do not represent, for example, the age structure of all students or all armed forces resident in the UK, since many students and members of the armed forces live in private households rather than communal establishments.

Figure **9.24**

Age-sex structure of people living in 'other' types of communal establishment[1,2], 2001

United Kingdom

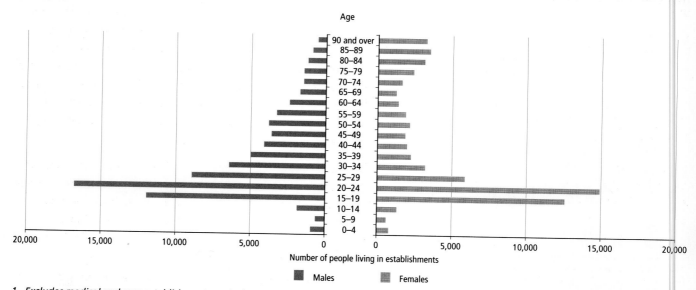

1 *Excludes medical and care establishments and education, defence and prison service establishments. 'Other' establishments include guest houses, hostels for the homeless and probation hostels – see appendix for a full list of establishment types.*
2 *Includes residents, resident staff and their families.*

Source: 2001 Census – Office for National Statistics, General Register Office for Scotland; Northern Ireland Statistics and Research Agency

Residents of 'other' types of communal establishment, such as hostels and guest houses, are predominantly young adults (Figure 9.24). In 2001, 49.6 per cent of such residents were aged 15 to 29, with males aged 20 to 24 being the largest group. Many of these people may be living in temporary accommodation and the small numbers of children in this category are likely to be living in such accommodation with a parent. The presence of some people aged 65 and over within this group may result in part from the misclassification of a small number of medical and care establishments as 'other' (see the appendix for information on this).

Some people will be a part of the communal establishment population for many years, while others will spend only a brief proportion of their life in this type of accommodation. The length of time that people spend living in a communal establishment varies considerably according to the purpose of their stay. The 2001 Census asked whether respondents had been living in the same establishment one year previously. Some people who were living in communal establishments were counted in the census as living at their usual address rather than at the establishment because they had been resident for less than six months, so the turnover in the communal establishment population is likely to be higher than the census figures might suggest.

Just over half (54 per cent) the UK's communal establishment population had been living in the same establishment for over a year, while 46 per cent had either joined the communal establishment population recently or moved from another establishment in the previous 12 months. This proportion varied considerably by type of establishment (Table 9.25).

Those living in defence, educational and prison service establishments tend to be much more mobile than other communal establishment residents. Almost three-quarters (70 per cent) of those living in educational establishments had been living elsewhere one year prior to Census day, as had 60 per cent of residents in prison service establishments and 52 per cent of those living in defence establishments. This reflects movement both between establishments, such as the movement of armed forces between bases, and into establishments from private households, for example among students moving from the parental home into a hall of residence.

In contrast, only 28 per cent of residents in medical and care establishments had been living elsewhere 12 months previously. This indicates that the majority of those in residential care and nursing homes, psychiatric hospitals and other, similar institutions tend to stay in the same establishment for more than one year.

Table **9.25**

Residents in communal establishments, by whether living in same establishment one year previously, 2001

United Kingdom   Percentages and thousands

	Lived at same communal establishment one year ago	Lived elsewhere one year ago	Total residents (thousands)
Medical and care establishments	72.4	27.6	512.2
Educational establishments	29.6	70.4	282.9
Defence establishments	47.9	52.1	56.9
Prison service establishments	40.1	59.9	51.6
Other	46.5	53.5	143.2
Total	54.4	45.6	1,046.7

Source: 2001 Census – Office for National Statistics; General Register Office for Scotland; Northern Ireland Statistics and Research Agency

Summary

Over one million people were living in communal establishments, according to the 2001 Census. This static population group covers a diverse set of people and the characteristics of this population vary considerably by the type of establishment. Census data show that residents of medical and care establishments were predominantly older people and the majority had been living in the same establishment for at least one year. Those living in defence, prison service and educational establishments tended to be much younger and more mobile in terms of moving in and out of establishments.

Summary – special and communal populations

This chapter has described how some population groups within the UK differ from the UK population as a whole. These static populations have a very different demographic profile from each other and from the rest of the UK population. For example, men considerably outnumber women in the armed forces and prison populations, while the reverse is true for full-time students and those living in medical and care establishments.

Static populations are also concentrated in particular locations. Portsmouth and Plymouth Unitary Authorities are home to the largest numbers of UK armed forces, while the London GOR has a greater concentration of full-time students in its population than any other part of the UK.

Finally, static populations change in size from year to year, for reasons that may be unrelated to demographic change. For example, the number of people living in nursing and residential homes might be expected to increase in future due to the demographic effects of the UK's ageing population. However, social policies relating to the care of older people and the availability of suitable accommodation will also affect the future numbers of people resident in such homes. Similarly, the size of the populations of prisoners, students and armed forces will be affected to some extent by demographic factors but also by government policies relating to justice, education and defence.

Static population groups will continue to be an important part of both the national population and local populations. Accurate data on these populations at the local area level will remain a central requirement for planning and service provision.

Notes and references

1. When rolling forward population estimates from one year to the next, groups such as armed forces must not be 'aged-on' each year with the rest of the population, otherwise these populations will appear to get progressively older each year. Further details can be found in *Making a population estimate in England and Wales*, National Statistics Methodology Series No.34: www.statistics.gov.uk/StatBase/Product.asp?vlnk=575

2. More details on the methodology used to make a population estimate can be found at: www.statistics.gov.uk/about/data/methodology/specific/population/PEMethodology/

3. UK regular forces include nursing services but exclude full-time Reserve Service personnel, Gurkhas, the Home Service battalions of the Royal Irish Regiment, mobilised reservists and Naval Activated Reservists. They include trained and untrained personnel.

4. The Naval Services include the Royal Navy and the Royal Marines.

5. The armed forces population spans the ages 16 to 55 and over, but the number aged over 55 in the armed forces is very small. Due to this limited age distribution, comparisons between the armed forces and the UK population aged 16 to 55 have been made where data are available.

6. The proportion identifying with a non-White ethnic group is even higher among the equivalent age group. For example, 9.3 per cent of those aged 16 to 54 in Great Britain identified with a non-White ethnic group in the 2001 Census.

7. Includes those with an unrecorded ethnic group and non-responses to the question.

8. Marital status definitions used in the 2001 Census and for the Army, Navy and Royal Air Force are described in the appendix.

9. Marital status estimates for years between censuses are produced for England and Wales only.

10. Figures in this section comprise UK regular forces, both trained and untrained, located within the UK. They therefore exclude Ghurkhas, full-time Reserve Service personnel, the Home Service battalions of the Royal Irish Regiment and mobilised reservists. Naval Services personnel on sea service and those serving in flights at sea are included within the local authority containing the home port of their ship or the base airfield of their flight.

11. Taken from TSP 10: *UK Regular Forces Distribution across UK at 1 July 2004.*

12. A large proportion of armed forces will be usually resident on the base at which they are posted. A smaller proportion will be usually resident off the base and commute to work at the base. They may be usually resident in a different local authority district to that of the base. The Office for National Statistics assigns armed forces to their local authority of usual residence for the purposes of population estimates.

13. The remaining countries of the UK do have populations of foreign armed forces but their numbers are very small.

14. More information on these prisons can be found at the following websites: HMP Rye Hill in England: www.hmpryehill.co.uk; HMP Parc in Wales: www.securicor.com/uk/uk-services/uk-services-justice/uk-services-justice-custody_rehab/uk-services-justice-adult-custody.htm; HMP Kilmarnock in Scotland: www.sps.gov.uk/establishments/home/prisoninfo.asp?estid=10&page=6.

15. The Scottish and Northern Irish legal systems are different from that of England and Wales. The greatest difference between judicial systems is in the nomenclature of offences. For example, in Scotland the most similar offence class to 'burglary' is 'housebreaking'. There may also be differences between the judicial systems in sentence length handed to offenders (a full discussion is outside the scope of this report). Information on the different judicial systems can be found at www.homeoffice.gov.uk/rds/cjschap1.html for England and Wales or in *Crime and Criminal Justice in Scotland* by Peter Young (The Stationery Office, 1997).

16. Rendall, M S and Smallwood S (2003) Higher qualifications, first-birth timing, and further childbearing in England and Wales. *Population Trends* **111**, 18–26.

17. 'Full-time students' are those responding 'yes' to the question: 'Are you a schoolchild or student in full-time education?'

18. The economically active are defined as employees, the self-employed and the unemployed, while the economically inactive may be retired, students, people looking after home/family, permanently sick/disabled or 'other'. Full-time students (see note 13) may be economically active or inactive.

19. Economically inactive part-time students are those who responded 'no' to the question: 'Are you a schoolchild or student in full-time education?', were classified as economically inactive (see note 14) and who ticked the box stating that they were a student in the week prior to the 2001 Census.

20. The proportion of older students identified by the census is lower than the proportions noted in data from the Department for Education and Skills (DfES) because census data include a large number of 16-year-old students in their final year of compulsory schooling.

21. Department for Education and Skills (DfES) *Education and Training Statistics UK 2004* Tables 3.8 and 3.9: www.dfes.gov.uk/rsgateway/DB/VOL/v000538/index.shtml

22. Department for Education and Skills (DfES) *Education and Training Statistics UK 2003* Table 3.11: www.dfes.gov.uk/rsgateway/DB/VOL/v000431/index.shtml 2002/03 data on new entrants in further education are not available.

23. Department for Education and Skills (DfES) Education and Training Statistics UK 2004 Table 3.11: www.dfes.gov.uk/rsgateway/DB/VOL/v000538/index.shtml

24. Census data for age 16 include a large number of students in their final year of compulsory schooling.

25. See the appendix for definitional differences between 1991 and 2001.

26. The population aged 16 increased by only 8 per cent between mid-1991 and mid-2001, so the increase in full-time students aged 16 between 1991 and 2001 is not purely due to an increase in the number of 16 year olds.

27. Higher Education Statistics Agency (HESA): www.hesa.ac.uk

28. Department for Education and Skills (DfES) *Education and Training Statistics UK 2004* Tables 3.8 and 3.9: www.dfes.gov.uk/rsgateway/DB/VOL/v000538/index.shtml

29. Department for Education and Skills (DfES) *Education and Training Statistics UK 2004* Table 3.7: www.dfes.gov.uk/rsgateway/DB/VOL/v000538/index.shtml

30. Department for Education and Skills (DfES) *Education and Training Statistics UK 2004* Table 3.5:
www.dfes.gov.uk/rsgateway/DB/VOL/v000538/index.shtml

31. All data on people living in communal establishments in this chapter include resident staff and their families as well as the residents themselves. The reason for this is explained in the appendix.

32. For more information on definitions relating to communal establishments and their residents in the 2001 Census, see paragraphs 4.14 to 4.22 and paragraphs 4.63 to 4.67 in *Census 2001: Definitions* at:
www.statistics.gov.uk/statbase/Product.asp?vlnk=12951

The UK population in the European context

Roma Chappell, David Pearce,
François Carlos-Bovagnet and Denis Till

Chapter 10

Introduction

This chapter builds on existing demographic analyses and includes recent population statistics published by international organisations, including Eurostat and the Council of Europe.[1,2,3] The statistics are used to compare the demographic position of the UK at the start of the 21st century mainly with the other countries of the European Union (the EU25, see Box 1). Population size and structure, population growth (or decline) and the demographic factors driving those changes, as well as some aspects of families across Europe are considered. This chapter aims to identify ways in which the UK is demographically similar to other European countries and ways in which it differs.

The UK's population estimates are constructed for the mid-year, 30 June, but the population statistics presented in this chapter are for a first of January reference date, to facilitate international comparisons. Although not identical, the UK's population estimates shown in this chapter are consistent with the mid-year population estimates for the UK shown elsewhere in this publication. Likewise some other UK figures shown in this chapter may not be identical to corresponding figures in other chapters. For example, to ensure comparability with other international estimates, the population density figures in this chapter are based on 2001 data, whereas in Chapters 1 and 2 the latest available population density estimates for the UK are given, which are for mid-2004.

Population

The population of the 25 countries of the European Union — the EU25 — was 456.9 million at the beginning of 2004. The UK was one of the largest of the 25 countries in terms of its population size and around one in eight residents of the EU lived in the UK. Figure 10.1 shows the EU25 countries ordered by their population size at the start of 2004. Only Germany had a much larger population than the UK (82.5 million), while France had a similar number of people and Italy slightly fewer. Many countries in the EU25 were relatively small in terms of their population size. Together, the six countries with the largest populations accounted for nearly three-quarters of the total population of the EU and 13 of the 25 countries had a population of fewer than ten million.

In 2003 the UK was the third most densely populated country of the 15 members of the EU prior to its enlargement to EU25 (Box 1), with a population density of 244.3 residents per km². The two most densely populated were the Netherlands and Belgium, with 480.3 and 340.0 residents per km² respectively. The least densely populated was Finland with 17.6 residents per km². These national measures of density disguise variations between the densely and sparsely populated areas of a country. Scotland, for example, has a low population density, despite being a constituent part of the UK, whereas the Government Office Region of London, in the densely populated south east of England, had a population density of over 4,000 people per km² in 2001.

Figure 10.1

Population size, EU25 countries, 1 January 2004

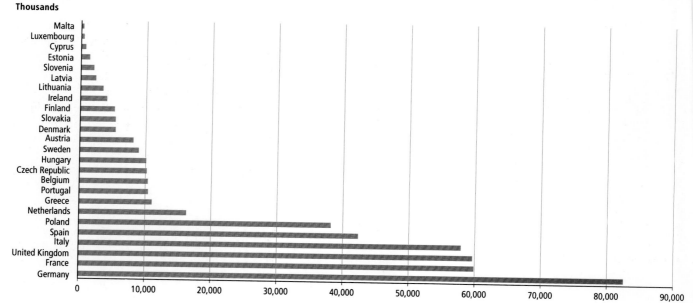

Source: Eurostat

Box 1

Timeline guide to key events in the formation of the European Union

Selected key events	**Member states**
1951 European Coal and Steel Community established	1951 Belgium, France, Germany, Italy, Luxembourg, the Netherlands are the six founding Community member states
1957 Treaty of Rome signed and two more communities set up: European Economic Community European Atomic Energy Community	
1967 Merging of three communities to form single European Commission, Council of Ministers and European Parliament	
	1973 Denmark, Ireland, United Kingdom join European Commission to give nine member states
1979 First direct elections to European Parliament (these are held every five years)	
	1981 Greece joins, giving a European Commission of 10 member states
	1986 Spain and Portugal join, giving a European Commission of 12 member states
1992 Treaty of Maastricht adds new forms of co-operation between governments to the community system and creates the European Union	
	1995 Austria, Finland and Sweden join to give 15 members of the European Union, the EU15
	2004 Ten new member states join: Cyprus, the Czech Republic, Estonia, Hungary, Latvia, Lithuania, Malta, Poland, Slovakia, Slovenia. These are the accession countries. The European Union is now a union of 25 member states, the EU25.

Source: European Commission[4]

Population change

Europe's share of the world population has been declining for many years. In 1960 about one in eight of the world's people lived in the area that is now the EU but by 2004 this had declined to one in 14.[3] The population of the EU25 grew by just over seven million between 2000 and 2004, a growth of 1.6 per cent. In the world context this is a relatively modest growth. The population of the world grew by 293 million, nearly 5 per cent, between 2000 and 2004. The population of the US grew by 11 million (around 4 per cent) in the same period. The fastest growing countries in the world were, in general, the less developed nations, where fertility rates remain relatively high. Generally speaking, fertility rates are much lower in Europe and natural increase (where population grows as a result of the number of births outnumbering the number

Table **10.2**

Population change, EU25 countries, 2000 to 2004

Thousands and rates

	Population 1 January 2000	Natural change[1] (per thousand)	Net migration and other changes[2] (per thousand)	Total change (per thousand)	Population 1 January 2004
European Union (25 countries)	449,716.3	2.3	13.6	15.9	456,863.0
European Union (15 countries)	375,230.0	3.6	16.3	20.0	382,721.3
Latvia	2,381.7	−20.7	−5.6	−26.2	2,319.2
Lithuania	3,512.1	−10.0	−8.8	−18.8	3,445.9
Estonia	1,372.1	−15.7	0.4	−15.4	1,351.1
Hungary	10,221.6	−14.7	4.5	−10.3	10,116.7
Czech Republic	10,278.1	−6.6	0.2	−6.5	10,211.5
Slovakia	5,398.7	0.1	−3.5	−3.4	5,380.1
Poland	38,263.3	−0.1	−1.8	−1.9	38,190.6
Slovenia	1,987.8	−2.4	6.7	4.3	1,996.4
Germany	82,163.5	−5.3	9.8	4.5	82,531.7
Finland	5,171.3	5.6	3.8	9.4	5,219.7
Greece	10,903.8	−0.3	12.9	12.6	11,040.7
Denmark	5,330.0	5.4	7.3	12.7	5,397.6
Sweden	8,861.4	0.2	12.7	12.9	8,975.7
United Kingdom	58,785.2	4.8	10.3	15.1	59,673.1
Belgium	10,239.1	3.2	12.2	15.4	10,396.4
Italy	56,929.5	−1.7	18.5	16.8	57,888.2
Austria	8,002.2	0.5	16.7	17.2	8,140.1
France	58,748.7	15.7	3.9	19.6	59,900.7
Malta[3]	380.2	10.0	12.8	22.8	388.9
Netherlands	15,864.0	15.5	9.3	24.8	16,258.0
Portugal	10,195.0	3.3	24.1	27.4	10,474.7
Luxembourg	433.6	15.0	26.5	41.5	451.6
Cyprus	690.5	17.4	40.4	57.8	730.4
Spain	39,960.7	4.8	54.9	59.7	42,345.3
Ireland	3,777.8	30.6	35.5	66.1	4,027.7

1 *Where natural change is positive, the number of births exceeded the number of deaths during the period. Where natural change is negative, the number of deaths exceeded the number of births.*
2 *'Net migration and other changes' refers mainly to international migration. Other small changes include changes in the numbers of armed forces.*
3 *Figures provided by Malta Statistics Authority and are not reflected in EU totals.*

Source: Eurostat

of deaths) is becoming less important as a cause of population growth. It is being overtaken by net migration from the rest of the world as the main driver of population change in Europe.

Although the populations of most of the countries of Europe have grown in recent years, not all 25 countries of the EU have done so. Table 10.2 shows population change for the 25 countries of the EU between 2000 and 2004, shown in ascending order of the size of the total change. The first seven countries listed had a fall in population over this four year period: Latvia, Lithuania, Estonia, Hungary, the Czech Republic, Slovakia and Poland. The remaining 18 countries are listed in order from the slowest growing, Slovenia, at 0.43 per cent, through to the fastest growing, which was Ireland, at 6.61 per cent.

Two causes of population decline are apparent. In Latvia, Estonia, Hungary and the Czech Republic, decline was driven by natural decrease (an excess of deaths over births), whereas, in Slovakia and Poland, it came about through net out-migration. In Lithuania, both factors were important in contributing to the population decrease.

Overall, net inward migration has played a much bigger role in population change in Europe than natural change in recent years, accounting for around 85 per cent of the total growth between 2000 and 2004. Even though some countries exhibited a natural decrease in their populations over this four year period, their populations still grew due to net inward migration that more than compensated for the natural decrease. This was the case for Germany, Italy, Slovenia and Greece.

The increased importance of migration as a driver of population growth reflects shifts that have occurred over the last 40 years in the relative contributions of net international migration and natural change to total population change. Figure 10.3 shows how these contributions have altered since the 1960s, for both Europe as a whole, Figure 10.3a, and for the UK, Figure 10.3b.

The four fastest growing countries of the EU25 between 2000 and 2004 were Ireland, Spain, Cyprus, and Luxembourg. Net inward migration was the biggest factor in the population growth for all these countries but population growth was also

Figure **10.3a**

Population change, EU25, 1960 to 2003

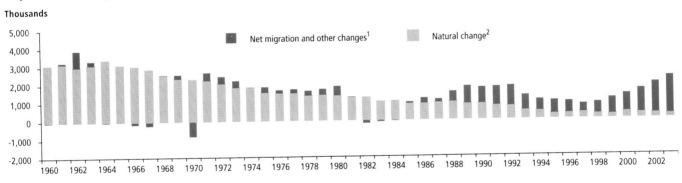

Source: Eurostat

Figure **10.3b**

Population change, UK, 1960 to 2003

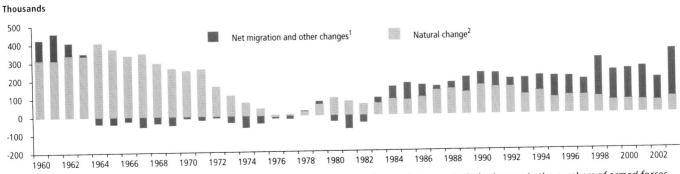

1 'Net migration and other changes' refers mainly to international migration. Other small changes include changes in the numbers of armed forces.
2 Where natural change is positive, the number of births exceeded the number of deaths during the period. Where natural change is negative, the number of deaths exceeded the number of births.

Source: Eurostat

driven by natural increase, particularly for Ireland. Even though the importance of natural change is declining in Europe as a reason for population growth, between 2000 and 2004 there were three countries where natural increase was the primary cause of population growth: France, the Netherlands and Finland.

Population growth in the UK between 2000 and 2004 was 1.5 per cent, which was around the value for the EU25 as a whole and put the UK at the middle of the table of countries ordered by size of total population change. The UK's 1.5 per cent growth was less than in France, the eighth fastest growing country at 1.96 per cent, but slightly greater than Sweden or Denmark's growth of 1.3 per cent. As was the case for most countries in Europe, the UK's growth was mainly driven by net in-migration from abroad. However, natural increase was also an important driver of change in the UK, accounting for around 30 per cent of the total increase between 2000 and 2004.

Fertility rates

There has been a general decline in fertility rates across Europe in the last 30 or so years, although towards the start of the 21st century there was a slight recovery in the total fertility rate[5] (TFR) in some countries of the EU25. Figure 10.4 shows the TFRs in descending order for the 25 countries of the EU in 2003. Within the EU25, TFRs were highest in Ireland (1.98), France (1.89), Finland and Denmark (both 1.76), the Netherlands (1.75), and the UK and Sweden (both 1.71). Fertility was lowest in southern, central and eastern Europe, for

example, in Slovakia (1.17), Poland (1.24), Greece (1.27), and Spain and Italy (both 1.29).

Europe is an area of the world that has moved through the first demographic transition. This is characterised by moving from high fertility and mortality rates, through lower mortality and on to lower fertility rates. Comparing fertility rates of EU countries over recent years shows that the range of rates has shrunk. Table 10.5 shows for the 25 countries of the EU how fertility rates have fallen and the range of rates has converged between 1985 and 2003. In 1985 the TFRs ranged between 1.37 and 2.47 but by 2003 this range had narrowed to between 1.17 and 1.98.

Table **10.5**

Total fertility rates, EU25 countries, 1985 and 2003

	1985	2003
European Union (25 countries)	1.70	1.48
Slovakia	2.25	1.17
Czech Republic	1.96	1.18
Slovenia	1.72	1.22
Poland	2.33	1.24
Lithuania	2.10	1.25
Greece	1.67	1.27
Spain	1.64	1.29
Italy	1.42	1.29
Latvia	2.09	1.29
Hungary	1.85	1.30
Germany	1.37	1.34
Estonia	2.12	1.35
Austria	1.47	1.39
Malta	1.96	1.41
Portugal	1.72	1.44
Cyprus	2.38	1.46
Belgium	1.51	1.61
Luxembourg	1.38	1.63
Sweden	1.74	1.71
United Kingdom	1.79	1.71
Netherlands	1.51	1.75
Denmark	1.45	1.76
Finland	1.65	1.76
France	1.81	1.89
Ireland	2.47	1.98

Source: Eurostat

Figure **10.4**

Total fertility rates, EU25 countries, 2003

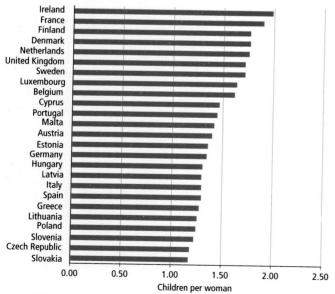

Children per woman

Source: Eurostat

The decline in fertility across Europe has brought rates to below the replacement level of 2.1 in all European countries.[6] If the fall in fertility rates across Europe is measured using the last year for which the TFR was at or above replacement level, the change to lower fertility levels first took place in some northern and western European countries – Sweden, Luxembourg, Finland, Denmark and Germany – in the late 1960s. These countries were followed by other western European countries during the early 1970s, including the UK. The change to low fertility was not seen in southern Europe until the 1980s. In central and eastern Europe there was an abrupt drop in fertility rates in 1989.[7] In recent years the rates have risen slightly in northern and western Europe and in the UK, though it is too early to tell if these increases will be sustained.

Table 10.6

Mean age of mother at first birth, EU25 countries, 1975 to 2003

Country	Year				Change from 1975 to 2003
	1975	1985	1995	2003	
Belgium	24.4	25.5	27.3	...	...
Czech Republic	22.5	22.4	23.3	25.9	3.4
Denmark[1]	23.9	25.5	27.4	27.7	3.8
Germany[1]	24.5	26.1	27.5	28.2	3.7
Estonia[2]	23.6	23.2	23.0	24.6	1.0
Greece	24.5	24.5	26.6	27.9	3.4
Spain[2]	25.1	25.8	28.4	29.2	4.1
France[1]	24.5	25.9	28.1	27.9	3.4
Ireland	25.5	26.1	27.3	28.2	2.7
Italy	24.7	25.9	28.0	...	...
Cyprus	24.0	23.7	25.5	26.9	2.9
Latvia	...	23.0	23.3	24.9	...
Lithuania	...	24.1	23.1	24.5	...
Luxembourg	25.5	...	27.9	28.7	3.2
Hungary	22.5	22.8	23.8	26.1	3.6
Malta	...	...	...	...	...
Netherlands[2]	25.2	26.6	28.4	28.7	3.5
Austria	...	24.3	25.7	26.9	...
Poland	23.0	23.5	23.8	24.9	1.9
Portugal[2]	...	24.2	25.7	26.8	...
Slovenia	23.0	23.1	24.9	27.3	4.3
Slovakia	22.8	22.6	23.0	24.9	2.1
Finland	...	25.9	27.2	27.9	...
Sweden	24.4	26.1	27.2	28.5	4.1
England and Wales	24.2	24.8	26.6	26.9	2.7

1 Data in 2003 column are for 2000 and change where available, is from 1975 to 2000.
2 Data in 2003 column are for 2002 and change, where available, is from 1975 to 2002.
... data not available

Source: Council of Europe

Age of mother at first birth

A postponement by mothers of their first birth and a rise in the level of childlessness have likewise been universal trends in Europe, and fertility patterns in the UK over the last 30 or so years have contributed to this pattern. Table 10.6 shows for all countries of the EU25 how the age of the mother at first birth has risen over the last three decades or so, typically by around three years. The highest increases in the mean age of women at the birth of their first child were in Slovenia, Spain and Sweden, all of which experienced an increase of over four years. The countries where the mother's mean age, at the birth of her first child, was highest were Spain (29.2), Luxembourg and the Netherlands (both 28.7), and Sweden (28.5). In England and Wales the mean age of women having their first child in 2003 was 26.9 years. This was a rise of 2.7 years from 24.2 in 1975.[8]

Rising levels of childlessness

The UK, Ireland and the Netherlands stand out as European countries in which the levels of childlessness have substantially increased. In Ireland one in 20 women born in the 1940s were childless by the end of their childbearing years but this had risen to around one in six for women born in 1958. Around one in ten women in the UK born in the mid-1940s were childless. The figure has risen to around one in five for women who are currently reaching the end of their fertile life (women who were born in the late 1950s). This rising trend has not been seen in Denmark or Spain, where the proportion of women who are childless has remained relatively constant at around one in ten, nor in France, where it has remained at around one in 12. In Portugal, the proportion of childless women has always been relatively low (lower than one in ten) while, in Finland, the level has always been relatively high (around one in six).[9]

Age structure and population ageing

Figure 10.7 shows two population pyramids, one for the 25 countries of the EU as a whole and one for the UK. The population pyramids depict the age structure of the population in 2004, reflecting past patterns and changes in fertility, mortality and, to a lesser extent, international migration. The bases of the population pyramids reflect the numbers of babies and infants aged under five in the EU25 and the UK respectively in 2004. These numbers are relatively low because birth rates at the end of the 1990s and at the start of the 21st century were low. The European pyramid demonstrates clearly that birth rates have fallen since the 1960s as the size of the cohorts has become progressively smaller, by descending age group from age 35 to 39 down to the under fives. The bulge at

ages 35 to 39 corresponds to the baby boom of the mid to late-1960s and is followed by smaller cohorts at older ages, reflecting the low fertility during World War II and in the 1930s, as well as the impact of mortality at older ages. The gender imbalance at older ages is due to the lower mortality rates and higher longevity of women.

The UK pyramid has similarities to the EU25 pyramid (the 1960s bulge at ages 35 to 39, for example) but also demonstrates some differences. In the UK there is a noticeable blip for people in their late 50s in 2004, which is not observable in the EU25 pyramid. This corresponds to a high birth rate in the UK after the end of World War II. Looking at young ages between 0 and

Figure **10.7a**

EU25 population by age and sex, 2004

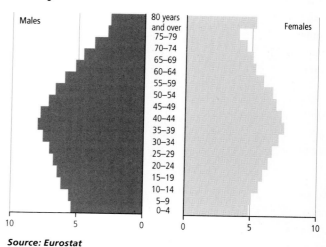

Source: Eurostat

Figure **10.7b**

UK population by age and sex, 2004

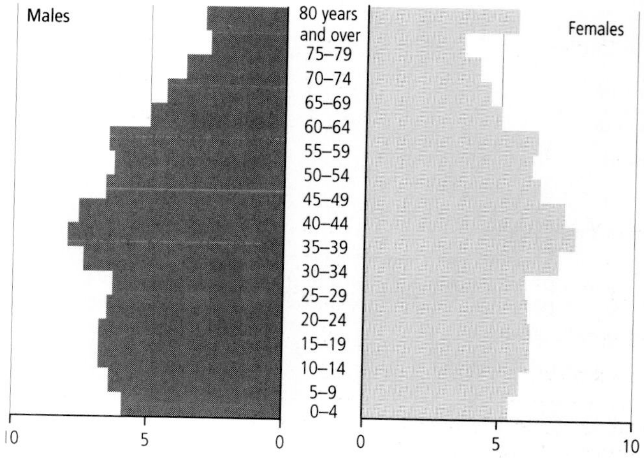

Source: Eurostat

29, it appears that, while fertility rates declined between the early 1970s and 2004, this did not happen in the UK in a steady way, as appears to be the case for the EU25 as a whole. Very low fertility rates in the UK during the late 1970s have resulted in 2004 in small cohorts of young adults in their mid to late-20s. However, the pyramid shows larger cohorts of people in their teenage years in 2004 than had been the case five to ten years previously. A combination of slightly higher fertility rates since the 1970s, and the larger cohorts of women born in the 1960s, who became mothers during the 1980s and 1990s, was the cause of these slightly larger cohorts of teenagers in 2004. Even so, fertility rates were low in the UK throughout this period relative to the 1960s.

Table 10.8

Proportions of population aged under 16 and 65 and over, EU25 countries, 1985 and 2004

| | Proportion of the population who are aged: | | | | Ratio of 65 and over to under 16 | |
| | Under 16 | | 65 and over | | | |
	1985	2004	1985	2004	1985	2004
European Union (25 countries)	22.0	17.6	13.0	16.5	0.59	0.93
Belgium	20.3	18.5	13.7	17.1	0.67	0.93
Czech Republic	24.8	16.5	11.8	13.9	0.48	0.84
Denmark	20.0	20.0	15.0	14.9	0.75	0.75
Germany	17.6	15.9	14.5	18.0	0.82	1.13
Estonia[1,2]	23.7	17.6	11.5	15.9	0.48	0.87
Greece[2]	22.6	15.6	13.3	17.5	0.59	1.12
Spain	25.2	15.6	11.9	16.8	0.47	1.08
France	22.9	19.9	12.8	16.4	0.56	0.82
Ireland [3]	30.5	22.3	11.0	11.1	0.36	0.50
Italy	21.3	15.2	12.9	19.2	0.61	1.26
Cyprus[1]	27.2	21.6	10.8	11.9	0.40	0.55
Latvia	22.5	17.0	11.8	16.2	0.52	0.95
Lithuania	24.7	19.2	10.3	15.0	0.42	0.78
Luxembourg	18.7	20.0	13.2	14.1	0.71	0.71
Hungary	23.0	17.1	12.3	15.5	0.53	0.91
Malta [4]	23.5	19.7	11.0	13.0	0.47	0.66
Netherlands	21.5	19.8	12.0	13.8	0.56	0.70
Austria	20.0	17.5	14.1	15.5	0.71	0.89
Poland	26.8	18.7	9.4	13.0	0.35	0.69
Portugal	25.6	16.9	11.7	16.8	0.46	1.00
Slovenia	23.8	15.9	10.1	15.0	0.42	0.95
Slovakia	27.9	19.1	9.4	11.5	0.34	0.60
Finland	20.8	18.9	12.4	15.6	0.60	0.83
Sweden	19.5	19.1	17.1	17.2	0.87	0.90
United Kingdom	20.9	19.6	15.0	16.0	0.72	0.82

1 Under 16 in 1985 estimated from under 15.
2 Figures in 2004 columns are for 2003.
3 Figures in 1985 column are for 1986.
4 Figures in 1985 columns are for 1995.

Source: Eurostat

An ageing population is one where the proportion of the population who are children under 16 is falling and the proportion who are aged 65 or over is rising. Falling fertility rates, together with falling mortality rates, are key drivers of population ageing. It has long been recognised that Europe has an ageing population[10] and the low fertility rates in Europe, apart from being associated with relatively modest population

Table **10.9**

Old-age dependency ratios, EU25 countries, 1985 and 2004

Old-age dependency ratio[1]	1985	2004
European Union (25 countries)	20.0	25.0
Belgium	20.8	26.6
Czech Republic	18.6	20.0
Denmark	23.1	22.9
Germany	21.3	27.3
Estonia [2,3]	17.7	24.0
Greece	20.8	26.2
Spain	19.0	24.9
France	19.9	25.7
Ireland [4]	18.8	16.7
Italy	19.6	29.3
Cyprus [4]	17.3	17.9
Latvia	18.0	24.2
Lithuania	15.9	22.9
Luxembourg	19.4	21.4
Hungary	18.9	23.0
Malta [5]	16.7	19.4
Netherlands	18.0	20.9
Austria	21.5	23.2
Poland	14.8	19.0
Portugal	18.7	25.4
Slovenia	15.3	21.8
Slovakia	15.0	16.6
Finland	18.5	23.8
Sweden	26.9	27.0
United Kingdom	23.4	24.8

1 Population aged 65 and over as a percentage of population aged 16–64.
2 Under 16 in 1985 estimated from under 15.
3 Figures in 2004 columns are for 2003.
4 Figures in 1985 column are for 1986.
5 Figures in 1985 columns are for 1995.

Source: Eurostat

growth, have also helped to 'fuel' this trend. Table 10.8 shows for the 25 countries of the EU how the proportion of population aged under 16 fell between 1985 and 2004, while the proportion aged 65 and over rose.

Table 10.8 also shows the ratio of the population aged 65 and over to the population aged under 16. In 1985 the value of this ratio was less than one because the under-16 population outnumbered people aged 65 and over in all the EU25 countries. By 2004 there were four countries – Italy, Greece, Germany and Spain – where the value of the ratio was greater than one because the proportion of the population aged 65 and over exceeded the proportion who were under 16. Though population ageing is a feature of UK society, it is happening more slowly in the UK than elsewhere in Europe. According to UK population projections, the proportion of the population who are aged 65 and over is not expected to exceed the proportion who are children until 2014.[11]

The ageing population is a source of concern for some policy analysts, particularly in the arena of pensions policy.[12] One issue is whether there are enough working people to pay the pensions of the retired. The dependency ratio is the ratio of the dependent population to those of working age, where the dependent population consists of people under 16 and those of state retirement age and over. The dependency ratio is often analysed separately for the young dependent population and the older dependent population. Table 10.9 shows old-age dependency ratios for all of the countries of the EU25 that, in nearly all cases, were higher in 2004 than in 1985. The biggest increases in the ratio over this period were in Italy, Lithuania, Portugal, Slovenia, Estonia and Latvia. In the UK, the value of the old-age dependency ratio in 2004 was slightly below average for the EU25 and the increase in the ratio between 1985 and 2004 was slight compared with a typical increase for the EU25 over the same period.

Ageing within the population of working age

Table 10.10 shows the median age of the population of working age for the EU25 countries, for 1985 and 2004. It shows that the median age has risen over the last 20 years in all of the EU25 countries, the highest rises being in Finland and the Netherlands. Rises are to be expected due to population ageing; they reflect the recent low fertility and the ageing of the baby-boom generations.[13, 14]

The median age of the working-age population in the UK is 39.7 years which is the average value for the EU25. The change in the median over the last 20 years in the UK has also been at the average rate for Europe as a whole.

Table **10.10**

Median age of working-age population, EU25 countries, 1 January 1985 and 2004

	1985	2004
European Union (25 countries)	37.4	39.7
Belgium	37.5	40.3
Czech Republic	37.9	39.4
Denmark	37.4	40.8
Germany	38.4	40.8
Estonia	38.3	39.2
Greece	38.6	38.8
Spain	37.0	38.0
France	36.7	39.7
Ireland[1]	35.2	36.9
Italy	38.4	40.0
Cyprus[2]	34.7	38.2
Latvia	38.8	39.2
Lithuania	37.2	38.7
Luxembourg	37.6	39.6
Hungary	38.7	39.6
Malta[2]	38.5	40.2
Netherlands	35.9	40.3
Austria	37.4	40.0
Poland	35.7	38.5
Portugal	36.8	38.8
Slovenia	36.9	39.7
Slovakia	35.6	37.7
Finland	36.9	41.6
Sweden	38.3	40.6
United Kingdom	37.3	39.7

1 *Figures in 1985 column are for 1986.*
2 *Figures in 1985 columns are for 1995.*

Source: Eurostat

In the UK the average age at which men exit the labour force[15] is the highest (64.2 years) of the countries for which 2003 estimates are available. The age for women (61.9 years) is the fourth highest. In the UK there is a 2.3-year gap between the ages at which men and women leave the labour force, with women leaving at a younger age. This gap does not reflect the five-year difference in the UK state retirement age for men and women but it is in line with women leaving the labour force at a younger average age. In most of the EU15 countries women left the labour force at a younger age than men but on the

Table **10.11**

Life expectancy at birth and infant mortality, EU25, 1960 to 2003

	Life expectancy at birth		Deaths of children under one year	
	Males	Females	Thousands	Per thousand live births
1960	67.1	72.6	255	36.5
1965	67.7	73.6	206	28.8
1970	68.0	74.4	162	24.7
1975	69.0	75.6	120	19.9
1980	69.8	76.8	86	14.6
1985	70.9	77.8	64	11.6
1990	71.7	78.8	50	9.2
1995	72.8	79.7	32	6.7
2000	74.4	80.8	25	5.2
2003	74.8	81.1	22	4.6
(EU15) 2003	75.8	81.6	17	4.3

Source: Eurostat

whole the age gap was less than in the UK and was less than a year. In the future it is likely that the age gap will narrow in the UK as, phased in between 2010 and 2020, women's state retirement age is changing to come into line with that of men.

Mortality

As a result of decreasing mortality rates over the last 40 years, the annual number of deaths has remained relatively stable in Europe, despite a growing, and ageing, population. Since 1980 the annual number of deaths in the EU25 has been about 4.5 million.

Two other key measurements of mortality are life expectancy[16] and the infant mortality rate.[17] Table 10.11 provides these measurements for selected years since 1960.

Table 10.11 shows that, over the last 40 years, life expectancy at birth in the EU25 countries has increased by 7.7 years for men and 8.5 years for women. Perhaps even more striking has been the fall in infant mortality, from 36.5 deaths of infants under one year old per 1,000 live births in 1960 to a current level of about 4.5 per 1,000 live births, an eight-fold decrease. The decrease in infant mortality has been universal throughout the EU, as Figure 10.12 shows, in descending order of the rate in 1960.

Figure **10.12**

Infant mortality rate, EU25 countries, 1960, 1980 and 2003

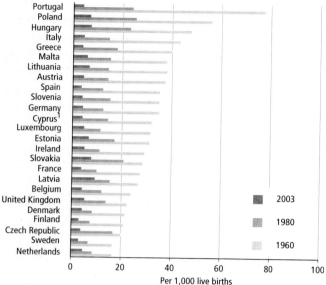

1   *1960 data refer to 1965.*

Source: Eurostat

Figure **10.13**

Life expectancy at birth, EU25 countries, 2003[1]

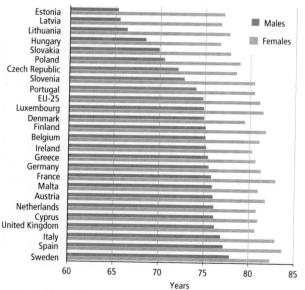

1   *For Belgium, Estonia, EU25 as a whole, Hungary, Ireland, Luxembourg, Malta, Slovakia and Slovenia, the data refer to 2002. For Cyprus, the data refer to 2001.*

Source: Eurostat

Sweden had the lowest infant mortality rate in 1980 and 2003, with less than three deaths of infants aged under one year per 1,000 live births in 2003. Historically, infant mortality in northern Europe has generally been lower than in both eastern and southern Europe. This is no longer the case in southern Europe, with low rates prevailing in Spain (3.2), Portugal (4.0) and Italy (4.3) in 2003.

There are also variations in life expectancy between EU countries, as can be seen in Figure 10.13. In 2003 life expectancy at birth for males was highest in Sweden, at 77.9 years, and lowest in the three Baltic States (Estonia, Latvia and Lithuania), at around 65 to 66 years. In contrast, for females, life expectancy at birth was highest in Spain, at 83.7 years. Based on the 2003 mortality rates, 16 out of the 25 member states had a life expectancy at birth for women of over 80 years, (this would be 17 of the 25 member states if Slovenia were to be included, where the rate was 79.9 years in 2002).

Based on prevailing mortality rates, a man reaching the age of 60 in 1960 and living in the EU could have expected to live to age 76, on average. By the early 2000s such a man could expect to live to about 80 years. The corresponding figures for women are 79 years and 84 years. The figures for the UK show a similar trend. In the UK a man reaching 60 in 1960 could have expected to live to around age 75; by 2002 such a man could expect to live to 80. The corresponding figures for women are 79 and 83. There have been increases of four and five years in life expectancy at age 60 for men and women respectively over the last 40 years in Europe (five and four years, in the UK). This has had a significant impact on the numbers of older people and, with it, the demand for health and other services, and for the provision of benefits and financial support.

Migration

Migration estimates are an important demographic output for any national statistical institute. This is true in Europe because migration is a major determinant of population change for many countries. Migration topics are also important in the political arena and are relevant to a number of areas of social and economic policy. Eurostat organises a joint collection of migration data from national statistical institutes. It does this data collection jointly with other international bodies, including the United Nations Statistical Division, the Council of Europe and the International Labour Organisation. Organisations such as the United Nations and Eurostat have been prepared to expend significant efforts to establish principles and practices on population statistics that will aid comparability and coherence.[18,19]

Nevertheless, countries differ in the way they produce migration statistics and who they consider to be a migrant. In some countries, migration statistics are based on administrative data taken, for example, from systems for issuing residence permits or from a population register. Some countries use survey-based data. These variations in data sources and definitions need to be borne in mind when comparing the migrant estimates for different countries.

In 2002 around 1.7 million more people migrated into EU15 countries than migrated out. Spain, Italy, Germany and the UK together received 71 per cent of the net inflow of migrants into the EU15 member states.[1] (Migrants are people leaving or coming to a country for a period of at least a year.) The areas of the world that accounted for the largest net inflows to the UK between 1999 and 2003 were the Indian sub-continent (200,000), African Commonwealth countries (220,000), and the Middle East (80,000). In contrast, there were net outflows of migrants from the UK to countries such as Australia and the USA.[20]

There are large gross migration flows between the UK and the rest of Europe, though net flows can be relatively small. Between 1999 and 2003 there was a net inflow of 26,000 migrants to the UK from the rest of the EU25. This was accounted for by a net inflow of 101,000 migrants from the accession countries and a net outflow of 75,000 migrants to the countries of the EU15. Some people migrating from the UK to Europe may be European nationals returning home after working or studying in the UK for a year or more.

Many people who migrate to the UK subsequently emigrate again. It is estimated that almost half the overseas-born immigrants to the UK in the 1980s and 1990s emigrated again within five years.[21] Migration from source countries that have a GDP per capita similar to or higher than the UK is more likely to be transient, while migration from countries with a lower GDP per capita is more likely to be longer-term or permanent. Thus migration from countries such as Australia, the USA and many other EU countries may be transient and migration from countries such as those in the Indian sub-continent may be longer-term.

The second demographic transition in the UK and Europe

Significant socio-demographic changes have taken place in the UK in the last 30 or so years. These changes in society, brought about by shifting social attitudes and norms and a new emphasis on personal freedom of choice, are sometimes considered to represent a 'second demographic transition'[22]. They are marked by a number of changes in partnership and

Map **10.14**

Crude marriage rate per 1,000 population for selected European countries, 2003[1]

Rate per 1,000

- 6.50 and over
- 5.20 to 6.49
- 5.00 to 5.19
- 4.50 to 4.99
- 4.49 and under

Azores

Madeira

Canary Islands

Malta (not to scale)

Source: Eurostat; Council of Europe

1 2000 data used for Albania and Bosnia and Herzegovina; 2002 data used for Norway and Croatia.

family formation, such as an increasing prevalence of cohabitation and a large increase in the proportion of births taking place outside marriage. There has been an increase in the age at marriage and at first birth. These changes have typically taken place in countries in northern and western Europe and, more recently, in eastern Europe. A brief view of some of these changes is given in the last part of this chapter. More information about families in the UK can be found in the *Focus on Families* publication.[23]

In Europe the number of marriages each year has fallen since 1972 from 3.3 million to 2.2 million, a decrease of one-third. In the UK there was a rise in the number of marriages between 2001 and 2002 but, even so, there is a falling trend in marriage rates in this country as well. The number of marriages in the UK in 2001 was the lowest annual figure since 1897 and the number in 2002 was 18 per cent lower than in 1992. In the European context, the UK rates were about average. The lowest rates within Europe occurred in Slovenia, Latvia, Sweden, Estonia and Belgium. Marriage rates have remained high in Cyprus. This is illustrated in Map 10.14.

The fall in marriage rates in the UK has gone hand in hand with a rising age at first marriage. In England and Wales the mean age at first marriage has increased over the last ten or so years. In 1991 the mean age at first marriage was 27.5 for men and 25.5 for women. By 2002 this had risen to 30.9 for men and 28.7 for women. In the European context these ages at first marriage are slightly above average, as Map 10.15 shows, though changes in the UK are in line with the trend in Europe towards getting married later in life. In 1980 the average age at first marriage in Europe was 26 for men and 23 for women. Latest estimates show that these had risen to over 30 for men and 28 for women in 2003.

Changes in marriage rates and age at marriage are partly due to the rise in cohabitation. Cohabitation has been increasing in the UK, as in Europe, where such partnerships are referred to as consensual unions. Cohabitation is becoming more popular both before, and as an alternative to, marriage, and some people do not view it as being a different union from marriage.[24] In line with these changes in partnership formation in the UK and across Europe has been a trend towards more

Map **10.15**

Mean age of women at first marriage below age 50[1] for selected European countries,[2] 2003[3]

Mean Age
- 28.50 and over
- 27.50 to 28.49
- 26.00 to 27.49
- 25.99 and under
- No data available

Azores

Madeira

Canary Islands

Malta
(not to scale)

1 Includes a small number of brides over 50.
2 England & Wales data used for UK as UK data unavailable.
3 2000 and 2001 data used for Italy and Germany respectively; 2002 data used for Belgium, Estonia, Greece, Spain, Malta and Netherlands.

Source: Eurostat; Council of Europe; Office for National Statistics

births outside marriage. The change has been quite dramatic in Europe. In 1960 one in every 20 live births in the EU was outside marriage but, by 2003, this proportion had risen to nearly one in three. Rates tend to be low in southern Europe, for example in Cyprus, Greece and Italy, and high in northern and eastern European countries such as Sweden, Estonia, Latvia and Denmark as Map 10.16 shows. The UK rates are also high and similar to those in Denmark.

Divorce has become more prevalent in Europe over the last 30 years, though there is strong variation in rates between countries. Very low divorce rates still prevail in Italy, Ireland, Poland and Spain. The highest rates are observed in Scandinavia. The divorce rate[25] in Great Britain is among the highest in Europe. In 2004 there were around 14 people divorcing in Great Britain per 1,000 married people.

Summary

- The UK has a growing population; between 2000 and 2004 it was the twelfth fastest growing of the EU25 countries.

- Natural change is still a feature of population growth in the UK though, as in the rest of the EU, net migration is the most important driver of population change.

- UK fertility rates are higher than the average rate across the EU25. But rates have fallen since the 1960s and are low relative to the UK 1960s peak.

- The UK has an ageing population but this is not happening as fast in the UK as in many other European countries. The proportion of people over 65 at 16 per cent is now slightly below the EU25 as a whole (16.5 per cent), having been higher than the EU25 in 1985 (15 per cent versus 13 per cent).

- The UK is one of the highest receivers of migrants to Europe from the rest of the world. There is also a high volume of flows between the UK and the rest of Europe, although the net flows may be relatively low.

- Significant socio-demographic changes have taken place in the UK in the last 30 or so years. These have included an increased prevalence of cohabitation, which has gone along with a large increase in the proportion of births

Map **10.16**

Percentage of live births outside marriage for selected European countries, 2003[1]

1 2002 data used for Belgium, Estonia, France and Bosnia and Herzegovina.   *Source: Eurostat; Council of Europe*

taking place outside marriage, a rising age at marriage and later childbearing. These changes are in line with European trends.

Reporting on the population is a matter that captures public interest and can cause wide debate. This is partly because population change over time is often seen by the public as reflecting a country's social and economic climate. It is also because population statistics are widely used in public administration and planning. In an increasingly mobile and complex world, where populations are becoming harder to measure and estimate with certainty, more effort has been expended to provide assurances about the accuracy of official statistics.[26, 27] The UK is planning for the next census in 2011, which will provide the base for the following decade of population statistics. Official statisticians from the UK are working closely with colleagues in other census-taking countries, both in the EU and internationally, to share experience and lessons learned from the 2000 round of censuses.[28] In Europe the UN ECE recommendations for the 2010 round of censuses are being reviewed, with the help of member countries, to update the corresponding recommendations from the 2000 round of censuses for this UN region. Considerable efforts are in hand in the UK to improve, between now and 2011, the quality of intercensal population estimates for local areas and migration estimates.[29]

Notes and references

1. Eurostat (2004) *The statistical guide to Europe 2004 edition*. Office for official publications of the European Communities.

2. Council of Europe (2004) *Recent demographic developments in Europe*. Council of Europe Publishing: Strasbourg.

3. Pearce D and Bovagnet F-C (2005) The demographic situation in the European Union. *Population Trends* **119**, 7–15.

4. European Commission *The History of the European Union*. www.europa.eu.int/abc/history/index_en.htm

5. Total fertility rates: the average number of children per woman that would be born to a group of women if current patterns of childbearing persisted throughout their childbearing life.

6. Smallwood S and Chamberlain J (2005) Replacement fertility, what has it been and what does it mean? *Population Trends* **119**, 16–27.

7. Philipov D and Dorbritz J (2003) Demographic consequences of economic transition in countries of central and eastern Europe. *Population Studies* **30**. Council of Europe Publishing: Strasbourg.

8. Estimates of the average age of mothers at their first birth are given for England and Wales rather than the UK. In order to estimate the average age of mothers at their first birth it is necessary first to ensure that the birth is a first birth. At registration women are asked only about their previous births inside marriage. Thus survey data are used in conjunction with registration data to estimate the true order of births to mothers resident in England and Wales. True birth order estimates, and hence average age of mother at first birth, are not available on a consistent basis for all countries of the UK and are therefore not available for the UK as a whole.

9. Pearce D, Cantisani G and Laihonen A (1999) Changes in fertility and family sizes in Europe. *Population Trends* **95**, 33–40.

10. Schoenmaeckers R C (2005) Population ageing and its challenges to social policies. Paper presented at the European Population Conference 2005: Demographic Challenges for Social Cohesion. Council of Europe, Strasbourg, 7–8 April.

11. Government Actuary's Department (2005) *UK Population Projections 2004-based*. www.gad.gov.uk/Population/index.asp

12. Pension Commission (2004) *Pensions: Challenges and Choices. The First Report of the Pension Commission*. www.pensionscommission.org.uk/publications/2004/annrep/exec-summary.pdf

13. Punch A and Pearce D (2000) *Europe's population and labour market beyond 2000* Vol. 1. Council of Europe Publishing: Strasbourg.

14. Punch A and Pearce D (2000) *Europe's population and labour market beyond 2000* Vol. 2. Council of Europe Publishing: Strasbourg.

15. Average age of exit from the labour force: Eurostat publishes estimates for a number of countries of the average exit age from the labour force. These are based on a probability model that considers the relative change of activity rates from one year to another at a specific age. The activity rate represents the labour force (employed and unemployed population) as a percentage of the total population for a given age. The indicator is based on the EU Labour Force Survey. Estimates are available for 13 of the EU15 countries, including the UK.

16. Life expectancy is the average number of years a person would be expected to live if they were subject throughout their life to the current mortality conditions or age-specific probabilities of dying.

17. Infant mortality rate: the number of deaths of children under 1 year per 1,000 live births.

18. United Nations Statistics Division Publications (1998) *Recommendations on Statistics of International Migration*, Revision 1. Series M, No. 58/Rev 1. Sales Number: 98.XVII.14.

19. United Nations Statistics Division Publications (1998) *Principles and Recommendations for Population and Housing Censuses*. Series M, No. 67. Sales Number: 98.XVII.8.

20. Office for National Statistics (2005) *International Migration 2003* Series MN30.

21. Rendall M S and Ball D J (2004) Immigration, emigration and the ageing of the overseas-born population in the United Kingdom. *Population Trends* **116**, 18–27.

22. Van de Kaa D (1987) Europe's second demographic transition. *Population Bulletin* **42(1)**.

23. Office for National Statistics (2004) *Focus on Families*. www.statistics.gov.uk/focuson/families/.

24. Philipov D (2005) Portrait of the family in Europe. Paper presented at the European Population Conference 2005: Demographic Challenges for Social Cohesion. Council of Europe, Strasbourg, 7–8 April.

25. Divorce rates are the number of divorces per 1,000 married people. Their calculation requires population estimates by legal marital status, which are not available on a UK basis due to the lack of estimates for Northern Ireland. Thus the divorce rates quoted here are for Great Britain rather than the UK.

26. Office for National Statistics (2003) *A demographic statistics service for the 21st century*. www.statistics.gov.uk/about/ Methodology_by_theme/downloads/Demographic_Statistics_ Service.pdf

27. Jones J and Chappell R (2004) European wide issues in population statistics. *Population Trends* **104**, 17–22.

28. Benton P, Massingham R, Brown H and White I (2004) The 2011 Census: a proposed design for England and Wales. *Population Trends* **115**, 16–23.

29. Office for National Statistics (2004) *2001 Census Local Authority Population Statistics*. www.statistics.gov.uk/downloads/theme_ population/LAStudy_FullReport.asp

Appendix

Chapter 1: UK population: past, present and future

Population estimates and projections

Estimated and projected populations consist of those people who are usually resident in the constituent countries of the UK, whatever their nationality. Figures for the UK do not include the population of the Channel Islands or the Isle of Man. Members of HM Forces stationed outside the UK are excluded; those stationed within the UK are included. Students are taken to be resident at their term-time addresses.

The most recent set of national population projections published for the UK are based on the populations of England, Wales, Scotland and Northern Ireland at mid-2004. These were published in October 2005 and replace the previous interim 2003-based national projections. Further details of these can be found on the website of the Government Actuary's Department: www.gad.gov.uk.

Classification of ethnic groups

The recommended classification of ethnic groups for National Statistics data sources was changed in 2001 to bring it broadly in line with the 2001 Census. There are two levels to this classification. Level 1 is a coarse classification into five main ethnic groups. Level 2 sub-divides Level 1, and provides a finer categorisation. Level 2 (detailed) categories should be adopted wherever possible. The two levels and the categories are:

Level 1	Level 2
White	British
	Irish
	Other White background
	All White groups
Mixed	White and Black Caribbean
	White and Black African
	White and Asian
	Other Mixed background
	All Mixed groups
Asian or Asian British	Indian
	Pakistani
	Bangladeshi
	Other Asian background
	All Asian groups
Black or Black British	Caribbean
	African
	Other Black background
	All Black groups
Chinese or other ethnic group	Chinese
	Other ethnic group
	All Chinese or other groups
All ethnic groups	All ethnic groups
Not stated	Not stated

Direct comparisons should not be made between the figures produced using the new classification and those based on the previous one. More details can be found on the National Statistics website at: www.statistics.gov.uk/about/classifications/downloads/ns_ethnicity_statement.doc

Chapter 2: Where people live

For details on ethnicity, see the appendix notes for Chapter 1.

Housing completions

The Office of the Deputy Prime Minister (ODPM) considers a dwelling to be completed when it becomes ready for occupation, whether or not it is occupied. In practice, there are instances where delays to the schedule mean that completions are missed, for example where an owner has not requested a completion certificate.

Housing tenure

There are four tenure categories for dwelling stock and household figures used in tables 2.21 and 2.22. These are:

1   Owner-occupied (or private enterprise, in the case of house-building statistics, that is, dwellings built for owner-occupiers or for private landlords, whether people or companies). This includes accommodation that is owned outright or bought with a mortgage, and shared ownership (part rent, part mortgage).

2   Rented privately (defined as all non-owner occupied property other than that rented from local authorities and registered social landlords (RSLs), plus that rented from private or public bodies by virtue of employment. This includes property occupied rent-free by someone other than the owner).

3   Rented from registered social landlords (RSLs, but for stock figures non-registered housing associations are excluded and subsumed within owner-occupied).

4   Rented from local authorities. In Scotland dwellings rented from local authorities include those rented from Scottish Homes, formerly the Scottish Special Housing Association.

Chapter 3: The UK's major urban areas

Definitions of an urban area – differences within the UK

England and Wales

In 2004 the Office for National Statistics (ONS) published 2001 *Census Key Statistics* and *Census Area Statistics* for individual named towns and cities throughout England and Wales. These are based on a definition of urban land consistent with that used to report data from the 1981 and 1991 Censuses. This approach considers Ordnance Survey maps and identifies urban land uses. Once the extent of urban land use within an area is great enough, that area is deemed to be urban. There is no further breakdown into types of urban land.

A rural and urban area classification was published in 2004 as the result of a project jointly undertaken by the Countryside Agency; the Department for the Environment, Food and Rural Affairs; the Office of the Deputy Prime Minister; ONS; and the Welsh Assembly Government. The classification includes four settlement types: 'urban', 'town and fringe', 'village' and 'isolated dwellings', all of which are further split according to whether the population density is 'sparse' or 'less sparse'. *Key Statistics for the rural and urban classification 2004*, published in March 2005, provides statistics where Census Output Areas have been aggregated by classification type to county and unitary authority level. The classification is currently available for a range of different geographic areas: Census Output Areas, 2003 statistical wards, Census Area statistical wards, Lower Layer Super Output Areas and Middle Layer Super Output Areas.

The data given in Chapter 3 are consistent with the rural and urban area classifications put forward by this partnership of agencies. All areas with a population exceeding 10,000 reported in the *Key Statistics for Urban Areas and Census Area Statistics for Urban Areas* publications for England and Wales are deemed either 'urban sparse' or 'urban less sparse' under the rural and urban area classification. According to the 2001 Census, 0.2 per cent of the population of England, and 1.9 per cent of Wales, were living in part of a town or city described as 'urban sparse'. Residents in areas classified as 'urban less sparse' made up 80.4 per cent of England's population and 62.3 per cent of Wales' in 2001. The England and Wales urban areas reported on in chapter 3 are wholly classified as 'urban less sparse'.

Scotland

The General Register Office for Scotland published the *Scottish Executive Urban Rural Classification 2003–2004* in June 2004, which splits settlements into three urban categories and one rural. An urban settlement is one with a population of over 3,000. The smallest urban category (settlements with a population of between 3,000 and 10,000) and the rural category are further delineated by whether they are accessible or remote. Greater Glasgow is classified as a large urban area, consisting of settlements with a population greater than 125,000.

Settlements in Scotland and urban areas in England and Wales are composed of Census Output Areas. The manner in which Census Output Areas were configured differed between the countries. This may mean that an urban area in Scotland will include a greater land area and a larger population than would be the case in England and Wales. This difference does not invalidate any aspect of Chapter 3. However, the effects for smaller urban areas would mean that making reasonable comparisons would be more difficult.

Northern Ireland

The official urban-rural definition in Northern Ireland is outlined in the *Statistical Classification and Delineation of Settlements* report published in February 2005 – see www.nisra.gov.uk/statistics/financeandpersonnel/DMB/urban_rural.html

In Northern Ireland, settlements with a population of 4,500 or more are defined as urban. The Northern Ireland Statistics and Research Agency created Census Key Statistics using 100-metre grid blocks rather than the Census Output Areas that are used to disseminate detailed settlement data from the 2001 Census. See www.ninis.nisra.gov.uk for more details.

The Northern Ireland classification includes a further dimension not found in the Great Britain classifications. Urban areas in Northern Ireland can include discontinuous settlements, where the smaller settlement has become a clear, functional part of the larger settlement. It is argued that this approach results in better planning decisions for Northern Ireland than if the smaller settlements were treated separately.

Summary

The definition of an urban area is related to the population density and land use of the area in which it is situated. An urban area in one agency's classification can be rural in another. As long as the different organisations consider similar issues when designating urban and rural area classifications, they will make classifications that are fit for purpose and are broadly comparable.

Urban area case studies

The following section describes the ten urban areas that were analysed but are not contained in the body of the text, with comparisons made between areas.

1 Greater London Urban Area

Greater London Urban Area is roughly contained by the M25, with some spurs of urban land that extend beyond: Waltham Abbey, Cheshunt and Hoddeston to the north; Hemel Hempstead to the north west; Slough to the west; and Woking and Byfleet through to West End to the south west. There are large areas of land that are not part of Greater London Urban Area inside the southerly and easterly boundaries of the M25.

The administrative boundary of the Government Office Region (GOR) for London does not equate to the Greater London Urban Area, nor do subdivisions of the larger urban area equate to local authorities or London boroughs. The south west of the urban area, including the sub-divisions of Staines, Egham, Shepperton and Walton and Weybridge, is not part of the London GOR.

Greater London Urban Area experienced the highest proportional increase in population density between the 1991 and 2001 Censuses. Population density increased by 7.8 per cent to 5,099.4 people per km^2 in 2001.

Between the 1991 and 2001 Censuses, the land size of Greater London Urban Area increased by 0.4 per cent, while the population grew by 8.2 per cent. The growth in population and land size over the ten-year period between the censuses was a result of population growth in existing areas and the envelopment of an urban area. The sub-divisions of Swanscombe, Northfleet and Gravesend were separate from Greater London Urban Area in 1991 but part of it in 2001. The growth of the Swanscombe and Northfleet sub-divisions has been the result of a community regeneration project and further development is expected. The sub-division of Swanscombe increased by 9,416 people and 4.4 km^2 between the censuses.

2 West Midlands Urban Area

West Midlands Urban Area extends from the sub-division of Brownhills to the north, Coleshill (North Warwickshire) to the east, and Wolverhampton to the west. The major centre of Birmingham and the centres of Dudley and Walsall are located within West Midlands Urban Area. The sub-divisions of the larger urban area do not equate to local authorities of the same name.

The population and land size of West Midlands Urban Area decreased by similar proportions between the 1991 and 2001 Censuses. As a result, the population density has remained fairly constant, moving from 3,812.4 people per km^2 to 3,808.6 in 2001. There was a decline in population in most sub-divisions within the urban area. One exception was the sub-division of Brownhills, which experienced a 9.4 per cent increase in population. A new sub-division of West Midlands Urban Area, Yew Tree, was incorporated in the 2001 Census results. Yew Tree, south east of Walsall, incorporates a portion of what was Walsall in 1991 and a new residential area.

3 Greater Manchester Urban Area

This urban area is discussed in the text of Chapter 3.

4 West Yorkshire Urban Area

West Yorkshire Urban Area extends to include the following sub-divisions: Menston in the north; Leeds in the east; Holmfirth and Honley in the south; and Keighley in the west. Centres within the urban area include the sub-divisions of:

- Leeds, dominating the north east
- Bradford, taking up much of the north west
- Huddersfield, in the south west
- Wakefield, in the south east.

Results from the 2001 Census listed 26 sub-divisions of West Yorkshire Urban Area, none of which equates to local authorities. Twenty of these sub-divisions experienced an increase in population between the 1991 and 2001 Censuses; 22 became larger in area. The sub-division of Leeds had the highest population, 443,247, and largest area, 109.2 km^2, in 2001. Leeds also experienced the highest absolute change in population between 1991 and 2001, an increase of 19,053, and the largest absolute growth in land area, of 2.7 km^2.

5 Greater Glasgow

The sub-divisions of Greater Glasgow that form the outer bounds of the larger urban area are: Milton to the north west; Milngavie to the north; Wishaw to the south east; Airdrie to the east; Newton Mearns to the south west; and Kilbarchan and Howwood to the west. These sub-divisions do not equate to local authorities of the same name.

In 2001 the majority of the population of Greater Glasgow lived in the sub-division of Glasgow: 629,501 of a population of 1,168,270. The next largest population centre was Paisley with 74,170 people.

Data for the urban areas and settlements in Scotland from the 1991 Census are available based on the 2001 urban area and settlement boundaries. The sub-division that experienced the largest population increase was Howwood, with an increase of 45.0 per cent or 466 people over the decade. The population of Faifley had decreased by 19.0 per cent or 1,155 people to 4,932 by 2001. The largest absolute population gain was in Newton Mearns, which grew from 3,295 to 22,637. The largest absolute population loss was in the sub-division of Glasgow, where numbers fell by 28,878 people between 1991 and 2001.

6 Tyneside

Tyneside has seafront as its eastern border. The northern boundary is on the coast at the sub-division of Whitley Bay, and its southernmost tip is at the sub-division of South Hetton. Tyneside extends as far west as the sub-division of Ryton. It surrounds but does not subsume Sunderland Urban Area. The Tyne River runs roughly through the centre of Tyneside urban area.

The population and population density of Tyneside decreased between the 1991 and 2001 Censuses while the land size increased. The three most populous sub-divisions are Newcastle upon Tyne, which dominates the north west, South Shields, which sits at the mouth of the Tyne, and Gateshead, which lies across the river.

7 Liverpool Urban Area

The River Mersey forms the western and southern border of Liverpool Urban Area. Sub-divisions of the larger urban area do not equate to local authorities. The sub-division of Crosby forms the northernmost point of the urban area. Liverpool Urban Area extends east through a spur of urban land extending from the sub-division of Liverpool, through the neighbouring sub-divisions of Huyton-with-Roby, Prescot and St. Helens, to the sub-division of Haydock at its easternmost point.

The sub-division of Liverpool dominates the urban area. Liverpool accounts for 57.5 per cent of the population and 58.4 per cent of the land size. The boundary of the Liverpool sub-division roughly equates to that of the Liverpool local authority. Areas included in the urban area that are not in the local authority are the electoral wards of Cantril Farm, Haleswood West, Haleswood South and much of Haleswood East – all from Knowsley local authority,

Liverpool Urban Area was second only to Greater Glasgow in terms of the proportion of population loss between the 1991 and 2001 Censuses. It recorded the third highest decrease in population density.

8 Nottingham Urban Area

This urban area is discussed in the text of Chapter 3.

9 Sheffield Urban Area

Sheffield Urban Area is dominated by the sub-division Sheffield, which forms its western and southern borders. The sub-division of Mosborough and Highlane includes the urban area's south-easternmost point, the sub-division of Rawmarsh to the north east, and the sub-division of Chapeltown to the north.

Sheffield Urban Area experienced the second highest proportional increase in population density between the 1991 and 2001 Censuses. Over two-thirds of the population and land coverage of Sheffield Urban Area is accounted for by the sub-division of Sheffield. The second largest sub-division is Rotherham, located in the north east.

10 Bristol Urban Area

This urban area is discussed in the text of Chapter 3.

Chapter 5: Fertility and mortality

Births and deaths

Deaths data may be reported by date of occurrence (when the person actually died) or date of registration (when the death was registered). England and Wales data in Chapter 5 represent the number of deaths registered in each year up to 1992, and the number of deaths occurring in each year from 1993 to 2003.

Within England and Wales, births are assigned to areas according to the usual residence of the mother at the date of the birth, as stated at registration. If the address of usual residence is outside England and Wales, the birth is included in any aggregate for England and Wales as a whole (and hence in the UK total), but excluded from the figures for any individual region or area. Birth figures for Scotland include births to both resident and non-resident mothers. From 1981 onwards figures given for Northern Ireland exclude births to mothers not usually resident in Northern Ireland. However, the UK total includes such births.

Deaths in England and Wales, are normally assigned to the area of usual residence of the deceased. If this is outside England and Wales, the death is still included in any aggregate for these two countries as a whole (and hence in the UK total), but excluded from the figures for any individual region or area. Figures for Scotland and Northern Ireland include deaths of both residents and non-residents, as do data for the UK.

Births and Deaths data for Northern Ireland between 1901 and 1911 are estimates that have been produced by aggregating the births and deaths from Registrar General Reports for the counties of Antrim, Armagh, Down, Fermanagh, Londonderry and Tyrone. These counties were combined to constitute Northern Ireland.

Country of birth and ethnicity

In the absence of high quality ethnicity data on births, the country of birth of a child's mother is used as a proxy for the child's ethnicity. The mother's country of birth has been recorded at the registration of a birth since 1969 in England and Wales.

However, because many women in non-white ethnic groups are UK-born, country of birth cannot be taken as completely reflective of ethnic minority fertility. Analysing ethnicity by using country of birth alone would miss half the UK ethnic minority population; the 2001 Census showed that 50 per cent of the ethnic minority population of the UK were born in the UK. For more information, see: www.statistics.gov.uk/CCI/nugget.asp?ID=767&Pos=3&ColRank=2&Rank=448

Male fertility

Father's age at the birth of a child is recorded for:

- all births within marriage

- all jointly registered births, whether they are to parents who are living at the same or different addresses.

Father's age is not recorded for births that are solely registered by the mother, which have comprised between 6 and 8 per cent of all births in England and Wales for the last two decades.

Measures of male fertility, like the total fertility rate or age-specific fertility rates (described in Box 4, Chapter 5), require the father's age. Because of the lack of paternal data for sole-registered births, analysis of male fertility is usually based only on births within marriage or jointly registered births. However, the age distribution of mothers of sole-registered births is different from that of other mothers, and this is likely to also be the case for fathers of sole-registered births. It is likely that measures of male fertility based only on births within marriage or jointly-registered births do not accurately reflect male fertility.

In Chapter 5, rather than exclude sole-registered births from estimates of male fertility, the distribution of fathers' ages at these births has been imputed from that of fathers of jointly registered births, where the parents were living at different addresses. These fathers are considered to have more similar characteristics to fathers of sole-registered births than either married fathers or those who have jointly registered births while living at same address as the mother. This is because both sole-registered births and those which are jointly registered to parents living at different addresses are often assumed to be a proxy for births to lone mothers.

Births jointly registered by parents outside marriage before 1986 cannot be differentiated according to whether the parents were living at the same or different addresses. For sole-registered births before 1986, all jointly registered births were used as the basis for imputation of father's age.

Chapter 6: Internal migration

National Health Service Central Register (NHSCR) migration data

Estimates for internal population movements are based on the movement of NHS doctors' patients between former health authorities (HAs) in England and Wales and area health boards (AHBs) in Scotland and Northern Ireland. These transfers are recorded at the NHS Central Registers (NHSCRs) in Southport and Edinburgh, and at the Central Services Agency, Belfast.

Patient moves within HAs are excluded from NHSCR data as they do not constitute a move between HAs. NHSCR data are used to create internal migration estimates between countries in the UK and, for England, between the Government Office Regions (GORs) of England and the rest of the United Kingdom.

The estimates are adjusted to take account of differences in recorded cross-border flows between England and Wales, Scotland and Northern Ireland, and provide a detailed indicator of population movement within the UK. However, they should not be regarded as a perfect measure of migration as delays of varying lengths can occur between a person moving and their registering with a new doctor. Additionally, some moves may not result in a re-registration, for example an individual may migrate again before registering with a doctor.

The NHSCR at Southport was computerised in 1991. Before 1991, the time lag was assumed to be three months between a person moving and their re-registration with an NHS doctor being processed onto the NHSCR. (It was estimated that processing at NHSCR took two months.) Since computerisation, estimates of internal migration derived from the NHSCR are based on the date of acceptance of the new patient by the HA (not previously available), with a one-month time lag assumed.

Inter-regional rolling year tables are released every three months in March, June, September and December. Data for March are released in December of the same year. Data for June, September and December are released in March, June and September of the following year respectively.

Census

Migration data from the 2001 Census are produced from a question that asks the respondent their address from one year before. The options were:

- 'The address shown on the front of the form'
- 'No usual address one year ago'
- 'Same as person 1'. This option allowed multiple occupants sharing a residence to indicate that, 12 months previously, they had had the same residence as occupant 1 (the question was for respondent 2 and above)
- 'Elsewhere'.

If the respondent indicated that they lived elsewhere, a box was given in which they could write their previous address. This address was used to establish where the respondent had migrated from, using post codes if the previous address was in the UK, and country codes if the address was outside the UK.

An internal migrant in the 2001 Census was defined as someone who was resident in the UK on Census day and who was living at a different UK address 12 months previously. The question on 'address one year ago' included a box for 'No usual address one year ago'. A significant number of the UK population recorded this response: the figure for England and Wales alone was 420,000 or 0.8 per cent of the population aged over one (children aged under one were given the migration characteristics of their next of kin). Notably, 11 per cent of respondents in England and Wales who completed the 'No usual address one year ago' box also wrote something in the text box to describe where they were. However, the coding system took the tick box in preference to the written response.

Those responding 'No usual address' one year age have been excluded from some of the analysis in Chapter 6. This is to ensure that analysis of distance moved is correct; the origin of someone with 'No usual address' is unknown, therefore distance cannot be calculated. All census data include infants who had not reached their first birthday by the time of the census but were given the migration characteristics of their next of kin. The data exclude people who died or emigrated between making a move between addresses in the UK as well as those who moved from, and back to, an address within the 12-month period.

Individual sample of anonymised records

This is a dataset that contains a 3 per cent sample, of responses from the 2001 Census for England, Wales, Scotland and Northern Ireland, relating to some 1.8 million records. The data have been completely anonymised and disclosure control methods applied, so that no individuals can be identified.

The Individual Sample of Anonymised Records (ISAR) includes the following information for each respondent:

- main demographic (sex/age/marital status), health and socio-economic variables

- derived variables, such as social class and accommodation (for example, tenure, availability of amenities and access to a car)

- information about the sex, economic position and social class of the individual's family head

- limited information about other members of the individual's household (for example the number of pensioners).

National Statistics Socio-economic Classification

From 2001 the National Statistics socio-economic Classification (NS-SEC) has been used for all official statistics and surveys. It replaces Social Class based on Occupation (SC) and Socio-economic Groups (SEG). NS-SEC is an occupationally-based classification designed to provide coverage of the whole adult population. While designed to cover the entire population, much of the classification relates only to people aged between 16 and 74, although information is available for those aged 75 and over. With the exception of the Individual Sample of Anonymised Records (ISAR; see above), which uses a greater number of occupation classes, 40 in total, analysis in Chapter 6 uses the classification that has eight occupation classes, the first of which can be sub-divided. These are:

1 Higher managerial and professional occupations

   1.1 Large employers and higher managerial occupations

   1.2 Higher professional occupations

2 Lower managerial and professional occupations

3 Intermediate occupations

4 Small employers and own account workers

5 Lower supervisory and technical occupations

6 Semi-routine occupations

7 Routine occupations

8 Never worked and long-term unemployed.

More details can be found on the National Statistics website at: www.statistics.gov.uk/methods_quality/ns_sec/default.asp

Standard Industrial Classification

The UK Standard Industrial Classification of Economic Activities (UK SIC(92)) is used to classify business establishments and other statistical units by the type of economic activities they are engaged in. The classification provides a framework for the collection, tabulation, presentation and analysis of data and its use promotes uniformity. In addition, it can be used for administrative purposes and by non-government bodies as a convenient way of classifying industrial activities into a common structure.

The following table gives a broad comparison between the sections of UK SIC(92).

A Agriculture, Hunting and Forestry

B Fishing

C Mining and Quarrying

D Manufacturing

E Electricity, Gas and Water Supply

F Construction

G Wholesale and Retail Trade; Repair of Motor Vehicles, Motorcycles and Personal and Household Goods

H Hotels and Restaurants

I Transport, Storage and Communication

J Financial Intermediation

K Real Estate, Renting and Business Activities

L Public Administration and Defence; Compulsory Social Security

M Education

N Health and Social Work

O Other Community, Social and Personal Service Activities

P Private Households with Employed Persons

Q Extra-territorial Organisations and Bodies

More information can be found on the National Statistics website at: www.statistics.gov.uk/methods_quality/sic

District classifications

Figure 6.11 shows the 408 local authority areas of Great Britain, classified into 13 types, on the basis of the principles used by the Office of Population Censuses and Surveys (OPCS, 1981)[i] in its 'area types' of England and Wales. The classification has been developed in three ways from the original version:

1. Extension to Scotland, on the same principles

2. Distinction between 'accessible' and 'remoter' districts in the original mixed urban/rural and remoter, mainly rural types, on the basis of whether they lie less than 65km from a metropolitan boundary.[ii]

3. Revision, in the light of the 1990s' changes in local government areas. Areas were assigned on the basis of which area type the majority of the population was within.

References

i. Office of Population Censuses and Surveys (1981) *Census 1981, Preliminary Report, England and Wales*, OPCS, HMSO: London.

ii. Boyle P (1995) Rural in-migration to England and Wales, 1980–81. *Journal of Rural Studies* **11**, 65–78.

Chapter 7: International migration

How migration to and from the UK is estimated

Unlike some countries, the UK does not have a comprehensive register of all the people who live in the country, nor a comprehensive record of migration into or out of the UK. Most of the information about migration between the UK and other countries comes from the International Passenger Survey (IPS). The IPS operates at major routes into and out of the country: airports, seaports and the Channel Tunnel. Participation in the IPS is completely voluntary, and around 80 per cent of those who are asked to take part agree to answer the questions. It is also anonymous. The IPS is not just used to estimate migration, but has several other important applications such as estimating the number of tourists and the amount of money raised through tourism.

The survey interviews only a relatively small number of migrants: about 3,000 in all. This is around 0.5 per cent of the total. The results of the survey are scaled up to represent all migrants who could potentially have been interviewed. This is a complex statistical process called weighting. Like all surveys, the IPS is subject to error, both because the weighting

procedure cannot give perfect results, and for other reasons. Migration data published by the Office for National Statistics (ONS) are estimates, and should be interpreted with this warning in mind.

The IPS does not estimate all migration, even after weighting has been carried out, because the survey does not cover all types of migrant. For example, it is thought that many asylum seekers are not counted by the survey. For this reason, adjustments are made and other sources of data are used in addition to the IPS.

A migrant is defined as someone who changes their country of residence for at least a year. The IPS asks people their intended length of stay on arrival or departure. To account for people who do not realise their intended length of stay, two adjustments are made:

1 To account for people who initially come to or leave the UK for a short period but subsequently extend their stay for longer (visitor switchers).

2 For people who intend to be migrants but who, in reality, stay in the UK or abroad for less than one year (migrant switchers).

Home Office data on asylum seekers and their dependants are also incorporated into the estimates. Finally, estimates of migration between the UK and the Republic of Ireland are provided by the Irish Central Statistical Office.

These sources are combined to give estimates of total international migration (TIM).

The IPS started operating in 1964 and has been collecting migration data comparable to that collected today since 1975. The adjustments made to data from the IPS to give estimates of TIM have been made for each year from 1991. For earlier years the IPS alone has been used. It is important to bear this in mind when comparing estimates from years before 1991 to those from later years.

Publication of international migration estimates

International migration estimates for the UK are produced by the Migration Statistics Unit in ONS. Estimates of international migration for 2004, broken down by broad citizenship, were published in a press release in October 2005. At the time of writing, more detailed breakdowns by a number of different variables were available up to 2003. These were published in the 2003 reference volume in April 2005. The 2004 first release and 2003 reference volume, and, from spring 2006, the 2004 reference volume are available on the National Statistics website at: www.statistics.gov.uk/STATBASE/ Product.asp?vlnk=507

Estimates based on IPS data only

As detailed in the section on how international migration is estimated, estimates of TIM are based on the IPS, with adjustments derived from different sources. Sometimes, however, it is useful to present estimates based solely on IPS data. This is because it is possible to produce estimates broken down by a number of different variables, while the other sources do not always have this flexibility. Where estimates used in Chapter 7 have been based solely on IPS data, rather than TIM, this has been indicated in the text.

Migration estimates derived from census data

The 2001 Census gives information on migration derived from the question that asked where people were living one year previously. These census data are not the official ONS estimates of migration. They cover only one year: the year prior to Census day, which was in April 2001. Census data can tell us only about in-migration, because people who had left the country would, of course, not have been here to fill in a census form. Migration data derived from the census are not comprehensive: over 400,000 people stated that they had 'no usual address' one year prior to Census day. Also, response rates in key migration areas of the country tend to be lower than elsewhere. The process used to impute information about the people who did not complete census forms was not specifically designed to account for migration status. This means that these people were included in the population but their migration status may not have been accurately coded.

Census data do, however, give a high level of detail, which is why they have been used in some sections of this report to provide a fuller picture of migration. Where estimates in Chapter 7 have been based on census data, this has been indicated in the text.

Chapter 9: Special and communal populations

Armed forces

Marital status definitions

The definition of a married person differs between the 2001 Census and that used by the armed forces. Even within the armed forces the definition of a married person varies by service, as the table below illustrates.

Students

Students in the 2001 and 1991 Census

In 2001 students and schoolchildren in full-time education studying away from the family home were counted as resident at their term-time address (wherever they were enumerated). Basic demographic information only (sex, age, marital status and relationship) was collected at their 'home' or vacation address. The information on families, household size and household composition for their family home does not include them. In the 1991 Census, students and schoolchildren were treated as usually resident at their 'home' or vacation address and were included in the corresponding counts.

Marital status definition by data source

Data source	Definition of married	Definition of not married
2001 Census	Married, re-married, separated (but still legally married).	Single (never married), divorced, widowed.
Armed forces		
Naval services	Married, re-married.	Widowed, legally separated, divorced (Decree Nisi), divorced (Decree Absolute) and all other, including singles. Also includes those service personnel whose service spouse (either service personnel or civil service personnel) is receiving married personnel allowances.
Army	Married, re-married, legally separated, legally separated revoked, divorced (Decree Nisi) and divorced (Decree Nisi) revoked.	Single, single marriage annulled, widowed and divorced (Decree Absolute), all either with or without children.
Royal Air Force	Married, re-married, legally separated, divorced (Decree Nisi), and estranged/separated.	Single, widowed, divorced (Decree Absolute), marriage annulled and restatement case.

Source: 2001 Census form; TSP 10 - Defence Analytical Services Agency

The 1991 question included a separate category for full-time students. All full-time students were assumed to be economically inactive and were included in the 'Student' category under economically inactive. In 2001 information on the economic status of full-time students was collected and they were classified according to that status.

Stages of education in the UK

Education takes place in several stages: nursery (now part of the foundation stage in England), primary, secondary, further and higher education. It is compulsory for all children between the ages of 5 and 16 (4 to 16 in Northern Ireland). The non-compulsory fourth stage, further education, covers non-advanced education. This stage can be taken at further (including tertiary) education colleges, higher education institutions and, increasingly, in secondary schools. The fifth stage, higher education, is study beyond GCE A levels and their equivalent. For most full-time students, this takes place in higher education institutions.

Further education

The term 'further education' can be used in a general sense to cover all non-advanced courses taken after compulsory education. However, in its more common usage, it tends not to include studies taken by pupils staying on at secondary school or courses in higher education, for example courses in universities and colleges leading to qualifications above GCE A level, Higher Grade (in Scotland), GNVQ/NVQ level 3, and their equivalents. Since 1 April 1993 sixth form colleges have been included in the further education sector.

Higher education

Higher education (HE) is defined as courses that are of a standard that is higher than GCE A level, the Higher Grade of the Scottish Certificate of Education/National Qualification, GNVQ/NVQ level 3 or the Edexcel (formerly BTEC) or SQA National Certificate/Diploma. There are three main levels of HE course:

1. postgraduate courses leading to higher degrees, diplomas and certificates (including postgraduate certificates of education and professional qualifications), which usually require a first degree as an entry qualification

2. undergraduate courses, including first degrees, first degrees with qualified teacher status, enhanced first degrees, first degrees obtained concurrently with a diploma, and intercalated first degrees

3. other undergraduate courses, including all other HE courses, for example HNDs and Diplomas in HE.

As a result of the 1992 Further and Higher Education Act, former polytechnics and some other HE institutions were designated as universities in 1992/93. Students usually attend HE courses at HE institutions, but some attend at further education colleges. Some also attend institutions that do not receive public grants, such as the University of Buckingham, and these students are excluded from the tables.

Communal establishments

For the 2001 Census, a communal establishment was defined as an establishment 'providing managed residential accommodation', where 'managed' meant full-time or part-time supervision of the accommodation. People were assumed to be resident in a communal establishment if they had been living, or intended to live, there for six months or more. These cover universities/colleges, hospitals, hostels/homes, hotels, holiday complexes, defence establishments (but not married quarters) and prisons.

In most cases (for example prisons, large hospitals, hotels), communal establishments can be easily identified. Identification is less easy with small hotels, guest houses and sheltered accommodation. Special rules applied in these cases:

- Small hotels and guest houses were treated as communal establishments if they had the capacity for ten or more guests, excluding the owner/manager and their family.

- Sheltered housing was treated as a communal establishment if fewer than half the residents possessed their own facilities for cooking. If half or more had their own cooking facilities (regardless of use), the whole establishment was treated as separate households.

Any analysis of communal establishments and their residents and staff should take account of some anomalies in the data:

- Hotels and small guest houses with fewer than ten guests are special cases that were enumerated as households (see above), but some other small communal establishments, for example small care homes, were erroneously enumerated as households, rather than communal establishments.

- In England and Wales some monasteries and convents were enumerated as private households and some as communal establishments.

- In many places, students and older people live in self-contained flats within communal establishments, an example being a set of flats overseen by a warden. In some cases, the individual residences were enumerated in the census as separate households; in others, they were counted together as a single communal establishment.

- Many communal establishments did not return a communal establishment form, and of those that did, some had only the address completed. Where information could not be gathered in subsequent enquiries, establishments were coded to 'Other establishment: Other'. Many coded as such had no address recorded and no people. 'Other establishment: Other' accounts for 22 per cent of all communal establishments but only 8 per cent of communal establishment residents.

- There is also some blurring between 'residents (non-staff)' and 'resident staff and families' in the statistical tables. Many respondents did not answer the question on 'position in establishment' and there was some misinterpretation of 'resident' as 'living there' rather than 'non-staff'. There is some evidence that some communal establishment staff filled in the form for residents by proxy, and incorrectly recorded them as staff.

Communal establishments were broken down into the following classes in England and Wales in 2001:

Medical and care establishments

NHS

Psychiatric hospital/home

Other hospital home

Local authority

Childrens' home

Nursing home

Residential care home

Other home

Housing association

Home or hostel

Nursing home

Other

Residential care home

Childrens' home

Psychiatric hospital/home

Other hospital

Other medical and care home

Other establishments

Defence establishment (including ships)

Prison service establishment

Probation/bail hostel

Educational establishment (including halls of residence)

Hotel, boarding house, guest house

Hostel (including youth hostels, hostels for the homeless and people sleeping rough)

Civilian ship, boat or barge

Other

Symbols and conventions

Symbols and conventions

Rounding of figures. In tables where figures have been rounded to the nearest final digit, there may be an apparent discrepancy between the sum of the constituent items and the total as shown.

Billion. This term is used to represent a thousand million.

Provisional and estimated data. Some data for the latest year (and occasionally for earlier years) are provisional or estimated. To keep footnotes to a minimum, these have not been indicated; source departments will be able to advise if revised data are available.

Non-calendar years
Financial year – for example, 1 April 2001 to 31 March 2002 would be shown as 2001/02
Academic year – for example, September 2000/July 2001 would be shown as 2000/01
Combined years – for example, 2000-02 shows data for more than one year that have been combined
Data covering more than one year – for example, 1998, 1999 and 2000 would be shown as 1998 to 2000

Units on tables. Where one unit predominates it is shown at the top of the table. All other units are shown against the relevant row or column. Figures are shown in italics when they represent percentages.

Dependent children. Those aged under 16, or single people aged 16 to 18 and in full-time education.

Symbols. The following symbols have been used throughout the report:

..	*not available*
.	*not applicable*
-	*negligible (less than half the final digit shown)*
0	*nil*

Glossary

LIVERPOOL HOPE UNIVERSITY

Accession countries	The ten additional countries that joined the European Union (EU) on 1 May 2004. These were: Cyprus, the Czech Republic, Estonia, Hungary, Latvia, Lithuania, Malta, Poland, Slovakia and Slovenia.
Administrative geographies	Administrative geographies are the hierarchy of areas relating to national and local government in the UK. For example: Government Office Regions and Unitary Authorities in England; Council Areas in Scotland and District Council Areas in Northern Ireland.
Ageing index	Population above state pension age, per hundred children aged 0 to 15.
Ageing population	A population where the proportion who are children under 16 is falling and the proportion who are aged 65 or over is rising.
Age-specific fertility rate	The number of births in a year to women aged x, per thousand women aged x in the mid-year population.
Age-specific mortality rate	The number of deaths in a year of people aged x, per thousand people aged x in the mid-year population.
Age-standardised mortality rate	The mortality rate for a population after controlling for age structure.
Armed forces	A country's military forces, usually consisting of army, navy and air force personnel.
Baby boom	Period in which there is an unusually high number of births.
Census output area (OA)	Used across the UK as the base unit of census output. Census output areas were introduced in Scotland in 1991 and the rest of the UK in 2001. They replaced census enumeration districts, although these are still used for census data collection.
Child bearing ages	The ages at which women are able to bear children. Defined in this report as 15 to 44 inclusive.
Child dependency ratio	Number of children aged 0 to 15 relative to the size of the working age population.
Cohort	A group of people with a common experience, who are observed through time. For example the cohort of people born in 1970.
Cohort analysis	Analysis that reflects the actual experience of a cohort of people over their lifetime or over a specific period. (See also 'period analysis')
Cohort life expectancy	The average number of additional years a member of a cohort would live based on the mortality rates the cohort has experienced or is projected to experience. (See also 'period life expectancy')
Commonwealth countries	The Commonwealth is a voluntary association of independent sovereign states consulting and co-operating in the common interests of their peoples and in the promotion of international understanding and world peace. The association has no constitution or charter, but members commit themselves to the statements of beliefs set out by Heads of Government. The basis of these is the Declaration of Commonwealth Principles, agreed at Singapore in 1971, and reaffirmed in the Harare Declaration of 1991. Commonwealth countries can be divided into two broad groupings, the old and new commonwealths. See Old Commonwealth countries and New Commonwealth countries for a list of countries.

Communal establishment	Defined in the 2001 Census as 'providing managed residential accommodation'. People were assumed to be 'resident' in a communal establishment if they had been living, or intended to live there for six months or more. Communal establishments cover universities and colleges, hospitals, hostels and homes, some hotels and guest houses (with capacity for ten or more people), holiday complexes, defence establishments (but not married quarters) and prisons.
Completed family size (CFS)	The average number of children born to a woman by the end of her childbearing years. A cohort measure of fertility.
Conglomeration	A single unit formed from a combination of many different parts. In the context of Chapter 3, a conglomeration is a large urban area built up from a combination of smaller cities and towns.
Council area	The 1994 Local Government (Scotland) Act led to the abolition of the existing structure of nine regions and 53 districts, although the three island councils remained. Since April 1996 Scotland has been divided into 32 council areas, whose councils are unitary administrations with responsibility for all areas of local government.
Dependent age group	People aged between 0 and 15 or above state pension age.
Dependent child	Defined in the 1991 Census, the Labour Force Survey and the General Household Survey, as a childless, never-married child in a family, who is aged under 16 or aged 16 to 18 and in full-time education.
	The 2001 Census was revised to a person aged 0 to 15 in a household (whether or not in a family), or aged 16 to 18 in full-time education and living in a family with his or her parents.
Dwelling	Defined in the 2001 Census as a self-contained unit of accommodation, with all rooms behind a door which only the household can use.
Economically active	Employees, the self-employed and the unemployed (looking for work and available to start work within two weeks). Full-time students may be economically active or inactive.
Economically inactive	The retired, students, people looking after home or family, the permanently sick or disabled, or 'other'. Full-time students may be economically active or inactive.
Economically inactive part-time student	Defined by the 2001 Census as those who: 1. responded 'no' to the question 'Are you a schoolchild or student in full-time education?' 2. were classified as economically inactive 3. ticked the box stating that they were a student in the week prior to the census.
Employment rate	The percentage of working age people who are employed.
Enumeration district (ED)	Used across the UK for the purposes of census data collection. EDs were also the base unit of census output, until census output areas were introduced in Scotland in 1991 and the rest of the UK in 2001.
	For the 2001 Census, England and Wales had 116,895 EDs (the majority of which were different from their 1991 equivalents) with an average size close to 200 households (450 people). Scotland had 6,987 EDs at an average size of 328 households (730 people) and Northern Ireland had 2,591 EDs at an average size of 260 households (650 people).
Ethnic minority	May refer to ethnic groups other than White, or to ethnic groups other than White British. The term has no fixed meaning and the definition used is dependent on context. Unless otherwise stated, in this publication ethnic minority refers to ethnic groups other than White.

Ethnic group data	The information for the ethnic group of each respondent is based on the data and categorisation generated from the 2001 Census from the Office for National Statistics, the General Register Office for Scotland and the Northern Ireland Statistics and Research Agency.

In both 1991 and 2001 respondents were asked to which ethnic group they considered themselves to belong. The question in 2001 had more extensive categories than those of 1991 so people could tick 'Mixed' for the first time. This change in answer categories may account for a small part of the observed increase in the minority ethnic population over the period. Different versions of the ethnic group question were asked in England and Wales, in Scotland and in Northern Ireland, to reflect local differences in the requirement for information. However, results are comparable across the UK as a whole. |
| **European Union (EU)** | A union of 25 independent states based on the European Communities and founded in 1992 to enhance political, economic and social co-operation. The founding members were Belgium, Denmark, France, Germany, Greece, Ireland, Italy, Luxembourg, Netherlands, Portugal, Spain and the UK. New members since 1 January 1995 are: are Austria, Finland and Sweden. New members since 1 May 2004 are : Cyprus, the Czech Republic, Estonia, Hungary, Latvia, Lithuania, Malta, Poland, Slovakia and Slovenia. |
| **Family** | A married or cohabiting couple, with or without their never-married child or children (of any age), including couples with no children and lone parents with their never-married child or children. A family could also consist of a grandparent or grandparents with grandchild or grandchildren if the parents of the grandchild or grandchildren are not usually resident in the household.

Although definitions differ slightly across surveys and the census, they are broadly similar. In the Labour Force Survey, family units can comprise a single person or include non-dependent children, that is those aged 16 or over and not in full-time education who have never married and have no children of their own in the household. |
First demographic transition	The stages that a population typically goes through when moving from a pre-industrial population with high mortality and fertility rates to a modern industrial country with low mortality and progressively lower fertility rates.
Flow of international migrants	International migrants entering or leaving a country or migrating between countries. Or, for the UK: international migrations into or out of the UK, or between the UK and another country. See also International migrant.
Foreign armed forces	Members of another country's armed forces stationed on permanent bases in the UK.
Full-time student	Defined in the 2001 Census as a person responding 'yes' to the question 'Are you a schoolchild or student in full-time education?'.
Further education	Full- or part-time education for people over compulsory school age. Further education and is taught in a variety of settings including further education college, schools and work-based training.
Government Office Region (GOR)	Areas in England for which regional government offices are responsible. GORs were adopted in 1996 as the government's statistical regions.
Health authority (HA)	The intermediate level of health administration in England prior to the NHS restructuring in April 2002. There were 95 HAs at the time of abolition, reporting to eight NHS Regional Offices. They generally covered groups of one or more complete local authorities, but there were cases where local authorities were split. In addition, there were five HAs in Wales, reporting to the National Assembly. The HAs were built from groups of unitary authorities, each of which had its own Local health group (LHG). These HAs and LHGs were abolished when the Welsh NHS was restructured in April 2003.

Higher education qualifications	Often split into two types:
	1. Degree or equivalent, includes higher and first degrees, NVQ level 5 and other degree-level qualifications such as graduate membership of a professional institute.
	2. Higher education qualification below degree level, includes NVQ level 4, higher level BTEC/ SCOTVEC, HNC/HND, RSA Higher diploma, other higher education below degree level, and nursing and teaching qualifications.
Household	A person living alone or a group of people who have the same address as their only or main residence and with common housekeeping, for example the 2001 Census defined this as those who either share one meal a day or share the living accommodation. Although definitions differ slightly across surveys and the census, they are broadly similar.
In-migrant	In the UK context, an in-migrant is someone who enters the UK from another country to live for a year or more.
Individual Sample of Anonymised Records (ISAR)	Abstract of individual census records, made available with strictly protected confidentiality. ISARs are known more commonly in other countries as 'census microdata' or 'public use samples'.
Infant mortality rate (IMR)	The number of deaths of infants aged between 0 and 1 in a year per 1,000 live-births in the same year.
Internal migrant	Broadly defined in the UK context as a person changing address within the UK. The precise definition varies depending on the data source used:
	• 2001 Census – someone who had a different address within the UK 12 months before the Census
	• NHS Central Register – someone who registered with a new general practitioner (GP) in a different former health authority area to their previous GP
	• Patient register – someone who had a different home postcode from the one they had a year previously.
International migrant	Someone who changes their country of usual residence for a period of at least a year so that the country of destination effectively becomes the country of usual residence. This is the internationally agreed, UN-recommended definition of a long-term migrant. It is also the standard definition of an international migrant used by the Office for National Statistics.
	Information on international in-migrants is also derived from the question in the 2001 Census on place of residence one year previously. An international migrant is someone who is recorded by the 2001 Census as living outside the UK one year prior to Census day (29 April).
Labour Force Survey (LFS)	A quarterly sample survey of households living at private addresses in Great Britain. Its purpose is to provide information on the UK labour market that can be used to develop, manage, evaluate and report on labour market policies.
	The survey seeks information on respondents' personal circumstances and their labour market status during a specific reference period, usually of one or four weeks (depending on the topic), immediately prior to the interview.
Life expectancy	The average number of additional years a person would live under a given set of mortality conditions.
Local authority district	The lower level of local government within the two-tier structure that has remained in parts of England since local government reorganisation.
Local government district	Replaced Northern Ireland's two tier administrative structure in October 1973. Outside Northern Ireland, the 26 local government districts are known as 'district council areas'. They are unitary administrations and are responsible for all areas of local government, but their remit is more limited than that of local authorities in the rest of the UK.

London boroughs	The local government areas of Greater London. The borough councils are unitary administrations with a status similar to metropolitan districts, except that they are affected by policies implemented by the Greater London Authority (GLA). There are 32 London boroughs, but the City of London (which has a different legal status) is often considered as a borough for statistical purposes. The London boroughs and the City of London together cover the whole Greater London area.
Lone parent family	Defined in the 2001 Census as a father or mother together with his or her child or children, and the children do not have a spouse, partner or child in the household. Also can encompass a grandparent with grandchild(ren) where there are no children in the intervening generation in the household.
	The Labour Force Survey's definition is a lone parent, living with his or her never-married children, providing that these children have no children of their own living with them.
Maternal mortality	Deaths of mothers up to a year after childbirth.
Median age	The midpoint age that separates the younger half of a population from the older half.
Migrant switcher	A traveller who stated their intention, in the International Passenger Survey, to stay in a destination country for more than a year, and was therefore counted as a migrant, but who actually left sooner.
Military personnel	People employed by the armed forces, excluding civilians.
Mixed ethnic group	Includes the 'White and Black Caribbean', 'White and Black African', 'White and Asian' and 'Other Mixed' ethnic groups.
Natural change	The difference between the number of births and deaths over a period, often a year. (See 'natural increase' and 'natural decrease'.)
Natural decrease	When deaths exceed births over a specific period. If there is zero migration in and out of a population, a population experiencing natural decrease will be reducing in size.
Natural increase	When births exceed deaths over a specific period. If there is zero migration in and out of a population, a population experiencing natural increase will be growing in size.
Net migration	The difference between the number of in-migrants to an area and the number of out-migrants. If in-migrants outnumber out-migrants there is a net gain. If out-migrants outnumber in-migrants there is a net loss.
New Commonwealth countries	As at 2005: Anguilla, Antigua and Barbuda, Ascension Island, the Bahamas, Bangladesh, Barbados, Belize, Bermuda, Botswana, British Antarctic, British Virgin Islands, Brunei, Cameroon, Cayman Islands, Cyprus, Dominica, Falkland Islands, Gambia, Ghana, Gibraltar, Grenada, Guyana, India, Jamaica, Kenya, Lesotho, Malawi, Malaysia, Malta, Mauritius, Montserrat, Mozambique, Namibia, Nigeria, Pakistan, Papua New Guinea, St Helena and Tristan da Cunha, St Kitts, St Lucia, St Vincent, Seychelles, Sierra Leone, Singapore, Sri Lanka, Swaziland, Tanzania, Trinidad and Tobago, Turks and Caicos Islands, Uganda, Zambia, Zimbabwe and other Commonwealth Pacific islands.
	Cyprus and Malta joined the European Union on 1 May 2004. In Chapter 7 these countries are included in the New Commonwealth category for years up to 2003 but, not for 2004 when they are included in the European Union.
Non-White	People from all ethnic groups other than the 'White British', 'White Scottish', 'White Irish', 'White Other British' and 'Other White' groups.
North-south drift	The movement of people from northern areas of the UK to southern areas.

OECD countries	The 30 countries of the Organisation for Economic Co-operation and Development which share commitment to democratic government and the market economy. Member countries are Australia, Austria, Belgium, Canada, the Czech Republic, Denmark, Finland, France, Germany, Greece, Hungary, Iceland, Ireland, Italy, Japan, Korea, Luxembourg, Mexico, the Netherlands, New Zealand, Norway, Poland, Portugal, Slovakia, Spain, Sweden, Switzerland, Turkey, the UK and the USA.
Old-age dependency ratio	The number of people above state pension age relative to the size of the working age population. The higher the ratio, the more older people who are likely to be dependent on the population of working age.
Old Commonwealth countries	As at 2005: Australia, Canada, New Zealand, South Africa and United Kingdom.
Oldest old	People aged 85 and over.
Out-migrant	Out-migrant is someone who leaves the UK to live in another country for a year or more.
Pension/retirement age	Age 65 and older for men and age 60 and older for women.
Pension/retirement population	Population above pension or retirement age. (See 'pension/retirement age'.)
Period analysis	Uses data for people of all ages at a specific time or for a specific period. A period measure of fertility. For example, the total fertility rate (see 'total fertility rate') in 2004 would provide a snapshot of the level of fertility in the population in 2004. However, the total fertility rate does not represent the fertility of an actual group of women over their lifetimes. (See also cohort analysis).
Period life expectancy	The average total number of years that a person of a specific age could be expected to live, if rates of mortality at each age were those experienced in that period.
Population density	The number of people resident per land area, usually expressed as persons per km^2.
Population projection	A future or historical unknown size of population calculated according to predetermined changes in assumptions about the factors that affect population size. The primary purpose of the population projections produced by the Government Actuary's Department is to provide an estimate of future populations. Projections are produced for the UK and its constituent countries by age and sex. They span 25 and 75 years and are usually prepared every second year.
Public private partnership	A collaboration between public bodies, such as local authorities or central government, and private companies.
Replacement fertility level	The level of fertility required to ensure a population replaces itself in size.
Resident population	The estimated population of an area includes all those usually resident in the area, whatever their nationality. Members of Her Majesty's armed forces stationed in England and Wales are included at their place of residence but those stationed outside England and Wales are not included. Members of the US armed forces stationed in England and Wales are included at their places of residence. Students are taken to be resident at their term time address. Prisoners are regarded as usually resident at an institution if they have served (or are expected to serve) six months or more of a custodial sentence. Diplomats are excluded. The expected mortality rate when the observed age-specific mortality rates are applied to a given standard population. This is done to eliminate the effects of age structure on mortality rates.

Standardised rates	Standardised rates enable comparisons to be made between geographical areas, over time, and between the sexes, independent of changes in the age structure of the population.
Stock of international migrants	People residing in the UK who were born in or are citizens of another country.
Tenure	The legal right to live in a place or use land or buildings for a specified period. There are up to four tenure categories used in housing stock figures: owner-occupied; rented privately; rented from registered social landlords; and rented from local authorities.
Total fertility rate (TFR)	The average number of children a woman would have if she experienced the age-specific fertility rates for a particular year throughout her childbearing life.
Total international migration (TIM)	Estimates of migration to and from the UK produced by the Office for National Statistics by combining migration data from the International Passenger Survey, Home Office data on asylum seekers, data on migration between the UK and Ireland, and adjustments for visitor switchers and migrant switchers.
UK regular forces	Trained and untrained personnel employed in the armed forces, including the nursing services but excluding full-time Reserve Service personnel, Gurkhas, the Home Service battalions of the Royal Irish Regiment, mobilised reservists and Naval Activated reservists. Naval Services personnel on sea service and those serving in flights at sea are also included and are counted within the local authority containing the home port of their ship or the base airfield of their flight.
Unemployment rate	The number of people unemployed per 1,000 of the population
Unitary authority	Area with a single tier of local government (as opposed to the two-tier county: district structure). In practice, the term is applied only to the 22 UAs established in Wales in 1996, and the 46 UAs established of England between 1995 and 1998. However, London boroughs and metropolitan districts in England, council areas in Scotland and district council areas in Northern Ireland are all also served by single-tier (unitary) administrations.
Urban-rural shift	The movement of people from inner cities to the suburbs and more rural areas.
Visitor switcher	People who enter or leave the UK intending to stay in their destination country for less than a year but who actually stay for a year or longer.
White	The term 'White' refers to individuals from the 'White British', 'White Scottish', 'White Irish', 'White Other British' and 'Other White' ethnic groups.
Working age	People aged between 16 and state pension age (currently age 65 and over for men and age 60 and over for women).
Young adults	People aged 16 to 24.